AF598761

READING CHINESE PAINTING

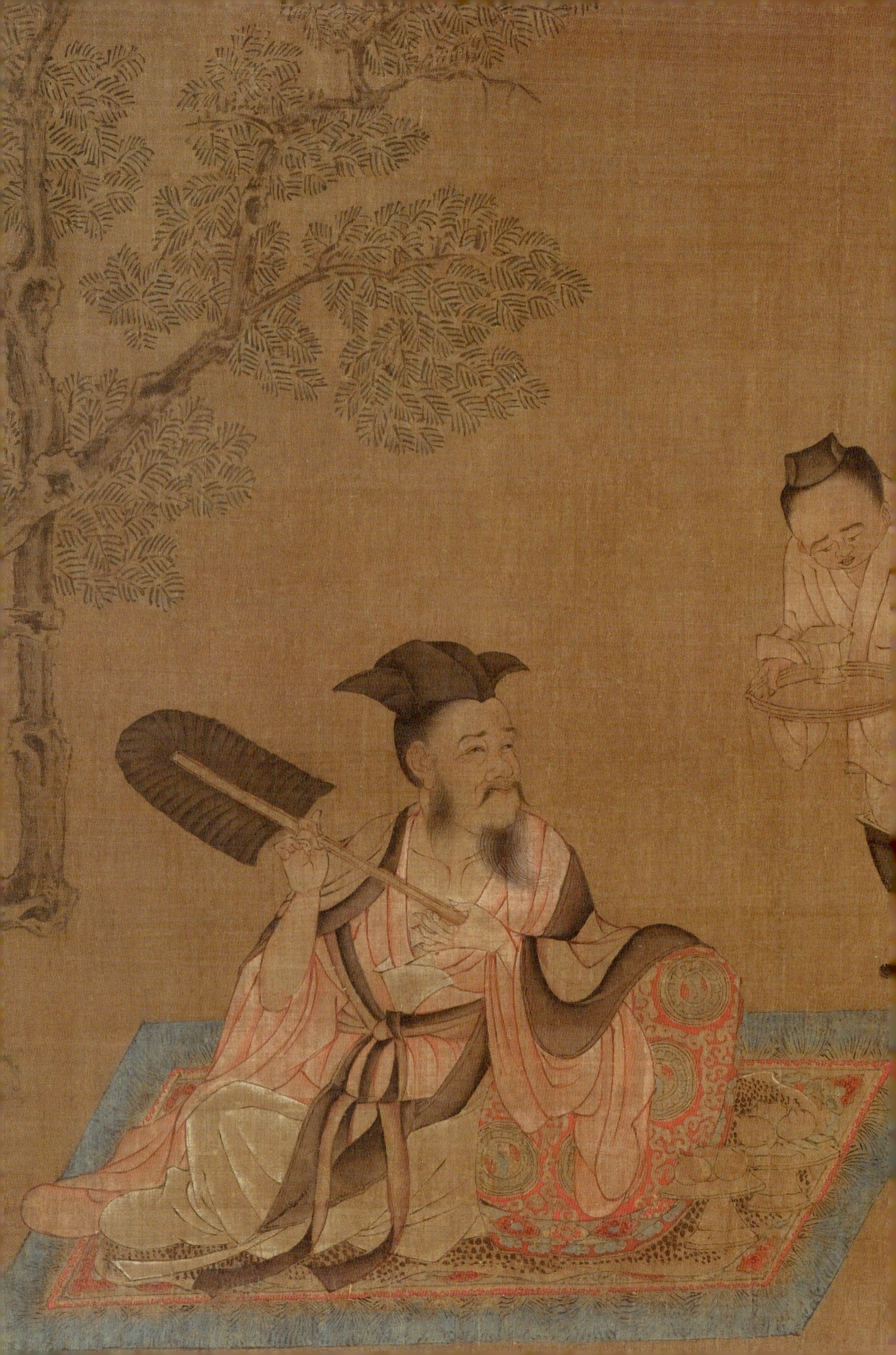

READING CHINESE PAINTING

Beyond Forms and Colors, a Comparative Approach to Art Appreciation

Better Link Press

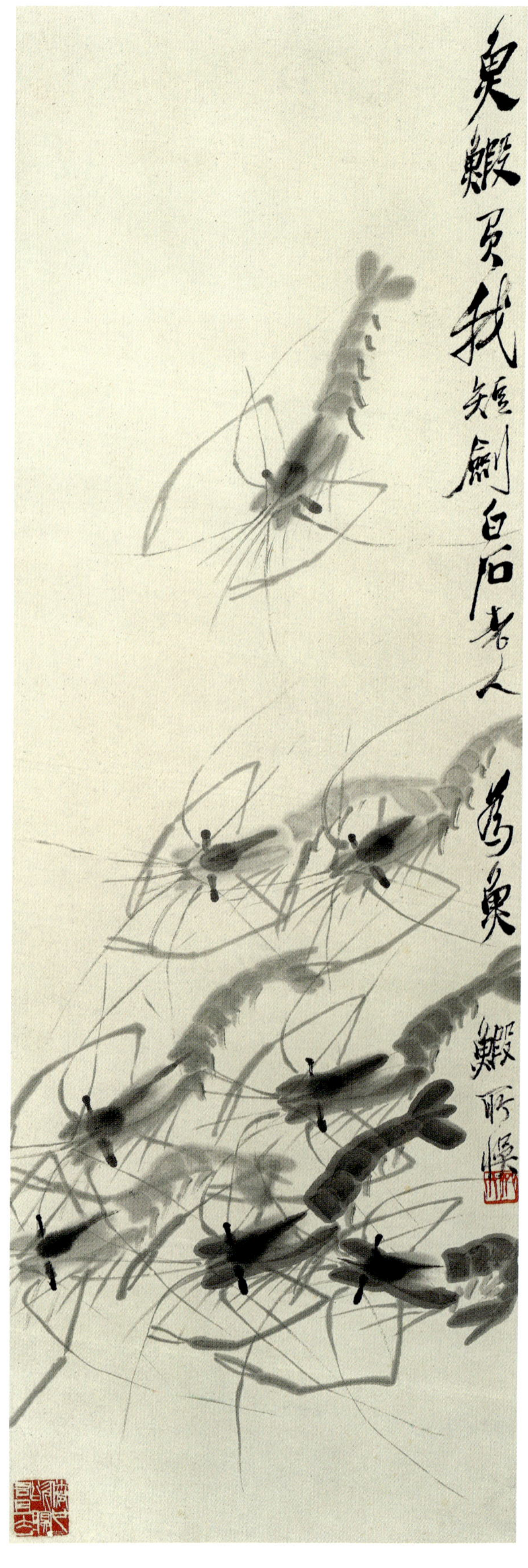

Fig. 3 *Ink Shrimps*
Qi Baishi (1864–1957)
Ink on paper
Height 102.5 cm × Width 34.5 cm
Liaoning Provincial Museum

There is no background in any of Qi Baishi's paintings of shrimps. Nevertheless, the lively shrimps sparkle with translucence and life. It is the *liubai* (leaving black) area of the background that so aptly makes us imagine that it is a limpid lake with the quality of a mirror. On the other hand, there would be nothing to marvel at had the background been painted in.

This book is edited and designed by the Editorial Committee of *Cultural China* series

Text by Sophia Suk-mun Law
Translation by Tony Blishen

Cover Design: Wang Wei
Interior Design: Li Jing, Hu Bin (Yuan Yinchang Design Studio)

Editor: Wu Yuezhou
Editorial Director: Zhang Yicong

Senior Consultants: Sun Yong, Wu Ying, Yang Xinci
Managing Director and Publisher: Wang Youbu

ISBN: 978-1-60220-024-1

Address any comments about *Reading Chinese Painting: Beyond Forms and Colors, a Comparative Approach to Art Appreciation* to:

Better Link Press
99 Park Avenue
New York, NY 10016
USA

or

Shanghai Press and Publishing Development Company, Ltd.
F 7 Donghu Road, Shanghai, China (200031)
Email: comments_betterlinkpress@hotmail.com

Printed in China by Shenzhen Donnelley Printing Co., Ltd.
1 3 5 7 9 10 8 6 4 2

Quanjing provides the images on pages 12, 13, 16, 17, 18, 30, 31, 33, 34, 49 (bottom), 52, 54, 70, 71, 72, 79, 80, 94 (top), 104, 113 and 127 (top).

CONTENTS

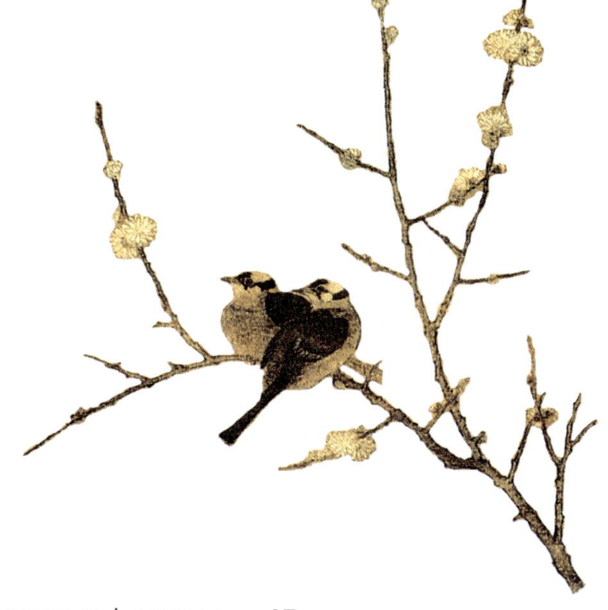

CONTENTS

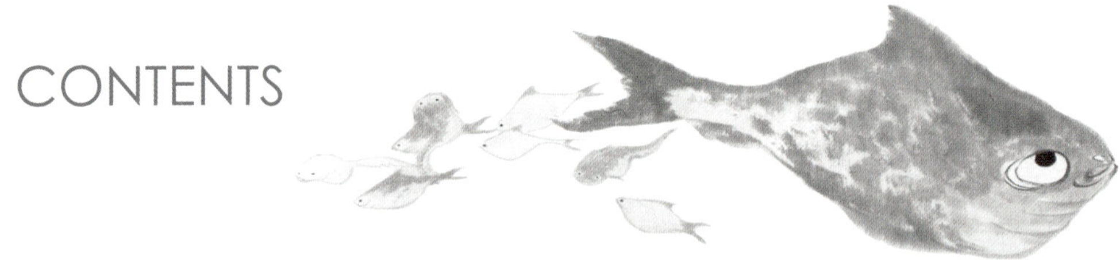

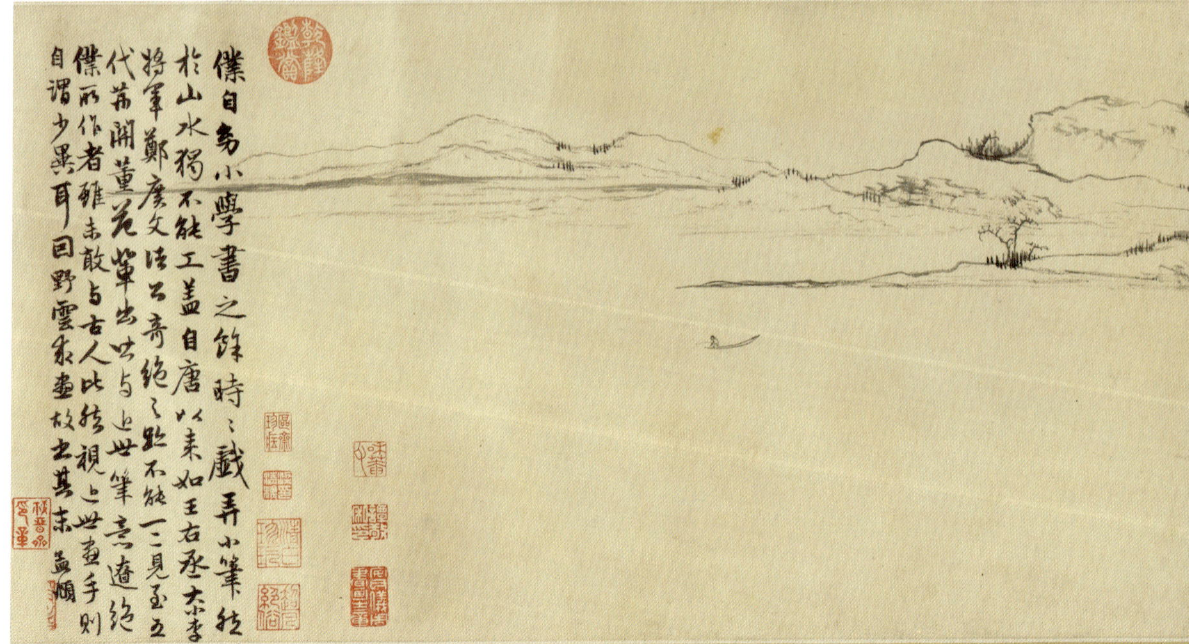

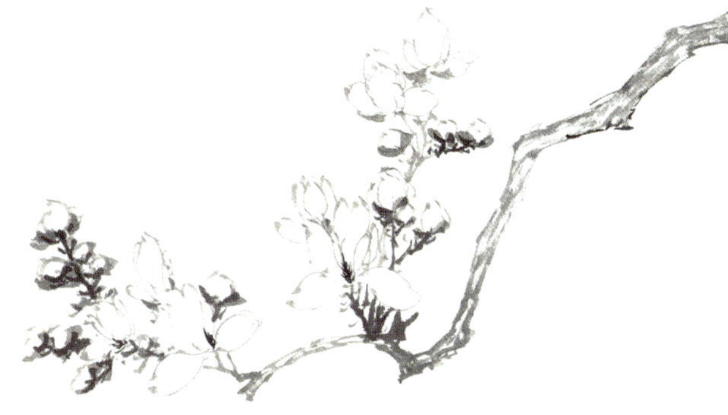

CONTENTS

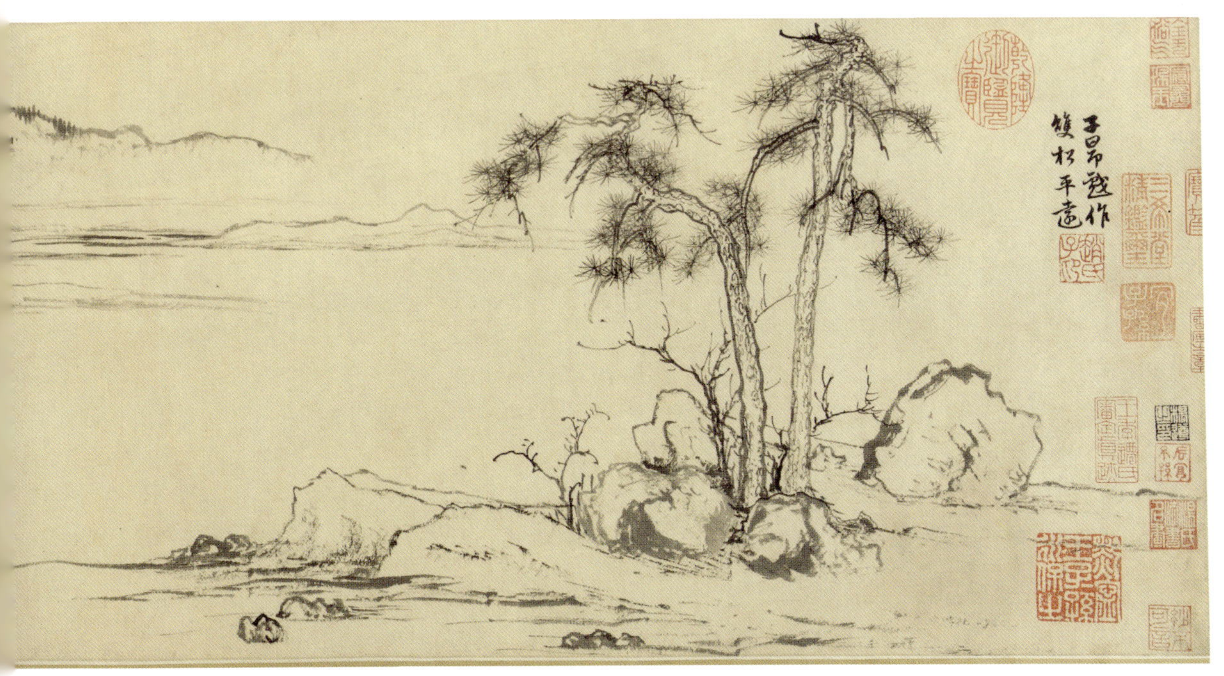

Page 1

Fig. 1 *Pines amongst Ravines* (detail)

Please refer to page 83.

Pages 2–3

Fig. 2 *Elevated Ease* (detail)

Please refer to pages 58–59.

Pages 6–7

Fig. 4 *Two Pines in Level Perspective*

Zhao Mengfu (Yuan dynasty, 1254–1322)
Ink on paper
Height 26.7 cm × Width 107.3 cm
The Metropolitan Museum of Art, New York

"*Qi*" is an expression of strength. In traditional painting, there is a kind of brushwork known as "flying blank" (*feibai*), where the artist, in the process of painting, does not touch the paper with the tip of the brush and produces no brushwork. However, because there has been no real pause in the movement of the brush, which continues in the same breath, the brushwork produced the next time the tip touches paper, though seemingly disconnected from the previous brushwork, gives a sensation of continuity. This is the meaning of the phrase "the brush may stop but the vital energy (*qi*) does not." See, for example, the line of the stones in the bottom righthand corner of this picture.

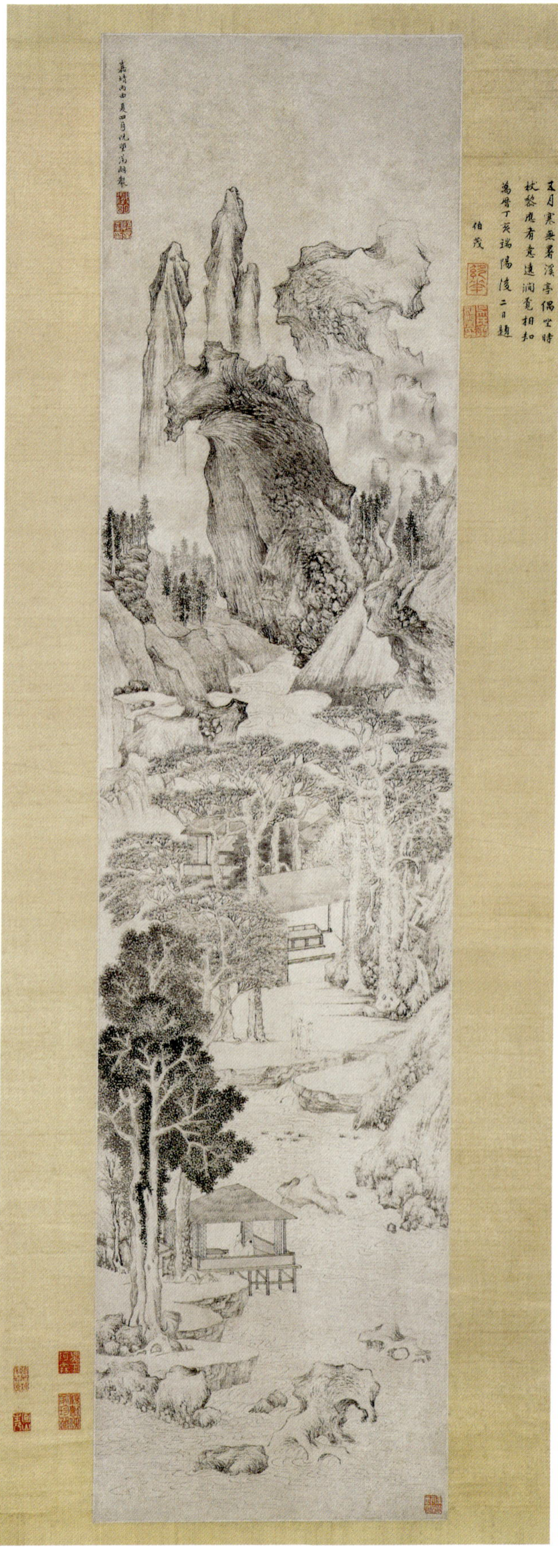

Fig. 5 *Deep River in the 5th Month*

Wen Zhengming (Ming dynasty, 1470–1559)
Ink on Paper
Height 127.5 cm × Width 31 cm
Suzhou Museum

Traditional Chinese paintings with natural scenery as their subject are known not as landscapes but as *shanshui* (hills and water). However, are *shanshui* landscapes or not?

INTRODUCTION

It is always difficult to compare the appeal of traditional Chinese painting with that of western art. In many years of university teaching I have found that students almost always fall for western art but treat traditional Chinese painting with distant respect. For example, in the same year, there could be over 150 students taking the history of western art in the first semester, but by the second semester the number studying the history of Chinese painting could have dropped to less than 40. When you ask why, the answer is: "Traditional Chinese painting is too profound." But if you do not study it, how can you understand its profundity?

Students tend to feel that at first sight, western painting is the more attractive. In landscapes, figure painting, still life and abstracts the themes are obvious and easily understood. Moreover, there is a diversity of colors and styles. Purely in terms of visual appreciation there is an abundance of riches. Traditional Chinese painting by contrast seems inferior. There seems nothing outstanding in the themes of most traditional Chinese paintings. On inspection, the scenery in landscapes does not resemble the natural landscape that we know (fig. 5), the paintings of figures do not resemble real people (fig. 6 on page 10) and what is even more baffling, how can those flowers and plants, sparsely sketched in two or three ink strokes with neither detail nor color, display the brilliance of the exuberantly colored floral world (fig. 7 on page 11)? Furthermore, the style and techniques of traditional painting apparently differ very little from dynasty to dynasty, thus making it difficult to distinguish the characteristics of one dynasty from another. These seem to be reasonable if impressionistic judgements that account both for the "distant respect" with which the majority of students regard traditional Chinese painting and also for their inability to enter its world.

The phenomenon of distant respect is not confined to students alone, a similar reaction can be observed on the part of many viewers and readers on their first contact with traditional Chinese painting. In point of fact this phenomenon is due to the observer mis-focusing his view of Chinese traditional painting. These impressions of indistinct styles, ill-defined imagery and lackluster color all derive from feelings created by the students' appreciation of the norms of western art. It is a little known fact that Chinese and western painting both originated and developed along different trajectories. The great 20th century master of Chinese painting Pan Tianshou (1897–1971) put it thus: "East and West, the two great systems of painting, each have their own greatest achievements. They stand between the continents of Europe and Asia facing each other like two great peaks of immeasurable height." These two peaks of Chinese and western painting have their own artistic territory, climate and environment. So the flowers and plants that they nurture ought rightly to have different characteristics; to insist on seeking western flowers and plants amongst the hills and mountains of China is

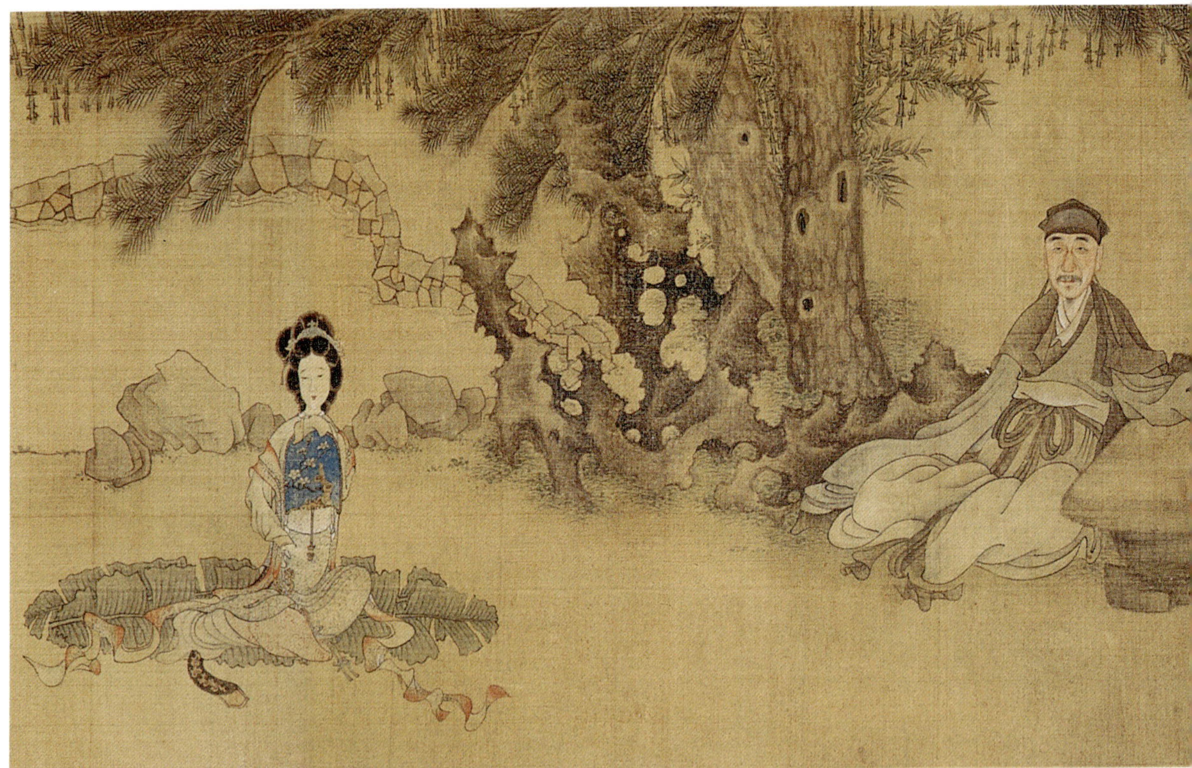

Fig. 6 *The Scholar He Tianzhang Listening to Music*
Chen Hongshou (Ming dynasty, 1599–1652)
Ink and color on silk
Height 25.3 cm × Width 163.2 cm
Suzhou Museum

It is difficult to make comparisons between figures in traditional Chinese painting and the portraits of Western art. Do these figures really derive from reality?

to adopt a mistaken perspective that naturally limits clarity of vision and must lead to a loss of elements of the sublime.

Western norms and values form the main stream of contemporary society and they determine our attitudes and judgements. It is natural for students who view traditional Chinese painting against the norms of western art to find the artists of ancient China less able than their western counterparts in their use of color, in composition, in managing light and shade and in their handling of three-dimensional space. Why really bother to look therefore? In fact, what they do not understand is that these skills are basically not the point of traditional Chinese painting and that to concentrate on these aspects alone is tantamount to viewing Chinese painting through a pair of unfocussed spectacles. To take it further, it amounts to an inability to see clearly the world that lies before them. Consequently, the first idea that I introduce to students of the history of Chinese painting and to those who hope to understand it, is this: Throw away the spectacles that you use to look at western art and readjust your focus, only then will you be able to perceive the essence and the look of traditional Chinese painting.

If we are to truly enter the world of traditional Chinese painting we must understand its historical and cultural background. According to present day understanding, art comprises creation in many different media and its appreciation is focused upon satisfying the visual and innovative senses, painting is merely one amongst a number of arts. At the same time, modern man generally regards artistic creation and its appreciation as a kind of cultural leisure activity. Such attitudes and understanding of art spring from the point of view of contemporary society, and are very

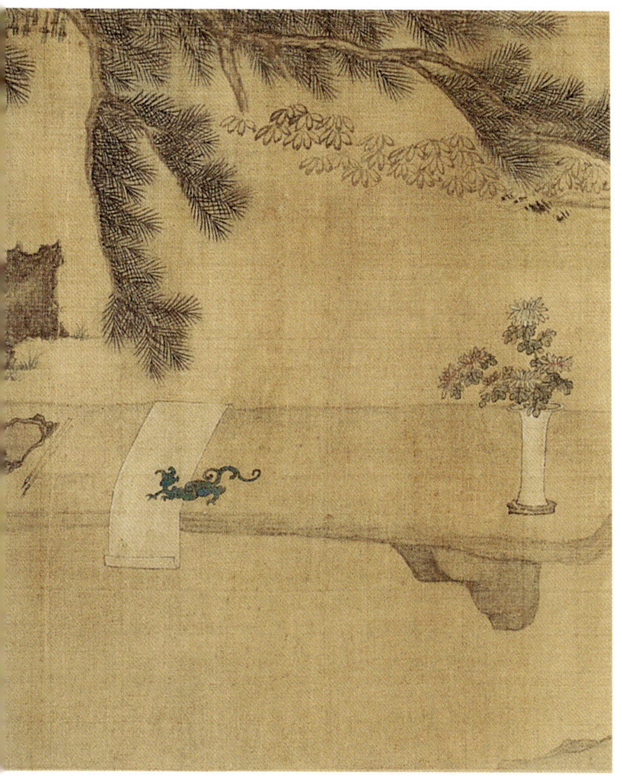

different from the artistic definitions and aspirations of pre-20th century traditional Chinese society.

In China, creative theories in calligraphy and painting developed continuously without interruption from the Han (206 BC–226 AD) to the Qing (1644–1911) dynasties, resulting in a rich accumulation of treatises on calligraphy and painting built up over the centuries. These classics of creative art took no account of creative activity in other fields such as Buddhist sculpture or folk handicraft. Consequently, in the eyes of the ancient Chinese, only calligraphy and painting could be truly regarded as creative art. The rest, for example architecture, sculpture and woodcut was merely handicraft. This view did not change until the 20th century. The *Compendium of Chinese Art* (*Zhonguo Meishu Quanzhi*) published in 1920, in addition to calligraphy and painting, included examples drawn from architecture, sculpture, and folk handicraft. The same can be seen with other histories of Chinese art compiled at the same time. However, the word *meishu*—art, was first used by an early 20th century writer on Chinese art history and was a borrowing of the Japanese word *bijutsu* (written with the same characters) used by a late 19th century Japanese scholar to translate the French *beaux-art* (fine art). The scope of "fine art" embraced music, poetry and literature, sculpture and architecture. This concept is comparable to our present-day idea of "art." It could be said that today's "art" and the concept of "fine art"

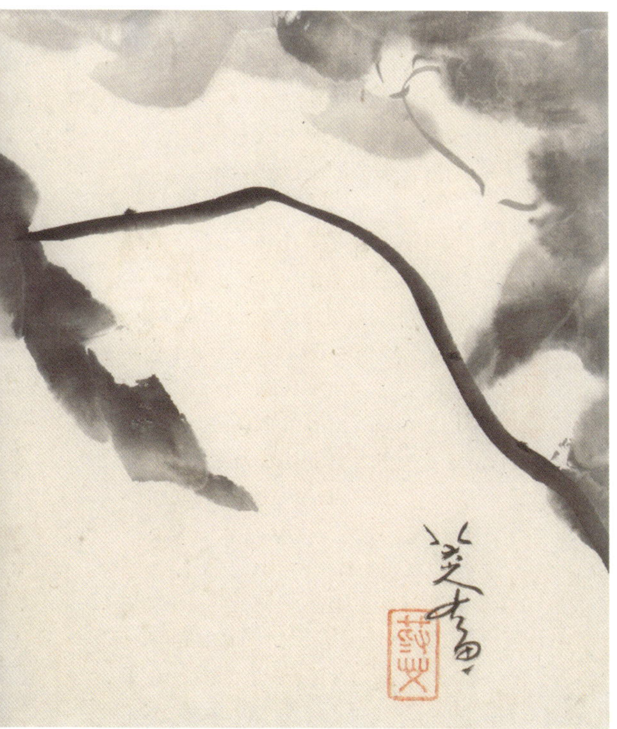

Fig. 7 *Lotus*
Bada Shanren (Zhu Da) (Qing dynasty, c. 1626–1705)
Ink on paper
Height 24.4 cm × Width 23 cm
Shanghai Museum

There are many examples of flowers and plants in ink in the traditional category of flower-and-bird paintings. They are simply constructed without clearly defined form or application of color. What are the criteria for the appreciation of this kind of painting?

when applied to traditional Chinese culture are both external and contemporary. In traditional Chinese culture there was no "fine art" just "art." It was this "art" that governed the development of Chinese painting.

The concept of "art" derives from the "six arts" (*liu yi*) of Confucian theory. These comprised ceremony, music, archery, chariot driving, literacy and arithmetic. Thus, Confucian educational philosophy promoted the personal implementation of six different forms of practical experience as a path towards the cultivation of morality. Although the six arts involved practical skills and training their main purpose was the moulding of character to produce dependability, a far cry from contemporary man's concept of art as a leisured cultural activity. For the ancients, creative art was confined to painting and calligraphy. Neither of these were part of the cultural amusements of the ordinary man. They were the cultural activities of scholars and officials. The calligraphers and artists who contributed to the history of Chinese art were philosopher sages who sought the ideals of morality and the realm of the spirit. It could be said that traditional Chinese painting was a form of "high art" that had a role in civilizing the person and cultivating the mind and was not purely a creation for the satisfaction of the visual senses and the expression of individual emotion. Consequently, the focus should not be upon parading the uniqueness of the individual or painting's stimulation of the visual senses.

Traditional Chinese painting is a kind of "art" that differs from "craft." Its development was based upon the pursuit of a conceptual sense (*yijing*) in traditional Chinese philosophy and classical literature. If Confucianism determined the content of developments in traditional painting, then Daoism guided its aesthetic sense. Traditional painting is focused upon the spiritual expression of spontaneity, evanescence and abstraction. It is always harmonious and tranquil, internal and abstract. The enjoyment of traditional painting should be attained through still contemplation and minute observation, the only way to perceive its inward delicacy. However, the frantic pace of modern society makes such an attainment easier said than done. When the ever present influence of western Modernism on our appreciation of traditional painting is taken into account, we seem to diverge more and more from the spirit of Chinese traditional art. As a result we can neither see nor perceive the sublime to be found in traditional painting.

The purpose of this book is to seek out a standpoint from which the reader may appreciate traditional painting and to give the reader clarity of vision and a grasp of its characteristics so that they can truly enter its world. This is the only way towards the beginnings of an appreciation and discussion

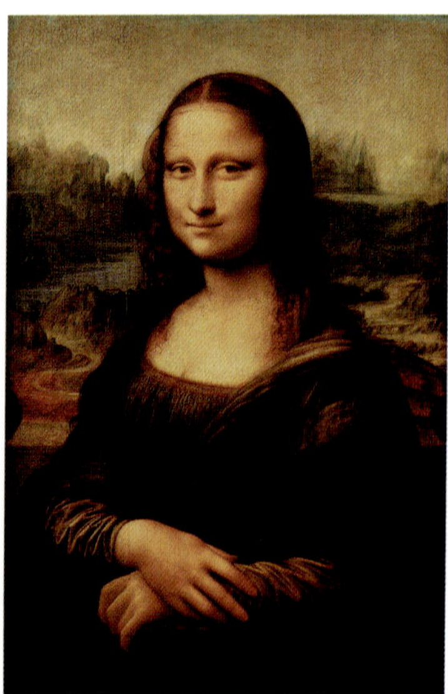

Fig. 8 *Mona Lisa*
Leonardo Da Vinci (Italy, 1452–1519)
Oil on poplar
Height 77 cm × Width 53 cm
Louvre Museum

Why are there no classic portraits like that of the *Mona Lisa* in traditional Chinese painting? Is traditional figure painting really portraiture or not?

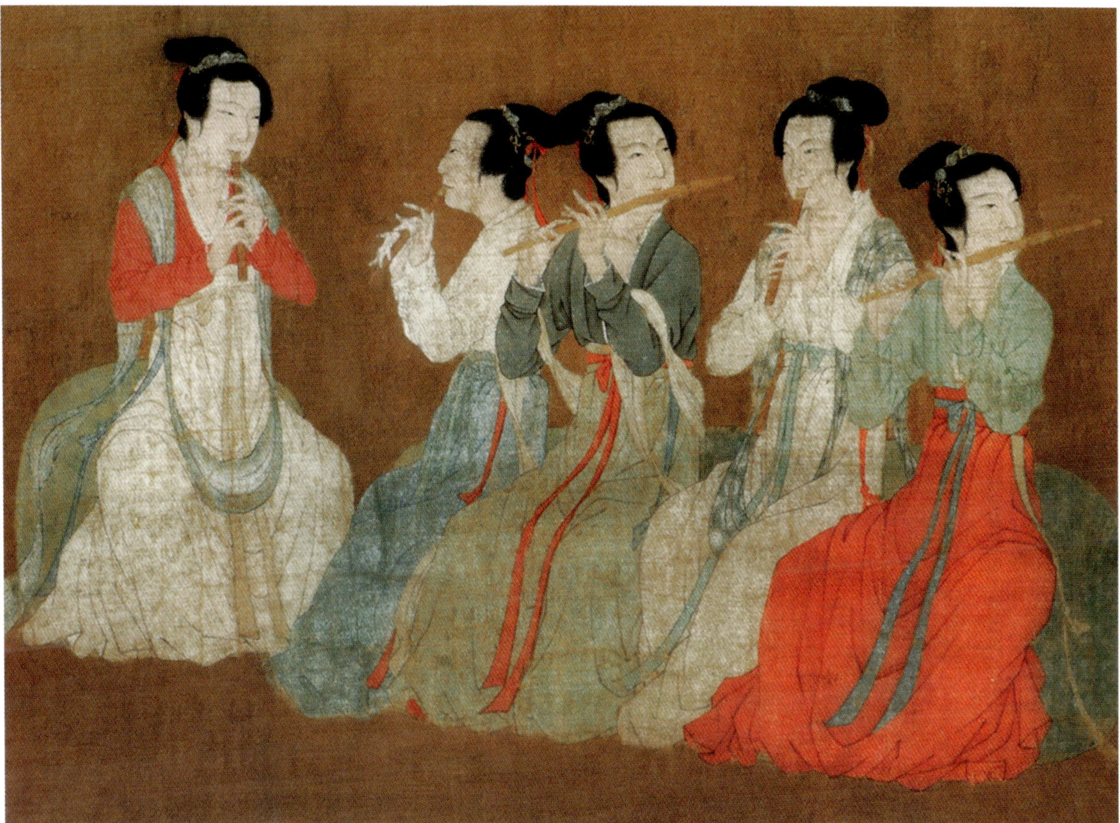

Fig. 9 *Chancellor Han Xizai's Evening Banquet* (detail)
Gu Hongzhong (Five Dynasties)
Ink and color on silk
Height 28.7 cm × Width 335.5 cm
Palace Museum, Beijing

The faces of figures in Chinese painting all seem to look the same, it is difficult to imagine that they are real people. So, are the figures in the paintings fabricated constructs?

of traditional painting. The first two chapters take two antithetical concepts as their center of focus, they are "Innovation versus Legacy" and "True Likeness versus Painterly Impression." These two concepts involve two fundamental points of view in the appreciation of Chinese painting upon which we can stand firm and examine its unique characteristics.

There are three main strands to traditional painting: figures, *shanshui*, and flower-and-bird paintings. In order to identify their unique characteristics we must first ask three obvious but rarely put questions: Why is there no Mona Lisa in traditional Chinese painting? Why do natural phenomena such as thunderstorms and avalanches never appear in *shanshui*? Do birds and flowers belong to the still life category? These questions strike at the crux of Chinese traditional painting since logic dictates that it was impossible that in ancient China there were no beauties worth a portrait or that in the past several thousand years there was not a single painter with an outstanding technique. Equally, it is also impossible that the painters of ancient China never encountered terrifying or unusual natural phenomena. Why then is there not so much as a brushstroke of this kind of scenery in the work of traditional *shanshui* painters? Furthermore, the flowers that appear in traditional Chinese flower-and-bird paintings are never thrust into vases as they so often are in Western compositions. So, can traditional Chinese flower-and-bird painting really be regarded as a form of still life? All these questions will be answered in chapters three, four and five and in the process the reader can explore the reasons layer by layer (figs. 8–12).

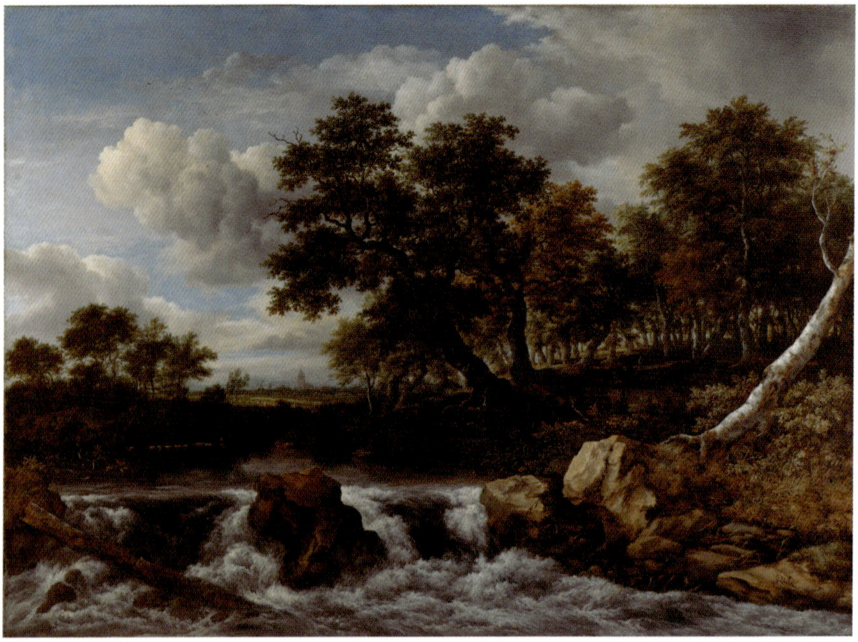

Fig. 10 *Landscape with Waterfall*

Jacob Isaacksz. van Ruisdael (Netherlands, c. 1629–1682)
Oil on canvas
Height 142.5 cm × Width 196 cm
Rijksmuseum

The minute depiction of objects in western landscapes allows the viewer to feel as if he is part of the scene.

Figure painting is the focus of the third chapter. In Western art, the *Mona Lisa* is the archetypal portrait. But in Chinese art, paintings of figures are never called "portraits." In that case, are figure paintings a type of portrait or not? Are the figures in figure paintings real people? Indeed, are there "portraits" in Chinese painting historically at all?

The fourth chapter deals with *shanshui*. Although nature itself is the creative stuff of all of them, Western artists call this class of subject "scenery" or "landscape" though the painters of ancient China called it *shanshui* (hills and water). So are *shanshui* a form of scenery? Do *shanshui* from the brush of traditional landscape artists derive from real hills and real water?

The fifth chapter looks at flower-and-bird paintings. In contrast to western painting, all traditional flower-and-bird painting, whether delicate and finely worked or rapidly sketched in ink, has a large expanse of blank space as background. In the vocabulary of Chinese traditional painting this is called *liubai* (literally, to leave blank). This chapter discusses the function of *liubai* and whether it is in fact a blank. At the same time, it also examines whether or not there is a difference between flower-and-bird painting and western still life.

The focus of the sixth chapter is brush and ink (*bimo*). *Bimo* is never far from us when looking at Chinese painting but to the ordinary viewer it is unfathomable. What is it that *bimo* actually tells us?

In the final chapter we focus on an unusual art form unique to Chinese painting, the handscroll. A good handscroll can take the viewer on a journey of wonderful fantasy.

To a greater or lesser extent the man of today harbors a degree of misconception about traditional Chinese painting. Even more, there are those who consider that traditional painting is actually out of kilter with the times. The aim of this book is not to discuss whether or not traditional Chinese painting is obsolete, since even if it is, it still retains a value in the field of appreciation. The problem is whether we can perceive and understand its inner meaning. For example, western painters of the early 20th century advocated the abstract, they emphasized the exploration of form and the expression of concept. By the same token, is the emphasis upon the exploration of *bimo* and

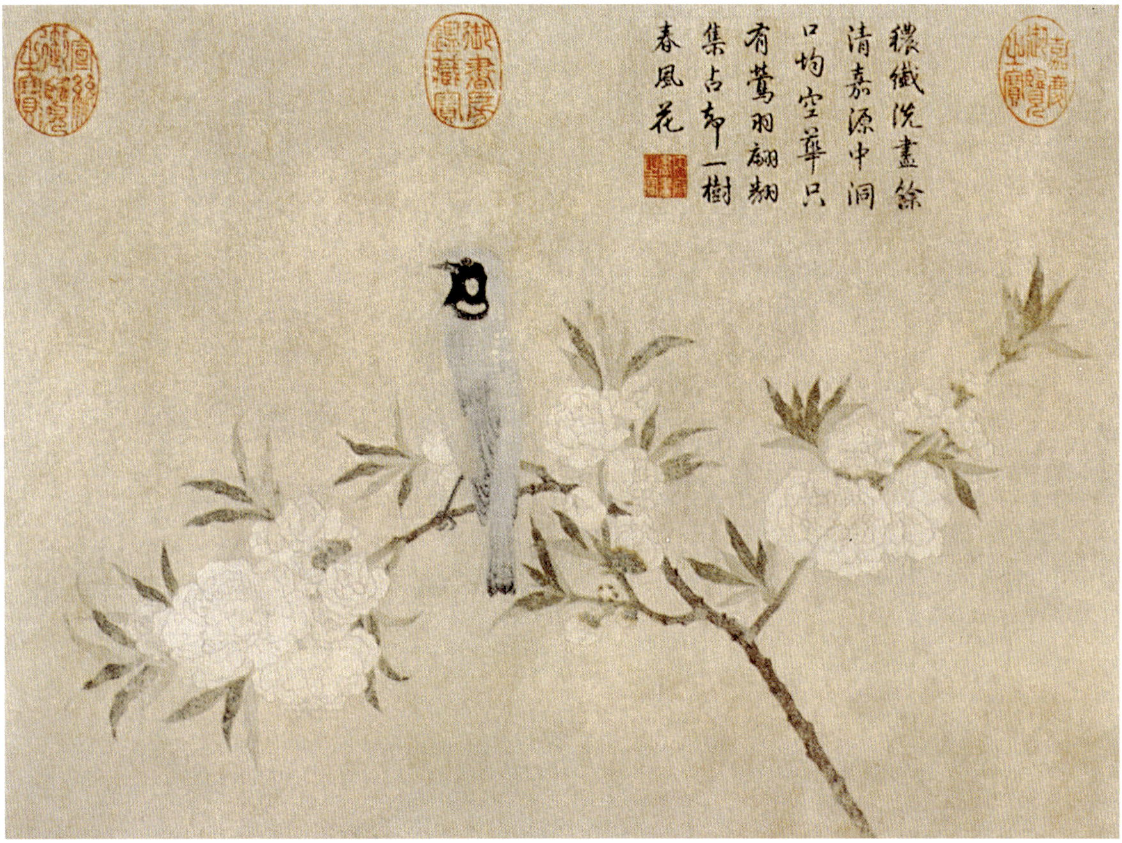

Fig. 11 *Flowers and Birds* (detail)
Qian Xuan (Yuan dynasty, c. 1239–c. 1300)
Ink and color on paper
Height 38 cm × Width 316.7 cm
Tianjin Museum

There are no flowers in vases in traditional Chinese flower-and-bird paintings as there so often are in western paintings. They are mostly "flowers on branches" (*zhezhihua*).

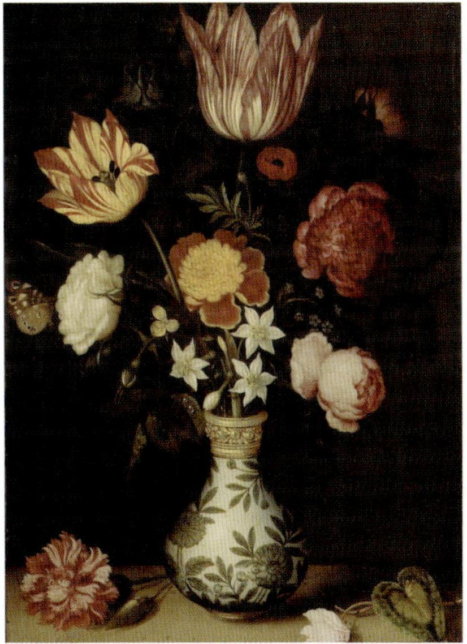

Fig. 12 *Still Life with Flowers in a Wan-Li Vase*
Ambrosius Bosschaert (Netherlands, 1573–1621)
Oil on copper
Height 31 cm × Width 22.5 cm
Rijksmuseum

It would be difficult to find this kind of composition in Chinese traditional painting. Do traditional flower-and-bird paintings fall into the still life category?

of expression through "painterly impression" on the part of the artists of ancient China also to be regarded as obsolete? Can that unique form of Chinese painting, the handscroll, act as a revelation to the modern artist?

If this book can open wide a portal to traditional Chinese painting for its readers, so that they can understand its unique characteristics and taste its essence, then it will have succeeded. As to whether or not traditional Chinese painting is out of date, that is a judgement for readers to make once they have truly entered the world of Chinese painting.

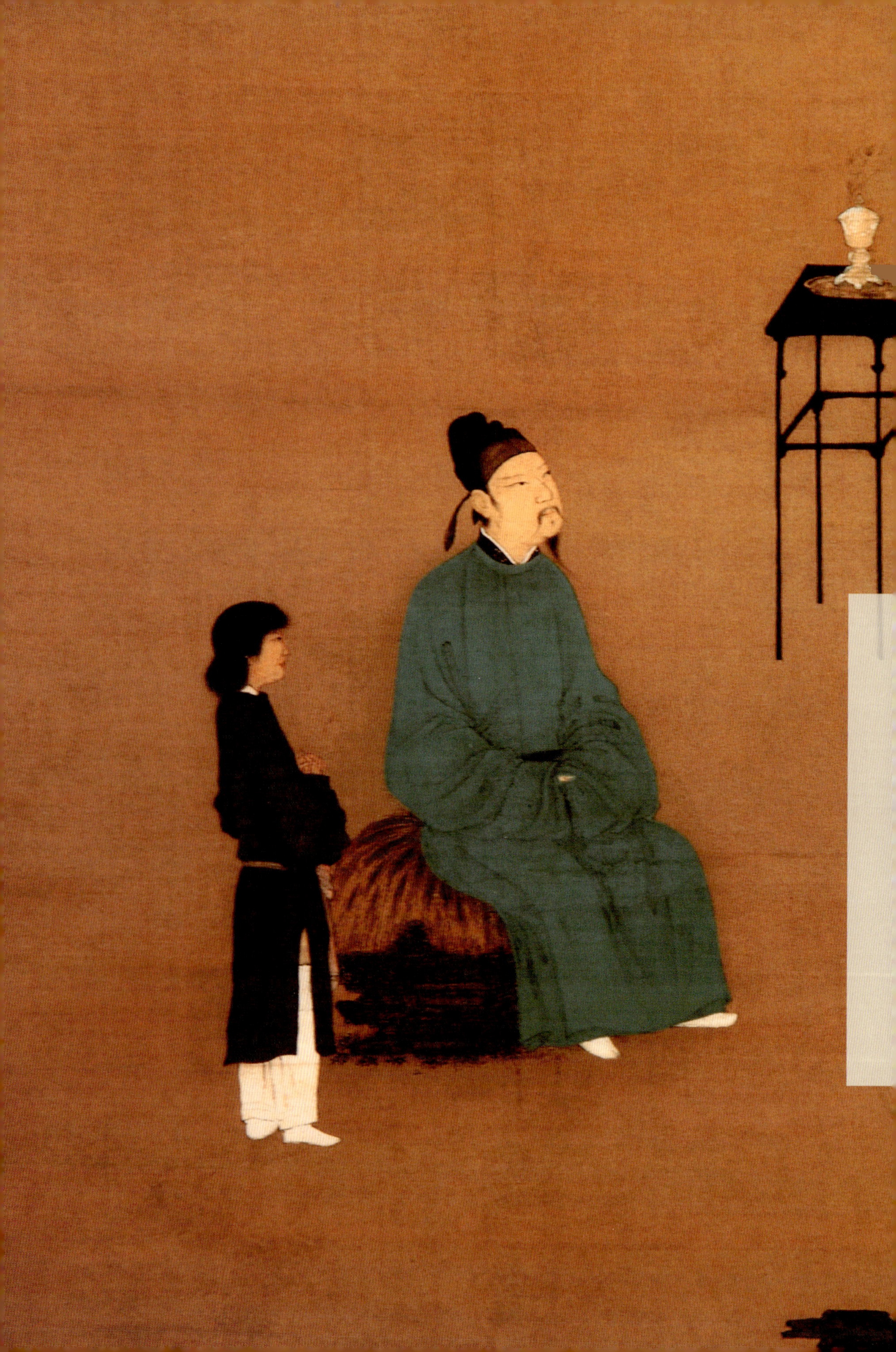

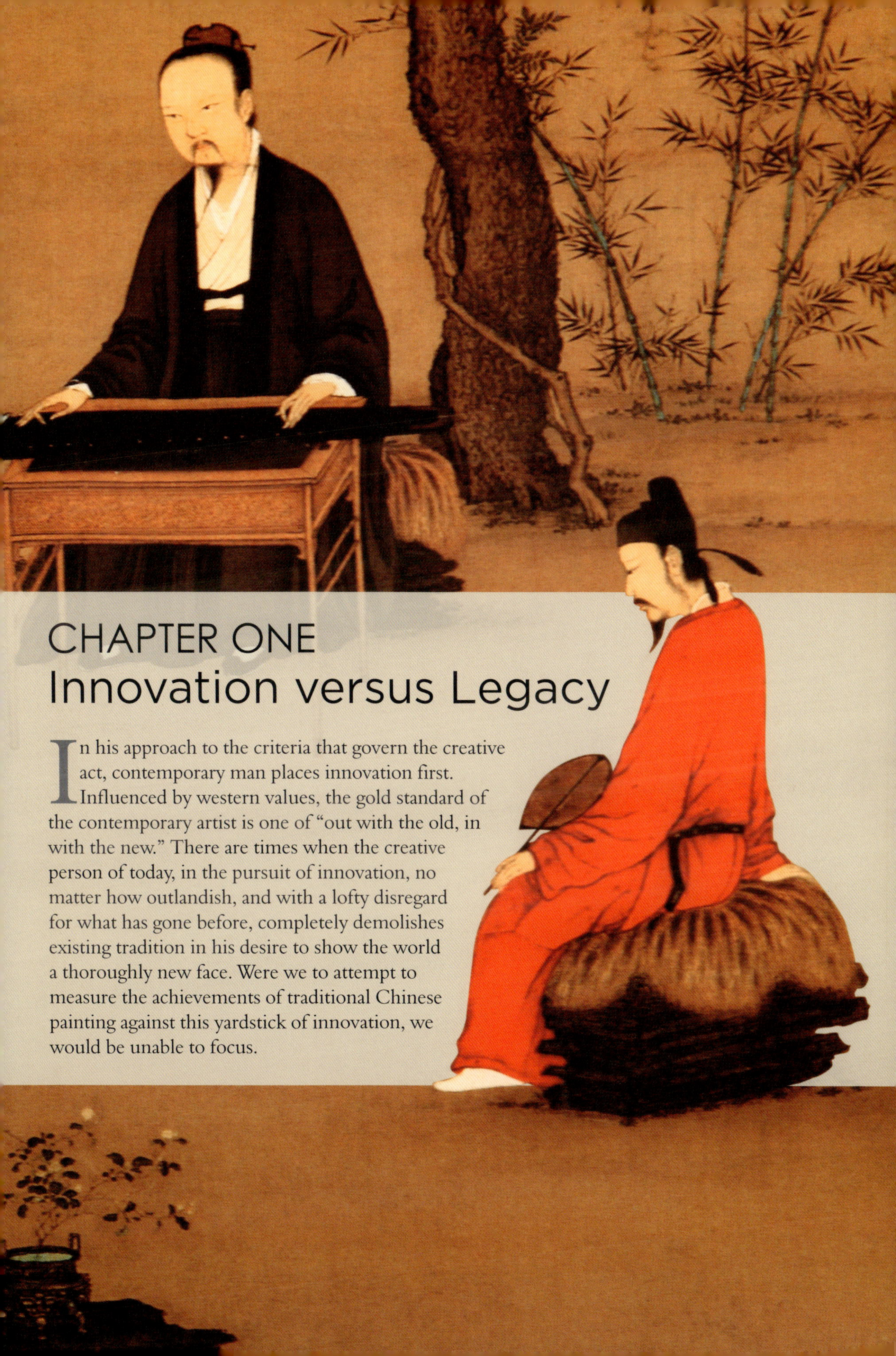

CHAPTER ONE
Innovation versus Legacy

In his approach to the criteria that govern the creative act, contemporary man places innovation first. Influenced by western values, the gold standard of the contemporary artist is one of "out with the old, in with the new." There are times when the creative person of today, in the pursuit of innovation, no matter how outlandish, and with a lofty disregard for what has gone before, completely demolishes existing tradition in his desire to show the world a thoroughly new face. Were we to attempt to measure the achievements of traditional Chinese painting against this yardstick of innovation, we would be unable to focus.

Innovation Is Not the Yardstick of Traditional Chinese Painting

In the appreciation of western art, stylistic changes are the overt features. In the development of western art, the birth of a new era arises from its clash with the artistic aspirations of the old era. Consequently, stylistic periods in western art are clearly marked and each period has its own easily distinguishable and distinctive appearance.

It is the same in Italian art for example. There is a very obvious difference between the religious paintings of the 16th century Renaissance and those of the 17th century Baroque (figs. 14–15), there is an obvious difference in style and the different periods have their own easily distinguishable characteristics: the former aspires to Greek perfectionism, the composition is balanced, light and shade are in proportion and the tones are harmonious; the latter strives for an instant of drama, the figures are no longer perfectly modeled and there is an intense contrast between light and shade. The difference in styles with the early 18th century Rococo and later Neoclassicism is even more pronounced and leaves no room for confusion.

Innovation is indubitably the major creative key in which western artists play. They challenge their predecessors to the tune of "out with the old, in with the new." Nevertheless innovation is not the tune of the historical development of Chinese

Pages 16–17

Fig. 13 *Listening to the Qin* (detail)

Zhao Ji (Song Emperor Huizong) (Northern Song dynasty, 1082–1135)
Ink and color on silk
Height 147.2 cm × Width 51.3 cm
Palace Museum, Beijing

Traditional Chinese painting contains a category known as "paintings of eminent men" (*gaoshi tu*) illustrating the activities of the scholarly leisured class.

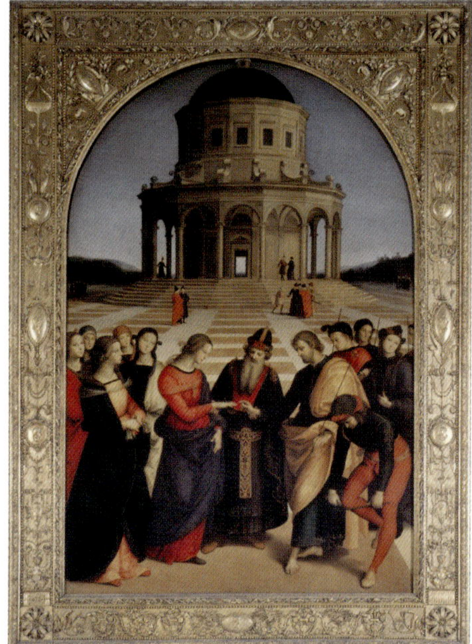

Fig. 14 *Marriage of the Virgin*

Raffaello Sanzio da Urbino (Italy, 1483–1520)
Oil on roundheaded panel
Height 170 cm × Width 117 cm
Pinacoteca di Brera, Milan

The Italian Renaissance glorified Greek Classicism and sought the artistic expression of a harmonious perfection. In the *Marriage of the Virgin* the composition has scenery above with figures beneath with a balance between left and right. The figures are delineated with a graceful line and the palette is soft. The lines of building and its surroundings that form the background display a perfect linear perspective.

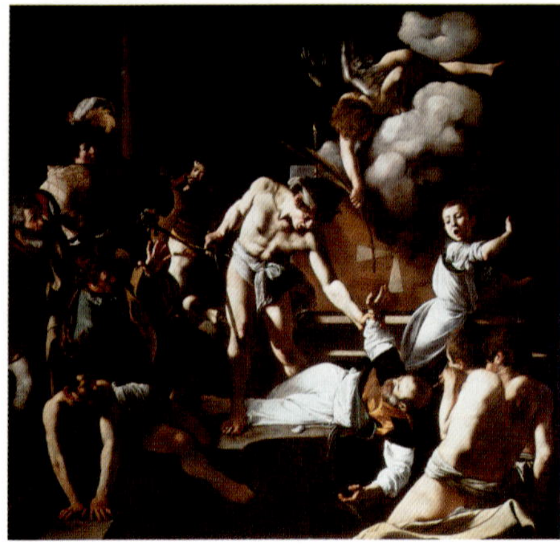

Fig. 15 *The Martyrdom of Saint Matthew*

Michelangelo Merisi da Caravaggio (Italy, 1571–1610)
Oil on canvas
Height 323 cm × Width 343 cm
San Luigi dei Francesi, Rome

Caravaggio was a master of the Italian Baroque whose works exhibit a strong contrast between light and shade that creates moments of high drama.

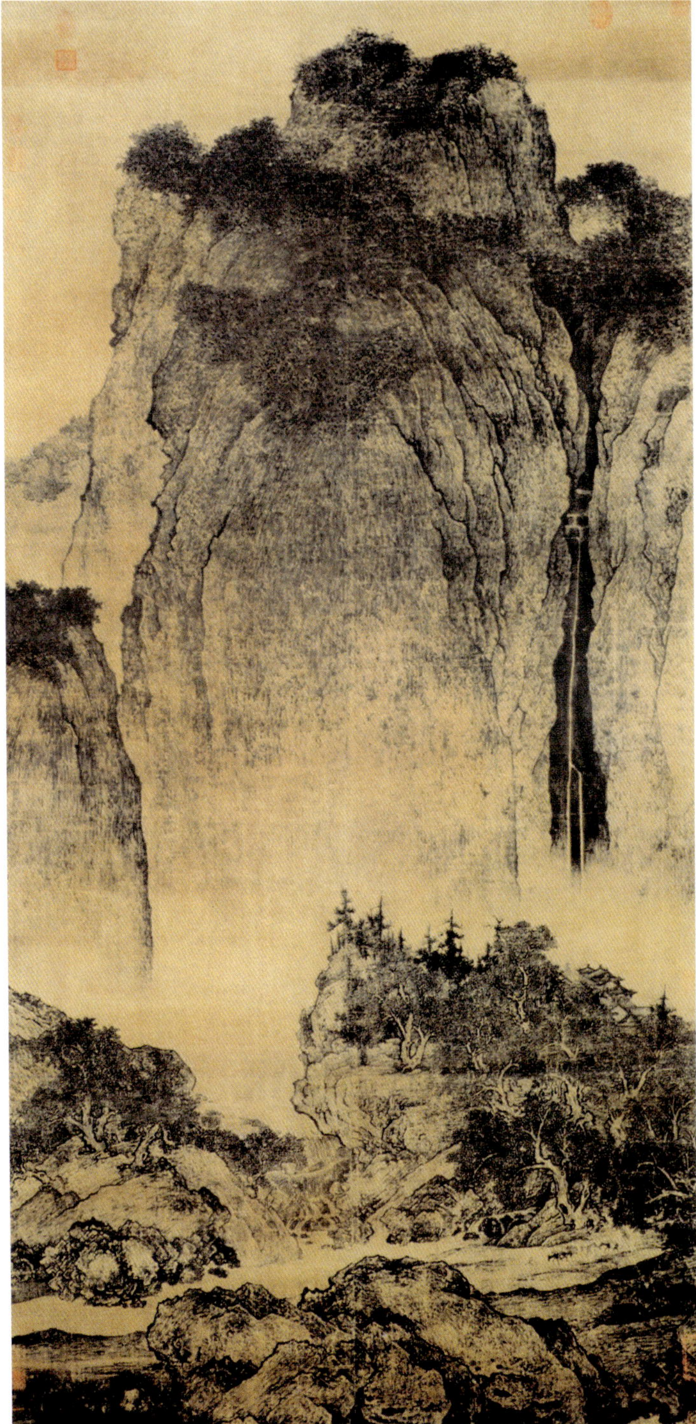

Fig. 16 *Travelers among Mountains and Streams*
Fan Kuan (Northern Song dynasty, 10th–early 11th century)
Ink and color on silk
Height 206.3 cm × Width 103.3 cm
Palace Museum, Taibei

Travelers among Mountains and Streams is the archetypal model of the Northern Song (960–1127) *shanshui*. The mountains, waterfalls, streams and miniscule human figures are frequent features of traditional *shanshui*.

painting. Consequently there is no head-on clash between the obvious characteristics of new and old. There are no traces of earth shattering transformations of style in the history of Chinese painting. Seen at a glance, Chinese traditional painting lacks a sense of the novel and the composition of some categories of painting is pedestrian and routine. There seems nothing exceptional in the characteristics of different dynasties as they appear from the brush of traditional artists.

In fact, there has never been an instance of overthrow followed by renewal in the history of Chinese painting and there have never been any cataclysmic changes of style. Nor have there been any epoch-making advances in theme or content. It has all been a monotonous procession of *shanshui,* figure, and flower-and-bird paintings. To take traditional *shanshui* as an example, the layout and composition of *shanshui* through the Song (960–1279), Yuan (1279–1368), Ming (1368–1644) and Qing dynasties engenders a feeling of familiarity, nothing but a few large hills and stretches of water furnished with waterfalls, streams and little bridges. At the very most there may be a few tiny figures fishing or hurrying along the road ... (figs. 16–18) at first sight it seems difficult indeed to make out the particular characteristics of different dynasties. As for figure paintings these are mostly paintings of ladies and eminent

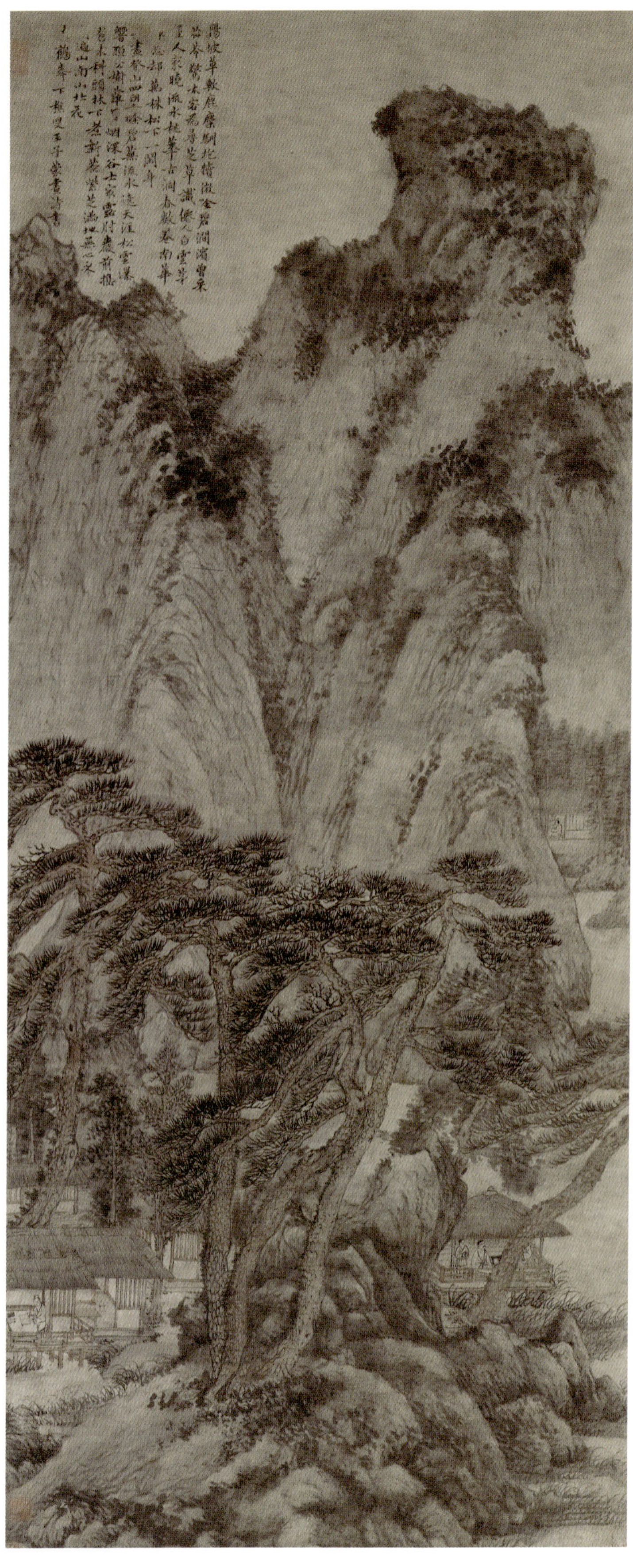

Fig. 17 *Reading in the Hills in Spring*

Wang Meng (Yuan dynasty, c. 1308–1385)
Ink on paper
Height 54.4 cm × Width 28.3 cm
Shanghai Museum

Wang Meng was one of the Four Yuan Masters, his *shanshui* are constructed on a grand scale.

men (*gaoshi tu*) (see fig. 13 on pages 16 and 17), of predictable content and confined to ladies standing holding flowers and literati playing the *qin* by a stream, difficult to view with either delight or surprise and with no outstanding sense of innovation.

The focus of the observations above has been upon innovation, a verdict on Chinese traditional painting reached from the point of view of western values which would be wrong to regard as incorrect. The problem is that neither "out with the old and in with the new" nor "innovation" is a measure of Chinese traditional painting and neither ever formed the creative focus of the artists of ancient China, "transmission" was the focus. In China's traditional culture, it was transmission from master to pupil that was important. Consequently the creative theory of these artists lay not in the overthrow of the achievements of their predecessors but in how best they could transmit their inherited experience onward.

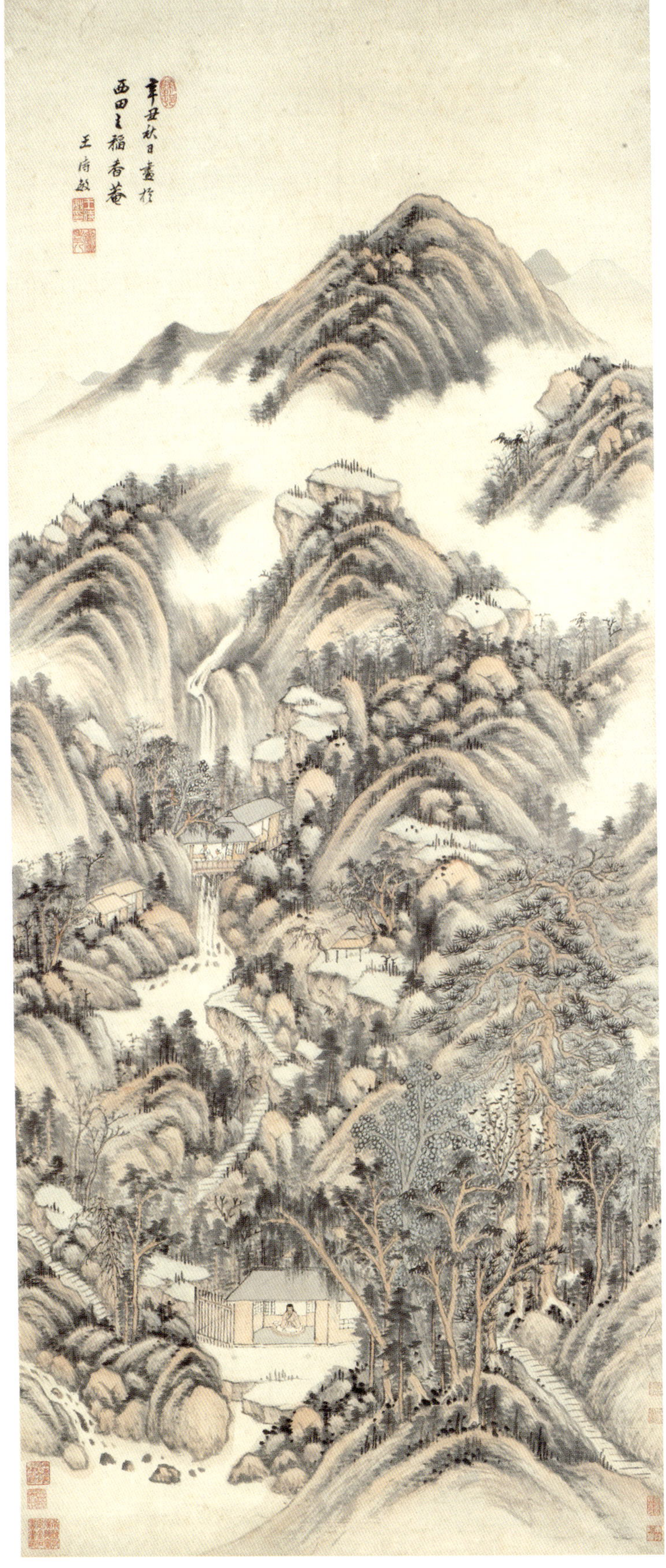

Fig. 18 *Mountains and Cloud*
Wang Shimin (Qing dynasty, 1592–1680)
Ink and color on paper
Height 171.7 cm × Width 60.2 cm
Shanghai Museum

Wang Shimin was one of the Four Wangs of the Qing dynasty. The layout and composition of his paintings seem to hold a sense of familiarity.

The Transformation of Transmission

Although "transmission" was the focus of traditional Chinese painting, that was not to say that traditional painting could not innovate. There is a Chinese saying that "ripe springs from raw" meaning that the achievements of the pupil outstrip those of the master but they do not completely overthrow him. Beyond praise for the pupil's achievements there is no sense of the master being supplanted. In the eyes of the ancient Chinese, the achievements of the pupil were built upon his master, a pupil without a master, however high his attainments, would in traditional society have been regarded as heretical and hence the target of abuse. Thus, as far as traditional creation was concerned, any "innovation" had to be founded upon "transmission." The idea of completely overthrowing one's predecessors is an utterly modern concept that belongs to a system of western values.

Of course, if it was purely a matter of transmission, and later painters were unable to surpass their predecessors however well they did, artistic development would stagnate, unable to continue. Historically, in fact, Chinese painting has never stood still. If we look at the records of works produced by painters starting with the Wei (220–265), Jin (265–420) and Northern and Southern Dynasties (420–589), right through to the end of the Qing dynasty in the early 20th century, it is easy to see that the development of traditional painting continued and broadened. A detailed study of the great painting masters of the past would tell us that that they were all well able to "receive from the past and

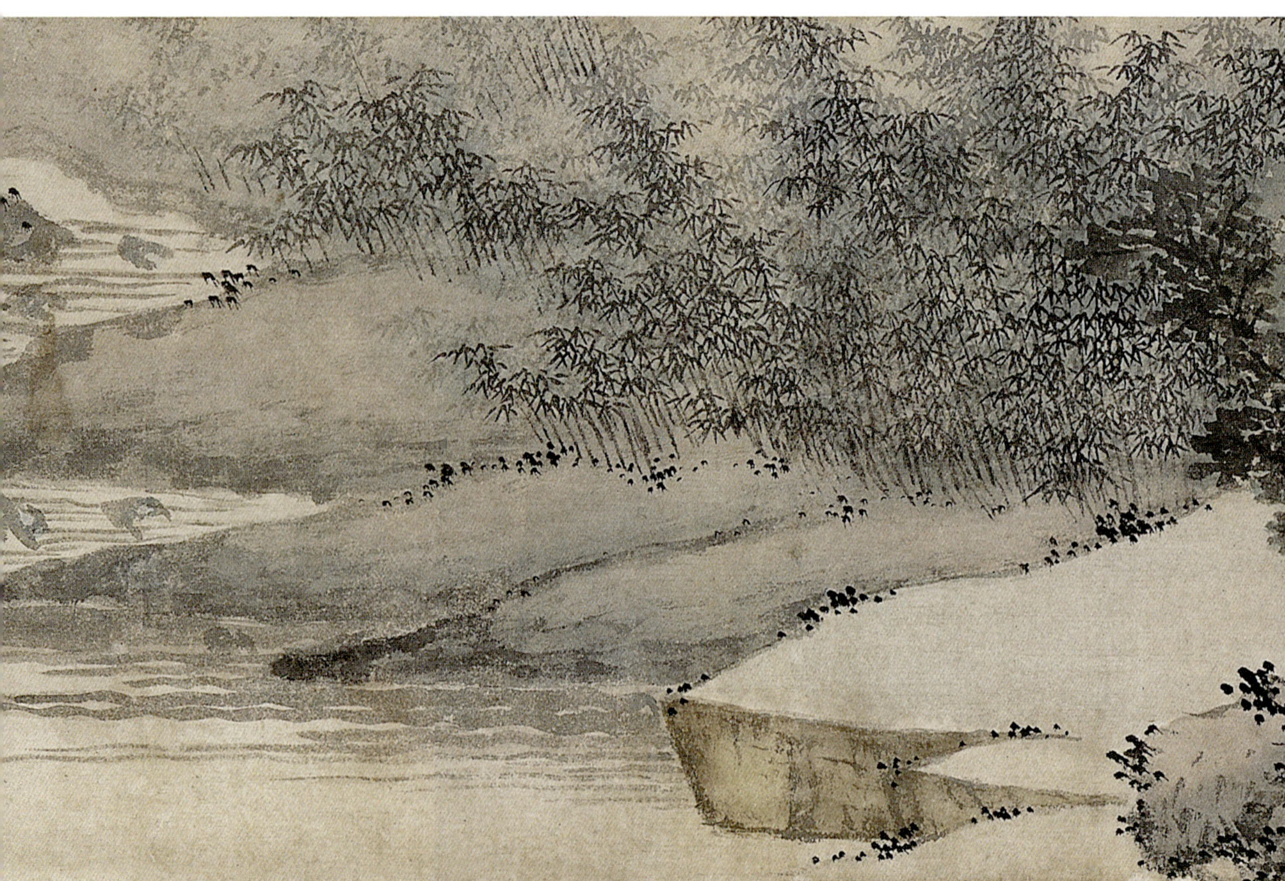

pass on to the future." The subtlety lies in the word "transformation," transformation does not require overthrow and a fresh start.

"Transmission" means being able to "receive from the past" and "pass on to the future." Throughout the historical development of Chinese painting, the works of the masters of each dynasty have on one hand displayed the obvious footprints of their predecessors confirming that they have accepted their artistic theories, and on the other have reflected their own individual flavor and the pulse of the dynasty in which they lived. It is just that the strong flavor of "transmission" bears easily identified elements of similarity, such as layout and composition, that obscure the distinctive features of innovation. In fact, constant observation and analysis and a grasp of the knack of looking at Chinese paintings allows one to see how the masters of each dynasty, based on the inheritance of different teachers, transformed the old tradition and developed their own differing idiosyncratic concepts of the new. Both the transmission and innovation to be found within the process are profoundly thought-provoking and of endless interest (fig. 19).

Fig. 19 *By the Bank of a Stream* (detail)
Shen Zhou (Ming dynasty, 1427–1509)
Ink and color on paper
Height 30.1 cm × Width 160.9 cm
Suzhou Museum

The rocks, bamboo and trees in this painting of elegant scholar hermits have been heavily influenced by the *shanshui* tradition of the Four Yuan Masters of the Yuan dynasty.

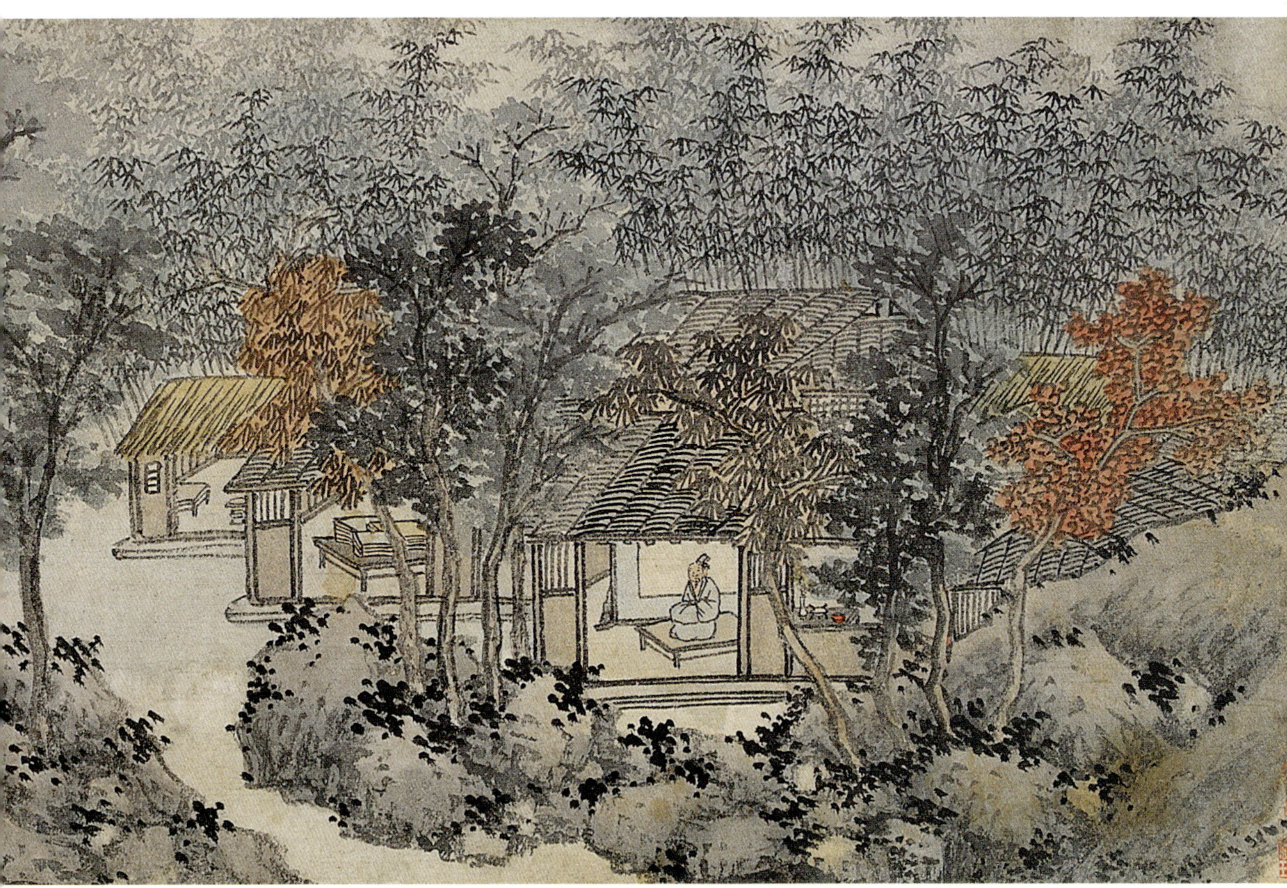

The Necessity of Copying

Because of the emphasis on transmission, it follows that copying (*linmo*) frequently occurs as a means of studying traditional Chinese painting. In ancient times, the artists used to say "learn from the ancients," meaning that they should take the ancients as their teacher and study the theory and technique found in the works of past masters. Copying consists of *lin* and *mo*, two means of studying the works of ancient artists. *Lin* is to have the original painting at one's side and to reproduce its form mechanically. *Mo* means to place semi-transparent paper over the original and then to carefully trace the shape of objects in it, brushstroke by brushstroke. Ideally, works produced by these two methods must resemble the original and on inspection must not seem like a lesser relative. It must be possible to confuse the artificial with the real.

Of course, counterfeiting is not the aim of copying. Copying is a kind of training and learning by duplicating the works of past masters and in the process of reproduction attempting to grasp the knowledge they had gained in the fields of composition, delineation, brushwork, color and the use of ink. A traditional painter once told the author that he had copied Fan Kuan's (10th–early 11th century) *Travelers among Mountains and Streams* at least three or four times and in the process had discovered something new each time, causing him to marvel at the profundity of the understanding of nature displayed by the Northern Song (960–1127) masters of *shanshui*, as well as at the precision of their creative thinking and their exquisite brushwork. This experience was only to be gained through a process of painstaking copying, stroke by stroke, so as to sense its essence for oneself. Once the copying was completed, and even if it was a perfect image of the original, the copyist then added his own name and title and amongst the inscriptions,

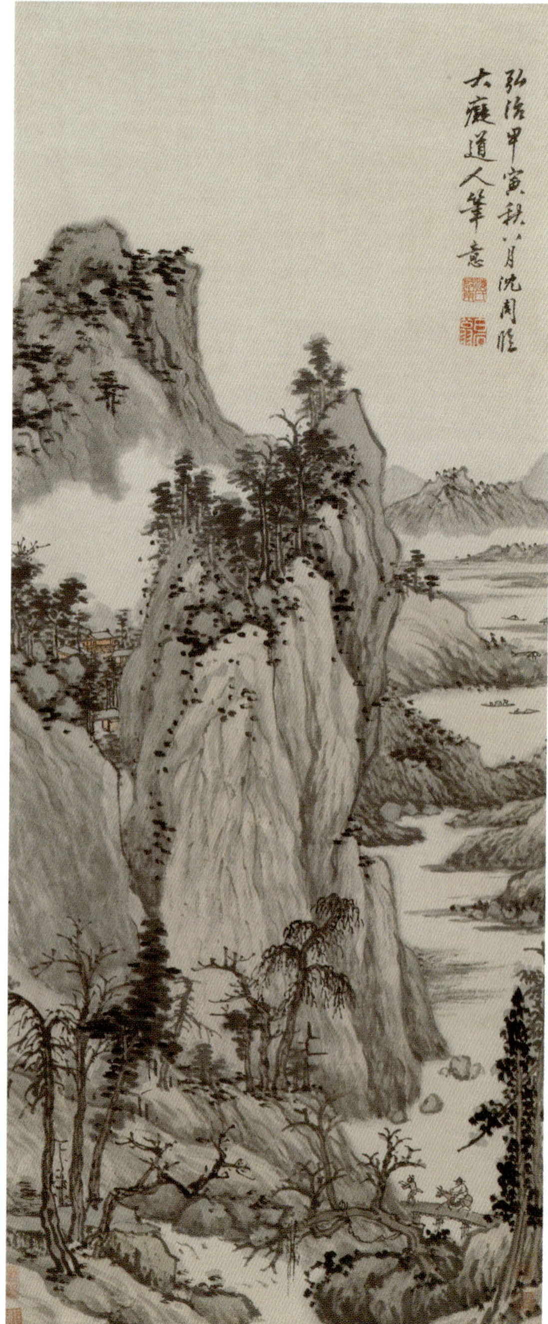

Fig. 20 *In the Style of the Shanshui of Da Chi (Huang Gongwang)*

Shen Zhou
Ink and color on paper
Height 115.5 cm × Width 48.5 cm
Shanghai Museum

Shen Zhou was a noted Ming dynasty painter whose *shanshui* continued the tradition of the Northern Song and of the Four Yuan Masters. The line and use of dotting in the depiction of the patterning of the rocks imitates the style of Huang Gongwang of the Yuan dynasty.

usually inserted a record of what he felt he had gained from the process of copying. These kind of paintings usually carried "copy of work by so and so" as a title, making it clear that it was just a copy (fig. 20). If the copyist not only failed to add his own name and then signed the name of the original master, the "copy" became a fake old master.

However close the copy it cannot surpass the achievements of the past. True artists and forgers have differing levels of requirement from the act of copying. When a forger copies, his attention is concentrated upon an object's shape, his aim to produce something that looks exactly like the original. However, for the painter of true artistic aspiration the shape of an object is merely a medium, that is to say the artist has to use a shape such as a tree, a hill or a flower in order to recreate the original painter's experience of the objects that lay beneath his brush at the moment of their creation. For an artist, the aim of copying is to understand the character and manner of the ancients by copying their brushwork and the abstract values that flow from it.

The forgery of ancient paintings has been common throughout the history of Chinese art. Documentary evidence suggests that the earliest examples occurred in the Jin and Tang (618–907) dynasties. Fake old masters are called *yanpin* (forgeries). By the Ming and Qing dynasties, and due to the speed of developments in society and the economy there was a definite demand for works of art and forgeries flooded the market, so much so that forgeries began to exhibit regional characteristics. Special names such as "Suzhou pieces," "Henan made," and "Kaifeng goods" were used by insiders in the trade to describe forgeries produced in other areas. In the 20th century the finest forger was Zhang Daqian (1899–1983) whose forgeries deceived not a few scholars and connoisseurs including Huang Binhong (1865–1955) and Chen Banding (1876–1970). A number of his forged "ancient paintings" were erroneously regarded as genuine by western museums and incorporated in their collections.

Historically, most of the masters whose paintings became the model for copyists were scholars and philosophers who had transcended material desire and aspired to the spiritual. They included Huang Gongwang (1269–1354) and Ni Zan (c. 1301–1374), two of the Four Yuan Masters and Bada Shanren (c. 1626–1705) and Shi Tao (1641–c. 1718), two of the Four Monks of the Early Qing. Two abstract concepts were involved, *xieshen* (imaging the spirit) and *bimo* (brush and ink). These will be explained in later chapters.

In the Manner of the Ancients

The pursuit of the abstract notions of spirit (*shen*) and brush and ink extends to a further means of studying to "learn from the ancients." This is *fang* (in the style of, or emulation). The process of emulation, is, in a way, the same as that of *lin,* a creation, so to speak, produced from the original painting. However, in this particular act of creation, the importance lies not in imitating the form of the original but in understanding the brush work and style of the original artists, including the way they used brush and ink and their composition and presentation. Consequently, the work that emerges from this process does not need to be precisely the same as the original. The emulator may, as it were, "tailor" the original or even alter its composition so that the external form of the original and its emulation bear no relation to each other, even though the brush work and style are born of the same breath and are similar in feeling.

In another way, an "emulation" may not require to have an original from a great master at hand and may be a completely new picture, but executed in the manner of the ancients and created merely on the basis of the

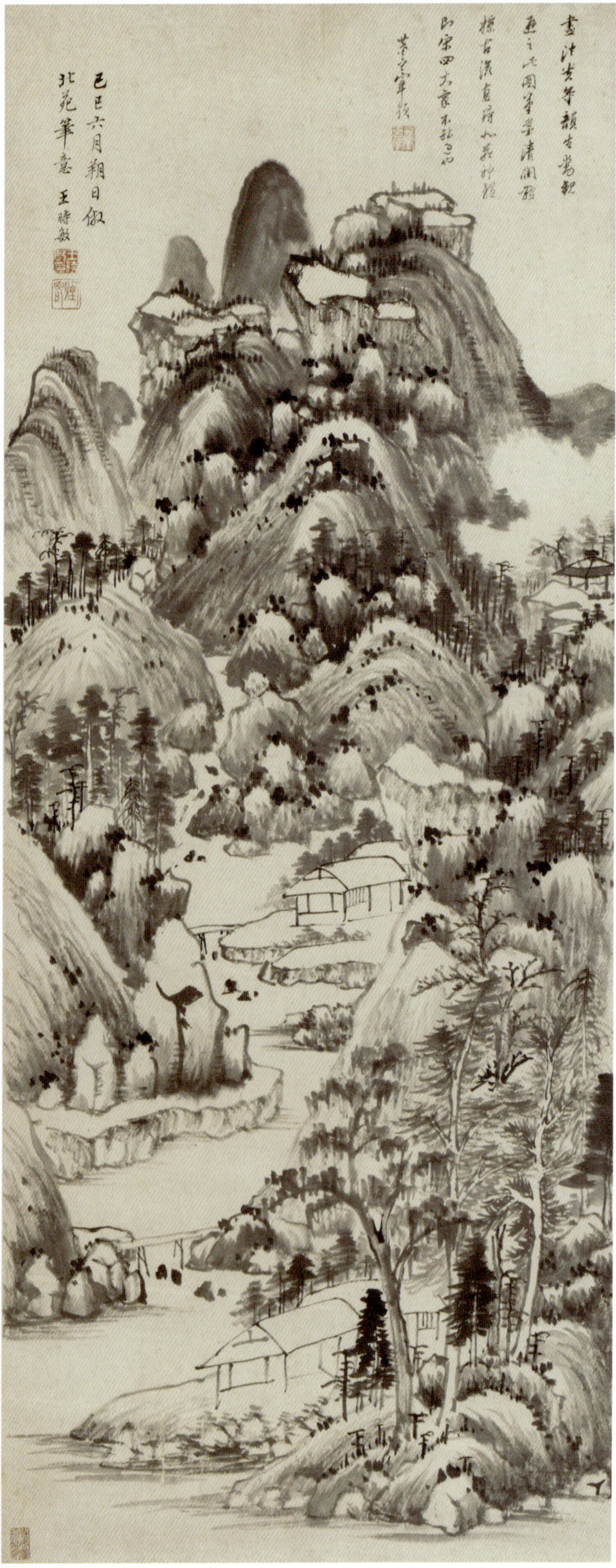

Fig. 21 Shanshui *Imitating Dong Yuan*
Wang Shimin
Ink on paper
Height 91.8 cm × Width 37.1 cm
Shanghai Museum

emulator's recollection of the manner and of his understanding of ancient brush work and style. These paintings usually bear the title "In the manner of master so and so." For those closely acquainted with ancient paintings, it is possible, without the need for any explanation, to detect the footprints of the ancients in these emulations, though clearly they are not ancient. In the history of Chinese painting, the most powerful emulators were Wang Shimin (1592–1680), Wang Jian (1598–1677), Wang Hui (1632–1717), and Wang Yuanqi (1642–1715) (figs. 21–23). These four recall the ancients with the admiration of their hearts and with the skill of their copying so that the brush and ink and manner of their work closely approaches the style of the ancients. The creative work of the "Four Wangs" is totally founded on the artistic concept of emulation, and their work was devoted to following and reflecting the styles of the *shanshui* masters of the Song and Yuan dynasties. They were highly esteemed in the Qing dynasty and came to be regarded as the orthodox school of painting (*huaxue zhengzong*), thereby demonstrating the value of transmission in traditional painting.

The quality of transmission can be found in all three genre of traditional painting from figure painting through *shanshui* to flower-and-bird paintings. For example, the paintings of court ladies by the Tang dynasty artist Zhang Xuan (active 714–741) directly follow the Tang artist Zhou Fang (8th–early 9th century); in *shanshui*, the great works of Dong Yuan (?–c. 962) and Ju Ran (fl. 960–985) of the Five Dynasties (907–960) and Northern Song dynasty became the models for

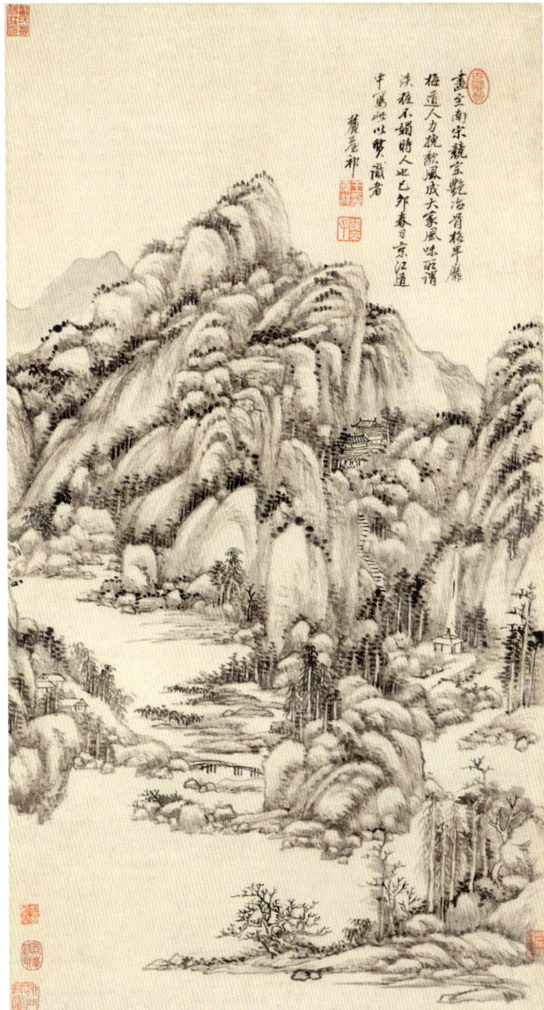

Fig. 22 *In the Style of the Shanshui of Wu Zhen*
Wang Yuanqi (Qing dynasty, 1642–1715)
Ink on paper
Height 141.7 cm × Width 51cm
Shanghai Museum

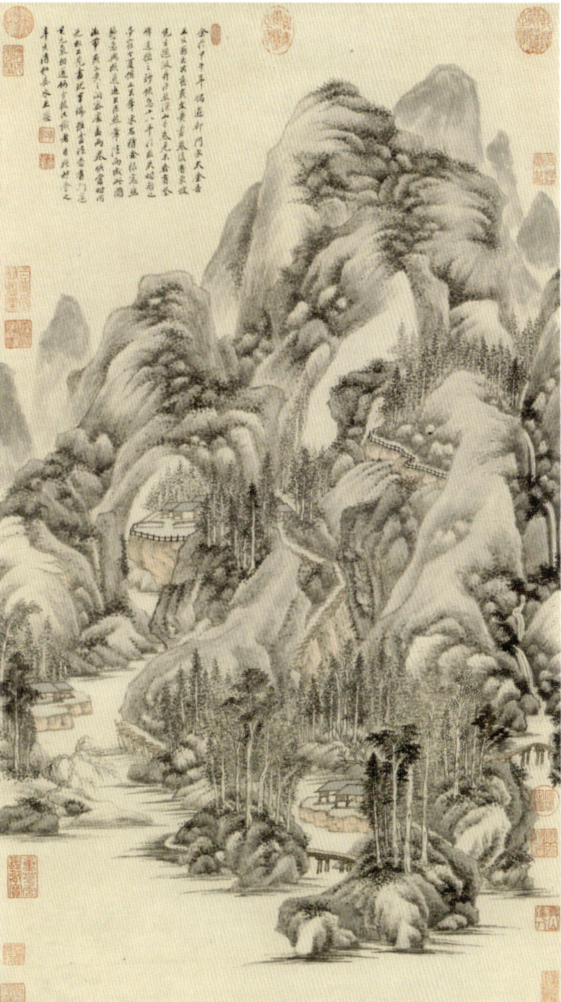

Fig. 23 *In the Style of a Ju Ran Shanshui*
Wang Jian (Qing dynasty, 1598–1677)
Ink and color on paper
Height 88.6 cm × Width 50.8 cm
Shanghai Museum

Figs. 21–23 The Qing tradition of the Four Wangs followed the artistic theory of "learn from the ancients" and strongly advocated the concept of "emulation." Their models for emulation were drawn from works of the Northern Song, Five Dynasties (907–960) and the Four Yuan Masters. In the process of creating a copy they strove to recollect the style and spirit of the ancients.

the literati painters of the Yuan, Ming and Qing dynasties; the Song Painting Academy tradition of flower-and-bird painting became the style so assiduously followed by later exponents of fine-work (*gongbi*) flower-and-bird painting.

In summary, the historical development of traditional Chinese painting lies not in innovation but in transmission, and it is in transmission that evolution towards change occurs. This is not only so in the expression of style but also in the artistic aspirations that lie behind the painting itself. This book will analyze the characteristics of transmission in Chinese traditional art on the basis of examples from the three genre of figure painting, *shanshui,* and flower-and-bird painting in order to see how the Chinese artists of the past developed painting through the dynasties without exaggerated self-promotion or a desire to upset the existing system of transmission from teacher to pupil. It is an interesting thought to ponder.

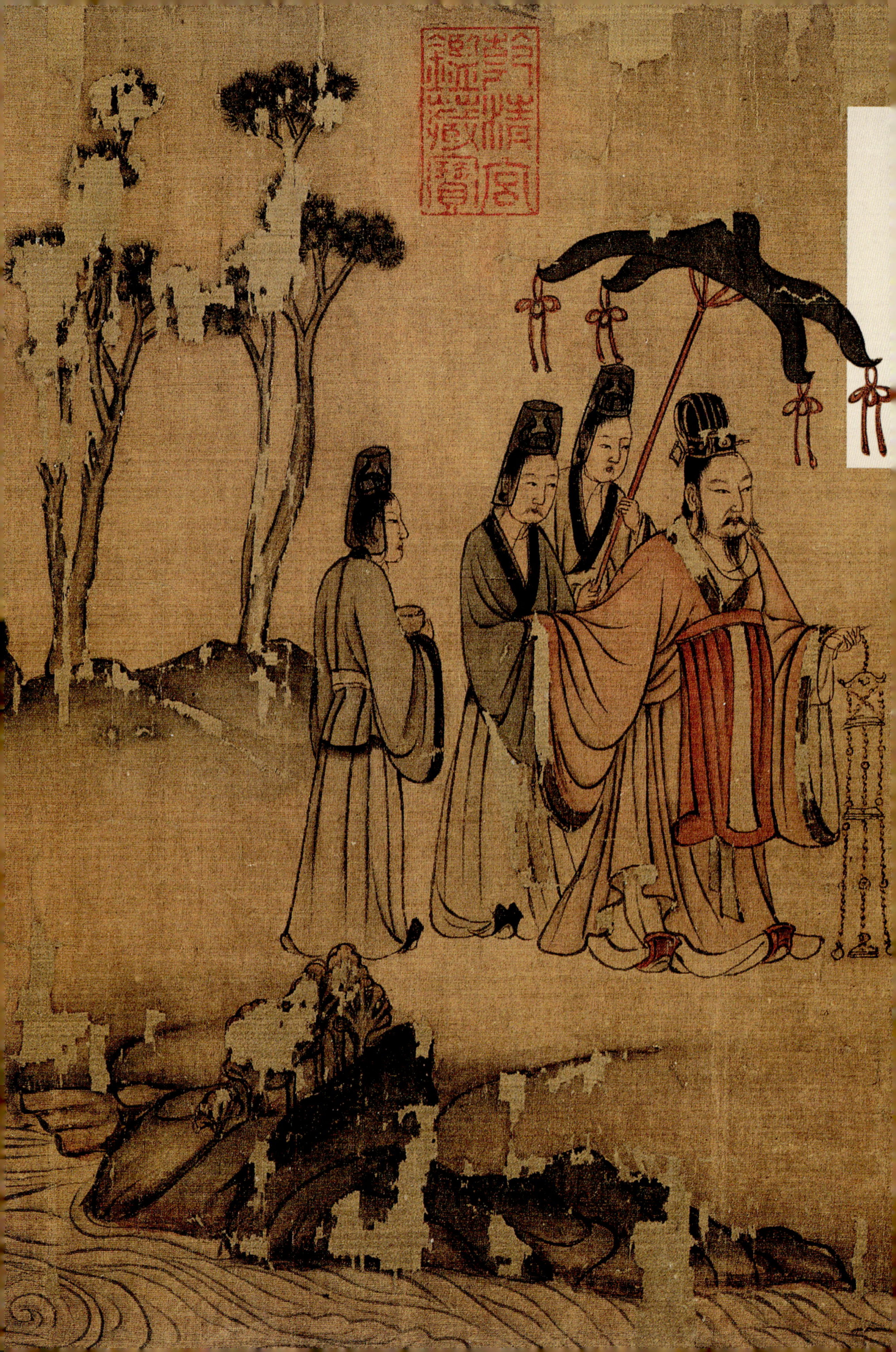

CHAPTER TWO
True Likeness versus Painterly Impression

"True likeness" (*xiezhen*) is the concrete and realistic manifestation of an object; "painterly impression" (*xieyi*) is the abstract manifestation of the externality of an image. Western painting is heavy with the flavor of true likeness, whilst in Chinese painting there is a greater emphasis upon "painterly impression." Consequently, the Chinese do not speak of "painting" a picture but of "writing" one. Compared with "painting" the importance of "writing" lies not in the detail but in the transmission of the sense.

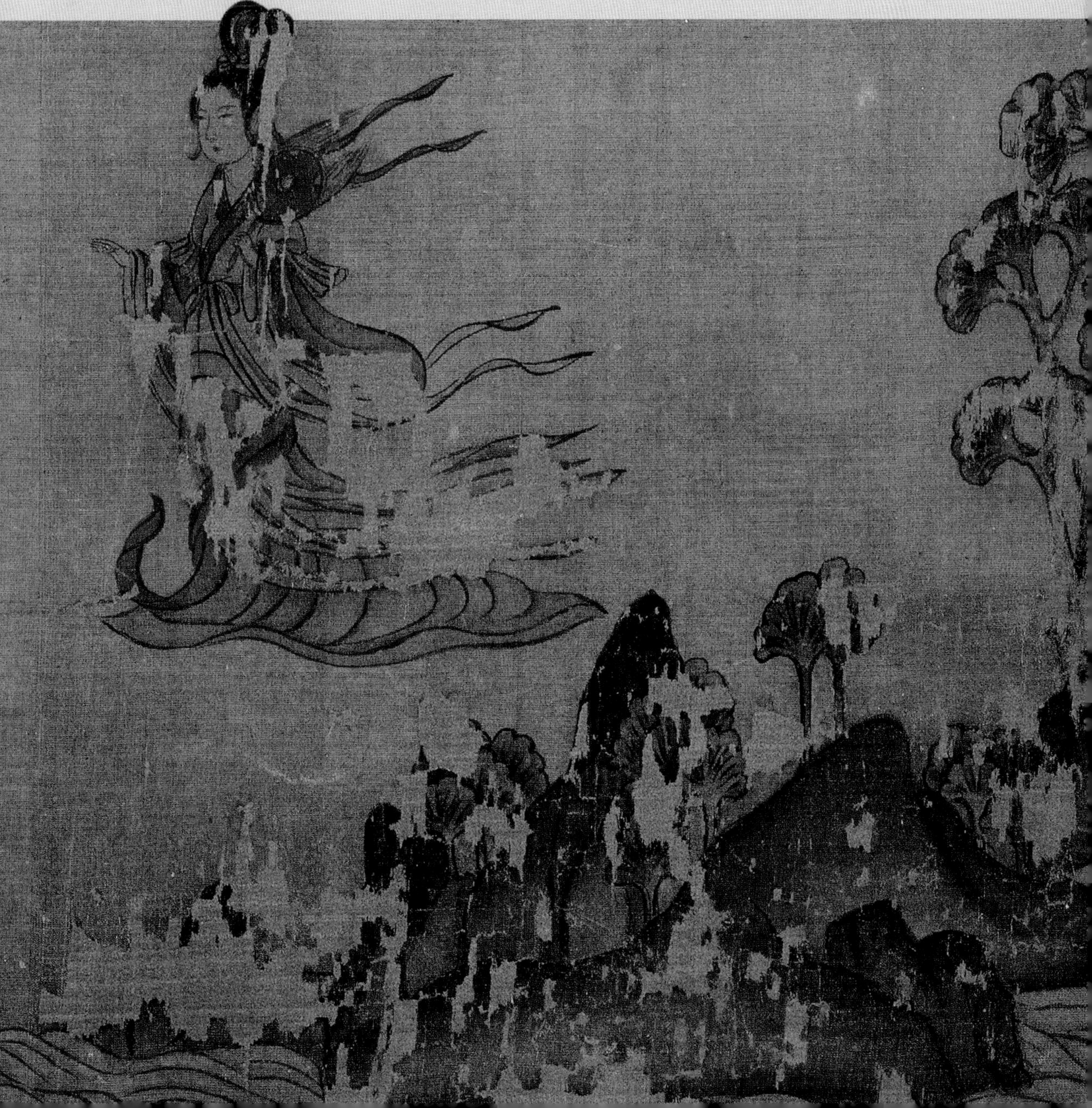

The Pursuit of *Xiezhen* and *Xieyi*

In China, the ancients did not refer to "painting pictures" but spoke of "writing pictures." There were two reasons for this. First, painting and writing in the Chinese context share the same tool and medium—brush and paper. Moreover the earliest pictograms of Chinese writing were fundamentally pictures that were "painted" rather than "written" and confirmed the theory that painting and calligraphy derived from the same source. Secondly, the most respected traditional painters and calligraphers of the ancient past were men of learning who, in their creative work, pursued art rather than handicraft. For these knowledgeable men there was no difference between painting and calligraphy, they were the same art of delineation. In fact, both Chinese painting and calligraphy can be seen as an art of lines. Once a particular theme and content had been established, the emphasis was not upon detail but upon conveying the spirit, the emergence of a kind of manner and temperament.

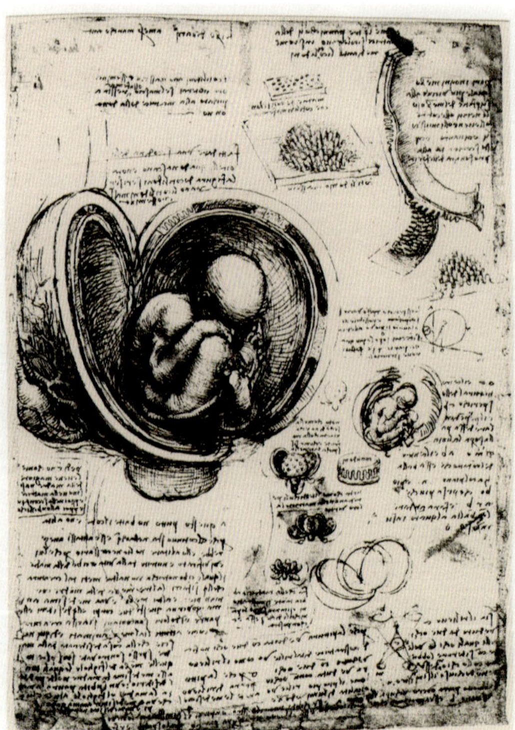

Fig. 25 *Drawing from Life*
Leonardo Da Vinci

Drawing from life is an indispensable part of training in the western art tradition. Its basic requirement is for detailed observation followed by the realistic and accurate depiction of the objects that lie before the eye. Masterpieces such as the life drawings of Leonardo Da Vinci are serious artistic creations as well as being practice pieces.

The art education of today is modeled on that of western art education, sketching and drawing from life is the indispensable basic primer to painting, as well as being the basis for the actual study of western art. From geometrical plaster shapes to plaster images, then on to drawing the human body, from simply composed still life drawing to outdoor sketching and then through training in sketching and drawing from life, the student acquires a grasp of the skills of showing the shape of solids, of managing light and shade and expressing space. The aim is to enable the student to display the world he sees before him realistically and faithfully in a drawing or painting. This is called *xiezhen* (fig. 25). Nowadays, drawing from life is generally regarded as a form of basic training rather than as a form of art. In a recent discussion of Renaissance drawings from life, a painter pointed out to the author that, at the time, drawing from life was a rigorous creative art form in its own right. A look at Da Vinci's drawings from life would show that they were no quick sketch or practice material. On re-examining historical art material the author discovered that there was much logic in the painter's point of view. However, the sketching and drawing from life discussed here relate to a generalized concept and to the demands of academic training.

One could say that the pursuit of *xiezhen* was a breakthrough continuously sought by western artists prior to the 19th century. We merely have to look at the development of western painting to discover that from

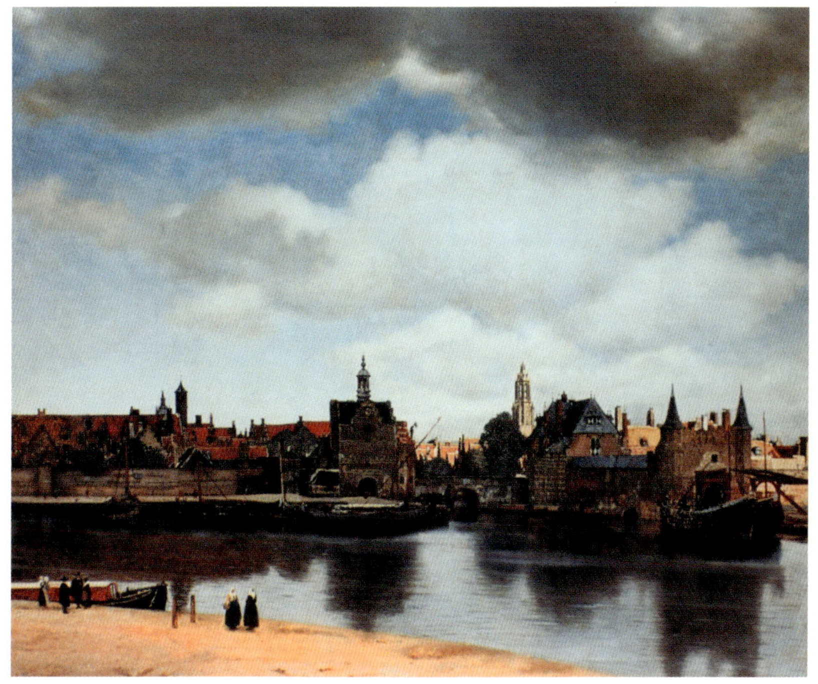

Pages 28–29

Fig. 24 Copy of Gu Kaizhi's *The Nymph of the Luo River* (detail)

Please refer to figs. 36–37 on pages 36 and 37.

Fig. 26 *View of Delft*

Johannes Vermeer (Netherlands, 1632–1675)
Oil on canvas
Height 96.5 cm × Width 117.5 cm
Mauritshuis, The Hague

Western artists of the Baroque reached the pinnacle of achievement in the painting skills of *xiezhen*. This view of 17th century Delft has a photographic quality.

the early Renaissance, and in the train of developments in scientific knowledge such as perspective and the principles of optics, western painters' grasp of the skills of *xiezhen* matured and quickened day by day, so that by the 17th century the western painters of the Baroque were able to produce uni-dimensional illusions of reality that were almost photographic (fig. 26). Later romantic painters began to move away from external representation and tended to a more internal form of depiction. For example, Goya's *The Third of May* (fig. 27) which depicts a scene of senseless tragedy in a Madrid square on 3 May 1808. French Napoleonic forces had occupied Madrid and there had been armed

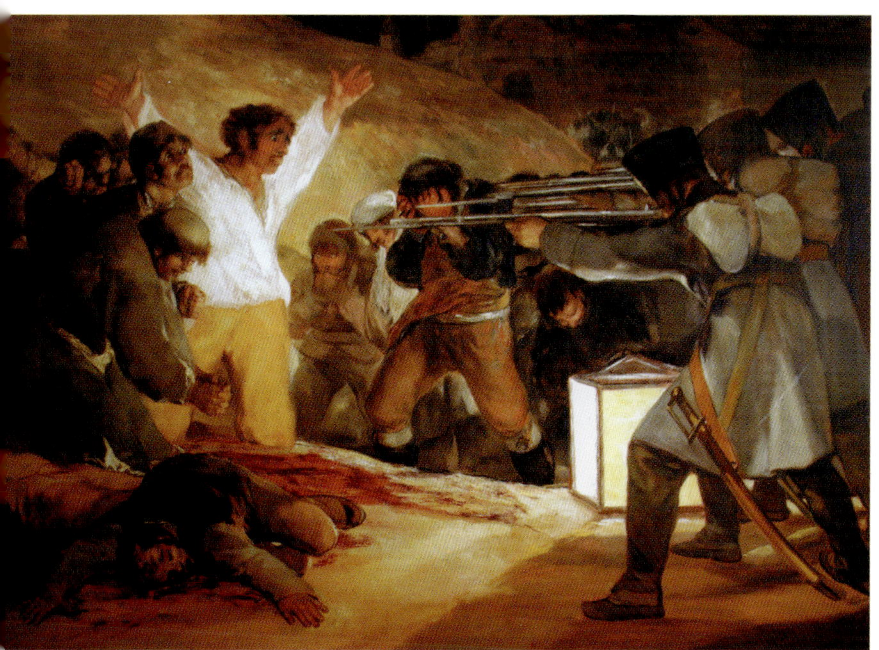

Fig. 27 *The Third of May 1808*

Francisco Goya (Spain, 1746–1828)
Oil on canvas
Height 266 cm × Width 345 cm
Prado Museum, Madrid

Western 18th century painters of the Romantic Movement began to move away from external representation. The focus of this painting of Goya's is upon the internal world portrayed in the face of the principal character and the sense of appalled helplessness that it shows.

clashes between the people of Madrid and French troops the previous day. The following day in an act of revenge the French slaughtered a number of Spanish civilians. The principal character in this painting is a Spanish civilian who stands in front of a rank of French soldiers with their weapons raised, his face filled with appalled helplessness in the face of such sudden tragedy. Although this painting records the senselessness of a historic tragedy and not the fate of a particular citizen, its principal theme is the internal world portrayed in the face of the principal character. In contrast, the other figures and the treatment of space still maintain the quality of *xiezhen*. We merely have to look at the self-portrait by the Qing artist Jin Nong (1687–1763) (fig. 28), one of the Eight Eccentrics of Yangzhou, to see immediately that the artists of the past in China placed no store at all by *xiezhen*. This painting is called an "image of self," but neither in the proportions of the figure nor in any characteristic expression of the face is there a trace of the "true likeness" of the western artist. Nevertheless, up until the 20th century birth of modernism, that quality was a predominant characteristic of the western painting tradition.

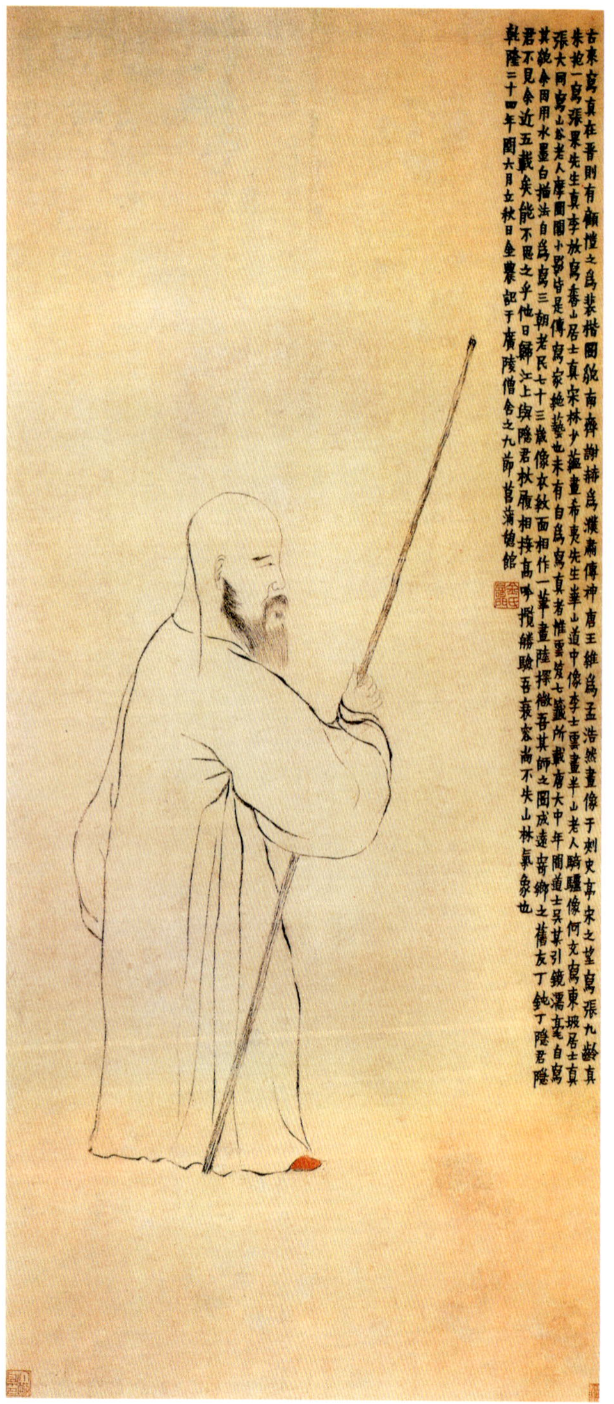

Fig. 28 *Image of Self*
Jin Nong (Qing dynasty, 1687–1763)
Ink on paper
Height 131.3 cm × Width 59.1 cm
Palace Museum, Beijing`

This painting is called *Image of Self*, but neither in the proportions of the body nor in the depiction of the characteristics of the actual figure would it be easy to regard it as a realistic representation.

The Division between Art and Handicraft

There is a fundamental parting of ways in the development of Chinese and western art. What is termed traditional Chinese painting is in no way a general kind of painting but a form of high art that belongs to scholars and the privileged classes. In the history of western art, painting and sculpture, architecture and even the decorative arts are all on a level. When considering each category of art and making their judgments, the focus of western art historians is wholly upon the achievements of the individual artist and not upon the difference between the various categories of art. Take Donatello's 15th century *David* (fig. 29) and Massacio's *The Tribute Money* (fig. 30) for example, though both

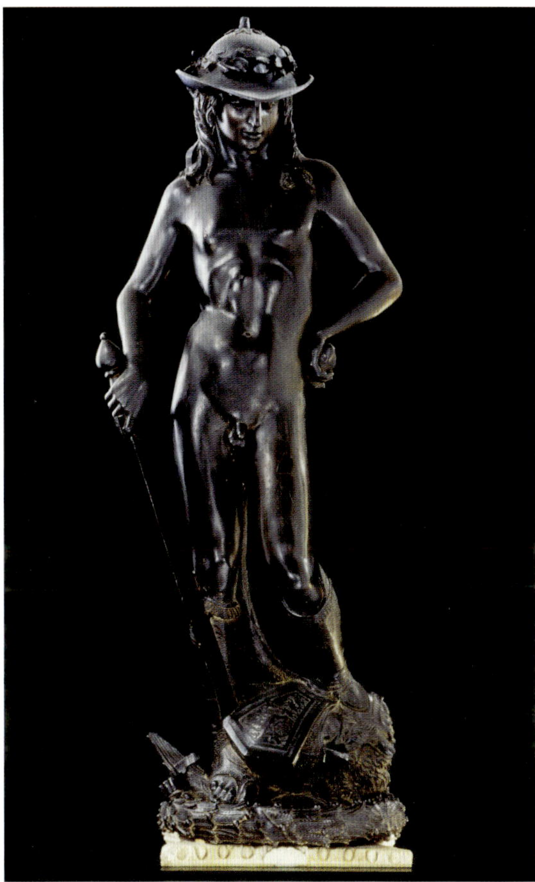

Fig. 29 *David*
Donatello (Italy, 1386–1466)
Height 159 cm

Donatello was a noted sculptor of the Early Italian Renaissance. In an illustration of the mythological story, David is depicted in the form of a young man grasping a sword and clad in boots with his foot on the decapitated head of the giant Goliath.

Fig. 30 *The Tribute Money*
Massacio (Italy, 1401–1428)
Fresco
Height 247 cm × Width 597 cm
Brancacci Chapel, Florence

Massacio was a noted painter of the Early Italian Renaissance. The modelling of his figures shows the influence of his predecessor Giotto. The spirit of Humanism and the spatial perspective in his work had a profound influence upon the subsequent development of the Italian Renaissance.

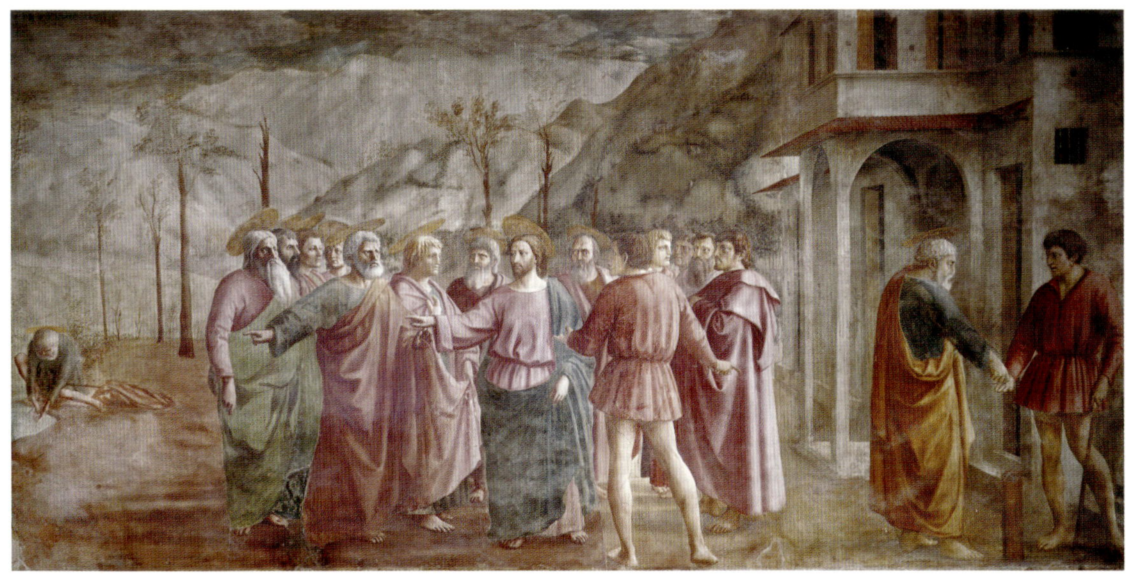

men were giants of the early Renaissance, the former was a noted sculptor and the latter was a painter, but both were highly influential in the development of the Italian art of the late Renaissance. Consequently they are of equal importance in the history of western art, in no way do their differing specialties affect their historical status. This kind of situation never existed in the history of Chinese art prior to the 20th century. In ancient China the status of a sculptor was not on a par with that of a traditional painter. This explains why, in pre-20th century histories of Chinese art, there are only great painters and calligraphers and no great sculptors or architects.

In the eyes of the art historians of ancient China, the fact that sculpture, architecture and the decorative arts had a functional role, merely placed them in the category of handicrafts, and not to be mentioned in the same breath as art. Furthermore, the definition of traditional painting included neither frescoes nor folk art so that these creations, which served both religion and the people, were regarded as the equivalent of the handicrafts of sculpture and architecture and not part of the canon of art. In ancient China, it was only calligraphy that could be viewed as being on equal terms with painting since both were scholarly arts in which the leading creative role was played by an educated elite (figs. 31–35).

Viewed separately, the creations of the artisans and artists of ancient China reflect the fact that painters and calligraphers were very aware, early on, of the division between "handicraft" and "art." The former speaks to skill and only the latter to artistic creativity. It is skill that is the focus of *xiezhen* and because, historically, traditional painters were conscious of this division between art and handicrafts, it made them dissatisfied with the concept of *xiezhen*. In short, traditional painters were not focused upon *xiezhen*.

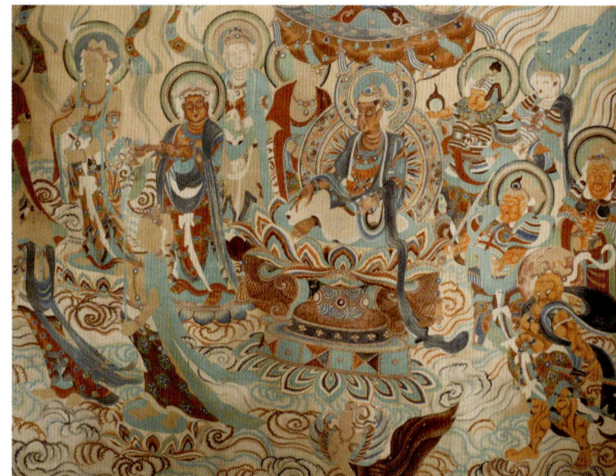

Fig. 31 Dunhuang fresco

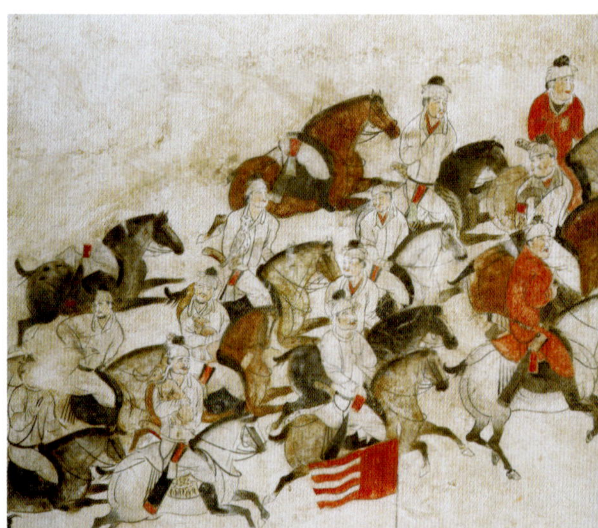

Fig. 32 Dunhuang fresco

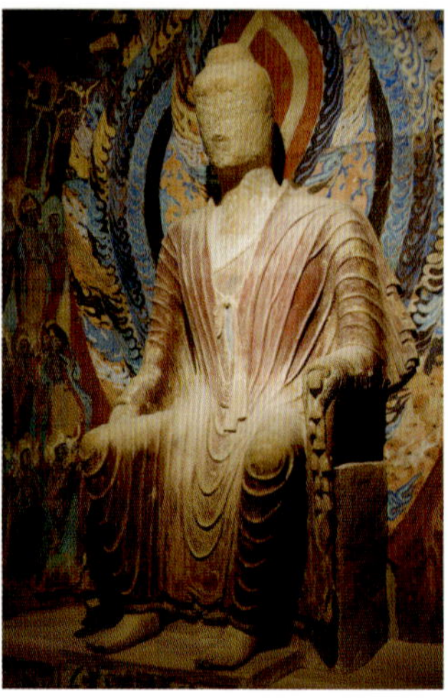

Fig. 33 Dunhuang sculpture

Figs. 31–33 In the eyes of the art scholars of ancient China, sculpture and frescoes were functional creations, handicrafts that were not to be regarded as art.

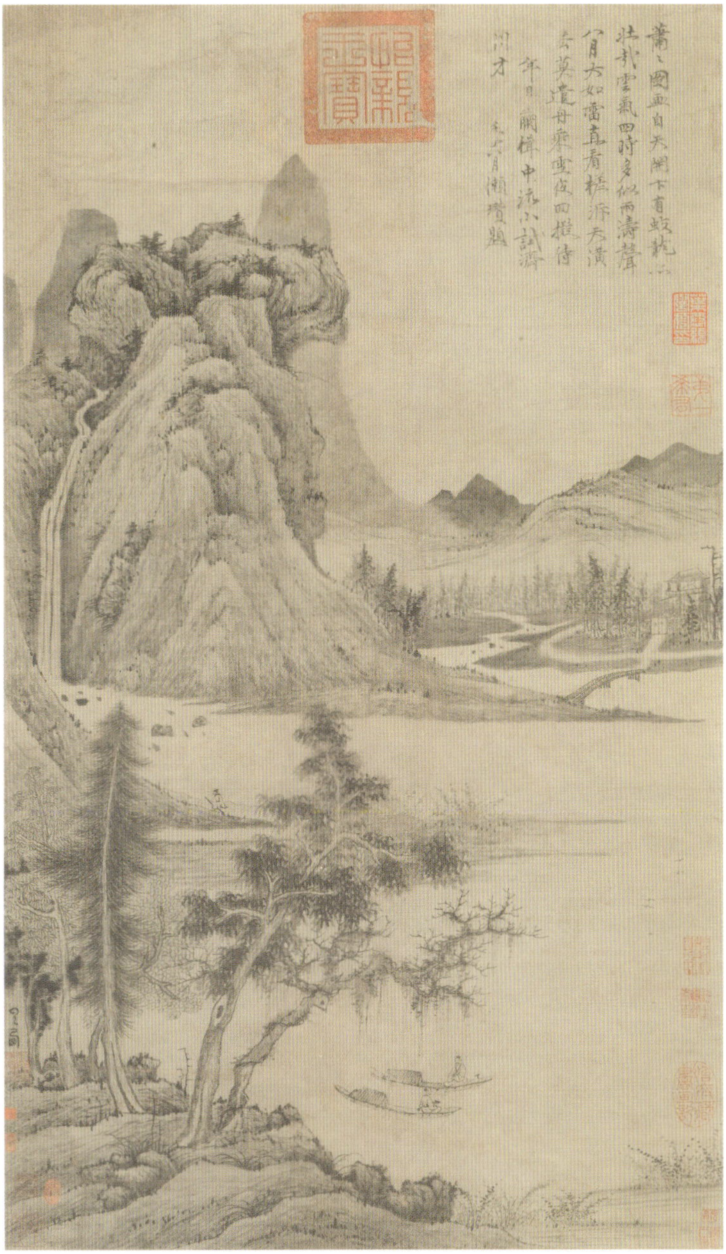

Fig. 34 *Hills and Streams with Boats*

Cao Zhibai (Yuan dynasty, 1272–1355)
Ink on silk
Height 86.3 cm × Width 51.4 cm
Shanghai Museum

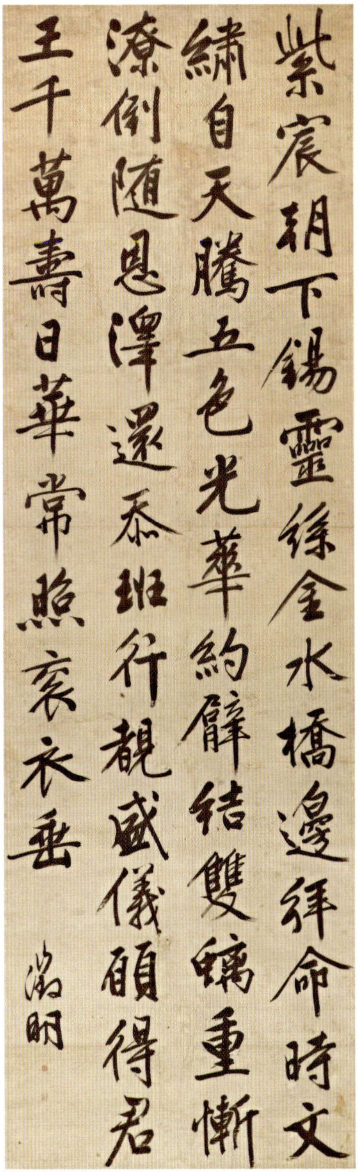

Fig. 35 *Hanging Scroll: Seven-Character Regulated Poem*

Wen Zhengming
Cursive script
Ink on paper
Height 315.5 cm × Width 98 cm
Liaoning Provincial Museum

Figs. 34–35 In the art histories of ancient China, only calligraphy and the paintings of an educated elite were regarded as true art.

The Artistic Theories of Likeness of Form and Likeness of Spirit

There is another respect in which there is an important divergence in the history of western and Chinese art and that is the question of the emergence of a theory of painting. An examination of the history of Chinese painting suggests that the development of Chinese painting was profoundly influenced by ancient theories of painting. In the West, by contrast, theoretical discussion of painting and records only appeared during the Renaissance and drew upon the flourishing developments in painting at the time. True critical discussion of painting by intellectuals other than artists had to wait until the end of the 19th century when they had significant influence on developments in western art.

However, in China where, historically, art theory and the art of painting itself seemed to have emerged almost simultaneously, it was another matter altogether. In the early fourth century the painter Gu Kaizhi (c. 345–409) a well known artist of the Eastern Jin dynasty (317–420) advanced his theory "On Transmitting the Spirit (*Chuanshen Lun*)." His paintings include a scroll entitled *Admonitions of the Instructress to the Court Ladies*, now in the British Museum which is the finest existing footnote to our understanding of "On Transmitting the Spirit," itself part of Gu's major theoretical work *On Painting*.

Gu was both a painter and a calligrapher and it was said of him that he "excelled in writing, in painting and in craftiness." His treatise *On Painting* is very short and concentrates on figure painting, its reasoning on the transmission of spirit is both cogent and exceptional. Gu believed that in figure painting external form and facial appearance were naturally important. Nevertheless, more important still was the ability to express the essential spirit of the person, that is, the person's soul and inner character. He also said that in *xieshen* or imaging the spirit, it was dotting in the eyes that was most important because the eyes were the seat of the spirit. Thus, the traditional painters of ancient China were already well aware of the sense of the modern saying that the eyes are a window into the soul. In the Beijing Palace Museum and the Liaoning Provincial Museum there is a painting entitled *Nymph of the Luo River* reputed to be by Gu Kaizhi (figs. 36–37), though scholars generally believe that it is a copy from later than the Jin dynasty (265–420). Even so, it is a work

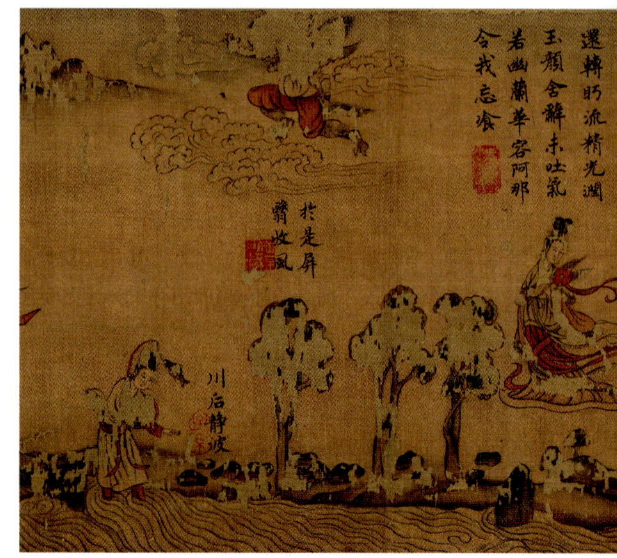

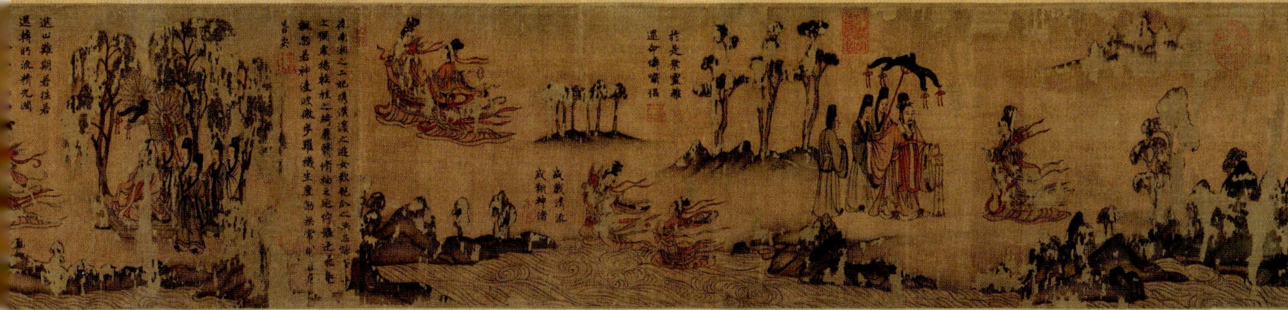

that is closest to the style of Gu Kaizhi and it is worth taking a look at the concept of the transmission of spirit exemplified in this painting.

Nymph of the Luo River is a handscroll based on a rhapsodic prose-poem of the same name by Cao Zhi (192–232) and illustrates his encounter with the nymph of the Luo River as man and nymph see each other, come to know each other and dream of nuptial delight. At the beginning of the handscroll, the refined Cao Zhi is seen on an outing in the countryside. Accompanied by an escort of officials he espies a water nymph holding a red fan and gazing at him from a distance. The arrangement of the figures in the scroll starts tightly and then relaxes. The expression in the exchange of gazes between the male and female characters is well caught and the background of mountain ranges and running streams extends naturally throughout the scroll, linking the development of the story from beginning to end. In the final scene, the red fan has found its way into Cao Zhi's hand signifying that the story has reached a happy conclusion. Gu's delineation is so delicate that his use of line was described in ancient texts like spring silkworms spitting silk

Figs. 36–37 Copy of Gu Kaizhi's *The Nymph of the Luo River* (detail)
Anonymous (Northern Song dynasty)
Ink and color on silk
Height 26.3 cm × Width 641.6 cm
Liaoning Provincial Museum

Nymph of the Luo River is a handscroll by Gu Kaizhi based on a revision of a rhapsodic prose-poem of the same name by Cao Zhi. This is a later copy. In his thesis *On Painting* Gu says that the most important aspect of figure painting is the ability to capture the essence of a person, that is, their soul and their inner character. According to ancient records, Gu Kaizhi's line was delicate and extended, like silkworms spitting silk, and was thus later known as "gossamer drawing."

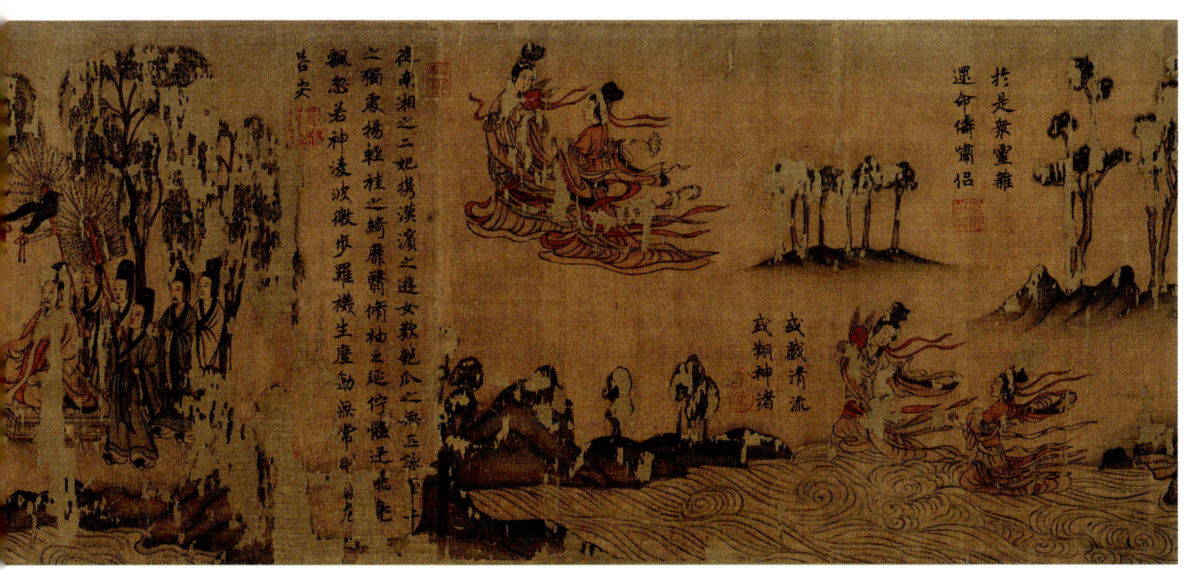

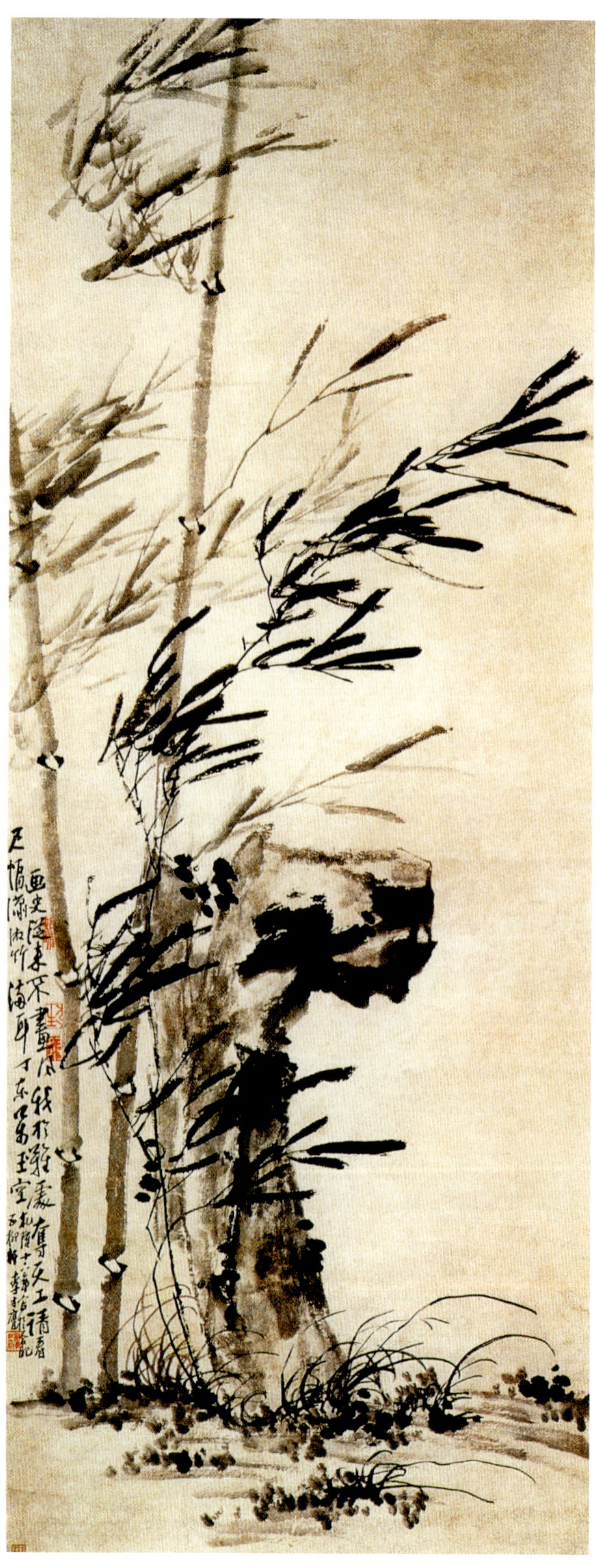

threads running through the elegant clothing, the streamers of the nymph and the billowing waves of the Luo River to embody the idea of the abstract in vivid and ethereal brush strokes. This is the home of the concept of the transmission of spirit.

The concept of the transmission of spirit had an important influence on the subsequent development and theory of painting and led directly to later Chinese painters not only concentrating upon an object's external shape but paying even more attention to its inner quality. In modern terms, the painter requires not only a photographic eye to capture the external shape but also a "mind's eye" that can see through to the inner quality of an object. The photographic eye takes only shapes; what the "mind's eye" captures is the very spirit of an object.

Traditional painting theory also contained the idea of "form and spirit both" (*xingshen jianbei*) designed to warn the painter that whilst the concrete nature of *xiezhen* should not be ignored in the creative process, equally, neither should the conceptual abstract essence of *xieshen*, in fact it would be better to overdo

Fig. 38 *Bamboos in the Wind*
Li Fangying (Qing dynasty, 1695–1754)
Ink on paper
Height 168.3 cm × 67.7 cm
Nanjing Museum

Xieyi (painterly impression) is an important concept in traditional painting and its sense lies in the fact that the important point of a painting is not the detail of form but the abstract conception of the subject. In this painting the artist favors the abstract expression of the totality of the wind over the detail of rocks and bamboo.

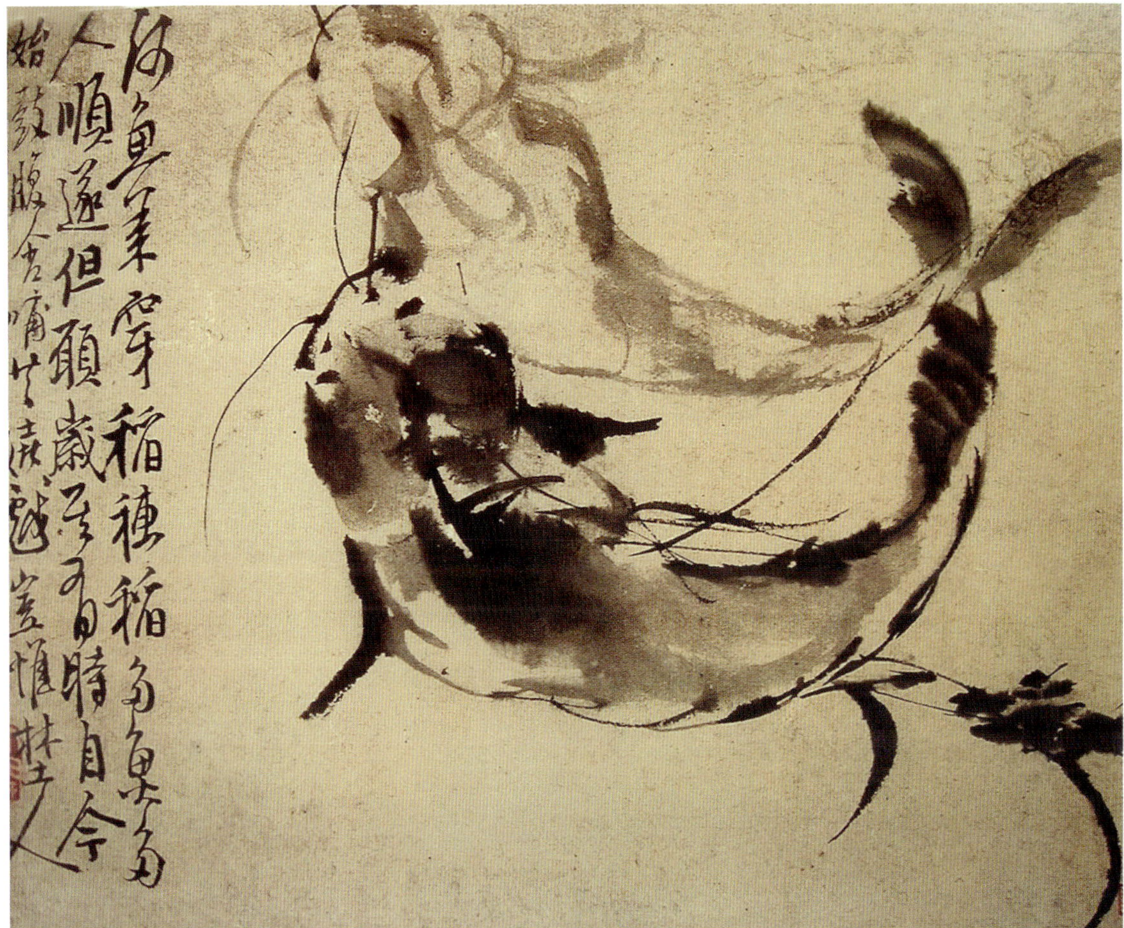

Fig. 39 *As One Would Wish Year upon Year*
Li Fangying
Ink on paper
Height 36.5 cm × 28 cm
Yangzhou Museum

From the point of view of style, in traditional painting *xieyi* refers to a way of painting that is the complete opposite of the meticulously detailed treatment of *gongbi*. Li Fangying was one of the Eight Eccentrics of Yangzhou. The brush and ink of this painting is exquisitely succinct, a few strokes capture the two tail-fins in the stream and vividly depict the fish amongst the rice-shoots.

the latter than not. According to the rules of traditional painting, a painting that was only inspired by *xiezhen* and had no element of *xieshen*, could only be regarded as the work of an artisan and was not to be called art. Consequently, in traditional painting the creative *schwerpunkt* was *xieshen* and not *xiezhen*.

Traditional painting theory contains two further technical ideas, those of fine-work (*gongbi*) and freehand (*xieyi*). The freehand described here is a style totally opposite to that of fine-work. Fine-work is delicate and meticulously detailed in its depiction of the form of objects, though good *gongbi* paintings (for example the flower-and-bird paintings in the tradition of the Song Painting Academy) still aspire to the ideal of "form and spirit both." In freehand the brush-work is simple and spontaneous with the emphasis not on detail but upon the abstract expression of the essential character of things. Nevertheless, in the same way, good examples of freehand, in addition to expressing the abstract, do not fail to display the actual appearance of things (figs. 38–39). Thus, in its narrow sense freehand is a kind of style but in a wider sense it is the expression of an aspiration towards the concept of the abstract.

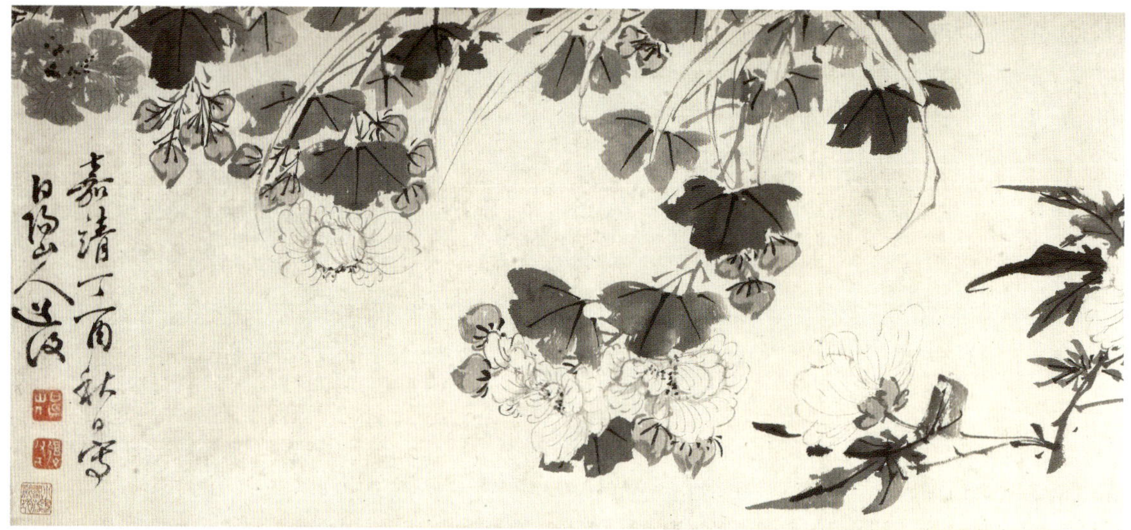

Fig. 40 *Flowers and Plants* (detail)
Chen Chun (Ming dynasty, 15th–16th century)
Ink on paper
Height 29.7 cm × Width 400 cm
Shanghai Museum

In traditional flower-and-bird painting there is generally no great achievement in the handling of external forms such as three-dimensional leaves and petals, light and shade, and the detail of background. In this scroll Chen Chun displays the vivacity and sense of life of flowers and plants in nature. Before putting brush to paper the artist makes numerous observations of all kinds of flowers and plants to acquaint himself with their state at different stages of growth. As he depicts their form on paper he uses *xieyi* to capture their abstract essence as well.

Xiezhen and *Xieyi* in Chinese and Western Painting

Xiezhen (true likeness) is founded upon the artist's detailed observation of objects and relies upon his visual experience; *xieyi* (painterly impression) is based upon a level of comprehension that, through the artist's observation and understanding of an object, draws out the inner sense that lies beyond its actual appearance.

A western painter friend on seeing the late handscroll *Flowers and Plants* by the Ming painter Chen Chun (15th–16th century) was astonished at its lifelike nature (fig. 40). However there were obvious differences when compared with the still life of western art (fig. 41). The fact that Chen Chun's work contained no light and shade or handling of space aroused my friend's curiosity about the concept of drawing from life in Chinese traditional painting.

In fact, the "drawing from life" aspect of the paintings of ancient China naturally contains an element of "learning from nature" meaning the collection of material from the observation of nature. At this level there is a relationship between the "from life" of Chinese art and that in western art. However the Chinese speak of "writing" as having the opposite meaning of "painting" and that *xieyi* is the opposite of *xiezhen*. As to the word "life" (*sheng*) its usage in China encompasses a number of abstract concepts such as *joie de vivre* (*shengqu*), vitality (*shengqi*) and liveliness (*shengdong*). Consequently, to the ancient Chinese "drawing from life" did not mean focusing on something and then creating a view through minute study of shape, light and shade and three dimensional construction. It meant rather, that the painter made his observations and studied the form of the object or objects so that having acquired a sense of the internal expression of the external form, he achieved a deeper understanding and knowledge of the object. Thereafter, he drew on its spirit and with simplicity of form but integrity of meaning and using freehand brush and ink he expressed, from memory, the sense of the feelings that the subject had engendered in

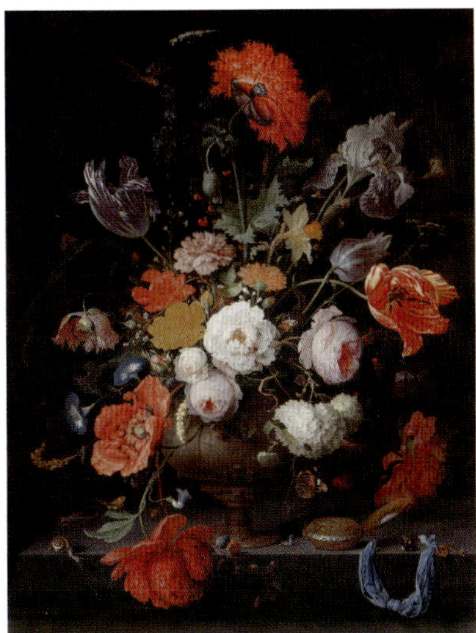

Fig. 41 *Still Life with Flowers and a Watch*
Abraham Mignon (Netherlands, c. 1660–c. 1679)
Oil on canvas
Height 75 cm × Width 60 cm
Rijksmuseum

In the still life of the Baroque era, everything from the appearance and texture of the object, to light and shade, and space is rendered in detail. The large, such as the appearance of blossom and petals and the management of space and background, and the small such as the thickness and texture of each object are so true to life that they seem to be before our very eyes.

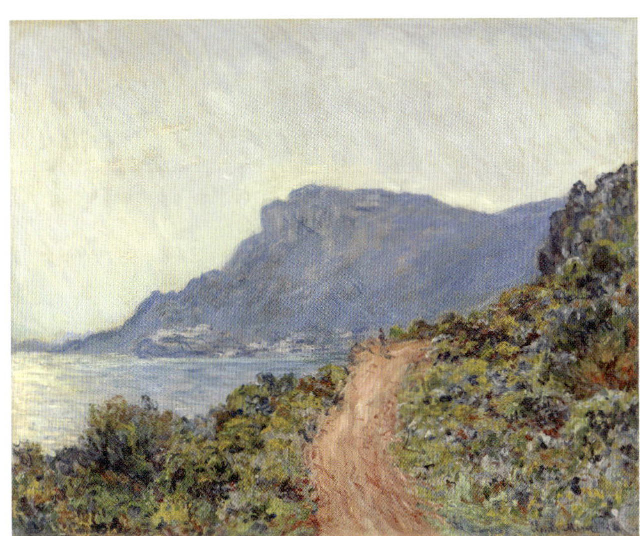

Fig. 42 *La Corniche near Monaco*
Claude Monet (France, 1840–1926)
Oil on canvas
Height 75 cm × Width 94 cm
Rijksmuseum

Most of the works of western landscape painters are views. As we look at this picture we can imagine the artist standing on a spot on this twisting road and recording in paint stroke by stroke, the mountain and sea in the distance and the road and vegetation close at hand.

him. The "drawing from life" of the western artist is based, on the other hand, upon detailed observation that displays the form of the subject on paper as near as possible to its real state. Naturally, good western life paintings ought to express sensibility as much as form and the best sketches and life paintings are not basic practice material. This is why that great master of 20th century Chinese art, Lin Fengmian (1900–1991) said: "The imitation of nature is at the heart of western art which results in a tendency towards realism; oriental art is, in the main, the depiction of impressions and this results in a tendency towards freehand."

The scroll of Chen Chun has neither light nor shade nor detailed form, yet the images within the painting are vibrantly life-like, precisely because, in the mind's eye of the artist, they are already as familiar as the back of his own hand, so that when the artist draws or paints his picture he vividly conveys an accurate sense of the image to paper. In the same way, the shape of the image, because of that element of lively attention, springs to life in the moment between nothing and existence. This example marks the freedom that *xieyi* enjoys over *xiezhen* in the creative process. Because *xieyi* transmutes visual experience into recollection, knowledge and emotion, there is no need to seek the direct likeness of a particular view during the process of creation, thus escaping the limitations imposed by drawing from the scene itself. In fact, the majority of the pre-conceived compositions—what they saw in their mind, of the artists of ancient China were not based on a particular visual environment. That is to say, most traditional paintings were not views and possessed more creative perspective compared with western artists, whose works, whether interiors or exteriors, are based on either specific scenes or views (fig. 42).

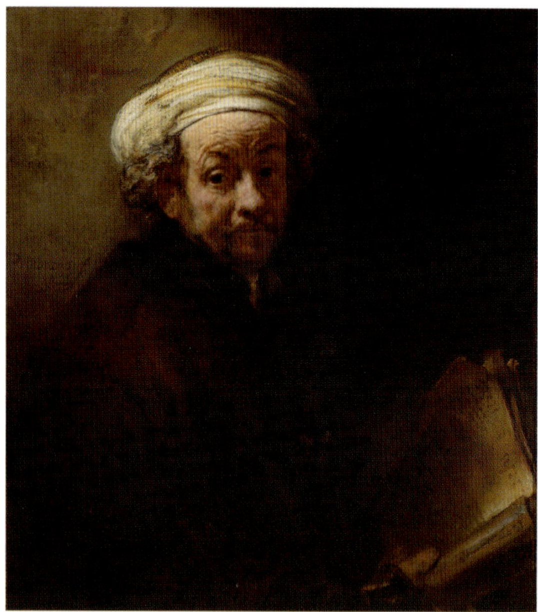

Fig. 43 *Self-Portrait as the Apostle Paul*
Rembrandt van Rijn (Netherlands)
Oil on canvas
Height 91 cm × Wdith 77 cm
Rijksmuseum

Rembrandt painted a number of self-portraits during his life, this one depicts his state of mind in old age.

In the hands of a true master of east or west, western *xiezhen* and oriental *xieyi* should reach the same heights but by different routes. Historically, the works of the great masters all display the same qualities of realism and abstraction. There is, perhaps, a subtle distinction between masters of the two traditions, western painting tends more to the true likeness of *xiezhen* where the internal spirit is expressed through likeness; the precise opposite is true of traditional Chinese painting where spirit is always to the fore, sometimes to the extent of masking likeness. An examination of the classic work of a western master may illustrate this subtle distinction.

Rembrandt's *Self-Portrait as the Apostle Paul* is recognized as a classic of the western tradition (fig. 43). Rembrandt painted a large number of self-portraits. Apart from recording his physical appearance during different stages of his life these portraits also display his internal world throughout those stages. In a late self-portrait his face bears the traces left by the years. The sagging muscles and the wrinkled forehead clearly depict the living Rembrandt, in detail and with a high degree of realism, as he was at the time. However, on another plane, behind that realistic image lies the expression of a complicated internal state. Through outstanding artistic technique, the deep expression in the eyes speaks as if alive, telling the viewer of the limitless emotion within and making us feel that this is a man with an unusual past. The artistic achievement of Rembrandt lies in his ability to express abstract feelings through his handling of detail. His *xieyi* is founded upon the highly skilled use of *xiezhen*.

The tendency towards *xieyi* in Chinese painting can only be understood in the context of attitudes towards the abstract. Nevertheless, shape and form is vividly expressed and accurately presented in the twists and turns and rise and fall of line that does not lack the quality of *xiezhen*. Similarly, the *xiezhen* of western art incorporates the transmission of elements of form and spirit both. Chinese painting is led by *xieyi* and at a glance it would seem difficult to discover the element of *xiezhen* within it. Western painting, by contrast, gives an immediate impression of *xiezhen*.

There are times when too much detail is a disadvantage in transmitting the spirit of a work. Too much detail can shift our focus on to the concrete form of an object thus obstructing our ability to absorb its abstract quality. The literati of ancient China led the development of traditional painting and their emphasis was not upon recording an event but on transmitting its spirit. Ni Zan, one of the Four Yuan Masters, put it bluntly: "My painting is mere dabbling, I do not aspire to likeness of form, I do it for my own amusement" (fig. 44). Thereafter, led by the literati, Chinese traditional painting more and more encouraged the concept of *xieyi,* reaching the point where the works

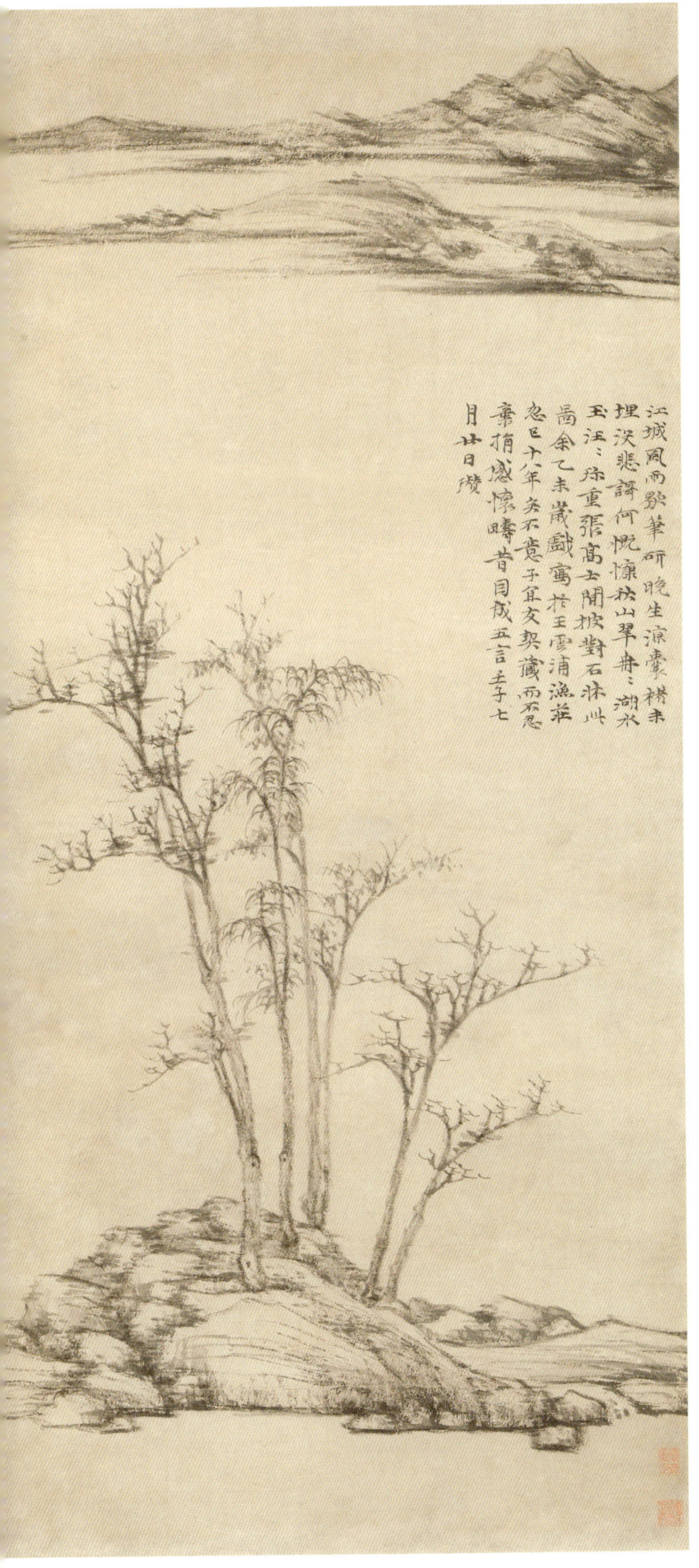

of a number of later painters completely abandoned the importance of form and became over-simplified and difficult to appreciate. In fact, however, the appreciative point of these pared down literati paintings lay in brush and ink and not in image. This will be covered in the chapter on brush and ink.

Once we realize that creation in Chinese painting is not about the creation of views or scenes and that the artists of ancient China inclined more to *xieyi* than to *xiezhen* we can begin to understand and even appreciate traditional figure painting, *shanshui* and flower-and-bird painting more. If we jettison the western approach of measuring art by the yardsticks of innovation and likeness, we can then imagine that the figures in Chinese painting are not run-of-the-mill portraits in the *xiezhen* category, that *shanshui* are not depictions of the scenery of specific views and understand how it was that so many simply constructed monochrome ink sketches of flowers and birds appeared. In the next chapter we shall be looking at figure paintings that are not portraits.

Fig. 44 *Fisherman's Hut beneath an Autumn Sky*

Ni Zan (Yuan dynasty, 1301–1374)
Ink on paper
Height 96.1 cm × Width 46.9 cm
Shanghai Museum

Ni Zan was one of the Four Yuan Masters. He regarded painting as a pastime. He did not aspire to likeness of form but sought to express an inner need to escape the world.

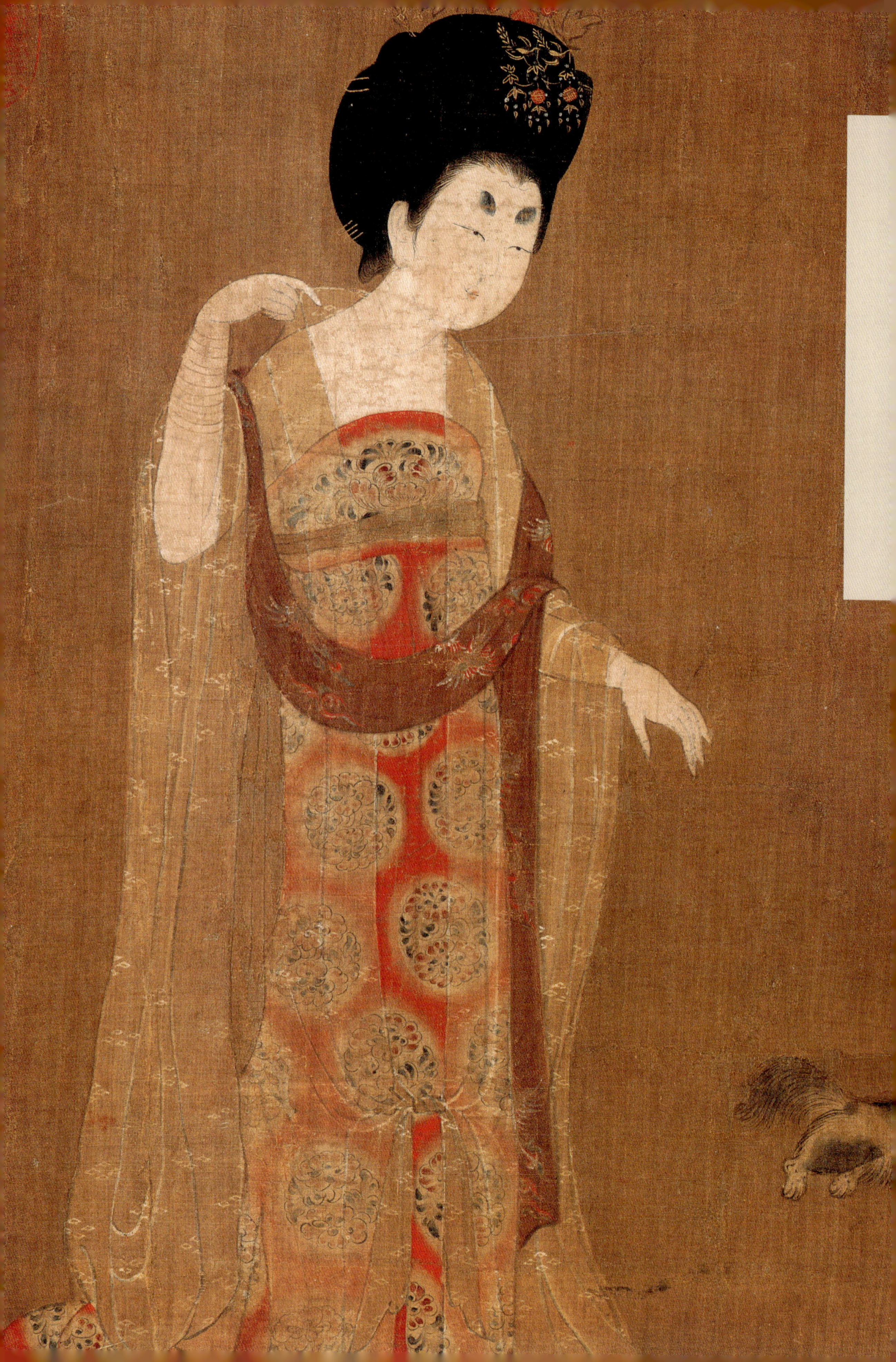

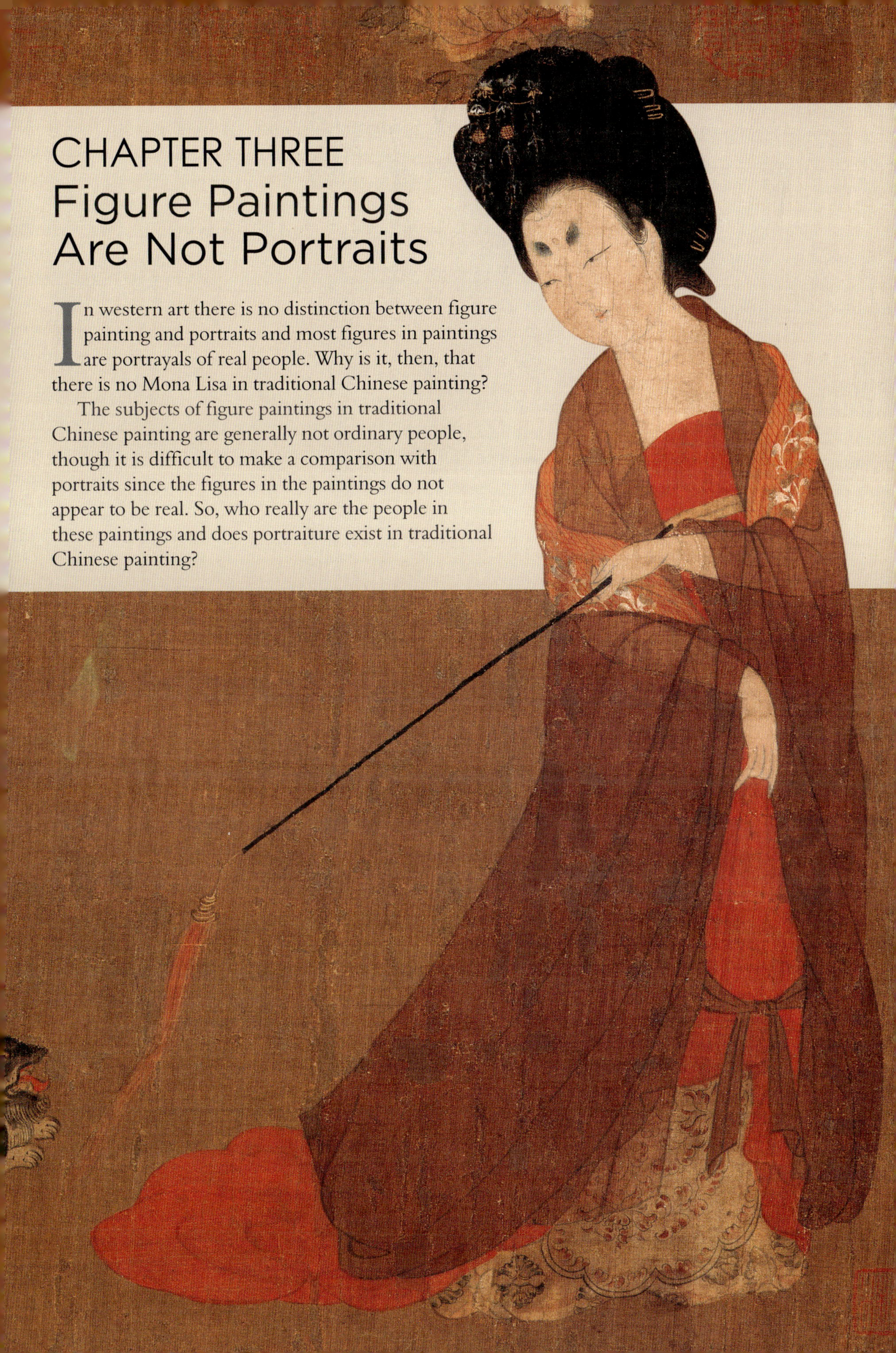

CHAPTER THREE
Figure Paintings Are Not Portraits

In western art there is no distinction between figure painting and portraits and most figures in paintings are portrayals of real people. Why is it, then, that there is no Mona Lisa in traditional Chinese painting?

The subjects of figure paintings in traditional Chinese painting are generally not ordinary people, though it is difficult to make a comparison with portraits since the figures in the paintings do not appear to be real. So, who really are the people in these paintings and does portraiture exist in traditional Chinese painting?

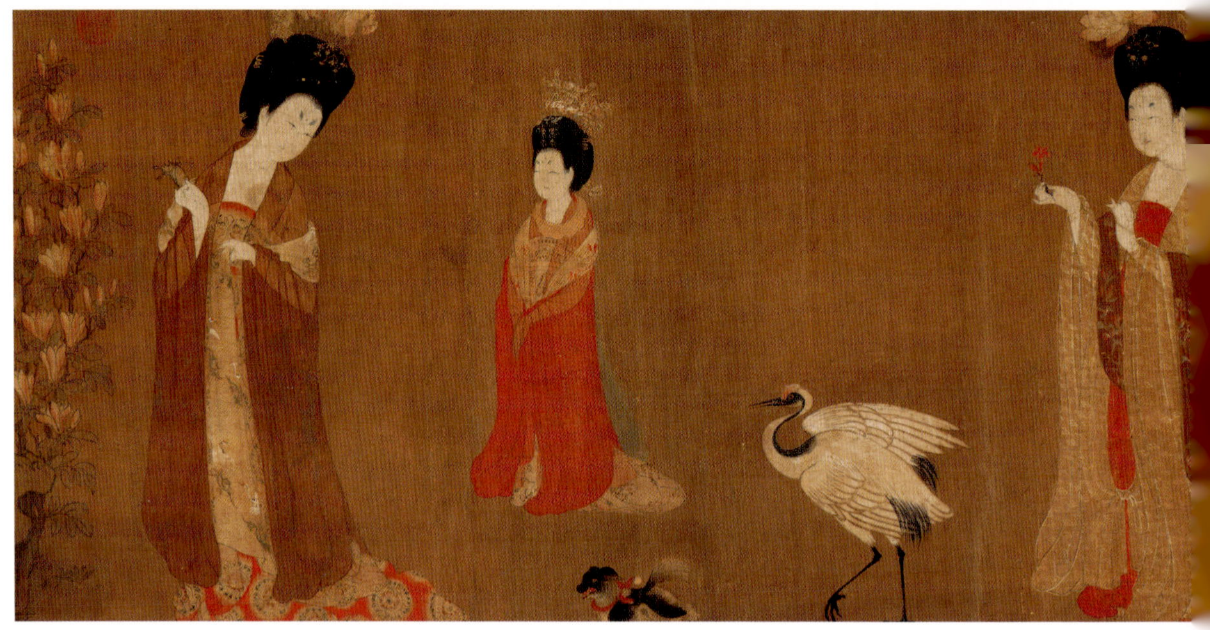

A Figure Painting Tradition of Its Own

When we speak of figure painting we immediately think of the classic painting by Zhou Fang, entitled *Court Ladies Adorning Their Hair with Flowers* (fig. 45 on pages 44 and 45, figs. 46–47), one of the jewels of Chinese art and one of the few genuine original examples of Chinese figure painting to have survived to the present. Zhou Fang was a Tang dynasty painter who came from a noble family and served as an official at the prefecture of Yuezhou. He excelled in

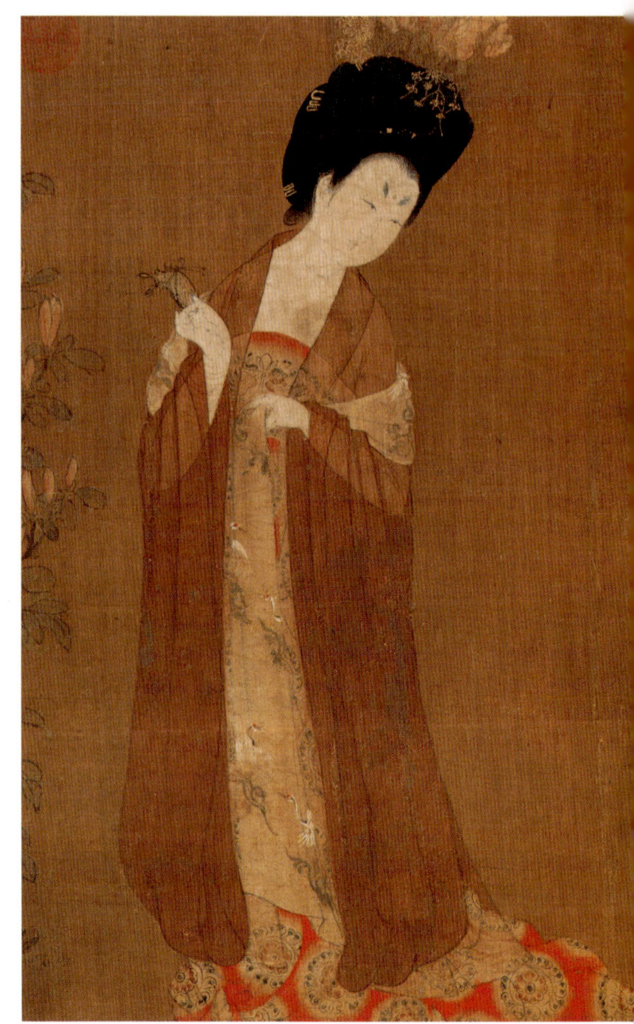

Figs. 45–47 *Court Ladies Adorning Their Hair with Flowers*
Zhou Fang (Tang dynasty, 8th–early 9th century)
Ink and color on silk
Height 46 cm × Width 180 cm
Liaoning Provincial Museum

Zhou Fang, style name Zhong Lang, who was active in the 8th and early 9th centuries, was a well-known Tang figure painter. *Court Ladies Adorning Their Hair with Flowers* is a representative work and the only surviving example of the Tang dynasty genre of paintings of ladies to have been verified by scholars. Its subject is the daily life of ladies of the nobility. It depicts, in fine-work and color, five ladies with flowers in their hair and a maid-servant with a fan, all in a garden, playing with a dog and a crane, picking flowers and chasing butterflies.

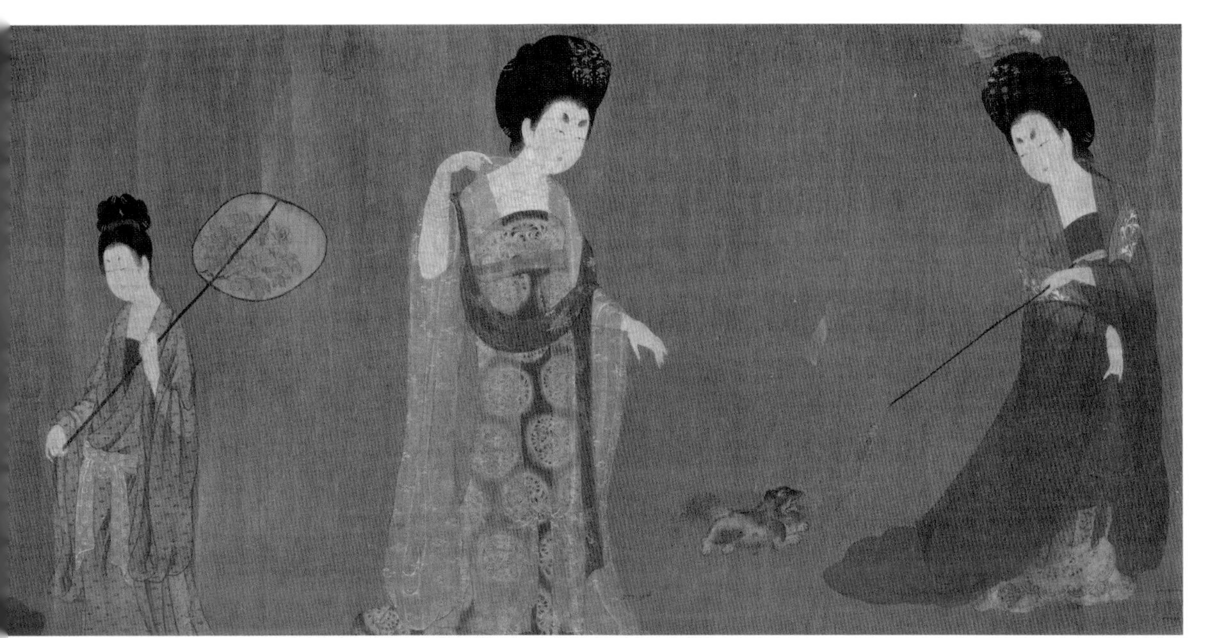

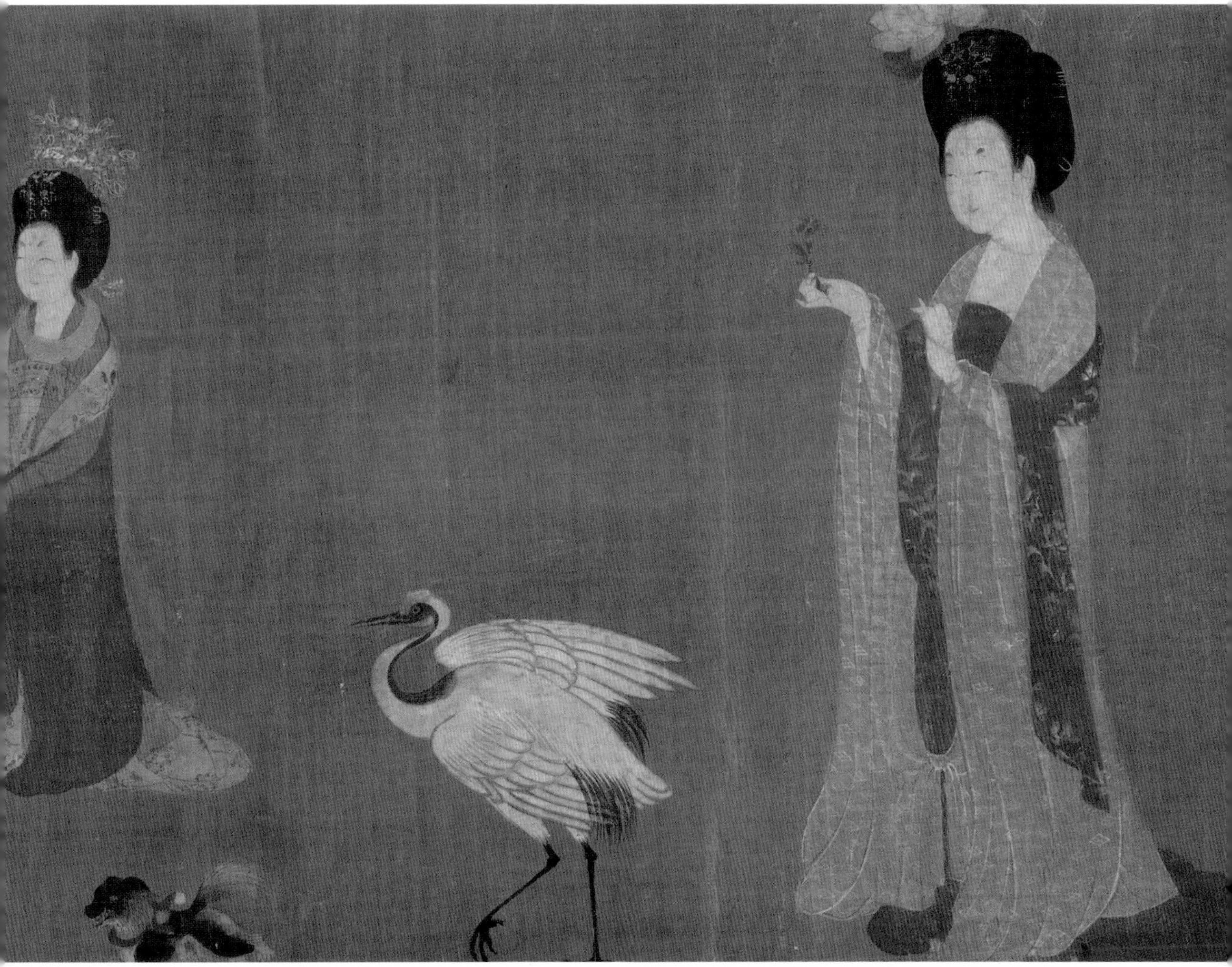

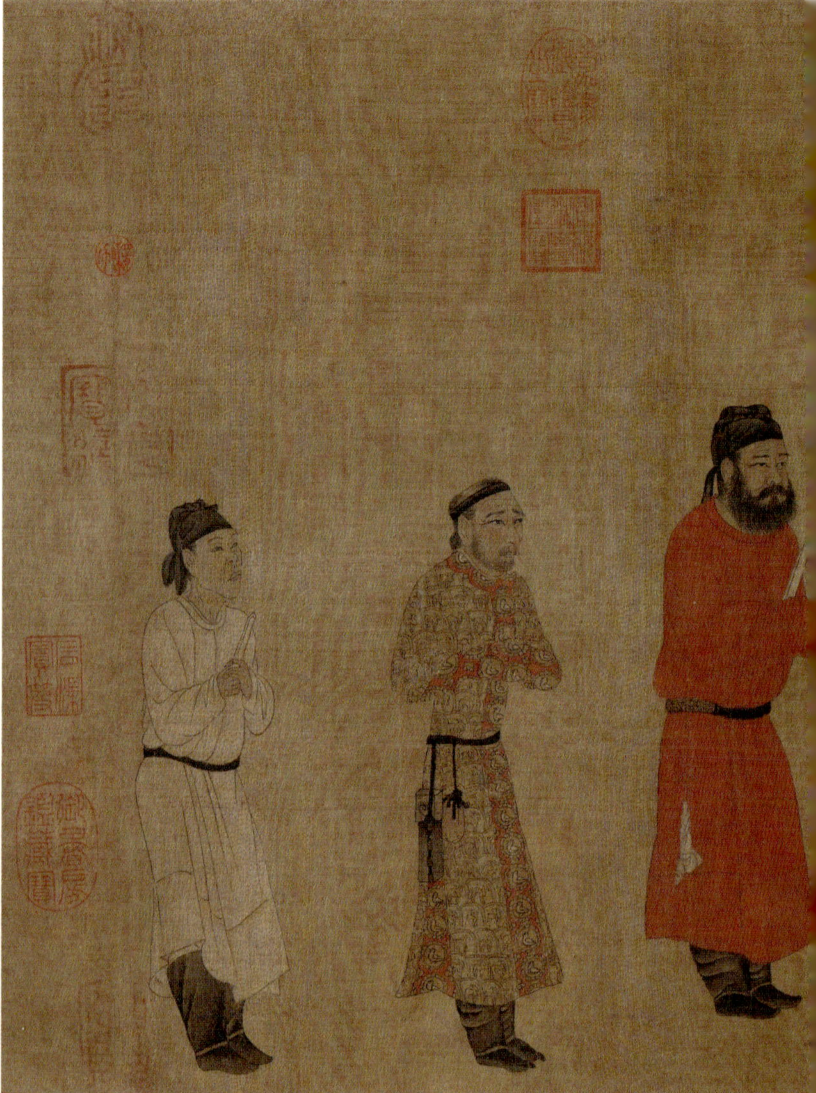

Fig. 48 *The Emperor Carried in Procession*

Yan Liben (Tang dynasty, c. 601–673)
Ink and color on silk
Height 38.5 cm × Width 129 cm
Palace Museum, Beijing

The Emperor Carried in Procession is a well-known painting by the Tang painter Yan Liben and is believed to be a copy made in the Song dynasty. It depicts the scene of an audience in 640 (14th year of Zhen Guan) between the Tang Emperor Taizong and Lu Dongzan, the emissary of the Tibetan Tubo dynasty. It emphasizes the diplomatic friendship between the two states rather than recording the likenesses of the Tang emperor and Lu Dongzan.

figure painting and on the orders of the Tang Emperor Dezong painted the frescoes at the Zhangming Temple. On their completion he was advanced to the first rank by the emperor and achieved considerable fame. *Court Ladies Adorning Their Hair with Flowers* is his representative work.

The Tang dynasty was the peak period for figure painting in China and marked the emergence of a number of masters of this genre. In addition to Zhou Fang they included Zhang Xuan, Yan Liben (c. 601–673) (fig. 48), and Wu Daozi (active 710–760), all historical masters of Chinese figure painting. Zhou and Zhang were famous for their paintings of court ladies. Although Zhang's paintings are now lost, the existing *Ladies Preparing Newly-Woven Silk* (figs. 51–52 on pages 52 and 53) is reputed to be a copy of the original by the Song Emperor Huizong (1085–1135) and can thus be consulted as an example of Zhang Xuan's style.

The existing *The Thirteen Emperors* (fig. 49 on page 50) is attributed to Yan Liben.

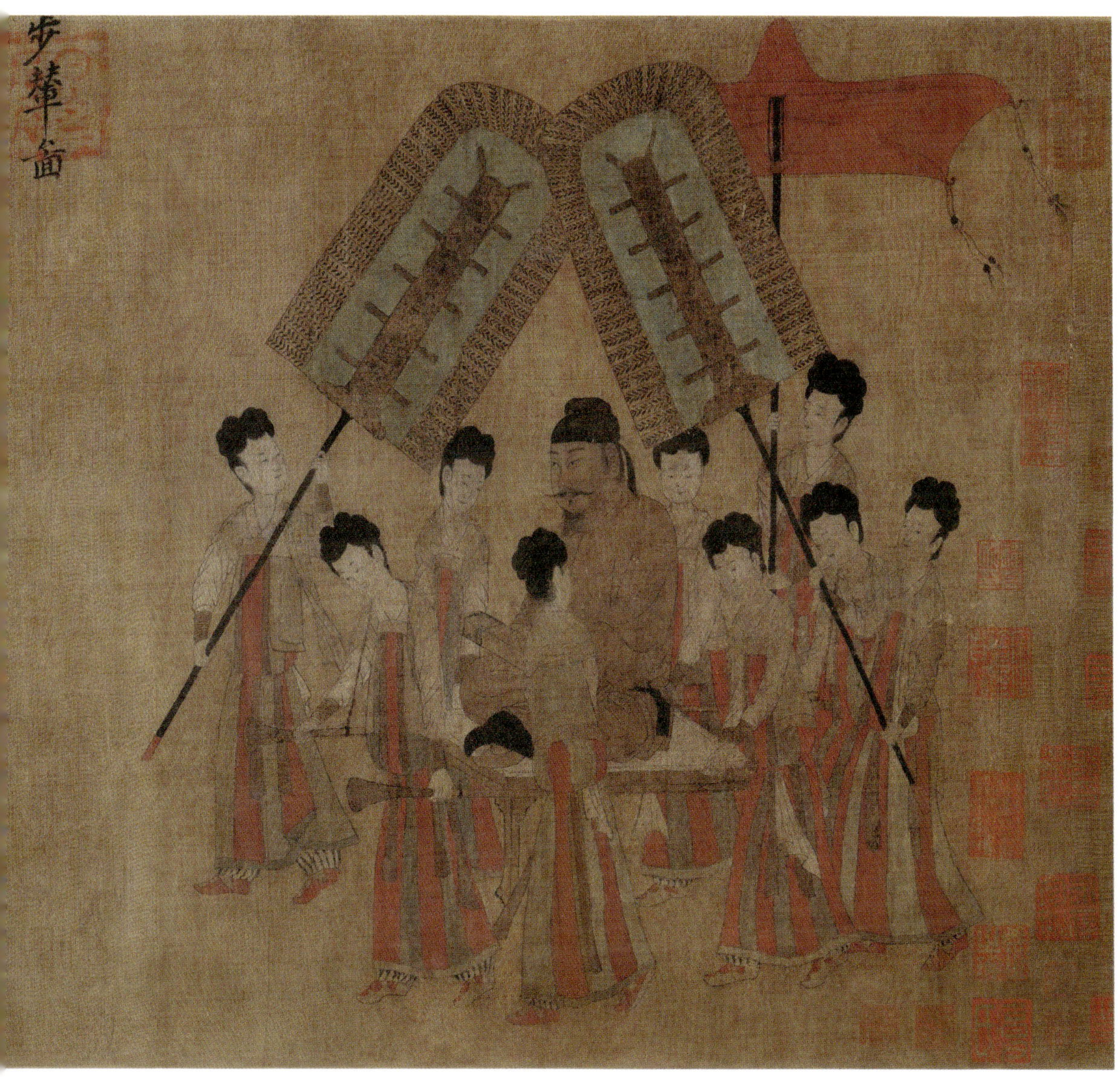

Although some scholars believe it genuine, this picture is not solely painted by Yan alone, though the style is believed to originate with him. Wu Daozi's main works were frescoes. The bulk of Tang dynasty wall paintings, apart from a few at Dunhuang, have not survived the ravages of time. However, we know from Tang and Song art histories that Wu Daozi was one of the Tang dynasty's much revered masters. His style was described as "white painting" (*bai hua*) meaning that his skilled use of line alone was able to encompass both the physical attributes and abstract aspects of his subject. Generally speaking scholars believe that the "high Tang" wall painting *Image of Vimalakirti* (fig. 50 on page 51) in cave 103 of the Mogao caves at Dunhuang approximates to the style of Wu's "iron line depiction" (*tiexian miao*) as described in early sources. The line in this painting has strength, tenses and relaxes and rises and falls, changing as it follows the shape of objects and provides a point of reference for the understanding of Wu Daozi's style.

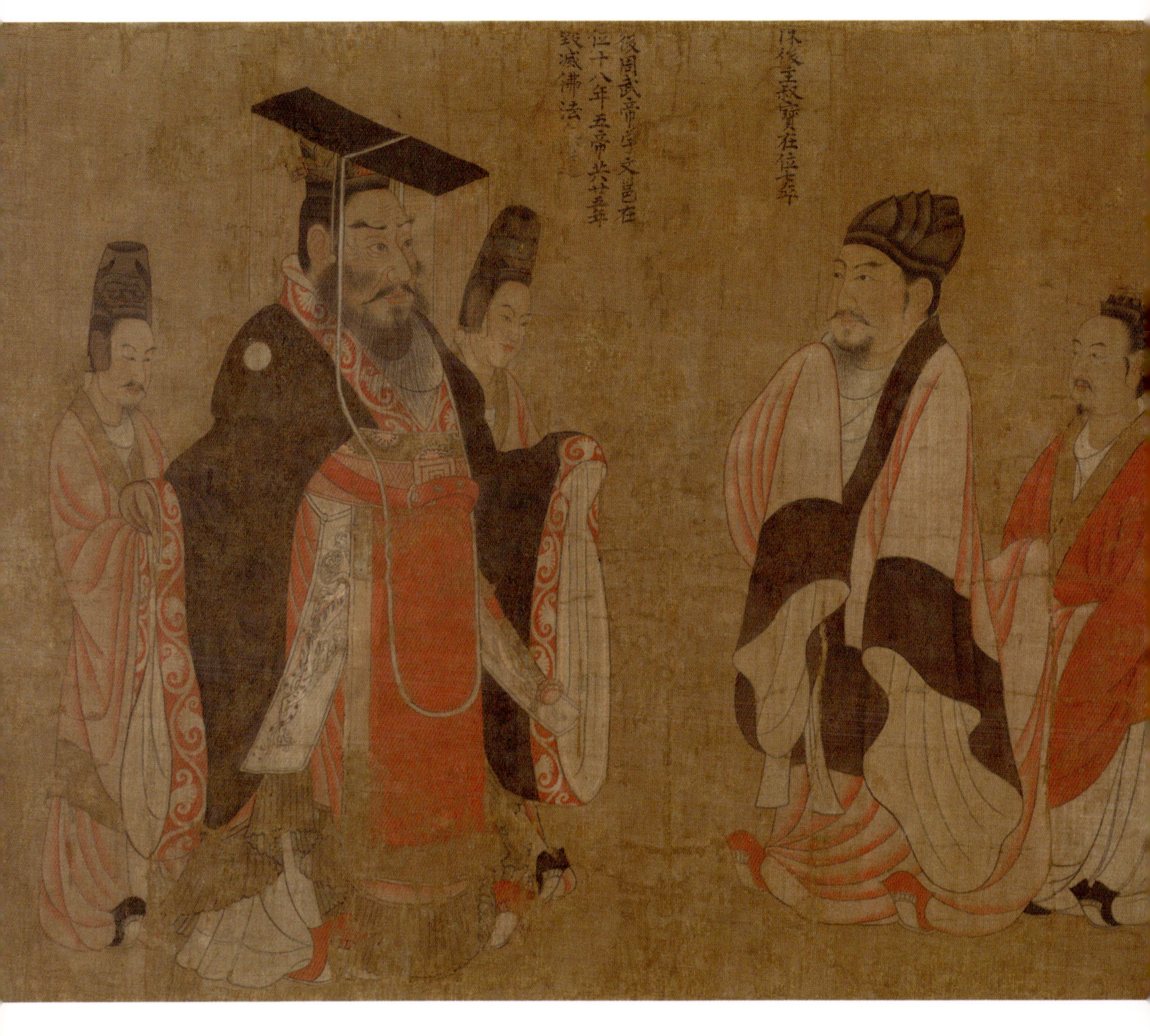

Fig. 49 *The Thirteen Emperors* (detail)
Attributed to Yan Liben
Ink and color on silk
Height 51.3 cm × Length 531 cm
Museum of Fine Arts, Boston

This scroll depicts the thirteen emperors from the Han to Sui (581–618) dynasties. Since they were all already dead Yan Liben would not have been able to portray them from life and his conceptual idea is based upon their historical achievements.

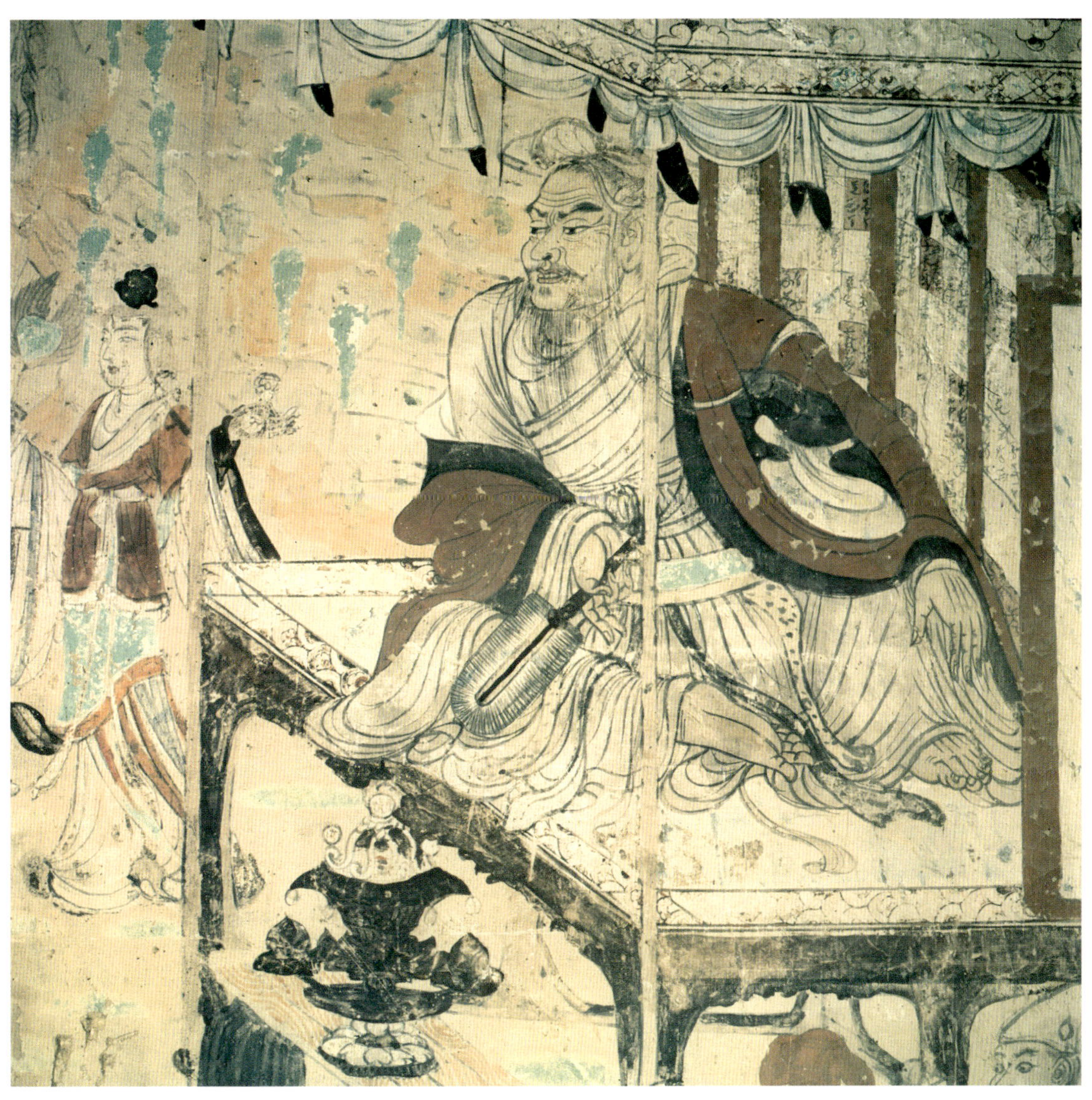

Fig. 50 *Image of Vimalakirti*

Anonymous (Tang Dynasty)
South face of cave 103, Mogao caves, Dunhuang

Of all the Tang dynasty images of Vimalakirti, this is the best known and the most vivid. It is filled with the style of Wu Daozi. Vimalakirti is depicted seated on a dais holding a deer's tail. He leans slightly forward with knitted eyebrows as if deep in thought. The artist has used a fluent and energetic line filled with the feeling of: "Flying dragon's whiskers, sprouting beard and strength to spare."

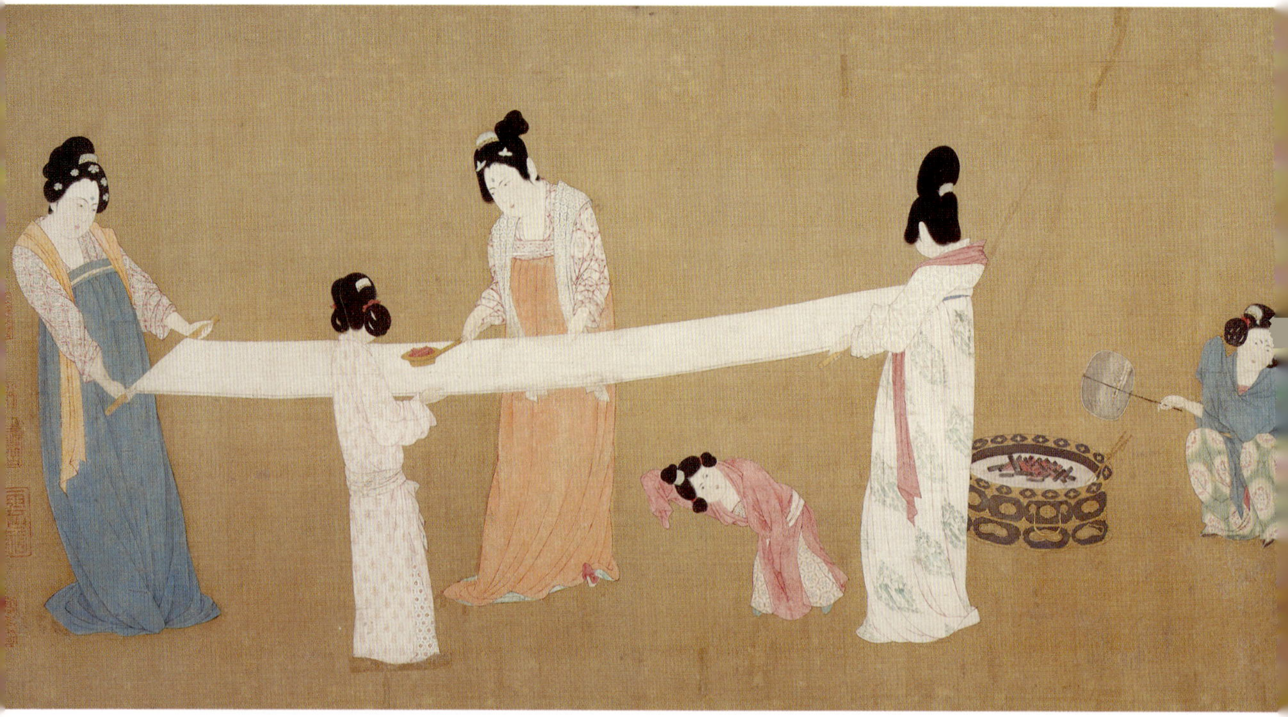

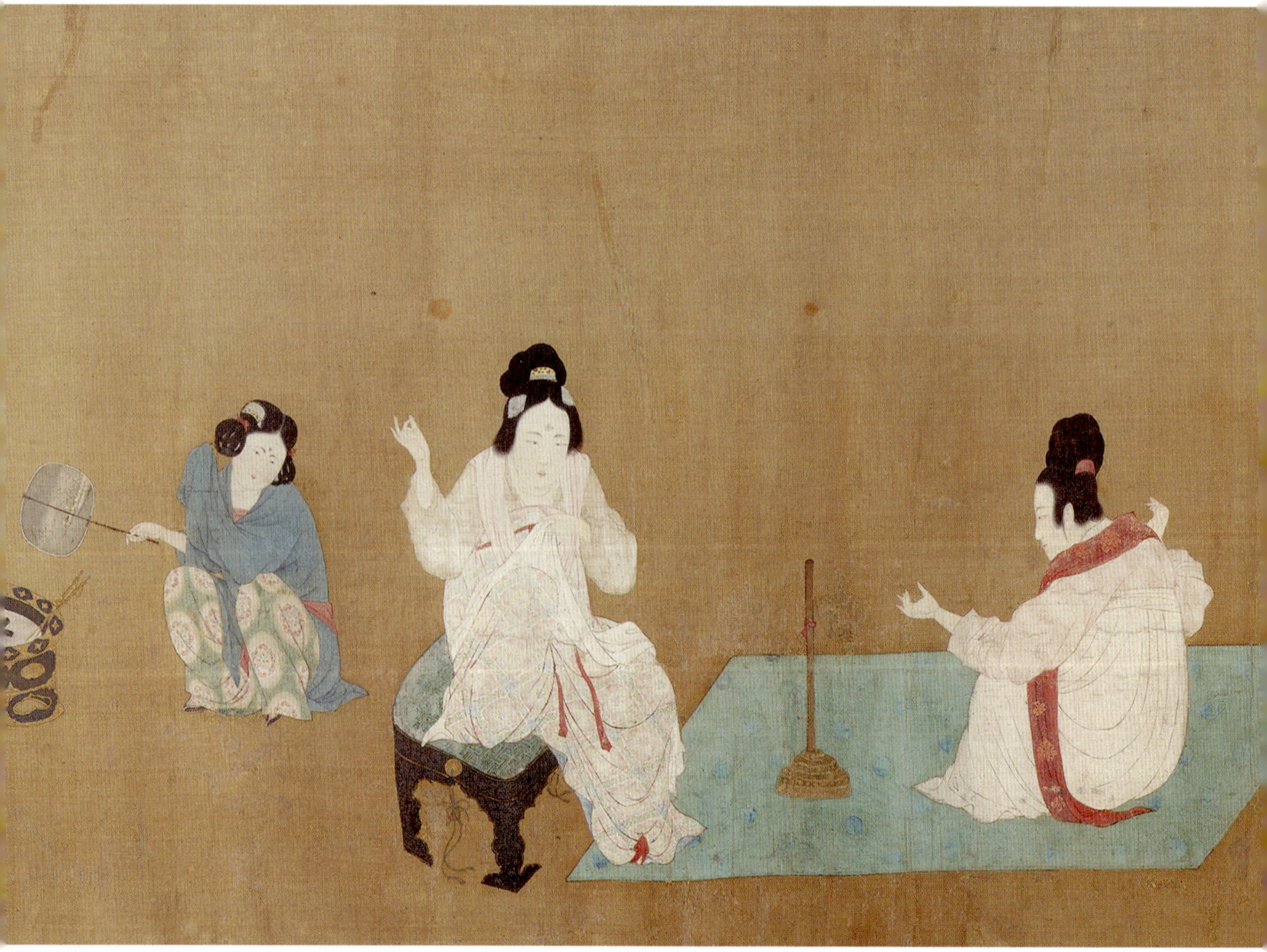

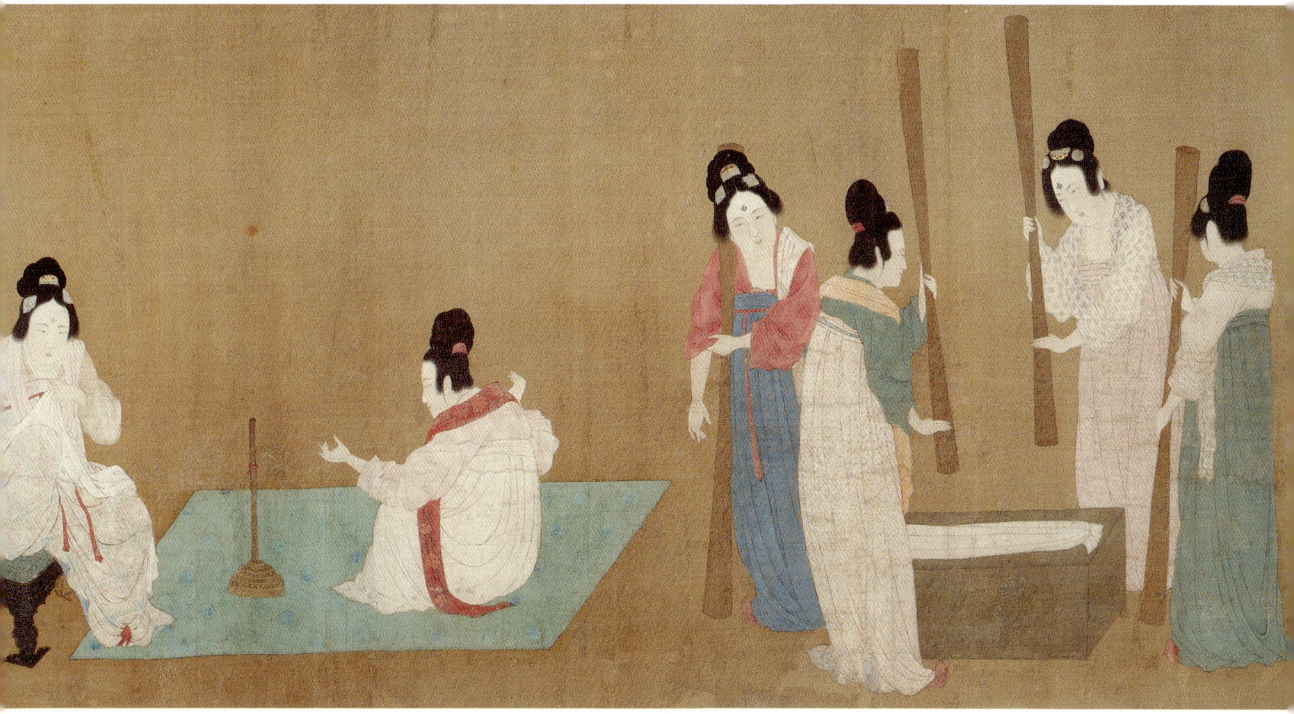

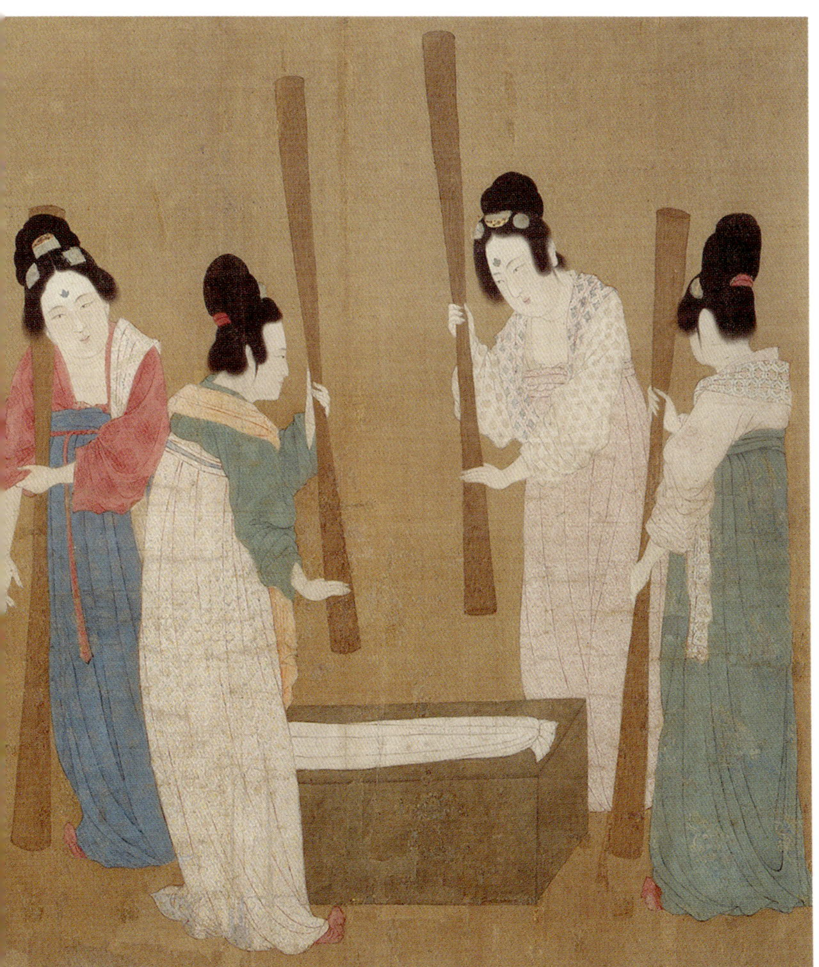

Figs. 51–52 *In the Style of Zhang Xuan: Ladies Preparing Newly-Woven Silk*

Zhao Ji
Ink and color on silk
Height 37 cm × Width 145.3 cm
Museum of Fine Arts, Boston

Zhang Xuan was a noted painter of the Tang dynasty who excelled in paintings of ladies of the nobility and was well known for his depictions of saddled horses and their riders. Historically, his reputation equaled that of the slightly later painter of ladies, Zhou Fang. A number of his paintings are recorded in the art histories of the Tang and Song dynasties but none survive. The present *Ladies Preparing Newly-Woven Silk* and *The Lady of Guo on a Spring Outing* are reputed to be copies of two scrolls of the same name by Zhang Xuan made by the Song Emperor Huizong. The scroll *Ladies Preparing Newly-Woven Silk* is a fine-work representation in color on silk of twelve ladies of the nobility preparing freshly washed new silk and stitching clothes. They are shown in three scenes of pounding, weaving and ironing.

Figures that Lack Individual Characteristics

The works of the figure painting masters that have been referred to previously, whether they be paintings of court ladies or of emperors, nobles, ministers and generals, all share something in common, none of the figures in them possess any individual characteristics. The facial features of some figures even bear a remarkable resemblance to each other and it is difficult to imagine that these are figures from real life. This is utterly different from western figure painting where the figures tend to possess striking individual characteristics and deeply memorable faces.

For example, the *Mona Lisa,* Rembrandt's self-portrait (fig. 53) and Vermeer's *Girl with a Pearl Earring* (fig. 54) are all household names in western portraiture. In each of them, the depiction, no matter whether of the features of their external appearance or of the state of their inner world is so detailed that we are profoundly aware of their age, social position, character and even of their inner being. It is this comprehensive depiction that leaves the viewer emotionally moved and it is precisely this depiction of individual characteristics that is lacking in the figure painting of the Chinese tradition and gives rise to the clear distinction that exists between Chinese

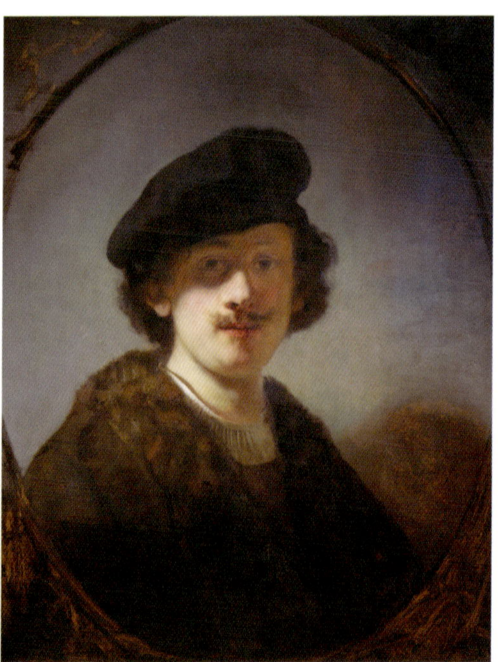

Fig. 53 *Self-Portrait with Shaded Eyes*
Rembrandt van Rijn
Oil on canvas
Height 48 cm ×Width 37.1 cm
Detroit Institute of Arts

Rembrandt painted over ninety self-portraits during his lifetime, ranging from youth to old age. The portraits not only recorded his external appearance at different ages but showed his state of mind at different stages of life. In the tiny space of the picture all life's emotions are displayed; confidence, anxiety, melancholy, tolerance and relief.

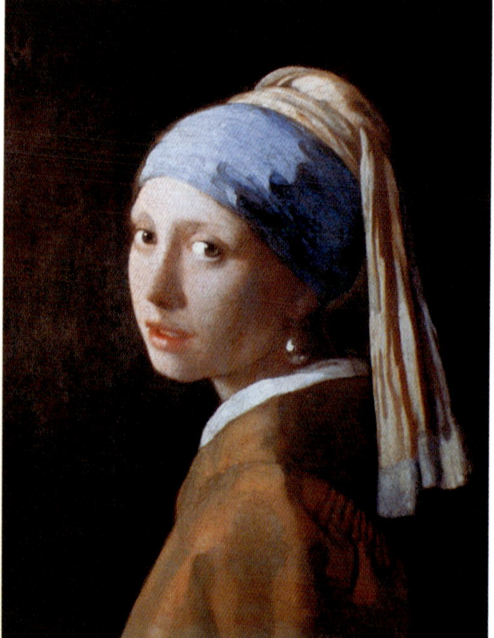

Fig. 54 *Girl with a Pearl Earring*
Johannes Vermeer
Oil on canvas
Height 44.5 cm × Width 39 cm
Mauritshuis Museum, The Hague

Western portrait painters emphasised the expression of a unique individualism in their portraits. The face, eyes, texture of skin and even the pearl earring and turban of the girl in this picture build up a quality of individualism. This depiction of individual characteristics was never the aim in Chinese figure painting.

and western figure painting. It is the great difference between a "figure" and a "portrait."

Western paintings that have people as their subject like the *Mona Lisa*, and *Girl with a Pearl Earring* are generally known as portraits whereas the classic Chinese paintings with people as their subject such as *Court Ladies Adorning Their Hair with Flowers* and *The Thirteen Emperors* are called figure paintings and never portraits. Taking these two works of Zhou Fang and Yan Liben as examples we can examine this tendency to attach little importance to individual characteristics in traditional Chinese painting in order to understand exactly what traditional Chinese figure painting is.

There are six people in *Court Ladies Adorning their Hair with Flowers*, the principal and easily distinguished main characters are the four noble ladies who are shown proportionately larger than the remaining two women, of whom one is a lady approaching from a distance and the other a maid in a minor role. The faces, adornments, physical carriage, posture and manner of the four main characters are all very similar and it is difficult to detect any difference in appearance or personality between them, leading one to wonder whether Zhou Fang painted four models of the same lady. At the same time this lack of individual characteristics in the models makes it difficult for the viewer to imagine that the ladies in the picture can be real people.

Yan Liben's *The Thirteen Emperors* shows the thirteen emperors from the Han to the Sui (581–618) dynasties. Although in point of appearance there are minor differences in the models of the thirteen, on inspection they do not resemble living people at all, let alone the fact that lacking cameras, how were the painters of the Tang dynasty to know the august visage of previous emperors? What was it that Yan Liben took as his conceptual model for the figures beneath his brush? A detailed analysis of these two paintings follows below.

Portrayals that Reject Individualism

Based on the observations described above we can conjecture that the conceptual model for the figures that appear in the paintings of the ancient masters were not real individuals and that the product of their brush was not a likeness of a particular person. In the two previous chapters we discussed the decisive influence that the concept of transmission and the reverence for freehand both had on the development of Chinese painting. In fact, there is a further point. Traditional Chinese culture placed little value on the individual, so that painters had no interest at all in the promotion of individualism.

In ancient Chinese society, the glory of the winner of the first place in the imperial examinations was reflected upon his extended family. That is to say, the greatest value of individual achievement lay in bringing honor to one's ancestors and not in a narrow, purely personal contribution. It is not easy to understand this system of values when approached with the mind-set of a modern person who is under the constant influence of western values.

Following the Romantic Movement of 18th century Europe, western artists pursued the goal of self-liberation to the point where individualism was rampant and innovation displayed an individual's special sense of artistic touch and promoted individual achievement. Consequently western painting from the 18th century on displays a marked tendency towards the expression of individual achievement and individual artistic concepts (figs. 55–56 on page 56). Put another way, individualism is not of the essence of traditional Chinese culture, so that figure painting whether in its creation or its appreciation does not focus upon individual characteristics. We may perhaps come to understand this line of reasoning through the poet Su Dongpo's (Su Shi) (1037–1101)

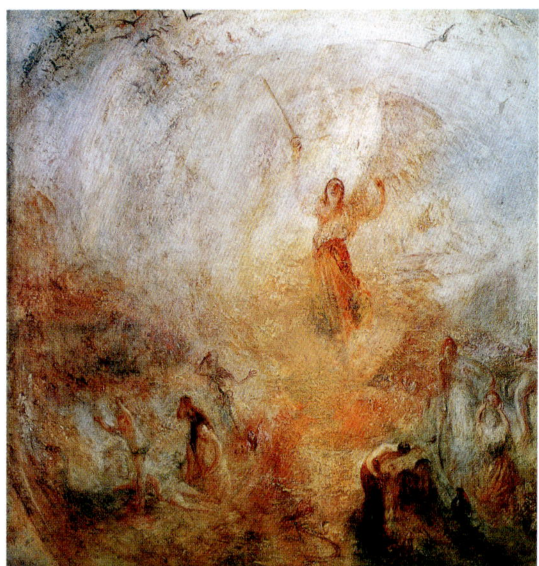

Fig. 55 *The Angel Standing in the Sun*
Joseph Mallord William Turner (UK, 1775–1851)
Oil on canvas
Height 78.5 cm × Width 78.5 cm
Tate Britain, London

The artists of 18th century western Romanticism sought self-liberation. Turner was an English master of Romanticism and the subject of this late work is the Last Judgement of the *Old Testament*. It expresses his pessimistic view of death.

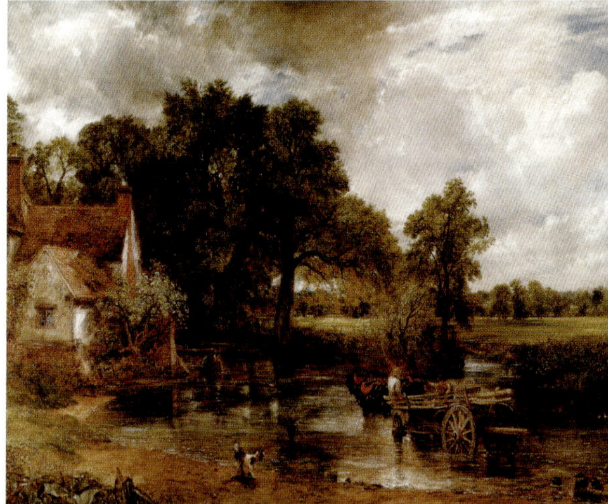

Fig. 56 *The Hay Wain*
John Constable (UK, 1776–1837)
Oil on canvas
Height 130.2 cm × Width 185.4 cm
National Gallery, London

Although also a representative of English Romanticism, Constable's style was far removed from that of Turner. *The Hay Wain* was the work that made his name. It captures a moment beside a stream at Flatford in the Suffolk countryside.

critique of two images of the scholar Ouyang Xun (557–641).

It is said that Su Dongpo once saw two paintings of Ouyang Xun. In the first, the image was painted in meticulous detail, the face was distinctly painted in and the general silhouette was outstanding. It was easy to imagine that it had been painted from Ouyang's appearance as it was in life, moreover there was an emphasis on *xiezhen* that enabled viewers of the painting to recall how he had looked before his death.

According to Su Dongpo's recollection the figure in the second painting was very simply delineated and apart from the positioning of the eyes, ears, nose and mouth there were no distinctively detailed features that allowed the viewer to make out Ouyang Xun's appearance as it might have been. However, considered as a whole there was an unaffected plainness about it caused by the economy of portrayal and simplicity of line, set off by the large expanse of white background, that gave the viewer a sensation of austere elegance. Su Dongpo said that he preferred Ouyang Xun as he appeared in the second painting, this was the man that he knew so well (fig. 57).

Su Dongpo's reasoning was quite simple. The first painting showed Ouyang Xun realistically, the artist had used his technical skills to portray him as he appeared in reality, much as in a photograph today. These "portrayals" are comparable with the portraits of the West and were known in ancient China as "images of the ancestors" (*zuxian xiang*), produced so that the descendants of the person in the painting could remember and worship them. Su Dongpo was not a descendant of Ouyang Xun and consequently had little feeling for this painting of "true likeness".

The second painting displays the scholarly

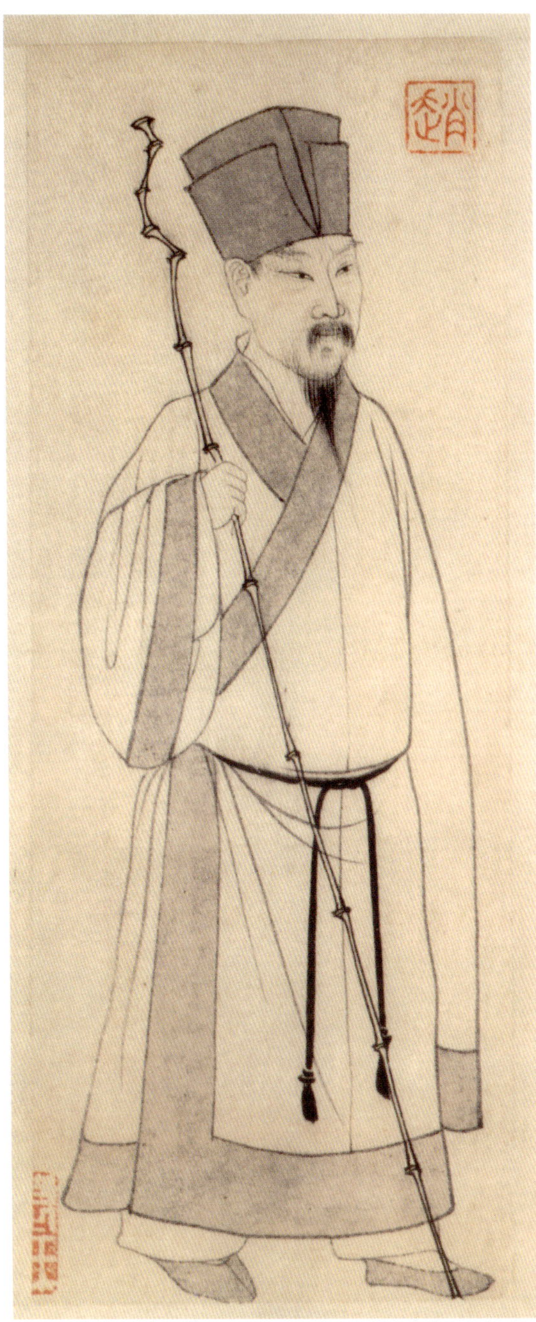

Fig. 57 *Portrait of Dongpo*
Zhao Mengfu
Ink on paper
Text of Su Dongpo's poem *Before the Red Cliff* with portrait of Su Dongpo at the head of the album, consisting of 935 characters in 81 lines
Height 27.2 cm × Width 11.1 cm (21 pp.)
Palace Museum, Taibei

Su Shi (1037–1101), otherwise known as Su Dongpo was a famed literary personality, calligrapher and artist of the Northern Song dynasty. He spent his life amidst the trials and tribulations of official life and was demoted and posted hither and thither thus suffering much hardship. His writings reflected his rich emotions. He liked to paint bamboos and stressed that paintings should carry spiritual connotation. The modelling of the figure in the painting has an elegant simplicity that reflects the indifference to material things and the desires and aspirations towards a spiritual life of the subject. The bamboo staff is a symbol of Su Shi.

inner temperament of Ouyang Xun and not his external characteristics, consequently the focus is not on how he looked or appeared but on the expression of his cultivated inner character and scholarly demeanor. Through spacious construction and simple line the artist evinces that lofty air of disdain for materialism combined with spiritual ardor that was the Ouyang Xun that Su Dongpo recognized, respected and understood. In sum, the first painting is a portrait or resemblance of Ouyang Xun and the second a representation of him as a literary gentleman.

Traditional Chinese painting did not promote individualism. However realistic the painting of individual characteristics, however heroic or charming, they just remained resemblances, portraits with no more significance than to serve as memorials and objects of worship for descendants. In the eyes of the traditional artists and historians of ancient China, this kind of *xiezhen* representation of people had only utilitarian and no artistic value. Consequently the focus of traditional figure painting was not on the *xiezhen* representation of individual figures but on commenting upon the level of society represented by the figure. Rather as if the painting of Ouyang Xun that Su Dongpo liked, was not an image of Ouyang Xun himself but a portrayal of the elevated moral character of a scholar and thus capable of arousing a sympathetic response from scholars generally.

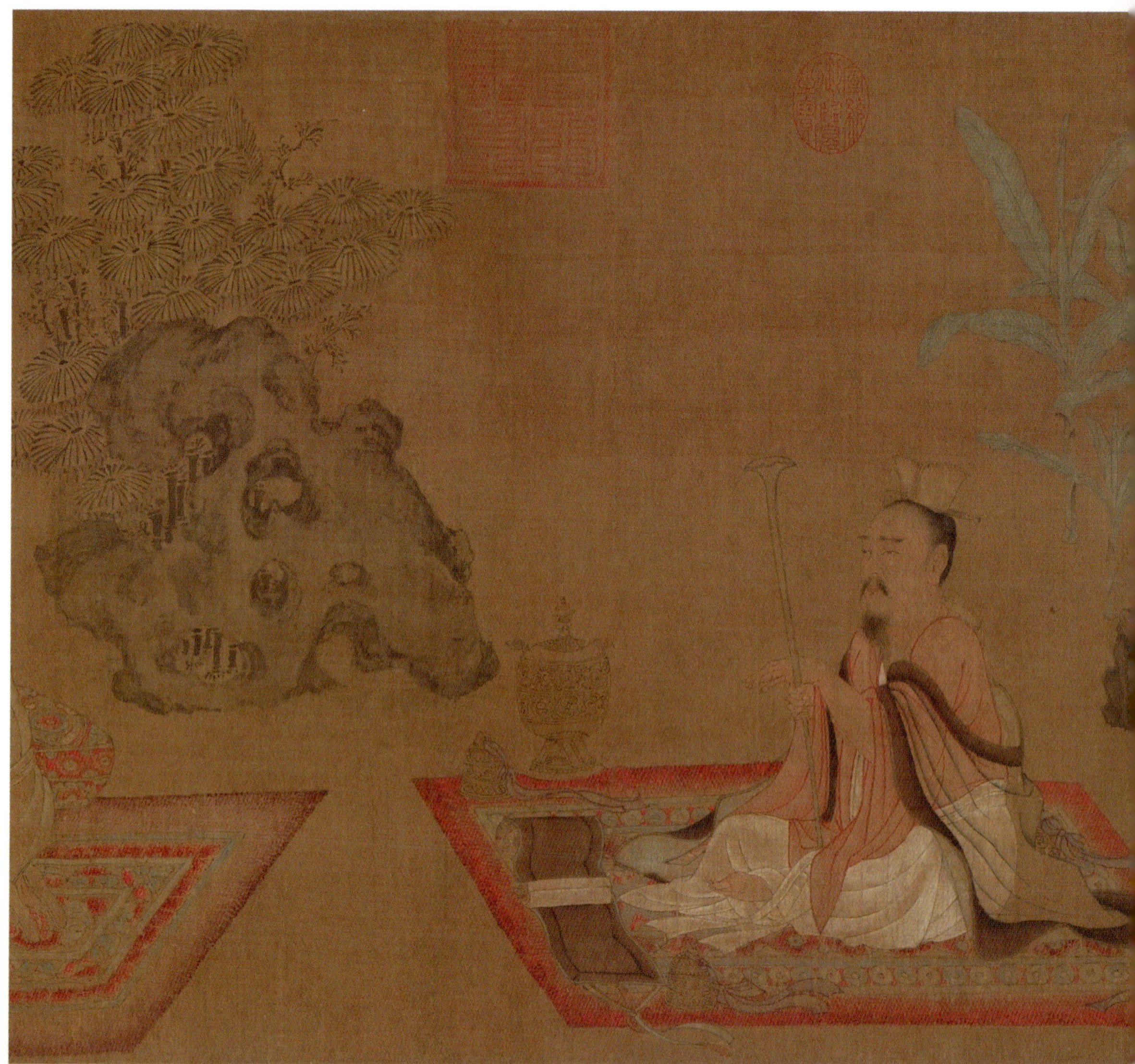

Thus it can be seen that there are broadly two kinds of figure painting by the artists of ancient China. First, *xiezhen* portraits, predominantly ancestor portraits, mostly by artisan painters and recording the actual appearance of the ancestor for commemoration by descendants, which, after the passage of time, are lost through natural damage and are consequently difficult to pass on to future generations. The majority of those ancestor portraits preserved today are works from the Qing dynasty and are in the collections of museums outside China. Just think, what Chinese would ever have an interest in somebody else's ancestors? An even more important reason why ancestor portraits were not well regarded by the Chinese themselves is that throughout Chinese history, histories of art and art theory have been the work of the scholar class with its prejudice against portraits and its belief that the work of artisans could not be regarded as art. Consequently they are rarely described in art histories or in the records of discussions about the theory of art.

The other kind is the only one referred to as figure painting in traditional art. The artistic achievement of this kind lies in its reflection of the concepts behind the figure. The subject is not the figure itself but the social strata it represents and their human values and ideals. The Tang writer Zhang Yanyuan

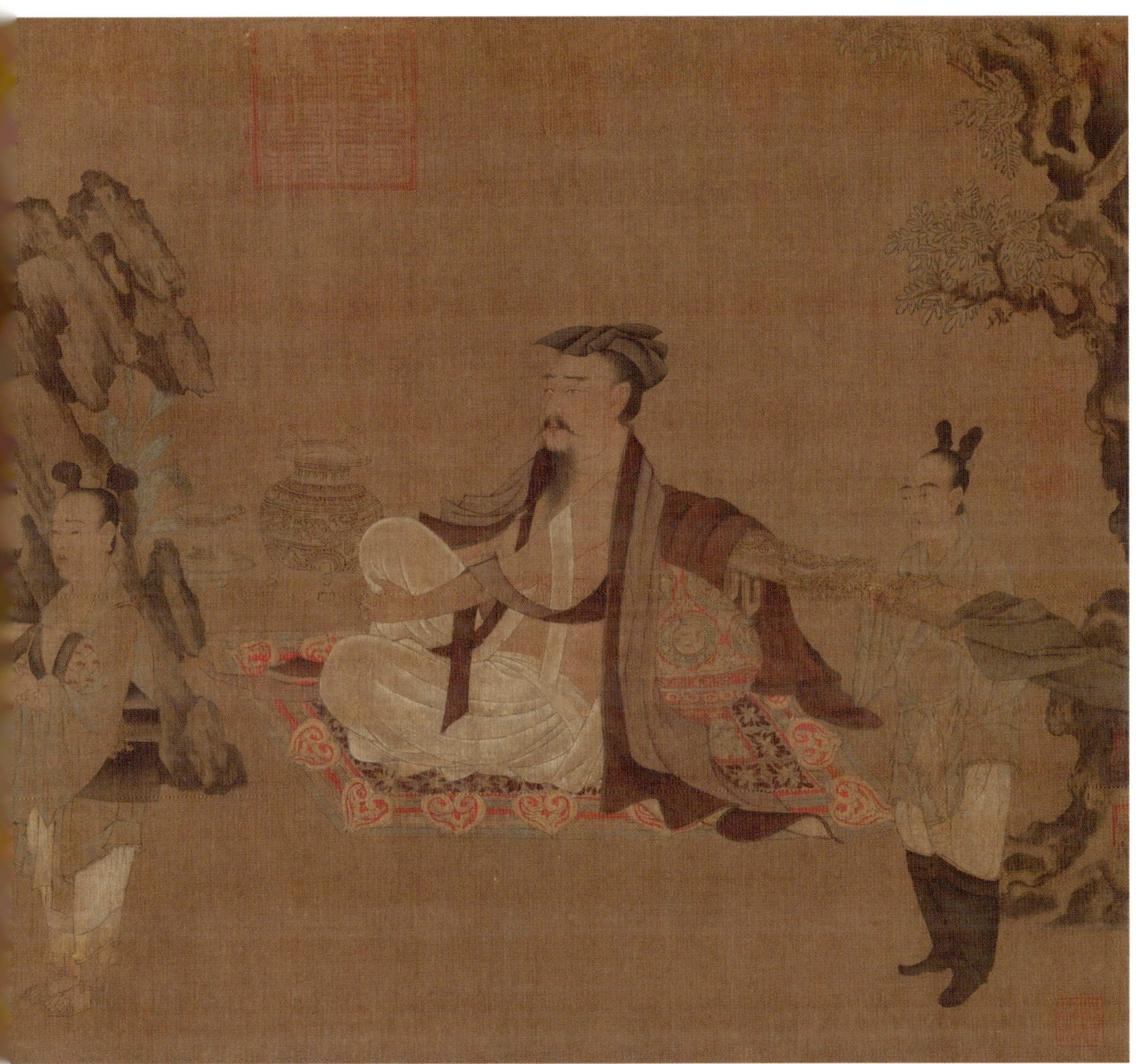

Fig. 58 *Elevated Ease* (detail)
Sun Wei (Tang dynasty)
Ink and color on silk
Height 45.2 cm × Width 168.7 cm
Shanghai Museum

Paintings of eminent men refers to a category of figure painting that takes the activities of the literati class as its subject. The focus of this category of painting is not on the tiny details of the life of any particular scholar, but on the ancient scholar class as a stratum of society that abhorred material desires and emphasised art and literature as a life-style that encouraged the cultivation of both body and mind.

(815–907) clearly and precisely pointed out in his *Record of Historical Paintings* (*Lidai Minghua Ji*): "The merit of painting lies in civilizing and assisting human relationships." Thus, in ancient Chinese society, one which did not promote individualism, the achievement of individual beauty was not the creative aim of the traditional masters of figure painting. Consequently traditional figure painting has never produced a western masterpiece such as the *Mona Lisa*. Traditional Chinese figure painting took people from different levels of society as its subject, divided, in the main, between the categories of ladies of position, eminent men and emperors, feudal chiefs, generals and ministers (fig. 58).

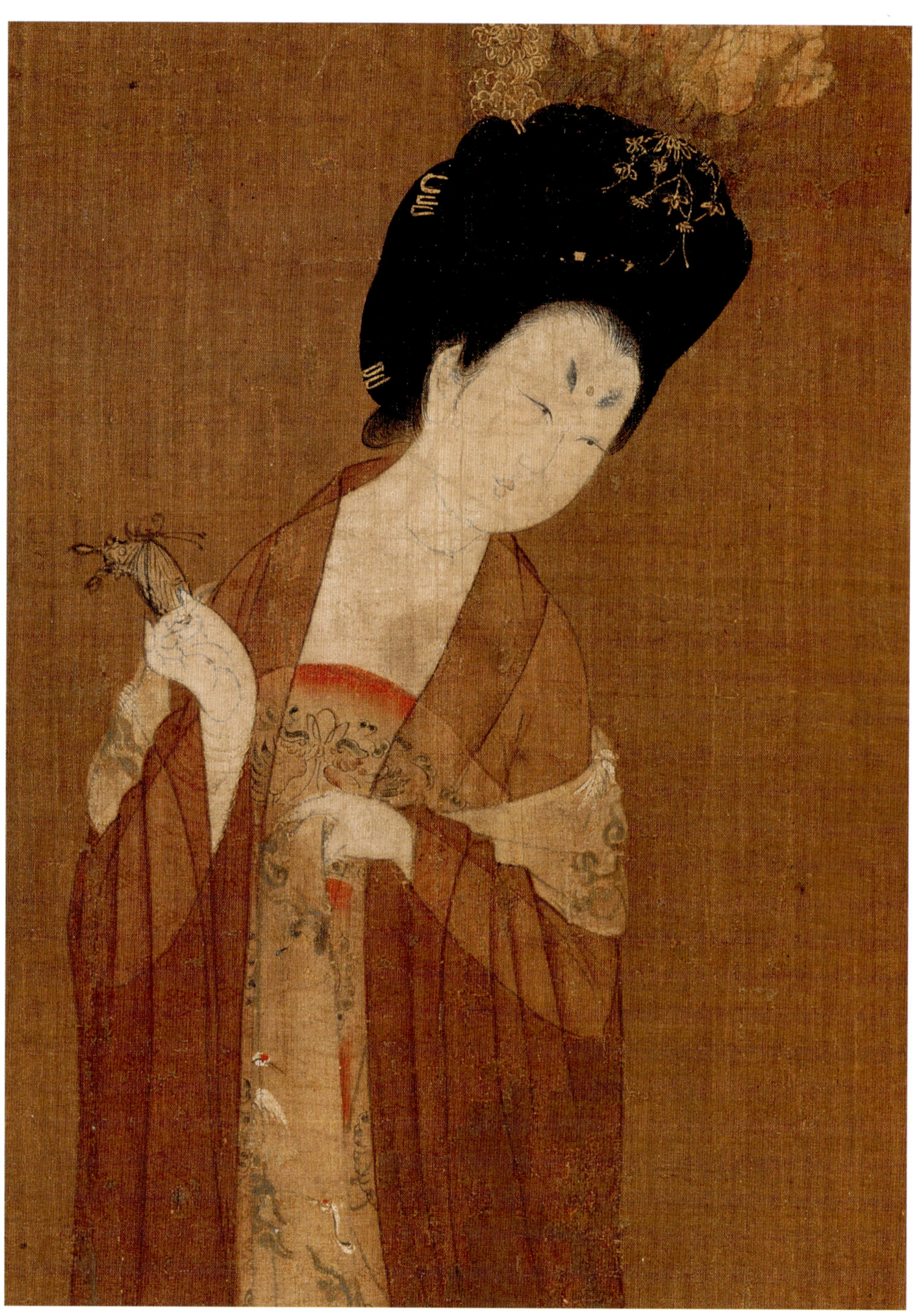

Fig. 59 *Court Ladies Adorning Their Hair with Flowers* (detail)

The Sociology of Chinese Painting

Having established that traditional figure painting is not portraiture of the individual but a creation that takes the various strata of society as its subject, we can take another look at Zhou Fang's *Court Ladies Adorning their Hair with Flowers* and Yan Liben's *The Thirteen Emperors* in order to better understand their significance.

Ladies of the nobility is the subject of *Court Ladies Adorning their Hair with Flowers*. The four ladies who are the principal characters in the painting are similar in clothing and countenance, their hair in high buns, ornamented with brightly colored sprays of flowers, eyebrows penciled like butterflies and wearing low-cut long skirts with shoulders covered by a muslin cape. A first impression of their elegant and graceful appearance tells the observer that these are no ordinary women but carefully made-up ladies of the nobility (fig. 59).

In fact, records indicate that the clothing and ornaments and mode of dress of the ladies of the Southern Tang (937–975) nobility were much the same as those in this picture. The first lady, with a whisk in her hand, leans back to play with the dog at her feet. The second lady faces the dog gazing at it as if she and the first lady are both playing with it. The third lady walks slowly to the left after a crane and is closely followed by a maid-servant holding a fan. The last lady stands by a group of flowers as if picking them, gazing back towards the crane on the right and the lady who follows it in.

Because of the lack of individual characteristics the four ladies look exactly the same, but it is their graceful deportment, elegant attire and leisured air that emphasizes the qualities that they have in common. The whole painting exhibits a strong sense of grace and leisure, this is the theme of *Court Ladies Adorning their Hair with Flowers*. Zhou Fang's intention was not to illustrate who amongst this group of noble ladies was prettier than the other, but to use their poised demeanor to show the appearance and bearing demanded of ladies of the ancient imperial family to reflect the style and sense of nationhood of the imperial Tang dynasty. In fact, we merely have to savor the sense of sumptuous magnificence exuded by this painting to discover that other artistic creations of the Tang dynasty, for example the pursuit of rule and order in calligraphy of the time or three-colored pottery are born of the same breath and share the same pulse.

Let us take another look at Yan Liben's *The Thirteen Emperors*. Yan's family were of Mongolian origin and his father and brother were painters. He excelled in figures and horses and chariots and was master of painting at the Tang court. As this court painter created *The Thirteen Emperors*, his aim was not to express his own inner feelings, nor indeed the individual characteristics of any particular emperor but the responsibility they had of "civilizing and assisting human relationships." There are thirteen emperors in this picture. Yan Liben's conceptual idea was not to present the real image and appearance of all thirteen emperors but to display their achievements and status and to evaluate their position historically through the different technical means of painting them. These included: "large face thick eyebrows," "tiger back bear waist," "soft and tender" and other models. If we take a look at the representation of the Zhou Emperor Wuwang (?–1043 BC) with his bristling beard and eyebrows as thick as a knife, glaring eyes, drooping earlobes and enormous body, the very image of majestic power, we see a representation of an "imperial visage" from the science of physiognomy. An inscription beside the image explains that this is the Zhou Emperor Wuwang. Any historically minded person seeing it would immediately thump the table and exclaim: "No wonder he's so impressive, it's the Northern Zhou Emperor Wuwang Yuwen Yong!"

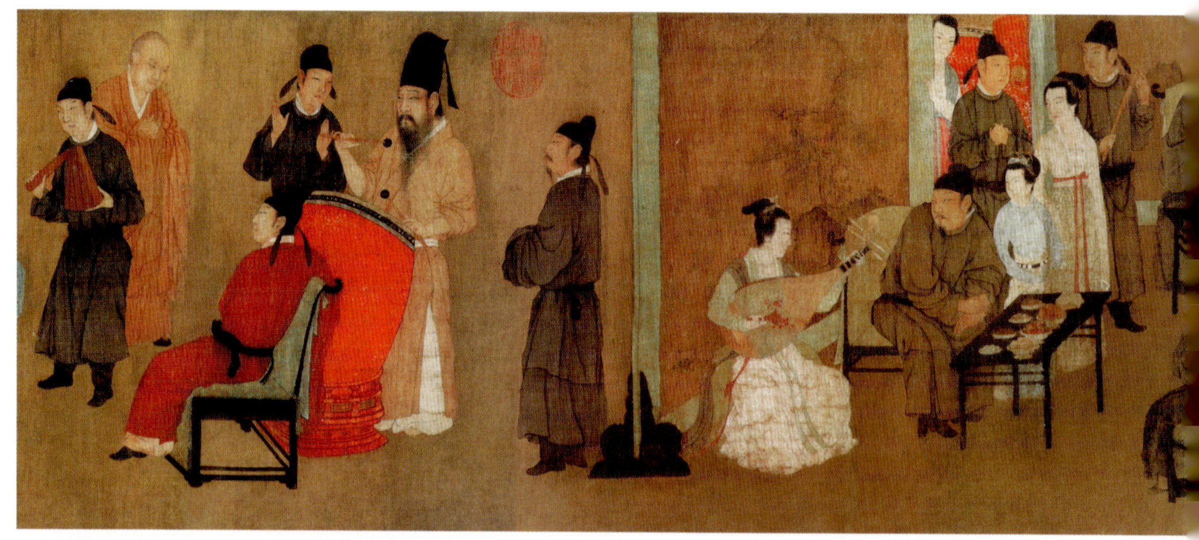

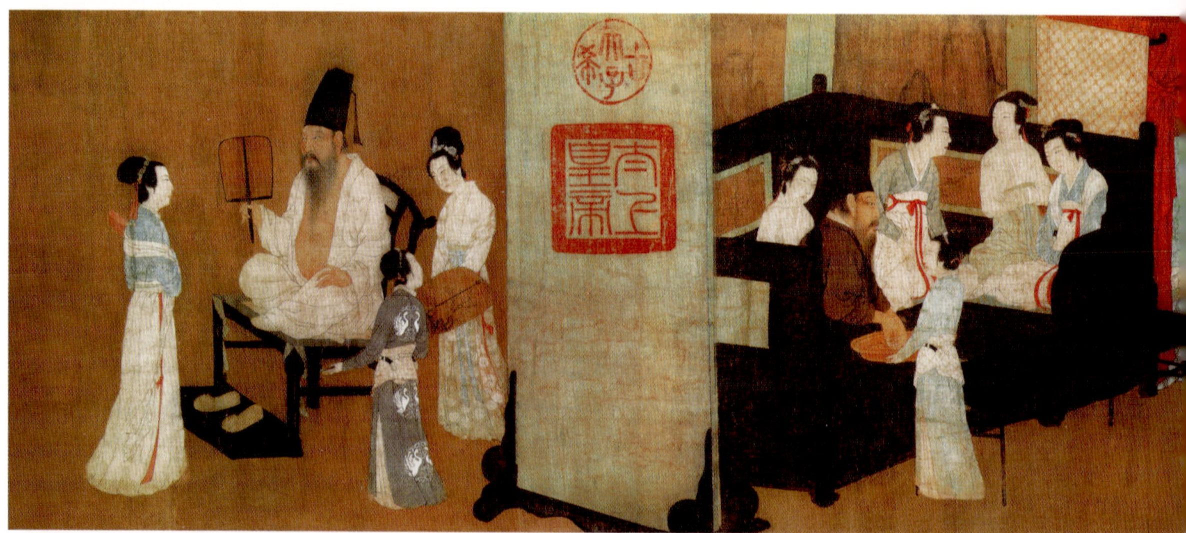

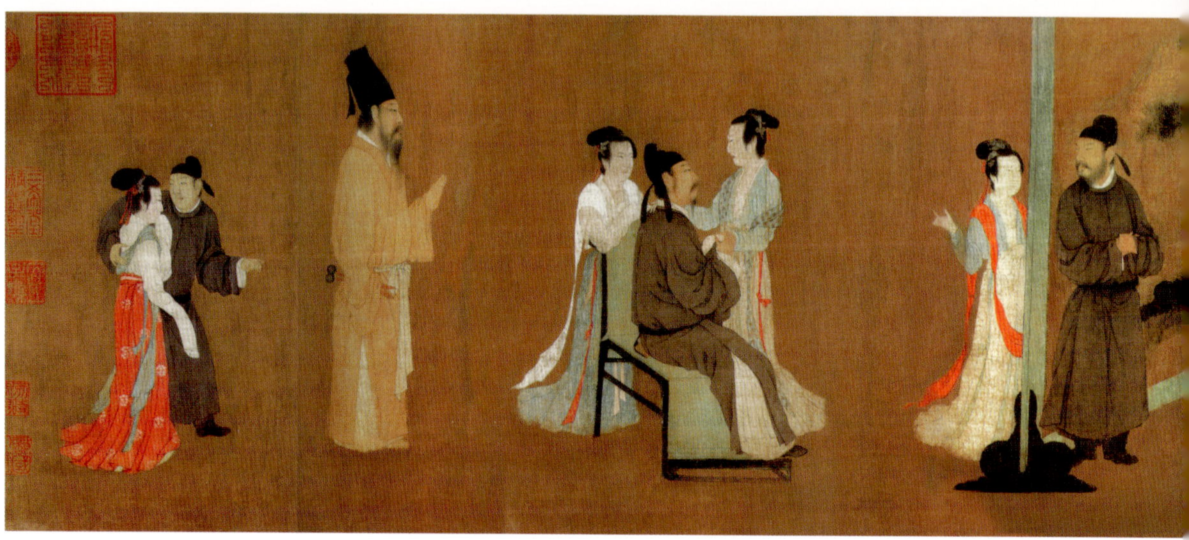

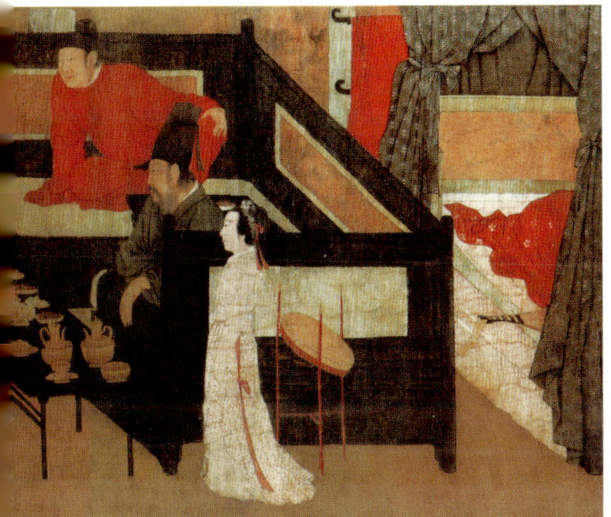

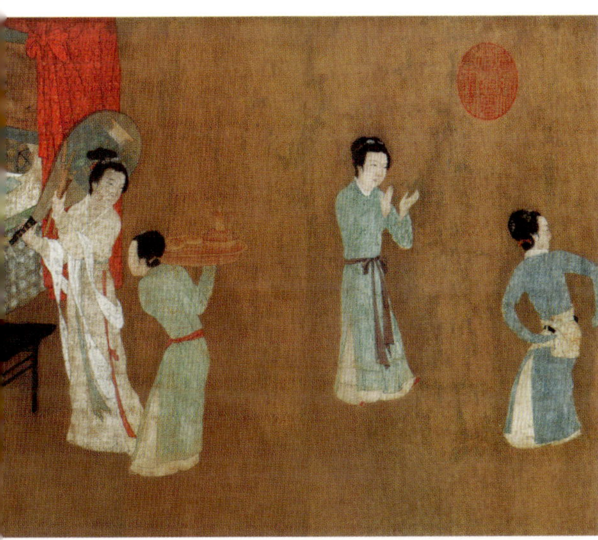

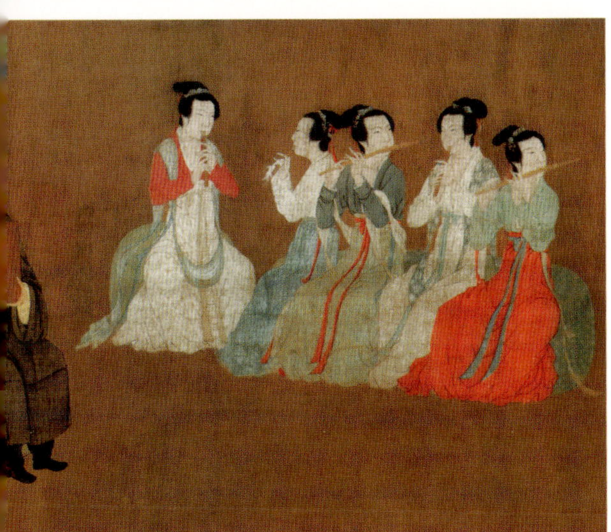

By the time of the Five Dynasties the archetypal work was the 10th century Gu Hongzhong's *Chancellor Han Xizai's Evening Banquet*. This bears the "*shaoxing*" seal of the Southern Song (1127–1279) Emperor Gaozong, and at the end of the scroll, an anonymous inscription which suggests that it is generally considered to be the work of Gu Hongzhong (figs. 60–62). Gu was a master of the painting academy under Li Yu (937–978) the final ruler of the Southern Tang period and Han Xizai was a Southern Tang minister who, out of favor with the court, took to women and drink and a dissolute lifestyle.

This painting was executed on Li Yu's instructions, following his order to Gu to investigate Han Xizai's life. It is a record of the latter's nightly banquets and dissolute lifestyle prepared for the emperor's information. Through the clever use of screens, Gu divides the whole scroll into five scenes, covering listening to string music, the watching of dancing, rest, wind music and bidding farewell to guests. Han Xizai, with bristling beard and wearing a square cap appears as the principal character in a number of different situations. Gu uses different apparel to represent the social position of

Figs. 60–62 *Chancellor Han Xizai's Evening Banquet*
Gu Hongzhong
Ink and color on silk
Height 28.7 cm × Width 335.5 cm
Palace Museum, Beijing

Gu Hongzhong was a member of the Southern Tang (937–975) painting academy during the period of the Five Dynasties and Ten States. *Chancellor Han Xizai's Evening Banquet* was painted on the instructions of the final ruler of the Southern Tang, Li Yu, that Gu should spy out the dissipated life-style of Chancellor Han Xizai and record "what the eye sees and heart perceives" in the scroll to reflect the ambience of Han Xizai's evening banquets.

The painting is divided into five sections covering listening to string music, the watching of dancing, rest, wind music and bidding farewell to guests. The sections are separated by gaps represented by screens or curtains. Han Xizai is shown in different attitudes in each of the five panels.

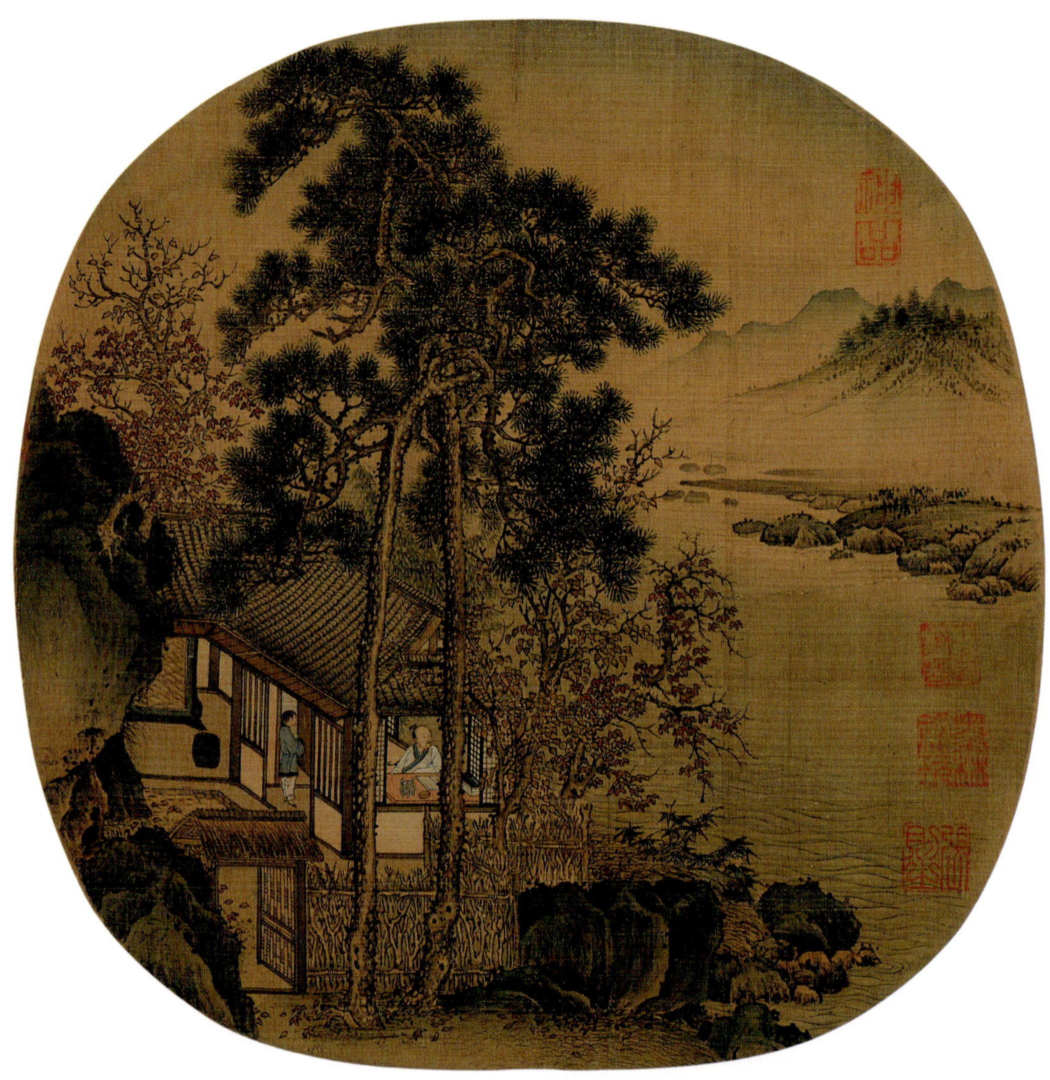

Fig. 63 *Reading at the Window in Autumn*
Liu Songnian (Southern Song dynasty, 12th–early 13th century)
Ink and color on silk
Length 25.8 cm × Width 26 cm
Liaoning Provincial Museum
Another painting that depicts the scholar class that has the same aims and characteristics as fig.13.

the other figures and depicts them in detail as they look about them and exchange glances, displaying their dissolute behavior, drunk with music, sex, wine and desire. This is a vivid pictorial record of the opulent atmosphere of a banquet in ancient times.

Although the subject of *Chancellor Han Xizai's Evening Banquet* is an actual person, the point of the painting is not the characteristics of the appearance of Han Xizai and his guests but the reflection of his dissipation and neglect of public office. Consequently, the question of who the dancers, singing-girls and guests were in reality is irrelevant, the important point was that the scroll should highlight and display Han's total absorption in sexual desire and his unfettered hedonism.

After the Song dynasty, traditional painting, in addition to depictions of ladies of the nobility and emperors, generals and ministers, also included numerous painting in the category of eminent men that took the literati class as their subject. The majority

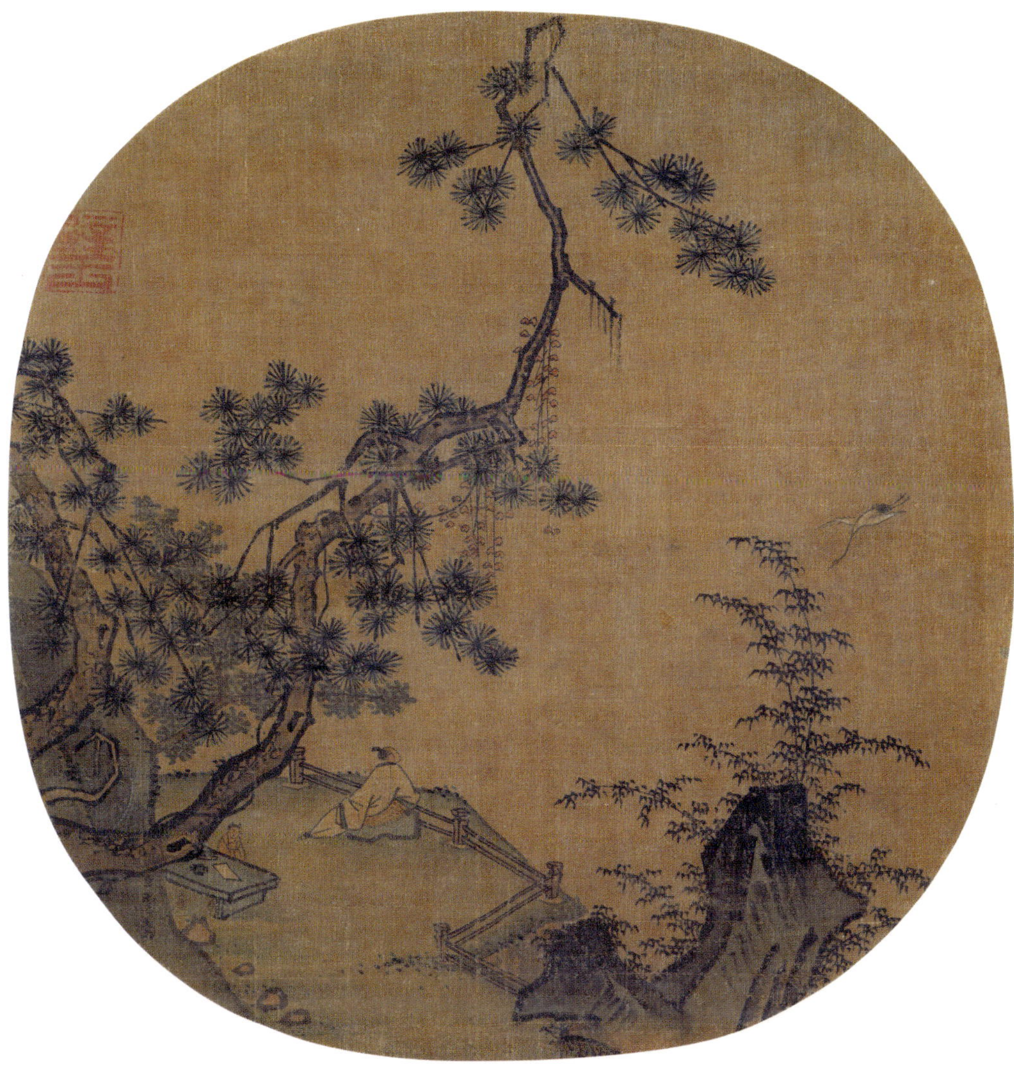

Fig. 64 *Humming beneath the Pines*
Ma Yuan (Southern Song dynasty, 12th–early 13th)
Light ink and color on silk
Height 24.5 cm × Width 24.5 cm
Shanghai Museum

In *Humming beneath the Pines*, a tiny figure has been placed in the midst of a vast open space. The large blank area helps build a state of leisured abstraction.

of these paintings focused on the activities of gentlemen scholars and reflected their aspirations for a life of the spirit. The eminent men category of Song academy paintings mostly show them listening to the pines, or gazing at waterfalls. Two notable examples are the Song painter Liu Songnian's *Reading at the Window in Autumn* (fig. 63) and Ma Yuan's *Humming beneath the Pines* (fig. 64). In common with other traditional figure paintings, the figures in both these paintings lack individual characteristics and bear no resemblance to real people.

For the same reason, the focus of *Humming Beneath the Pines* is upon an environment of leisurely contemplation and the experience of the abstract world that derives from the process of contemplation. Thus, the figure in the painting is relatively small and sits alone beneath a massive pine tree, beside a river. Most of the painting is executed in weak ink lightly applied, its aim to construct an abstract world from space.

Physical Shape Is Not Better than Spiritual Form

Western art was already known in China by the time of the Ming and Qing dynasties, though the literati painters who led the painting world evinced no great interest in the *xiezhen* aspects of western painting. Literati painters tended to prefer *xieyi* to *xiezhen* and drew a conscious line of demarcation between the artistic creations of painting and calligraphy and the mere products of handicrafts. The Qing painter, Zou Yigui (1686–1772) criticized western art in the following terms: "Though the work be skilled it is not painting," meaning that however refined the style and outstanding the technique, in the end it was just a handicraft and not to be mentioned in the same breath as art (figs. 65–66).

As a result and in the main, the painters of the Ming and Qing dynasties continued to retain the features of traditional painting. However, some professional painters skillfully incorporated western techniques into the requirements of traditional figure painting, adding a new meaning to them. Interesting examples from the Ming and Qing dynasties include the Qing painter Jiang Xun's *Portrait of Li Qingzhao*, Zeng Jing's (1568–1650) *Portrait of Wang Shimin*, Shi Tao's *Image of Tao Yuanming* and Ren Bonian's (1840–1895) portrait of Wu Changshuo under the title *The Impoverished Official*. Let us now look at the characteristics of these paintings.

Li Qingzhao (1084–c. 1151) was a noted woman poet of the Northern Song dynasty who came from a literary family and enjoys a high reputation in Chinese classical literature. Although *Portrait of Li Qingzhao* is that of a historical personage it lacks the features that would make Li Qingzhao a real person (fig. 67). At a glance it resembles a classic painting of ladies. But there is something special about its construction, which is not modelled on the whole figure construction of traditional figure painting but adopts the frequently

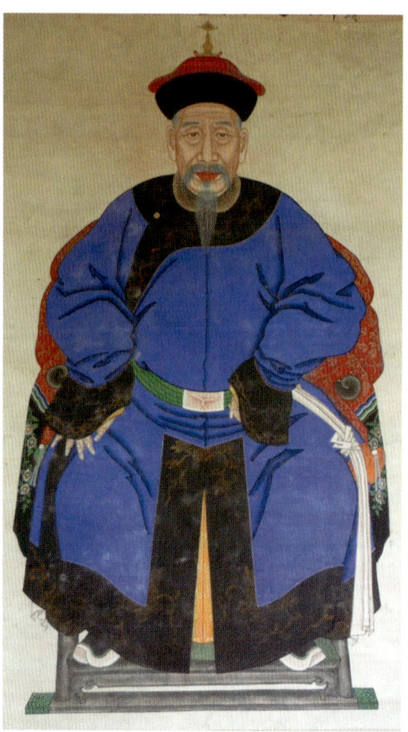

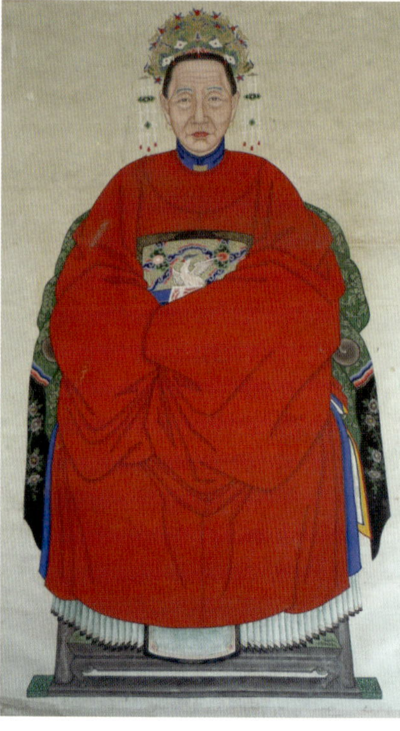

Figs. 65–66 *Portraits of Ancestors*

Most early Chinese portraits are generally portraits of ancestors painted for the purposes of commemoration or worship. They were generally executed by artisan painters and in the eyes of the educated elite were handicrafts and not works of art. Consequently they were neither recorded nor discussed in traditional art histories.

used western model of the half-figure, with a simply dressed and adorned half-figure image of a lady placed at the bottom of the picture. Moreover, there is no background at all, leaving a larger blank space at the top of the picture. Above, an inscription records that this is the famous woman poet Li Qingzhao. But for the explanation in the inscription we would not know that this was Li Qingzhao. Nevertheless, the abbreviated composition favored by the traditional literati painters gives us a clear impression of a temperament of elegant nobility, precisely that of Li Qingzhao herself.

Shi Tao was one of the Four Monks of the Early Qing. His original name was Zhu and he was a descendant of the Ming imperial family born into the turbulent times that preceded the fall of the dynasty. His father had proclaimed himself regent in Guangxi province and the whole family was later slaughtered by the Qing, leaving him the only survivor. In order to avoid capture by the authorities he had taken the tonsure as a buddhist monk at the age of five and had been given the religious name Yuan Ji. He promoted the idea of "method that is not method" (*yi wufa wei fa*) in painting and his unconventional spirit and freehand brush and

Fig. 67 *Portrait of Li Qingzhao*
Jiang Xun (Qing dynasty, 1764–1821)
Ink and color on paper
Height 115.8 cm × Width 26.7 cm
Wuxi Museum

Li Qingzhao was a woman poet of the Northern Song dynasty who enjoys a high reputation in the history of Chinese literature. The Li Qingzhao in the painting lacks any of the features of a real person and, at a glance, looks like one of the ancient paintings of ladies. However, the painter does not employ the full figure construction of traditional figure painting but places the frequently used western half-figure model at the bottom of the painting with a simply dressed and plainly adorned image of a woman, while the upper portion of the picture is occupied by a large blank space. The artist uses this simple layout to convey Li Qingzhao's air of simple elegance.

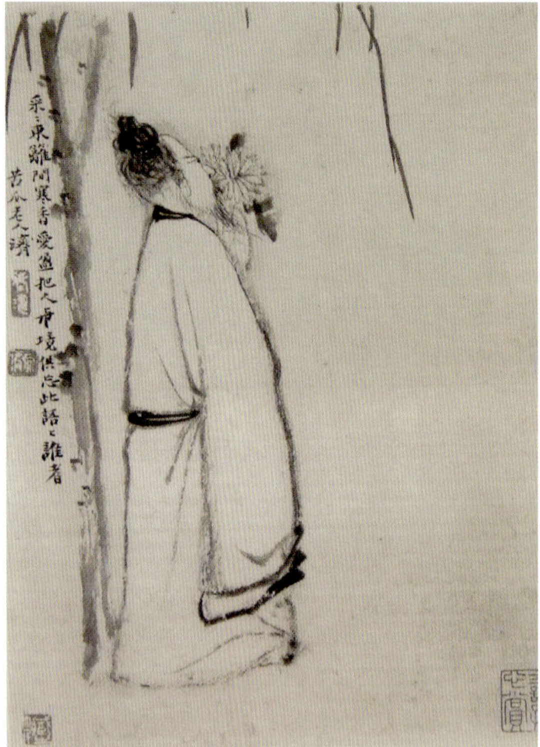

Fig. 68 Tao Yuanming painted by Shi Tao

Tao Yuanming (c. 365–427) was a well-known literary figure famed for the fresh natural style of his writing. When people thought of chrysanthemums they thought immediately of Tao Yuanming. The theme of the painting is not the figure, but Tao Yuanming's indifference to material desire encapsulated in the phrase "don't break your back for a peck of rice," demonstrating the literati painting tradition of "heavy in meaning but light in form." The figure in the painting in no way resembles a real person, even to the extent of ignoring its proportions. The whole painting is sparsely sketched, without superfluity, in a few brushstrokes with the focus upon the chrysanthemum in the figure's hand.

ink style deeply influenced later generations. His *Image of Tao Yuanming* was in the tradition of "heavy with meaning but light in form" of the literati painters (fig. 68). The figure in the painting bears no resemblance to a real person and at the time of creation no account at all was taken of its proportions. The painting's focus is upon the flowering chrysanthemum in the figure's hand which recalls lines from a famous poem of Tao Yuanming's: "I pluck the chrysanthemum bloom beneath the eastern fence / and see serene the southern hills." The painting is sparse in line without a superfluous dot or stroke and suits the aloof world of "Don't break your back for a peck of rice."

Zeng Jing was a well-known Ming dynasty figure painter who earned his living from painting. He painted portraits of many Ming literati artists. There is a certain expression of western individualism in his figure painting, though no loss in the requirements of the Chinese tradition. In 1616, he painted a likeness of Wang Shimin (fig. 69). Wang Shimin came from a distinguished literary family and was a senior official under the dynasty. He gave up his post on the accession of the Qing dynasty in 1644 and thereafter devoted himself to painting. This painting was completed in 1616 when Wang was only 24. The painting reflects his individual facial characteristics, not in excessive detail but just sufficiently to allow the viewer to imagine

Fig. 69 *Portrait of Wang Shimin*
Zeng Jing (Ming dynasty, 1568–1650)
Ink and color on silk
Height 64 cm × Width 52.3 cm
Tianjin Museum

Wang Shimin was one of the Four Wangs of the Qing dynasty. Zeng Jing painted this portrait in 1616 when Wang Shimin was 24. Zeng Jing uses a simple line to depict the plainly dressed young man as a gentleman scholar holding a whisk. The background consists of clear blank space that reflects the simplicity of the figure and matches Wang Shimin's aspirations to a life of hermetic retirement and inner cultivation. The emphasis is upon the inner and not the outer man. Consequently, although the face has its individual distinctive features, they are no more than touched in.

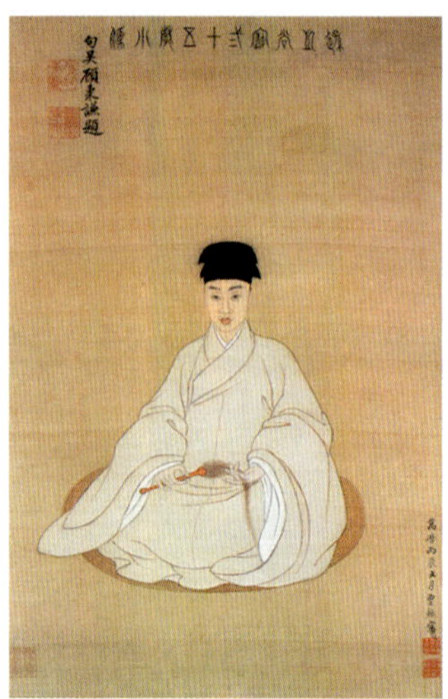

how the young Wang Shimin looked, just so much and no more. Zeng Jing uses a simple line to depict the plainly dressed young man as a gentleman scholar holding a whisk. The background consists of clear blank space that reflects the simplicity of the figure and matches Wang Shimin's aspirations for a life of hermetic retirement and inner cultivation.

Ren Bonian was a professional painter of the late Qing dynasty who excelled in flower-and-bird and figure painting. *The Impoverished Official* is a portrait of his friend, the well-known flower-and-bird painter Wu Changshuo (1844–1927) (fig. 70). Wu Changshuo had been, for the space of a month, resident magistrate in Dong'an county in Hunan province but unable to bear the dark and authoritarian ethos of officialdom had resigned to become a professional painter. Wu is shown in the uniform of a low grade official. The detail of clothing and decoration is swiftly sketched in with ink wash and the facial characteristics are simply outlined. The expression of unhappiness that shows contains an element of helplessness. The figure lacks any background but the inscription tells us that Ren Bonian met Wu, dressed as an official, in the street one day and instantly realized the misery that life as a minor official was causing him. The use of the description "impoverished" is actually an expression of sympathy for his friend and the *raison d'etre* of the painting.

The reference to the *xiezhen* portrait of Ouyang Xun earlier in the chapter demonstrated that early Chinese painters were well able to paint portraits, it was just that portrait was not historically and traditionally well regarded and was not the type of figure painting uppermost in the minds of painters. Many ancient portraits with a practical use have been scattered and lost over the generations and very few have survived. Consequently, the Song dynasty "portrait" inscribed: *Feng Ping, Retired Secretary*

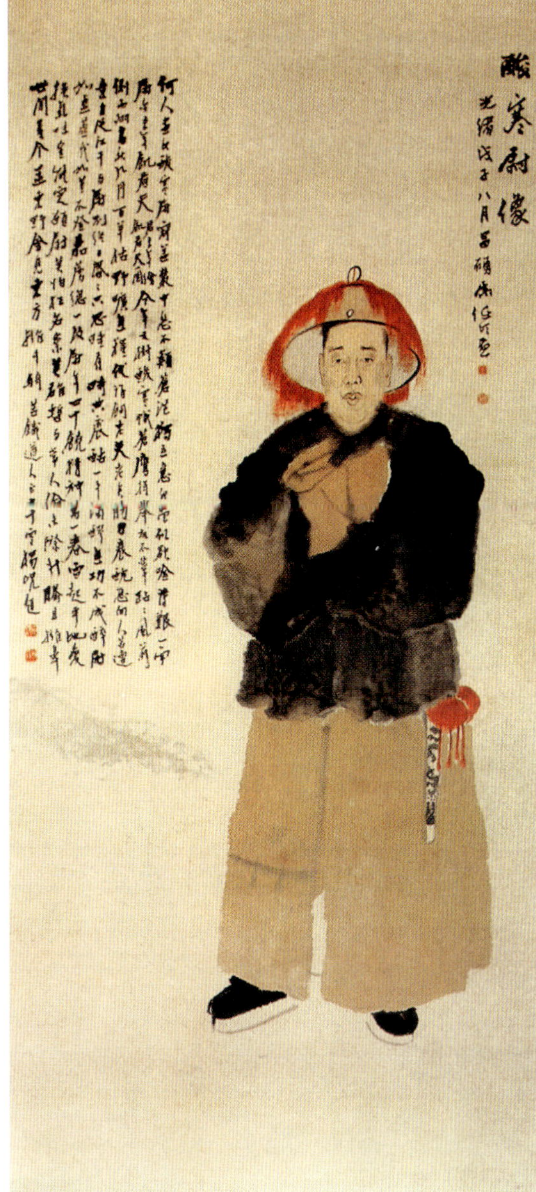

Fig. 70 *The Impoverished Official*
Ren Bonian (Qing dynasty, 1840–1895)
Ink and color on paper
Height 164.2 cm × Width 77.6 cm
Zhejiang Provincial Museum

Painted in 1888, this picture depicts Wu Changshuo at the age of 45. Wu had once spent a month as a minor official, but unsuited to the politics of the court, had resigned and supported himself by selling paintings. He later became a leading light of the Shanghai Painting School (*haipai*). Wu Changshuo and Ren Bonian were great friends. Wu is depicted in official uniform with a red tasseled hat and high soled boots. He wears a long dark yellow gown covered by a black silk jacket. There is a hint of helplessness in his expression.

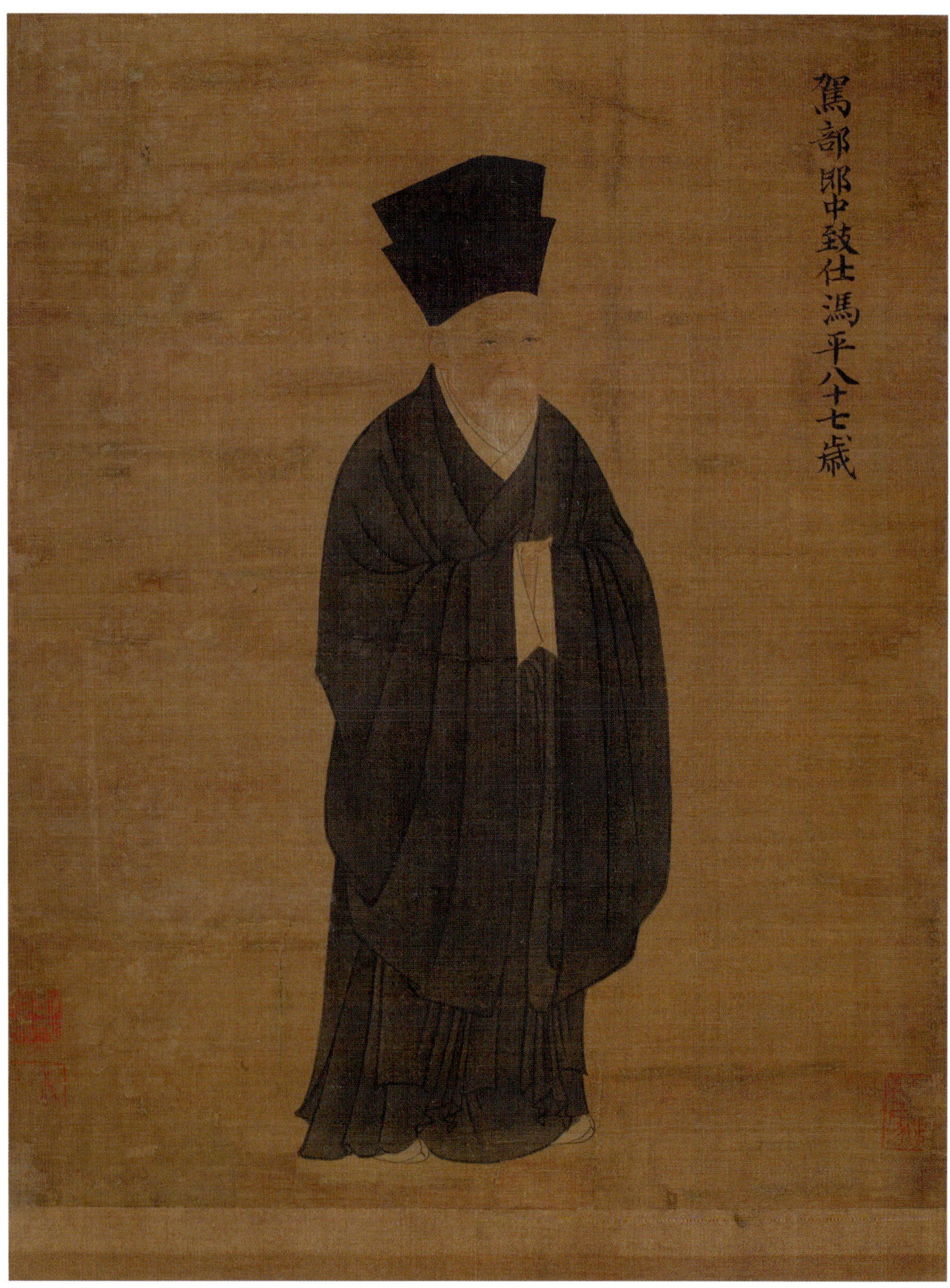

Fig. 71 *Portrait of Feng Ping*
Anonymous (Northern Song dynasty)
Ink and color on silk
Height 39.9 cm × Width 32.7 cm
Freer Gallery of Art and Arthur M. Sackler Gallery, Washington D.C.

This painting may be the earliest surviving portrait. The inscription explains that this is *Feng Ping, Retired Secretary of the Board of War, in His Eighty-Seventh Year.* It shows Feng Ping in official dress, in clear outline and aged in looks, it is easy to imagine that this is a portrait of a real person.

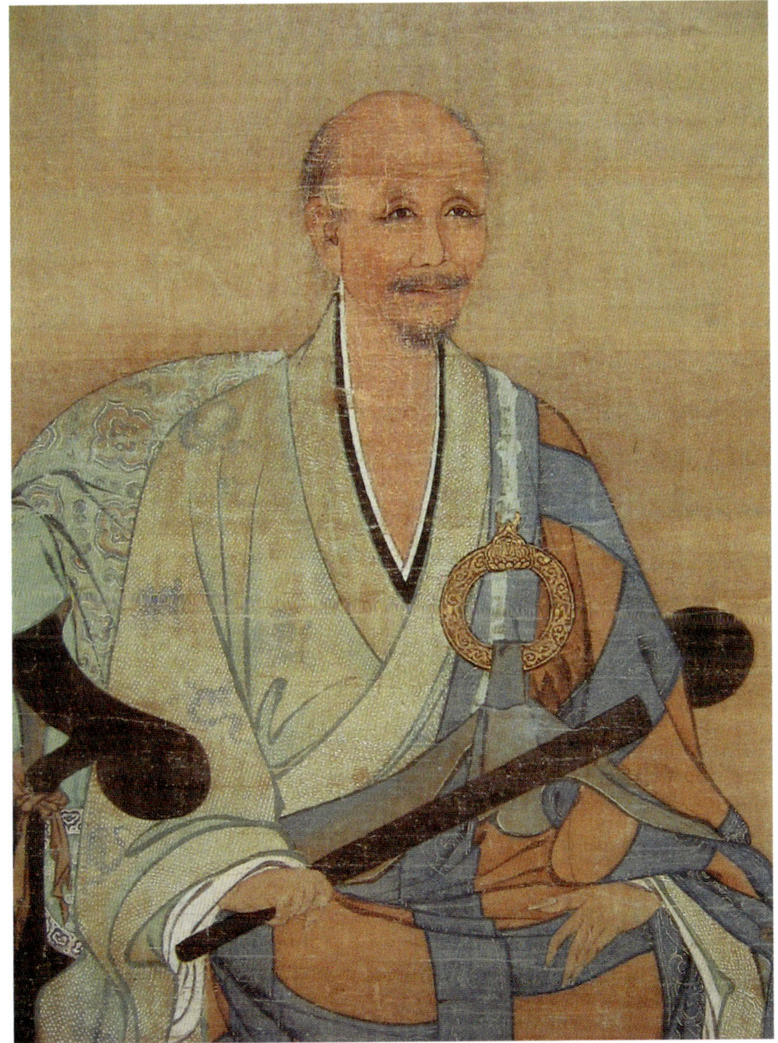

Fig. 72 *Zen Master of the Southern Song Dynasty (detail)*

Ancient China did not lack for skilled portrait painters. This painting of 13th century shows the spare outline and gleaming eyes of a Zen master, his face full of individualism.

of the Board of War, in His Eighty-Seventh Year is extremely valuable (fig. 71). It shows Feng Ping in official dress, in clear outline and looking aged and it is easy to imagine that this is a portrait of a real person. A further portrait is that of a Zen Master of the Southern Song dynasty now in a Buddhist monastery in Japan (fig. 72). The portrait shows the emaciated outline of an elderly Zen master with prominent features and gleaming eyes. Zen Buddhism flourished during the Southern Song dynasty when many Japanese students of Buddhism came to China to practice Buddhism under well-known Zen masters. On the conclusion of their studies they returned to Japan, often bearing portraits of the Zen masters, some of these portraits have survived.

The analysis above is probably sufficient to explain the reasons why the figures in traditional figure paintings are not those of ordinary people. The reason that no Mona Lisa is to be found in Chinese traditional art is not because there were no individuals who could act as models, or because there were no painters who possessed outstanding true to life technique but because the subject in traditional figure paintings focuses not on any particular individuals. Looking for a Mona Lisa in Chinese art is to set one's focus incorrectly and miss the point of figure painting. The true focus of traditional figure painting is in the expression of the values and ideals that the figures represent and not in the expression of the individuality of a particular person, this is where the appreciation of traditional figure painting should lie. There was indeed portraiture in ancient Chinese painting, it was just that, in the traditional society of the time, it did not fall within the scope of art and was thus ill-regarded. The West did not share this point of view and, by contrast, many Qing ancestor portraits have been collected by western scholars and even become research material.

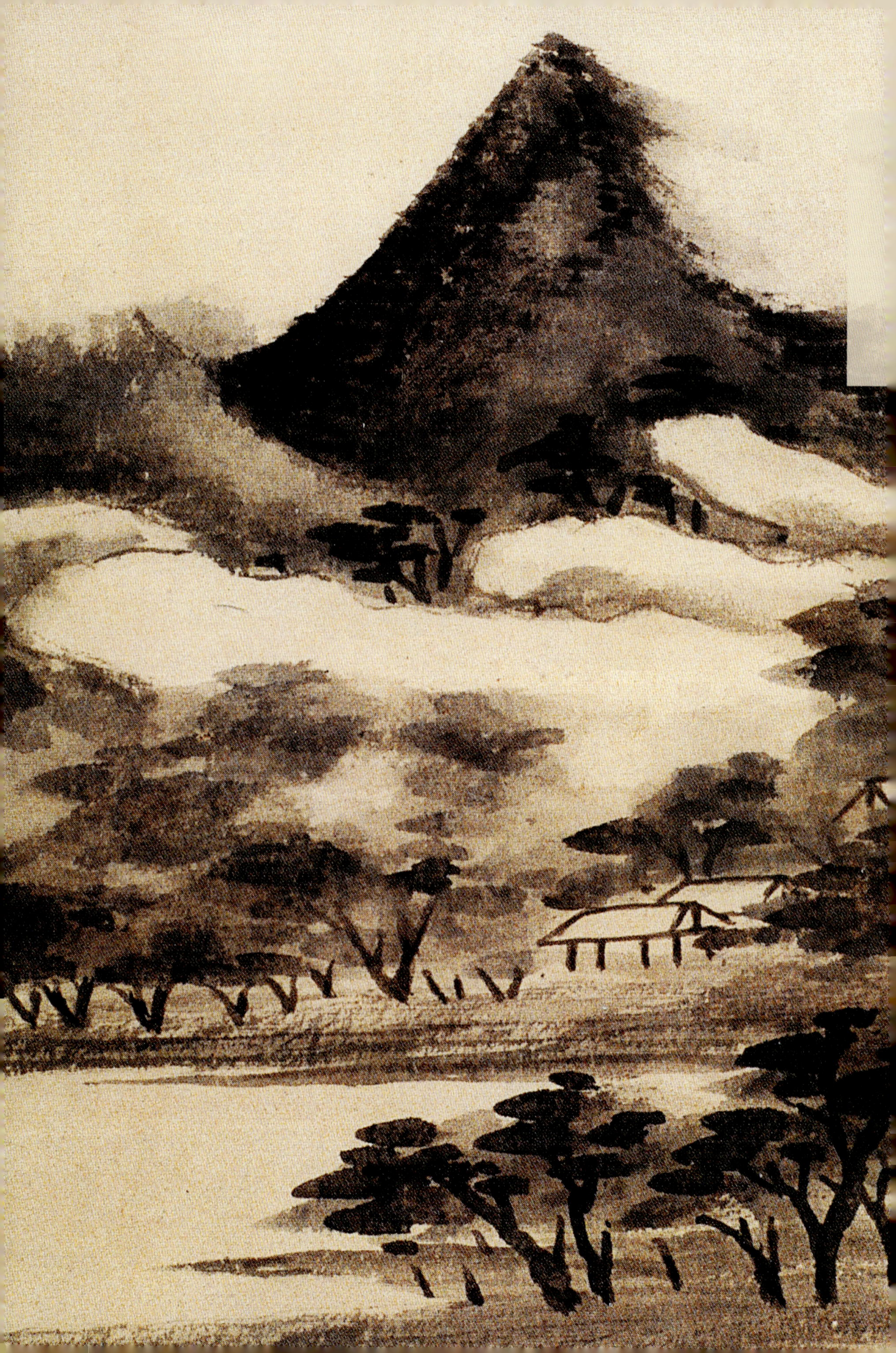

CHAPTER FOUR
Shanshui Differ from Landscapes

Nature is a source of creative inspiration for painters. In East and West many painters have taken natural scenery as a subject. We call works that have scenery as a subject landscapes; but in traditional Chinese painting they are not called landscapes but *shanshui* (hills and water).

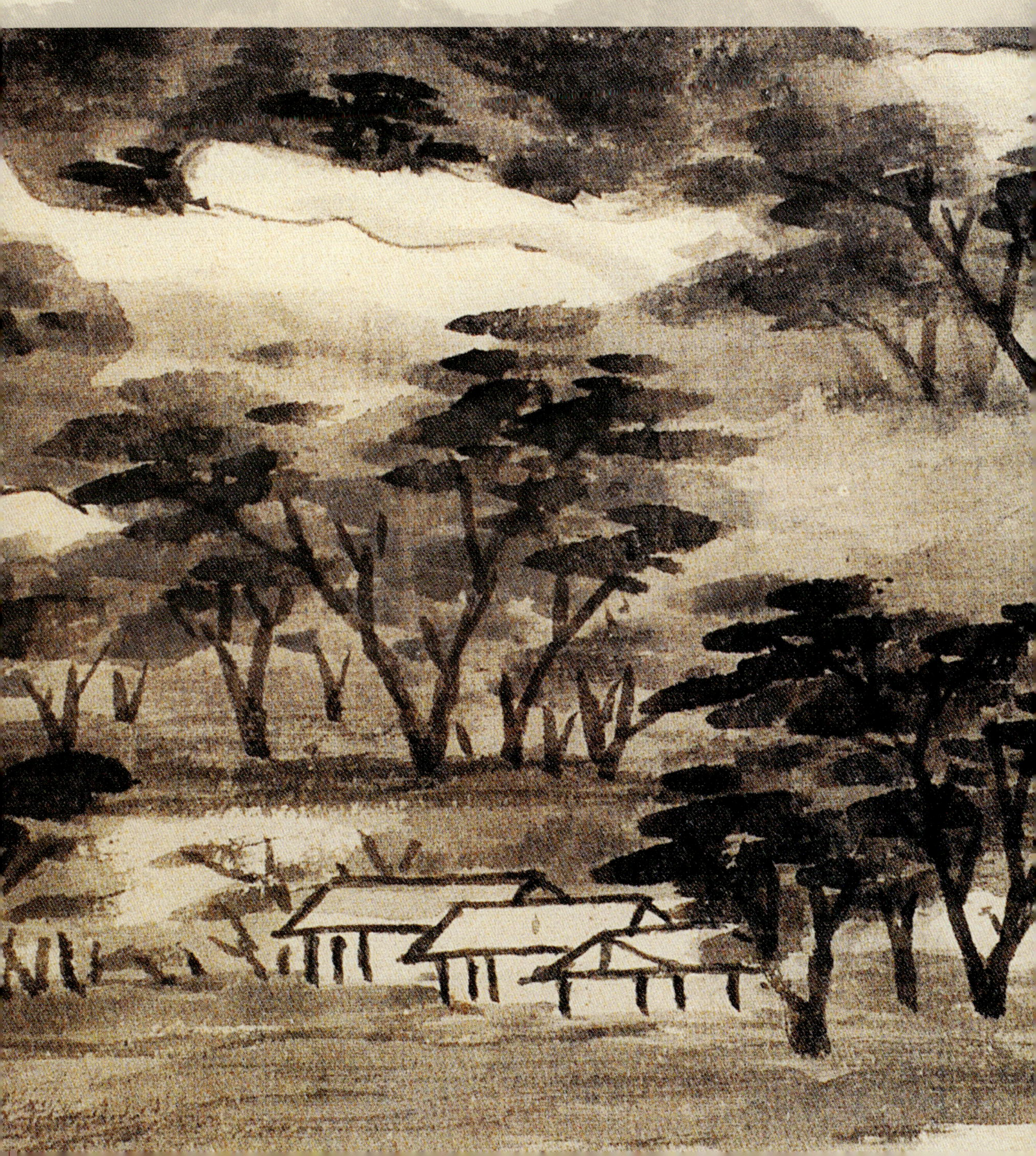

Shanshui Are Not Landscapes

I often like to place a western landscape alongside a traditional Chinese *shanshui* and then ask students what they see. The answer is straightforward and is, of course, "a landscape and a *shanshui*." However, when I ask them: "Can you call this landscape a *shanshui,* and can you call the *shanshui* a landscape?" the answer is no longer quite so straightforward. Some students begin to hesitate because they know that if they reply "no, a *shanshui* cannot be called a landscape," the next question will be "why not?" Some say that the images within a *shanshui* are mostly hills and water, hence the name. But western art does not lack for paintings containing hills and water. For example, the 19th century impressionist painter Monet's *The Cliffs at Etretat*, is all hill and water (fig. 74). Then, can we call it a *shanshui*?

I doubt if many people would call Monet's painting a *shanshui*; nor would many people call Ju Ran's *Crags and Trees* (end of 10th century) a landscape (fig. 75), the reason being that when you look at a *shanshui*, the scenery does not resemble a landscape but when you look at a western landscape the scenery in it is so real that it seems an actual physical landscape. Let us now look at the Dutch master of landscape Ruisdael's *Windmill at Wijk bij Duurstede* (1670) and examine the meaning of landscape (fig. 76 on page 76).

The subject of the *Windmill at Wijk bij Duurstede* is easily identifiable. It is a village scene in water-bound the Netherlands. It's focus is a large windmill that stands majestically towering over a river. Behind the mill the sky is filled with billowing clouds that occupy some two thirds of the painting. Beneath the mill there is an uneven line that runs across the whole painting, joining the terrain on the right to the water level on the left and dividing the painting into space on two levels, the sky above and the

Pages 72–73

Fig. 73 *Mountain and Mist in the Style of Mi* (detail)
Wen Zhengming
Ink on paper
Height 24.8 cm × Width 602 cm
Palace Museum, Beijing

A painting of trees and bushes. The horizontal double dot brush strokes are reminiscent of the Song dynasty "Mi-dot" tradition of Mi Fu (1051–1077).

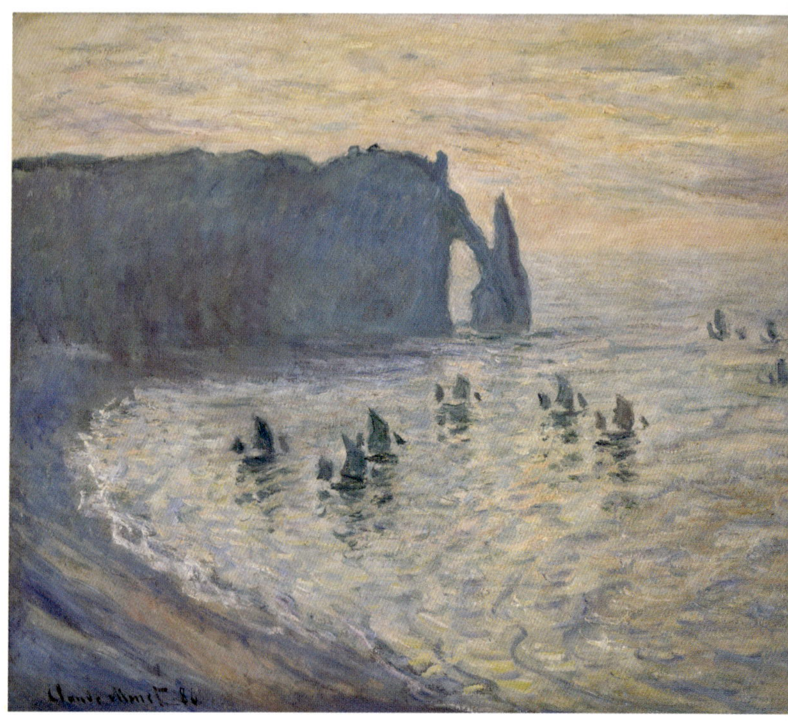

Fig. 74 *The Cliffs at Etretat*
Claude Monet
Oil on canvas
Height 66 cm × Width 81 cm
Pushkin Museum of Fine Art, Moscow

Western landscapes prompt the imagination, the actual scenery of a certain place at a certain time, just as this painting of a famous rock formation in north west France by Monet does.

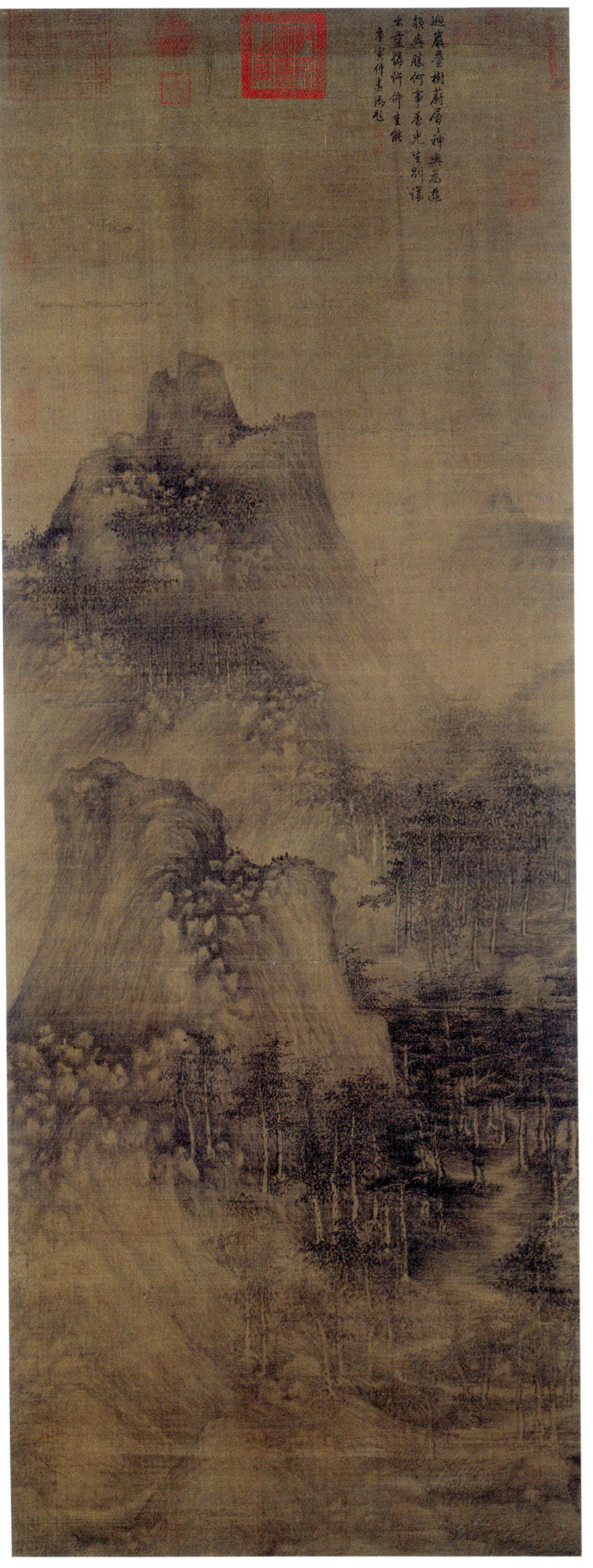

Fig. 75 *Crags and Trees*

Attributed to Ju Ran (Five Dynasties, fl. 960–985)
Ink on silk
Height 144.1 cm × Width 55.4 cm
Palace Museum, Taibei

The *shanshui* tradition of the Five Dynasties and Northern Song is the model for all *shanshui* art. Ju Ran was a painter of the Five Dynasties, a monk at the Kaiyuan Monastery and a pupil of Dong Yuan with whom he was known collectively as Dong-Ju. He had a considerable influence on later *shanshui* artists.

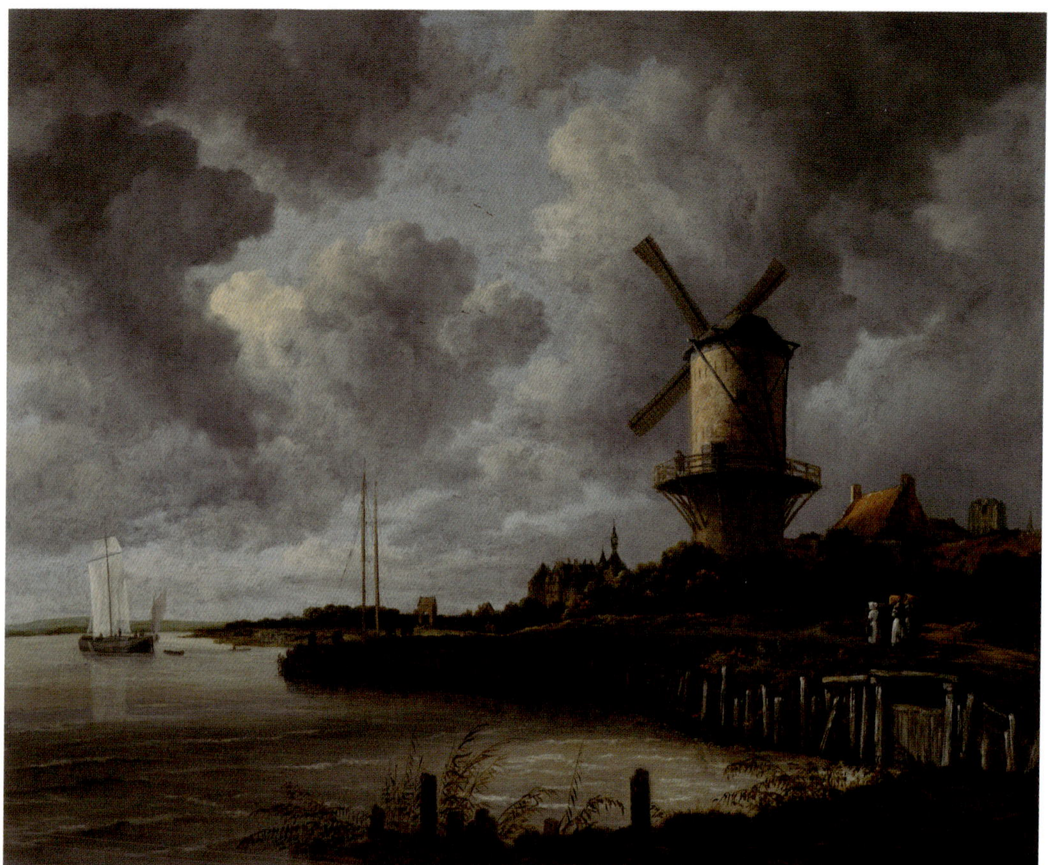

Fig. 76 *The Windmill at Wijk bij Duurstede*
Jacob Isaacksz van Ruisdael (Netherlands, c. 1629–c. 1682)
Oil on canvas
Height 83 cm × Width 101 cm
Rijksmuseum

The works of the Dutch landscape masters of the 17th century are not only detailed depictions of scenery but also of a particular moment in time. This painting captures the approaching shower of rain as well as depicting a Dutch riverside scene.

earth (water) below. The undergrowth in the picture has turned black beneath the dark clouds. Objects in the painting are richly and meticulously rendered. The waterside charm, even the approaching shower and the suddenly changeable weather unfold before the viewer as realistically as a photograph, making you feel that you are standing in a particular spot in a 17th century Dutch village awaiting the arrival of rain. This "on the spot" sense of locality is a feature of landscapes that is completely lacking in *shanshui*, and always prompts the question: "Is the scenery in *shanshui* real hills and real water?"

To understand the difference between landscape and *shanshui* we must first trace the origins and development of each in the histories of Chinese and western painting. Landscape flourished in the 17th century Netherlands. Western artists' attitude to nature was, in a sense, scientific and microscopic, a detailed observation of one place at one point in time that created an "on the spot" record from a fixed location. Consequently, on the one hand, they created comfortable, harmonious scenes of the ordinary, and on the other unusual scenes of imminent storms, shipwreck, avalanche and natural disaster (fig. 77). It is worth noting that the traditional Chinese *shanshui* usually displays scenes of tranquil harmony and not of nature at its most extreme.

The origins of Chinese *shanshui* painting can be traced back to the 4th century *Treatise on Shanshui* (*Shanshuihua Xu*) by Zong Bing (375–443) of the Southern Dynasties (420–589), the earliest work on *shanshui*, in which it is clear that Chinese *shanshui* appeared more than a thousand years earlier than the western landscape. By the time of the Five Dynasties and Northern Song the works of the great *shanshui* masters Dong Yuan, Ju Ran, Guo Xi (11th century), and Li Cheng (919–967) had become *shanshui* models for later generations. It should be pointed out that these artists of *shanshui* were not artisan painters but were Confucians and Daoists of whom the majority were hermits who subscribed to Daoist doctrine. Their motivation for creating *shanshui* was the integration of the Daoist Way that they sought amongst the hills and water of nature and not the expression of a single scene at onc point in time. Rather it was the expression of the spiritual aspects of the rhythm of nature, the wonder of the atmosphere and the constancy of harmony. Extreme natural events did not accord with the concept or Daoist Way of the constancy of harmony, they were abnormal phenomena that reflected an imbalance between man and nature and thus unsuitable material for their brush. This accounts for our inability to find natural disasters or even thunder and lightning in traditional *shanshui* paintings.

Despite the fact that nature was a subject for both Chinese and western artists there was a considerable difference in their creative artistic goals, so much so that, from the start, they developed along two different lines. The early 20th century master of Chinese painting Pan Tianshou pointed out: "In origin, Chinese painting is founded upon philosophy and western painting upon science, they proceed in opposite directions and each has its own criteria." This aptly identifies the reason for the difference between *shanshui* and landscape. *Shanshui* is not a landscape creation of a view, the point of interest is not the display of a particular scene at a certain place at a certain time but the expression of the artist's experience and his feelings for nature. If we compare Ju Ran's *Crags and Trees* with Ruisdael's *The Windmill at Wijk bij Duurstede*, we could say that Ruisdael painted a specific view and Ju Ran painted scenery and temperament, the view emphasized *xiezhen* but the scenery and temperament emphasized *xieyi,* the two represent two opposite systems of values and aesthetics.

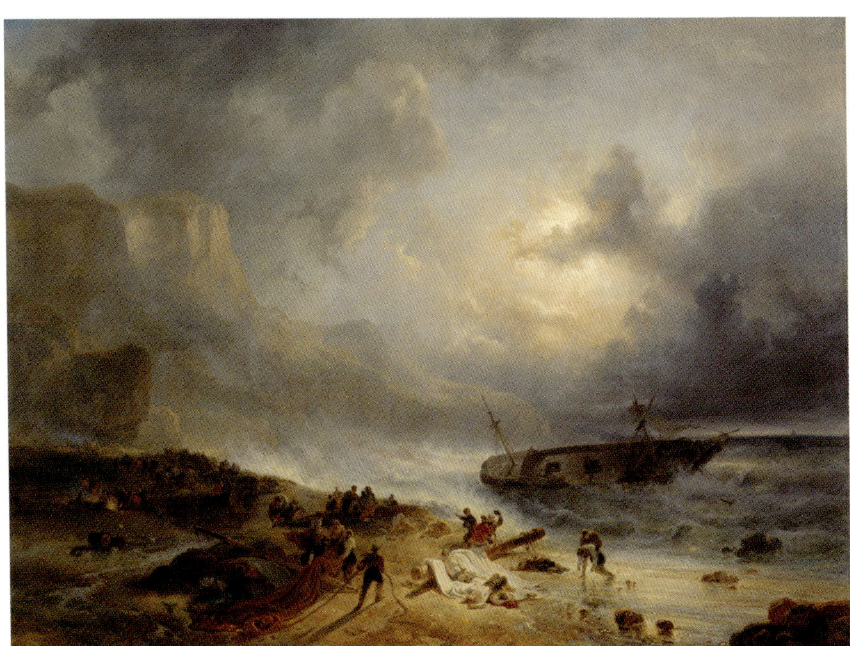

Fig. 77 *Shipwreck off a Rocky Coast*
Wijnand Nuijen (Netherlands, 1813–1839)
Oil on canvas
Height 154 cm × Width 206 cm
Rijksmuseum

Western landscape artists frequently took natural disasters as their subject. This kind of subject cannot be found in ancient *shanshui* art. Is there a particular underlying reason for this?

Shanshui, a Macroscopic Approach

It was the depiction of scenery and temperament and views that determined the differing approaches to the observation of nature taken by western and Chinese artists. Western artists took a microscopic and scientific approach, while the *shanshui* painters of China adopted an approach that showed an awareness of the macrocosm. There is no indication in Ju Ran's *Crags and Trees* of the location of the scenery in the painting, the hazy mists among the mountains and the thick covering of trees is not a display of the scenery of a particular mountain but of the moistly burgeoning vitality of mountain forest in spring and summer. The Song dynasty painter Guo Xi discussed how to paint *shanshui* in his famous treatise *The Acme of Forest and Springs* (*Linquan Gaozhi*) and set out in detail the macrocosmic attitude to nature of the artists of ancient China. A passage on the observation of mist and mountains says this: "In reality vapor in the mountains differs from season to season. In Spring it beautifies, in Summer it luxuriates, in Autumn it weakens, in Winter it darkens." He also had this to say: "In reality rising mist in the mountains differs from season to season. Spring mountains smile in splendor, summer mountains drip with verdant green, autumn mountains stand in clarity and winter mountains sleep in gloom." Guo Xi did not explain whether he was referring to the vapor

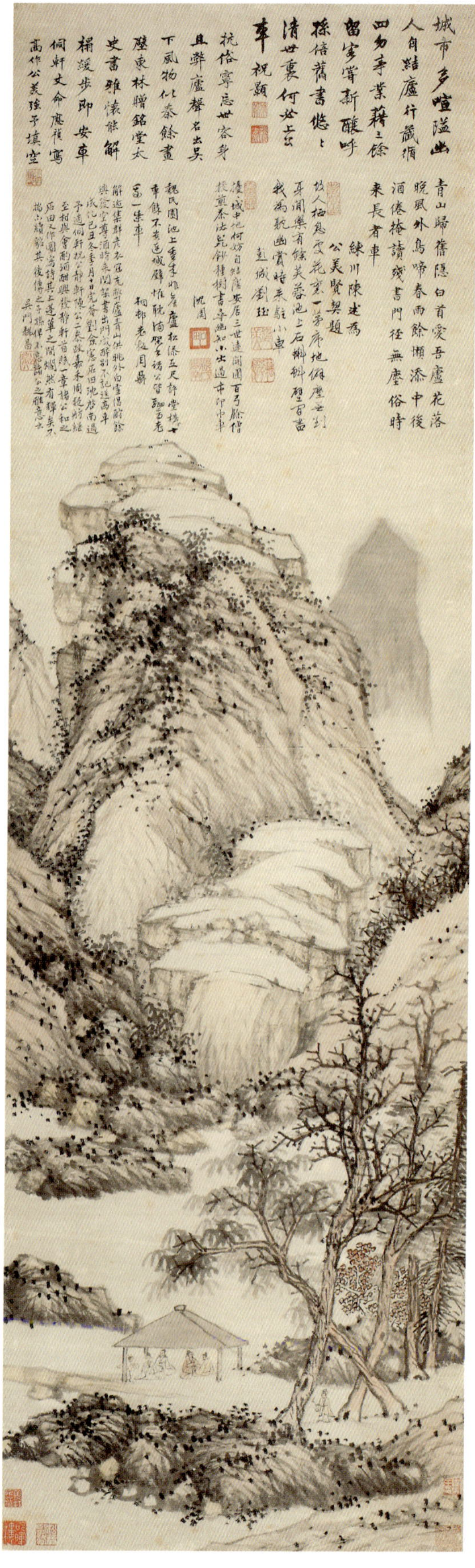

Figs. 78–79 *Elegant Gathering in the Wei Garden*
Shen Zhou
Ink and color on paper
Height 145.5 cm × Width 47.5 cm
Liaoning Provincial Museum

The Wei Garden actually occupies relatively little space in this painting and is lightly inked in. It is just a simple hut deep in the woods beneath the mountains. In fact the focus of the artist is not upon the Wei Garden itself but upon the eternal and harmonious relationship that the master of the Wei Garden enjoys with nature.

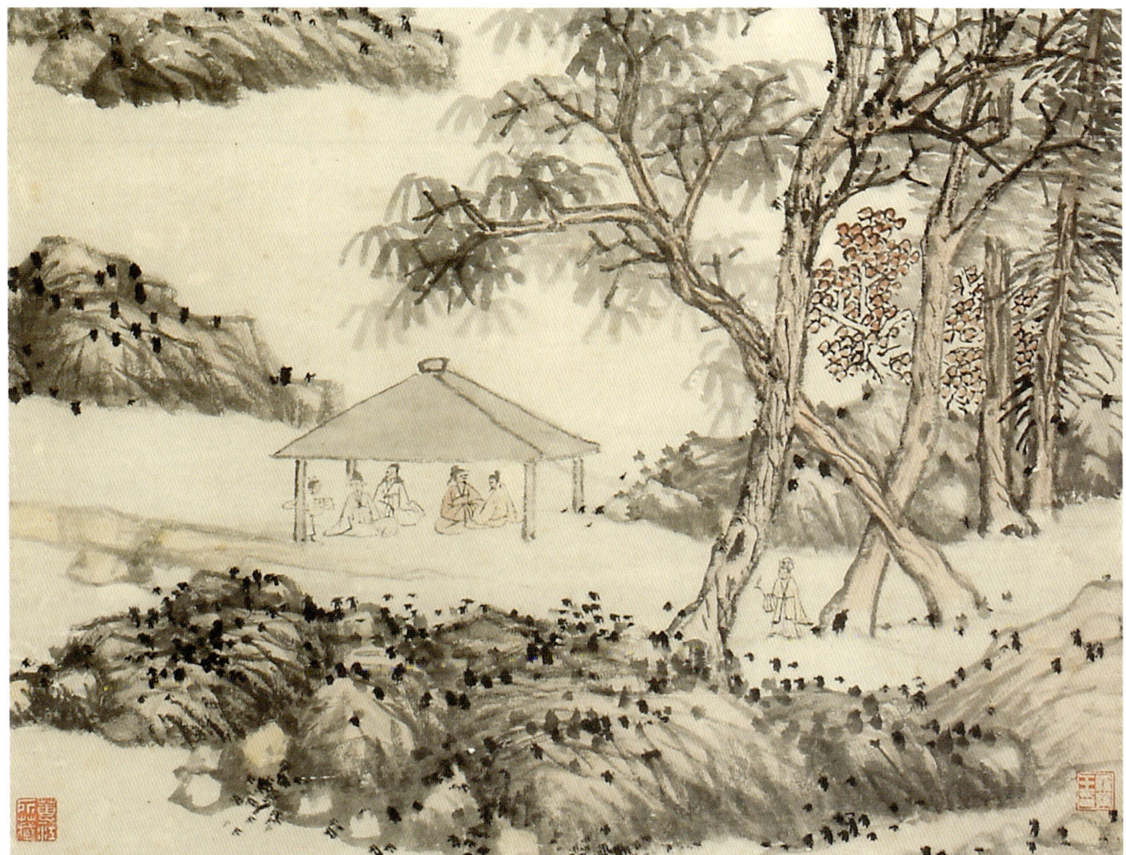

and mists of Huashan Mountain, Huangshan Mountain or Taishan Mountain, even less did he say that it was like this or that in any particular season. It was a general observation that made the point that mist and vapor had seasonal characteristics and ought to appear as described. All these descriptions simply and directly encompass the constant scenery of mountains in spring, summer, autumn and winter. They describe the laws that govern the orderly changes of nature.

After explaining seasonal characteristics, Guo Xi went on to point out the important point in the descriptions of *shanshui*: "Spring mountains smile in splendor, summer mountains drip with verdant green, autumn mountains stand in clarity and winter mountains sleep in gloom," "smiling," "dripping," "standing," and "sleeping" indicated both form and sense. Having once explained how the sense of nature differed season by season, Guo then likened nature's ordered sequence of change to the emotions of man: "The spring hills clothed in mist, so in man happiness; summer hills with the shade of trees, so in man ease; autumn hills bright and bold, so in man dignity; winter hills shrouded in gloom, so in man silence." All these are emotional states in man and represent the understanding of nature of the ancient Chinese.

The understanding of nature of the *shanshui* artists of ancient China did not relate to a single scene at one point in time but to their belief in a constant pulse and rhythm of seasons in nature derived from the influence of Daoist and Confucian philosophy (figs. 78–79). We have only to look at the references to hills and water and the descriptions of nature in the *Daodejing*, *Zhuangzi* and the *Analects*, to find out that the philosophers of ancient China transmuted the wisdom they gained from their observation of nature into human virtues. This was especially true of Daoist philosophy which regarded mankind and nature as one. Sayings such as "I exist with heaven and earth, at one with all things," "the complete man is together in virtue with heaven and earth," "benevolence resembles water," and "the wise take joy in water and the humane in hills," all describe the ability of man to perceive the truth and virtue that derive from an understanding of the natural universe.

Influenced by Confucian and Daoist philosophy, the ancient *shanshui* artists focused upon the manifestation of a constant natural law and not on the recording of a specific point in time and space. Guo Xi's treatise is a very good example. What these artists saw was a harmonious relationship between man and nature. *Shanshui* from their brush contained emotion and had an air of unhurried tranquility. Even in a scene of bitter winter it was possible to feel tranquility and not despair (figs. 80–81).

Figs. 80–81 *Tramping through the Snow to Visit a Friend*
Sun Zhi (Ming dynasty, 16th–early 17th century)
Color on paper
Height 148 cm × Width 37.5 cm
Suzhou Museum

The paintings of traditional *shanshui* artists were filled with emotion. Even in this scene of winter, man is not excluded but shown tramping through the snow to visit a friend in an expression of perpetual friendship.

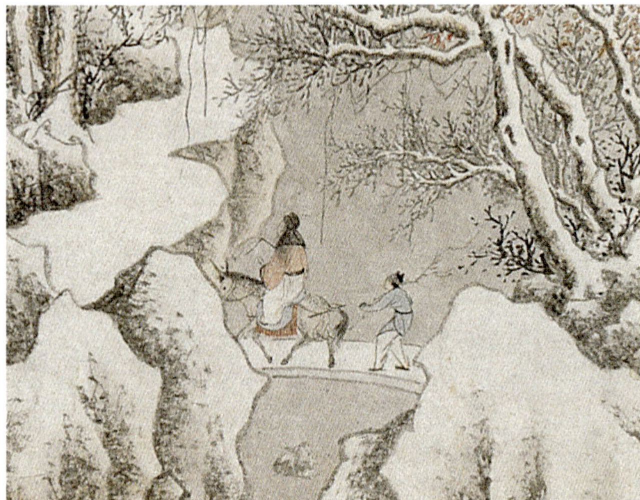

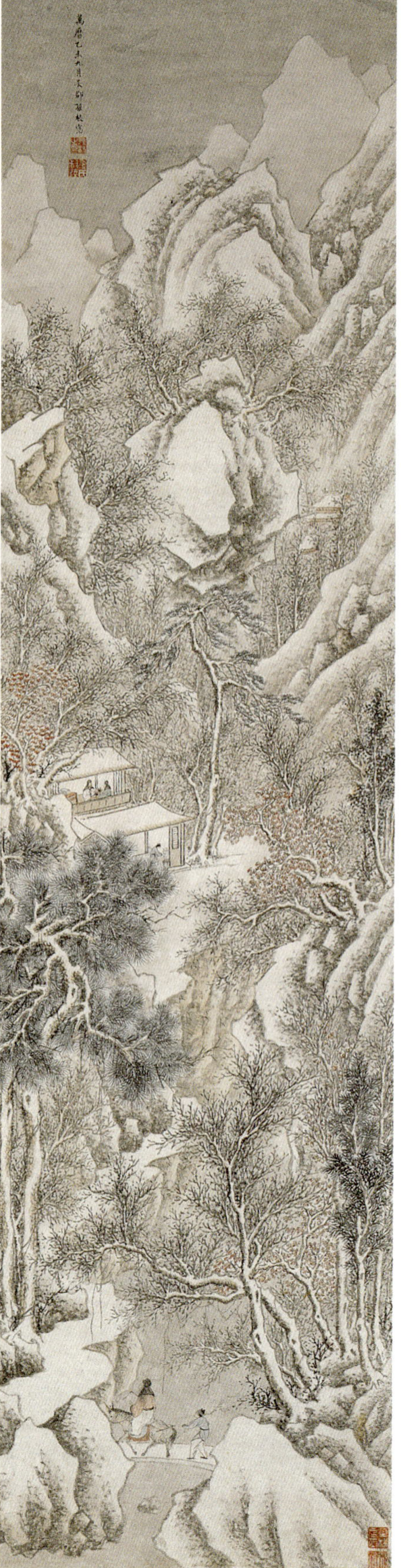

A Sense of Location Is Not the Aim of *Shanshui*

Since *shanshui* are not views, the conceptual idea of the artist cannot be a particular piece of scenery and the painting cannot have that real sense of on-the-spot location found in landscapes. On the contrary, a *shanshui* often induces a feeling of a kind of illusory reality. Let us take the Five Dynasties artist Ju Ran's *Crags and Trees* as an example (see fig. 75 on page 75).

Ju Ran lived during the Five Dynasties and the beginning of the Song dynasty. After the destruction of the Southern Tang period, he left his family to become a Buddhist monk at the Kaiyuan Monastery. He excelled in *shanshui* and liked to depict misty mountains and rivers in a pale ink wash, *Crags and Trees* is considered his masterpiece. It depicts layer upon layer of mountain peaks with a path seemingly winding through a darkened wood in the foreground. In the depths of the mountains distant misty peaks appear, one after the other, as if there were yet mountains beyond mountains, their end invisible to the eye. There is nothing in the painting that indicates either time or place and it is impossible to make out what mountain scenery this is. Even more, the whole scene expresses a strangely confusing sense of illusory reality. It is impossible to imagine what place in the real world it could be.

The comparative painting, Ruisdael's *The Windmill at Wijk bij Duurstede*, depicts a country scene in the 17th century Netherlands on a cloudy day as a shower approaches; the sense of locality is almost photographic. The technique of displaying observed three-dimensional space in a single plane is known as linear perspective, a form of scientific observation that accurately reflects the relationship between the size of an object and its distance from the observer. Put simply, if an artist wishes to depict the height of similar bamboos, the closer the bamboo is

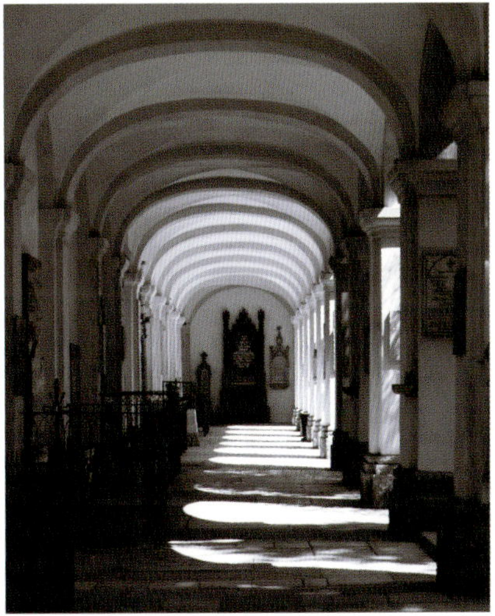

Fig. 82 Linear Perspective

Mastery of linear perspective enabled western artists to realistically represent three-dimensional space in a single two-dimensional plane.

to the artist the longer the vertical line that represents its height has to be, that is to say, the length of the vertical line becomes shorter with distance (fig. 82). Mastery of this technique gave western artists the ability to accurately and realistically reproduce on canvas the space and scenery that they had observed on the spot, so that the illusion of space modelled in the painting was exactly the same as the sense of space that we experience every day, we look at the painting and it is as if we are surrounded by reality.

Although in *Crags and Trees* Ju Ran took his material from real hills and real water, the painting does not display the result of a single journey amongst hills and water, it is a recollection of *shanshui* experienced within nature itself. This kind of painting, based on experience and recollection, does not suffer from the limitations of linear perspective. In the act of creation the artist may follow where his mind wills and use recollected imagery to proceed from different view-points, so that the scene that emerges from beneath his brush is sometimes seen looking up from the foot of a mountain and sometimes looking down from above, moving hither and thither freely. This technique of depicting, in the same picture, space observed from different points is known as multiple-point perspective.

Multiple-Point Perspective in Chinese and Western Art

Multiple-point perspective is a unique characteristic of traditional Chinese *shanshui* painting. This illusion of space seen from a number of angles offends our everyday visual sense since it is impossible to see views from two different angles simultaneously, that is to say, the space of our visual experience can only be the space of a fixed point perspective. Landscape perspective accords with the experience of our visual sense and it is thus not difficult to comprehend and appreciate the scene in the picture. By contrast, the multi-point perspective space of *shanshui* is not the space of our everyday experience and so appears extremely unreal and difficult to comprehend. It is not easy for the viewer to respond to, let alone understand and appreciate.

The emergence of the camera in the 19th century stimulated western artists into a re-examination of the significance of painting as an expression of the real external world. At the same time, Japanese *ukiyo-e* (pictures of the floating world) reached the west and their use of multi-point perspective broke the mold of western artists' perceptions of space and heavily influenced contemporary western painting. The works of the impressionist painter E. Degas (fig. 83), the post-impressionist painter Paul Cezanne and Vincent van Gogh all show signs of an exploration of multi-point perspective. By the beginning of the 20th century, multi-point perspective had become the basis of the birth of cubism (fig. 84).

The secret of multi-point perspective lies in the way in which it cleverly combines space observed from a number of different angles into one. In fact, we merely have to divide a *shanshui* into a number of panels or pictures to see that each picture immediately becomes an independent and easily viewed "landscape."

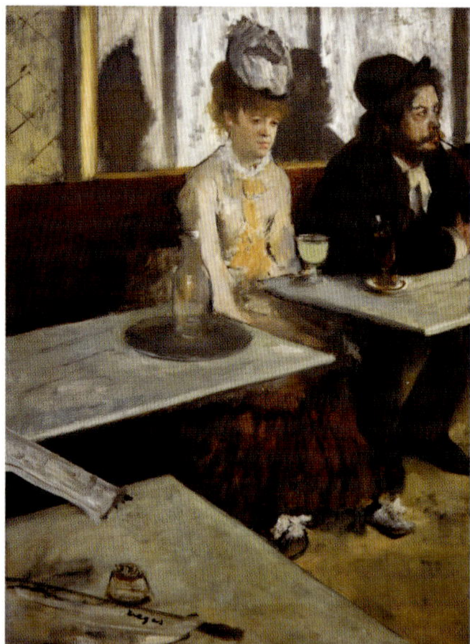

Fig. 83 *The Absinthe Drinker*

Edgar Degas (France, 1834–1917)
Oil on canvas
Height 92 cm × Width 68.5 cm
Musée d'Orsay

Influenced by oriental painting, especially the *ukiyo-e* of Japan, the western impressionist school began to attempt to incorporate different viewing points into the same picture. The table in the left foreground and the two seated figures are seen from different angles.

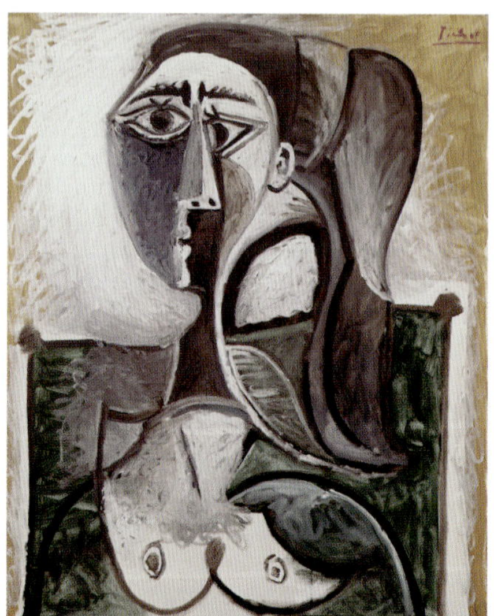

Fig. 84 *Bust of a Seated Woman*

Pablo Picasso (Spain, 1881–1973)
Oil on canvas
Height 100 cm × Width 81 cm
Musée Unterlinden

In the early 20th century the cubism of Picasso sought interesting relationships between form, plane and space.

Aware that the focus of *shanshui* painting is on *xieyi* and knowing that multi-point perspective is its secret, we can now view some of the classics of traditional *shanshui* painting and appreciate its particular characteristics.

The golden age of *shanshui* was the Five Dynasties and Northern Song dynasty. This period marks the emergence of a number of masters of *shanshui*. In the Five Dynasties they included: Jing Hao, Guan Tong (early 10th century) and Dong Yuan. In the Northern Song dynasty there were Ju Ran (fig. 85), Li Cheng, Guo Xi and Fan Kuan (see fig. 16 on page 19). They were all either Confucian or Daoist worthies and philosophers, deeply aware of the grandeur of creation and of the relationship between man and nature. The emotional environment of their *shanshui* paintings expresses the magnificence of nature. Consequently, *shanshui* of this period have a monumentality of construction that displays the majesty of the hills and the distant and limitless scenery before the viewer's very eyes.

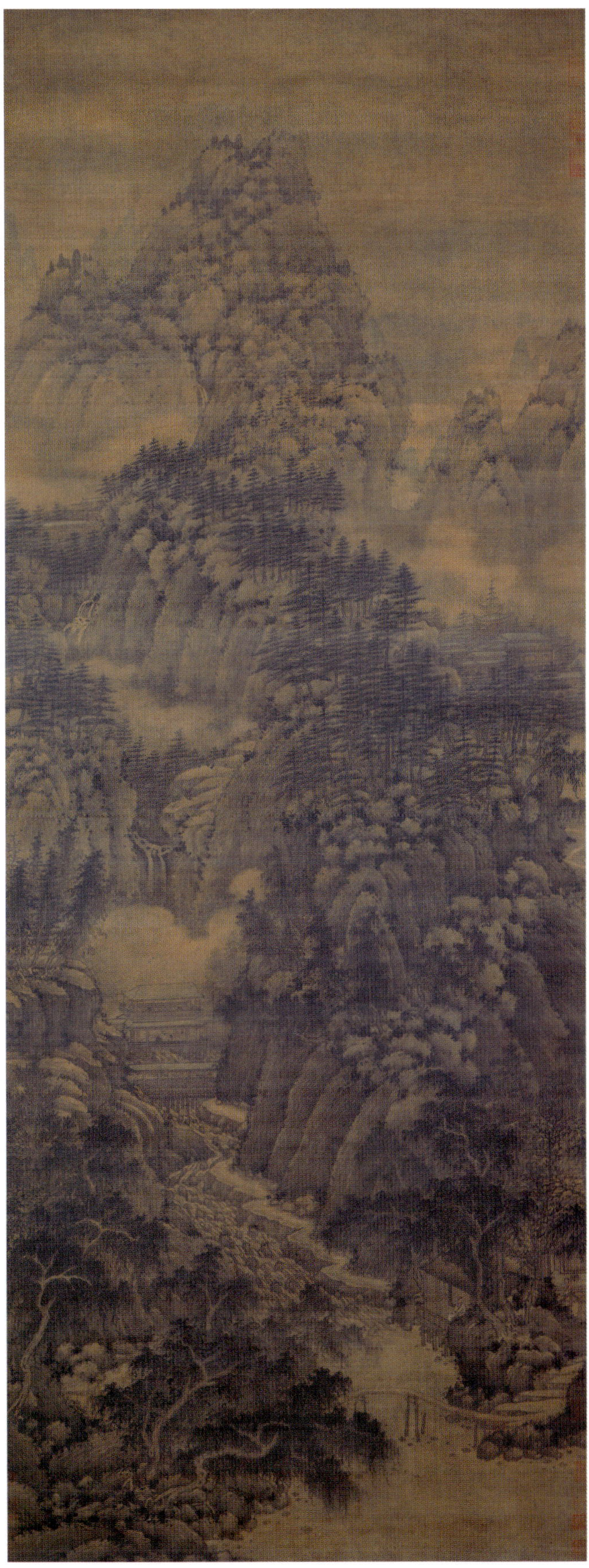

Fig. 85 *Pines amongst Ravines*
Attributed to Ju Ran
Ink on Silk
Height 200.7 cm × Width 70.5 cm
Shanghai Museum

Because of the passage of time, genuine examples of Song *shanshui* are extremely rare. The majority of works reputed to be by Ju Ran are later copies.

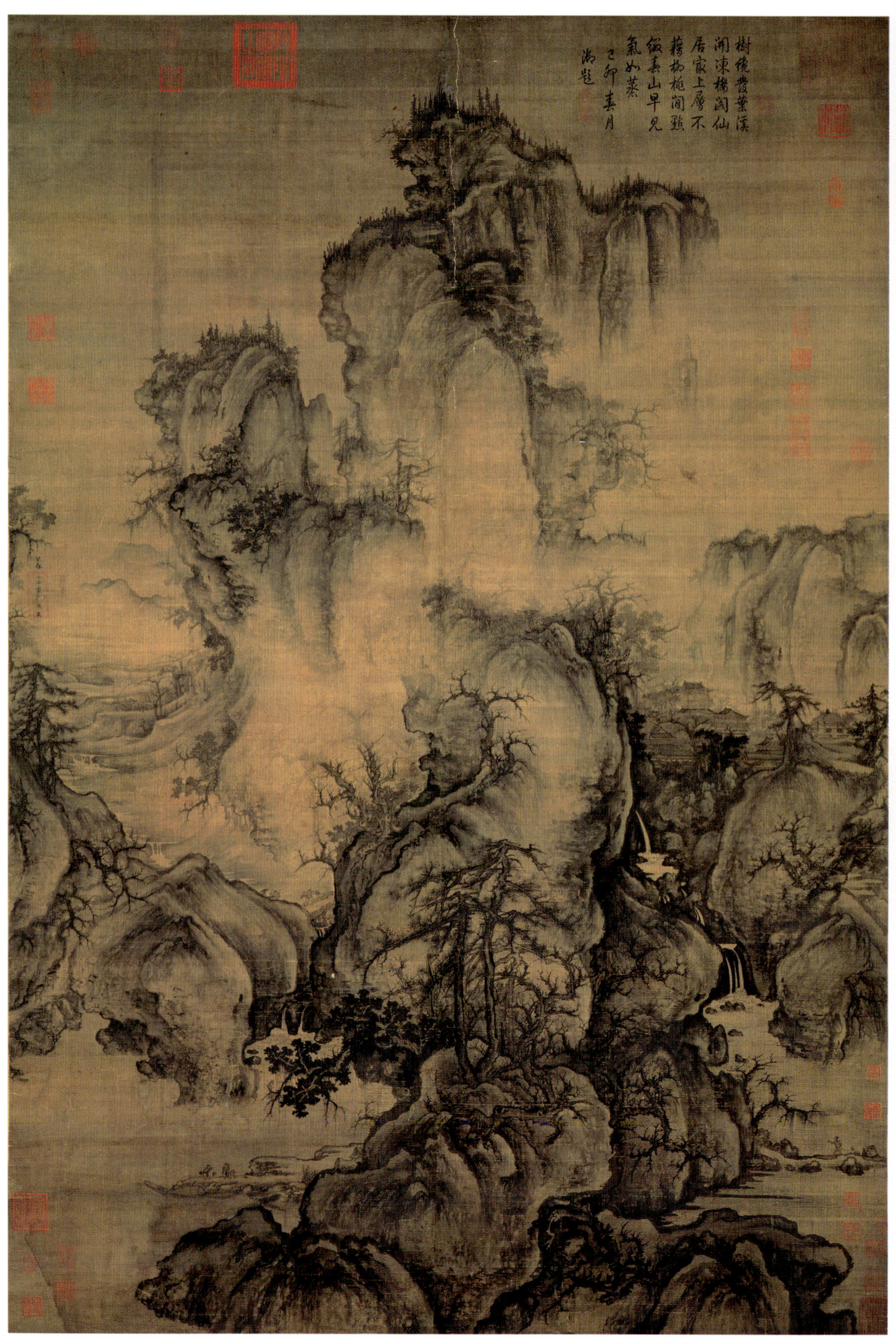
樹纔發葉溪
澗凍樓閣仙
居最上層不
藉柳桃間點
綴春山早見
氣如蒸
乙卯春月
御題

Three-Distance Perspective

Because of the sheer scale of the hills and rivers that appear in the construction of *shanshui* of the Five Dynasties and Northern Song, they were later known as "monumental landscapes" (*jubeishi shanshui*). The construction of *shanshui* of this period frequently combines perspectives from three different points of view. That is to say, close examination of a picture will reveal scenes observed from three different viewing points. This is known as "three-distance perspective."

Three-distance perspective refers to a horizon viewed from three different points. The first is known as upper distance (*gao yuan*), meaning someone standing at the bottom of a mountain and looking up towards the top of the mountain and seeing it towering over him. The second is level distance (*ping yuan*) where the observer is on the mountain and can see into the far distance as well as being able to take in the view below. The last is deep distance (*shen yuan*) where the observer is in front of the mountain looking through to its other side, from near to far, thus gaining a sense of depth. Taking the Northern Song painter Guo Xi's *Early Spring* as an example, we can see both the picture's unique three-distance perspective and the harmonious relationship between man and nature (fig. 86).

Fig. 86 *Early Spring*

Guo Xi (Northern Song Dynasty (11th century)

Ink on silk

Height 158.3 cm × Width 108.1 cm

Palace Museum, Taibei

Early Spring is one of the few paintings that scholars believe to be genuine examples of Guo Xi's work. There is an inscription "*Zaochun, Renzi Nian Guo Xi Hua*" ("Painted by Guo Xi in the Renzi year") on the left and a square vermilion seal "*Guo Xi Bi*" ("From the brush of Guo Xi").

Guo Xi, style name Chun Fu, was a native of Meng county in Henan province who used to work at the Imperial Academy of Painting. He left the academy in 1086 for political reasons. *The Acme of Forest and Springs* is the result of the work of a lifetime and was edited by his son Guo Si. His painting *Early Spring* is a classic and depicts the natural scenery of early spring at the end of a bitter winter.

The most eye-catching aspect of this painting is the curiously formed mountain that towers over the center of the painting, sprawling over the foreground and then rising upwards so that the upper part of the picture depicts, from left to right, a range of mountain peaks mistily shrouded in the depths of cloud. In the center of right of the picture there is a water course which flows down from a crack in the rocks. This is the harbinger of spring, a gradual thaw of the mountain's accumulated snow. The water flows silently through the mountain forest and falls behind a hill, emerging to join a river at the foot of the mountain. A figure has just reached the bank from the bridge over the river on the lower right and is making its way deep into the forest. The trees still stand in solemn winter array but soft buds are beginning to gently sprout on the bare branches in response to the thawing snow, once more bearing news of the arrival of spring. A boat has just touched shore at the bottom left of the picture, two fisherfolk are on their way home, the man carries a load suspended from his shoulder and the woman leads a child, a comforting expression of a normal life.

Early Spring does not say what village this is, or what mountain, or which river, but instead vividly presents a picture of nature at the point where hard winter turns to early spring, with its flavor of burgeoning spring

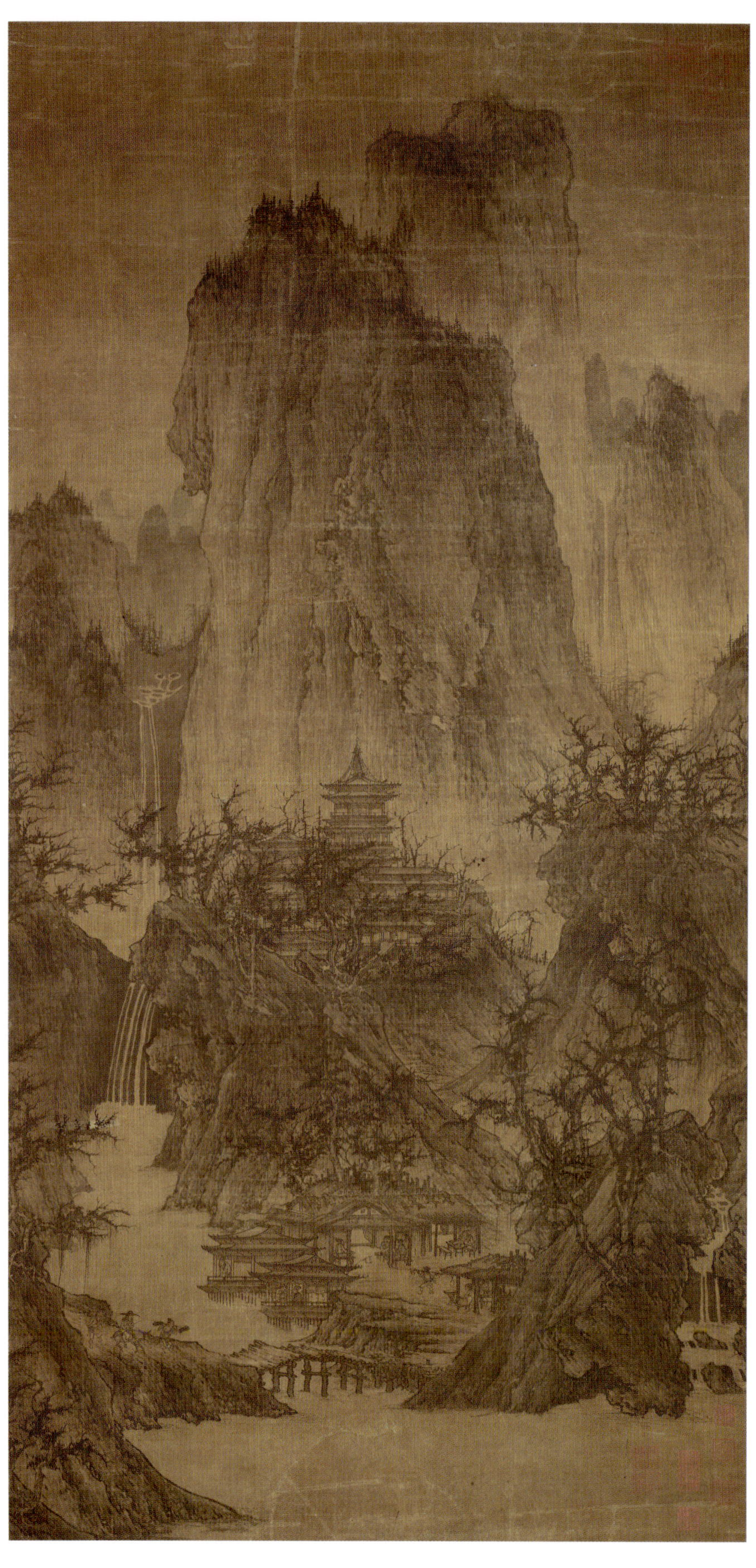

Fig. 87 *A Solitary Temple amidst Clearing Peaks*

Li Cheng (Five Dynasties, 919–967)
Ink and light color on silk
Height 111.4 cm × Width 56 cm
Nelson-Atkins Museum of Art, Kansas City

The Five Dynasties and Northern Song period was the era of the great masters of *shanshui*. In addition to the "Dong-Ju tradition" there was also the "Li-Guo tradition."

weather. The figures within the picture happily live the age-old life of the people within the laws of nature.

At first glance and because of the use of three-distance perspective, *Early Spring* does not resemble a recognizable scene. Guo Xi was the earliest artist to suggest the use of the technique of three-distance perspective in *shanshui*. In *The Acme of Forest and Springs* he had this to say about it: "In the mountains there are three distances; looking up to the top of a mountain from below, this called upper distance (*gao yuan*); looking through to the other side of the mountain from the front, this is called deep distance (*shen yuan*); viewing distant mountains from a nearby mountain, this is called level distance (*ping yuan*)." Once *Early Spring* is divided into three, an analysis of the picture shows that three-distance perspective is present throughout and we discover that the three individual pictures are not so difficult to understand after all and are actually quite "realistic" and easy to view.

Take a look at the mountain in the upper half of the picture. The artist is looking up at the mountain from below, that is to say, the artist must be positioned at the bottom of the mountain, this is "upper distance." But if you look at the trees and rocks in the lower half of the picture, most of the surface of the rocks and the tops of the trees are visible, thus the viewer must be looking down from above and seemingly positioned on the upper slopes of a nearby mountain, but, because of the height, also able to see mountains in the far distance. This is Guo Xi's "level distance." In this context, "nearby" does not refer to a position within the picture but to the theoretical view-point of the observer. Finally, looking at the left of the picture, you can see a path that winds towards the rear of the mountain, we are positioned just on this side of the path, looking towards the other side of the mountain. This is "deep distance." Viewed separately, these three perspectives are not in the least confusing and one has no difficulty in understanding them.

Li Cheng, style name Xian Xi, was another famous *shanshui* artist and a descendant of the ruling family of the Five Dynasties Southern Tang period. He spent his life in Chang'an (present-day Xi'an in Shaanxi province) and was of outstanding intellect with a reputation for the depiction of forests in winter. His *A Solitary Temple amid Clearing Peaks* in the Nelson-Atkins Museum of Art, Kansas City, bears a Northern Song official seal dating from between 1083 and 1127 and is recorded in the Song Painting Academy's *Xuan He Register of Paintings* (*Xuan He Huapu*) (fig. 87). It is believed that this painting must be a copy of a Li Cheng *shanshui* by an artist of the Northern Song period.

A Solitary Temple amid Clearing Peaks is constructed in the monumental style of vast peaks and rushing water. The upper half of the painting is occupied by a strangely shaped peak of lofty crags. In the center, an ancient temple sits atop a hill in the middle distance. Beside the river in the foreground there is a small village. On the left, two waterfalls link the river that flows from the distant heights into foreground. At first glance the picture seems to contain nothing but scenery. However, closer examination discloses a number of people. For example three people on their way home are about to cross the bridge in the bottom left hand corner. The first appears to be a woodcutter carrying firewood suspended from his shoulder while the one in the center is riding a donkey. On the bank to the left of the bridge one old person is leaning on a fence seemingly looking to see whether the people returning home are members of his family. There are a dozen or so houses in the village over the bridge with people both inside and out, some resting and some working in a scene of leisurely placidity.

Transmission and the Quest for Change Seen through the *Cun* Texture Method

The Confucian and Daoist intellectual background of the *shanshui* artists of the Five Dynasties and Northern Song caused the *shanshui* tradition that they established to become a model, both technically and spiritually, as well as the ultimate goal, for the *shanshui* paintings of later generations. Monumental style apart, the *shanshui* artists of this period employed different brushstroke techniques to express the quality of the texture of rocks. These techniques were known as *cunfa* or *cun* texture methods.

The *shanshui* masters of the Five Dynasties and Northern Song each had their own *cun* texture methods. Dong Yuan, for example, liked to use long thin lines to express the quality of the mountainous scenery of Jiangnan, these strokes resembled lines of hemp fiber and were later known as "hemp fibre *cun*" (*pima cun*). Ju Ran had been a pupil of Dong Yuan and added "alum-head *cun*" (*fantou cun*) to Dong Yuan's hemp fibre *cun*. The alum-head *cun* technique was used to depict the tops of mountains and the rocks that appear amongst trees and undergrowth with brush and ink form that rather resembles a Chinese steamed bun (figs. 88–89). Dong Yuan and Ju Ran also

Figs. 88–89 *Cun* refers to the brushstroke technique used to depict the texture of rocks. Dong Yuan and Ju Ran used vertical lines resembling strands of flax or hemp running from the top to the bottom of a mountain to represent the patterning of rocks. These were known as hemp fibre *cun*. Alum-head *cun* refer to the formations appearing on mountain tops and rather resembling a Chinese steamed bun (*mantou*). They represent cliffs and rocks protruding from amongst the trees on a mountain top seen from a distance.

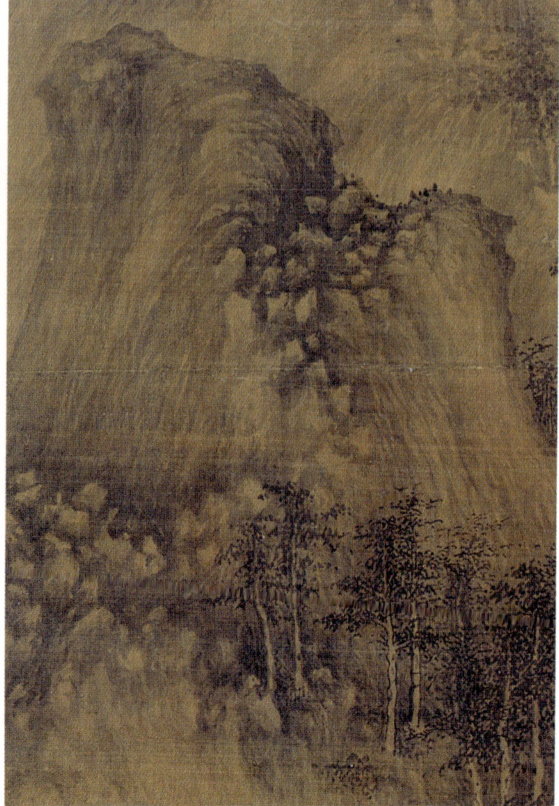

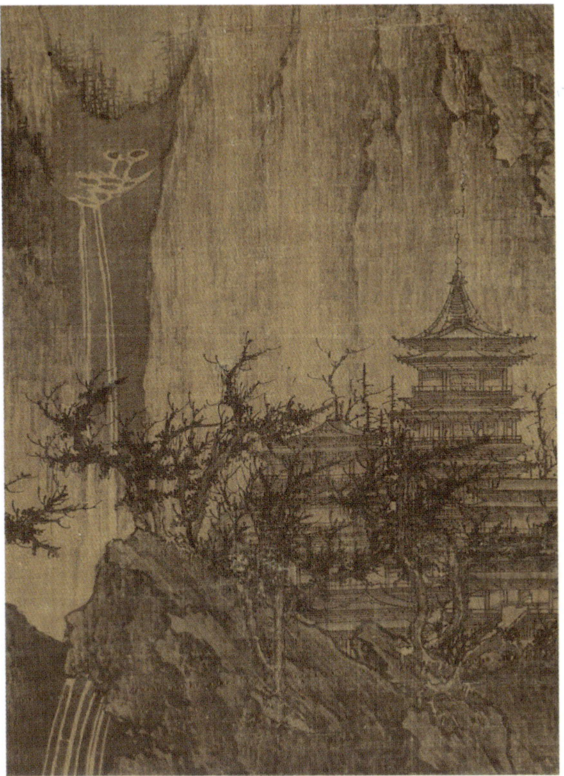

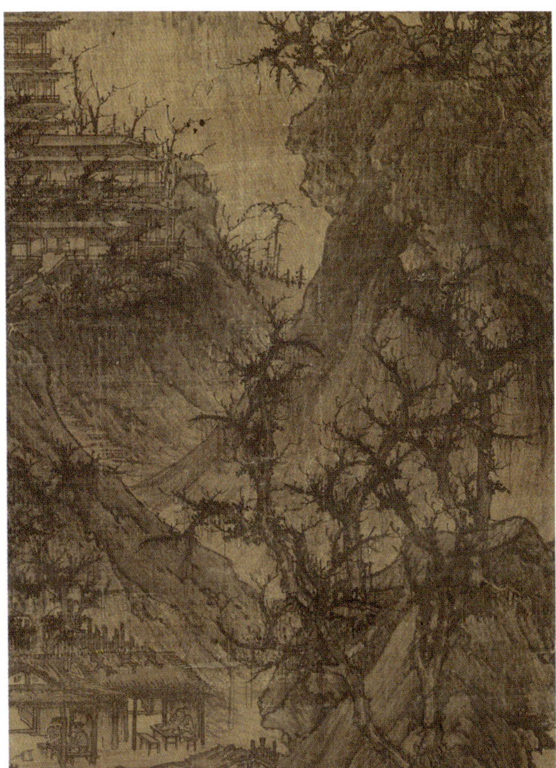

Figs. 90–91 *Solitary Temple amid Clearing Peaks* (detail)

Li Cheng excelled in sharply pointed brushwork that resembled the claw of a crab to depict the dessicated appearance of trees and to express a sense of wintry melancholy. This type of brushwork was later known as crab-claw *cun*.

used dots of ink to indicate woods and trees in the distance, this technique was known as "dotting" (*diantai*). The trees on mountain ranges depicted by this dotting technique always display a feeling of luxuriant growth. Later, the Song dynasty father and son Mi Fu (1051–1107) and Mi Yuren (1074–1153) often depicted the misty lushness of the scenery of Jiangnan. They inherited Dong Yuan's and Ju Ran's use of dots and modified the horizontal dot. Later generations called their dots the "big Mi-dot" and "little Mi-dot" (see fig. 73 on pages 72–73).

Dong Yuan and Ju Ran apart, the three other *shanshui* masters of the Five Dynasties and Northern Song, Li Cheng, Guo Xi and Fan Kuan were northern painters and it was the precipitous mountain ranges of the north that mostly appeared in their paintings. They laid particular emphasis upon the texture of the mountains, with strange craggy rocks and more rocks than trees. In form, the trees had more branches than leaves with a preponderance of trees in winter.

Li Cheng who was renowned for his scenes of trees in winter produced *shanshui* of withered trees and strange, desolate rocks. He excelled in sharply pointed brushwork that resembled the claw of a crab to depict the dessicated appearance of trees and to express a sense of wintry melancholy. This type of brushwork was later known as crab-claw *cun* (*xiezhua cun*) (figs. 90–91). The trees of the equally renowned Guo Xi inherited the crab-claw *cun* technique of Li Cheng. At the same time he favored a technique of "cloud-scroll *cun*" (*juanyun cun*) to depict the form of strange mountain and rock formations. Fan Kuan's *Travelers among Mountains and Streams* is one of the few existing paintings generally recognized to be an authentic Song work. In it, the autumn mountains have succeeded to

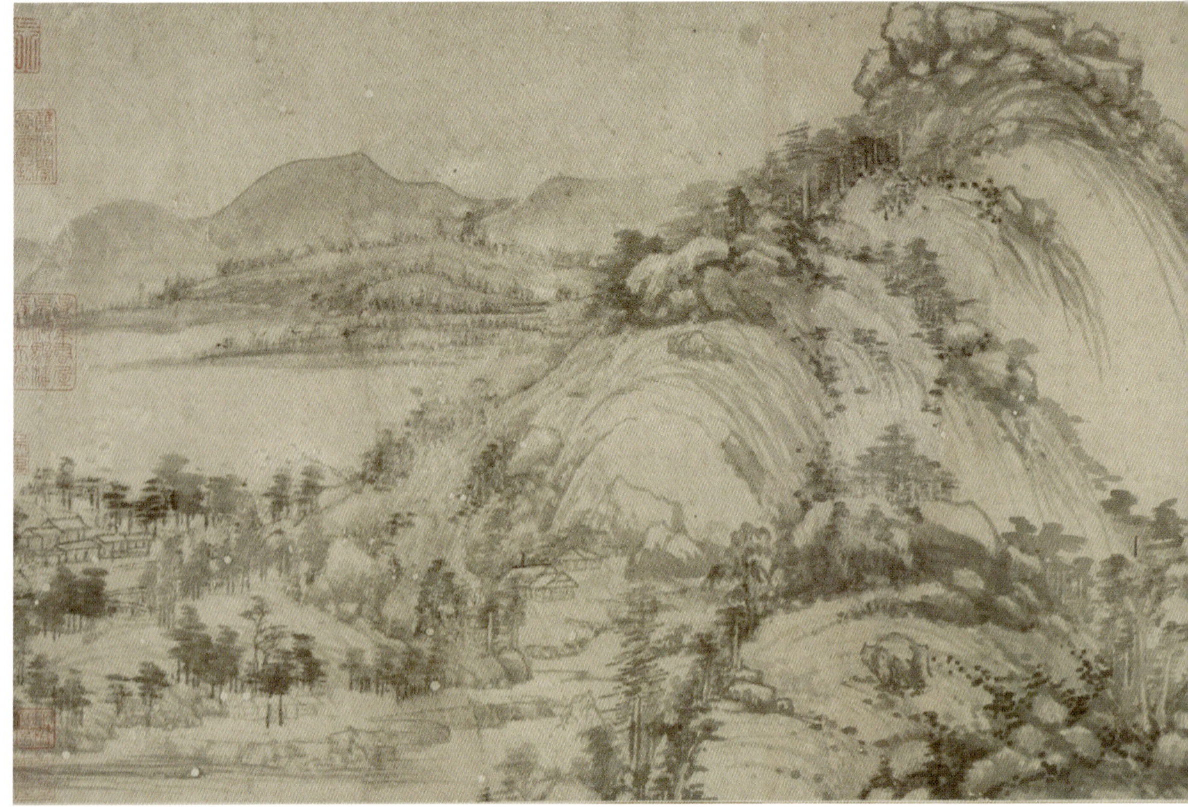

Fig. 92 *Dwelling in the Fuchun Mountains—The Remaining Mountain* (first half of the scroll, detail)

Huang Gongwang (Yuan dynasty, 1269–1354)
Ink on paper
Height 31.8 cm × Width 51.4 cm
Zhejiang Provincial Museum

At about the age of 82 the Yuan dynasty literati painter Huang Gongwang spent three years painting the long scroll *Dwelling in the Fuchun Mountains* for his friend Zheng Wuyong, the "Useless Master." One of the ten great paintings of China, it was highly esteemed by later collectors, particularly by the late Ming collector Wu Hongyu who attempted to make a burnt sacrifice of it shortly before his death, fortunately it was rescued from the fire by his nephew but it had been burnt into two fragments. The shorter fragment from the beginning of the scroll was repaired and called the *Remaining Mountain* and is now in the Zhejiang Provincial Museum. The remaining longer section is known as the *Useless Master's Scroll* and is in the Palace Museum, Taibei.

the monumental construction technique of the past. The mountains occupy the center of the picture standing like a huge slab of stone before the eyes of the viewer and making them gleam (see fig. 16 on page 19).

The *shanshui* masters of the Five Dynasties and Northern Song were outstanding in their understanding of the art whether in modelling or in the abstract expression of living nature. The *shanshui* world displayed in their works exceeds the ability of the visual senses to appreciate it. It is a harmonious vision of the unity of man with nature. Scholars and the literati yearned after his broad realm of spirituality and it became the basis for the later development of traditional *shanshui* painting.

Because of the relationship between inherited teaching and style, Dong Yuan and Ju Ran are often treated together and their style regarded as one, the "Dong-Ju tradition," while the styles of Li Cheng and Guo Xi are regarded as a separate network, known as the "Li-Guo tradition." Irrespective of whether it is the former or the latter, or even the monumental style of Fan Kuan, all had an extremely important influence upon the subsequent development of Chinese *shanshui* painting, though it was the Dong-Ju tradition that was most revered by later literati painters. For example, Huang Gongwang, one of the Four Yuan Masters, used a great deal of the "hemp fibre *cun*" to depict the modelling of hills and slopes in his *Dwelling in the Fuchun Mountains* (fig. 92). He also used closely packed "alum-head *cun*" and glistening dotting to express the texture of stone and the luxuriance of forest trees. The importance of the concept of transmission may be judged from these brush strokes which are in the direct line of the Dong-Ju tradition.

However, by the time of the Four Yuan Masters, modeling from nature and the depiction of the texture of rocks had both become secondary. For artists the emphasis was now upon the abstract values of brush and ink (*bimo*). Consequently, when the *shanshui* of Huang Gongwang are compared with those of Dong Yuan, the former are more graphic and abstract whilst the latter are more realistic. In truth, when compared with the *shanshui* of the Five Dynasties and the Northern Song there is something flatter and more level about the *shanshui* of the Four Yuan Masters. This is a characteristic of Yuan *shanshui*: born of the Five Dynasties and Northern Song tradition but with the focus upon *bimo* and expressing the character and the inner being and ideals of the artist. These abstract aspirations will be discussed in detail in the chapter on *bimo*.

In the Qing dynasty, the fashion for copying and works "in the style of the ancients" (*fang gu*) was widespread and the Four Wangs, with the addition of Wu and Yun, were known collectively as the Six Great Masters of the Early Qing Dynasty. We have mentioned the Four Wangs before; Wu refers to Wu Li (1632–1718) and Yun is Yun Shouping (1633–1690).

Apart from Yun Shouping whose flower-and-bird paintings were better than his *shanshui* the remaining five excelled in *shanshui*. The majority of their works were *shanshui* in the style of Dong Yuan, Ju Ran or the Four Yuan Masters. These works, in composition, *bimo*, and style reflected the Five Dynasties and Northern Song with the addition of a strong flavor of the Four Yuan Masters. At a glance there seems no sense of anything new about them, so much so that some people regarded them as unbearably oppressive.

However, if we look carefully, it is relatively easy to discover that the *shanshui* theories of the six were entirely different from those concepts to which the artists of the Five Dynasties and Northern Song aspired. Although they may have closely followed the *bimo* aspirations of the Four Yuan Masters, their focus was upon the copying of *bimo* brushwork, nature was not the master of the creative act and it was the paintings of the ancients that were their conceptual basis, a bottom up idea that resulted in formalization. Although macroscopic monumental style was the principal theme in the *shanshui* of the Four Wangs, in their paintings, layer upon layer of mountain peaks are piled high into a series of distinct mountain ridges which are called "dragons' veins." Dragon's veins are a particular compositional characteristic of Qing dynasty *shanshui*. This compositional formalism is very different from the *shanshui* inspired by nature of the Four Yuan Masters. Thus, although there is a very strong flavor of received tradition in the works of the six, they actually express an early Qing sense of period. Their artistic achievement lies in richness of brushstroke. Each of them had their own characteristics but it was Wu Li who introduced the influence of western painting into the *shanshui* tradition of the literati (fig. 93).

Vertical hanging scrolls and horizontal handscrolls are the commonest forms in which traditional *shanshui* are presented. There are also square album leaves. Most monumental style *shanshui* are presented as hanging scrolls. Because western artists think in terms of creating a view from a fixed point their composition always consists of fore, middle, and background. Traditional *shanshui* artists were not limited by this consideration and since the hanging scroll is an upright oblong, their compositional ideas did not proceed from front to rear but from bottom to top. In the hanging scroll model of *shanshui* the bottom half of the painting usually forms a foreground of scenery to the whole *shanshui*, consisting for the most part of objects like trees and little bridges, while the upper half of the painting is occupied by the most distant parts of the scene as a whole with towering mountain peaks backed by further vaguely distant mountains and mist and cloud. Closer inspection will reveal how through the skilful use of little paths, waterfalls in the rocks or thick mist and fog, the artist draws our line of sight upwards from the bottom, from near to far, linking the fore, middle and background that extends from the top of the painting to the bottom into a single whole. There is no detailed treatment of the distances and relationships between fore, middle and background. This is left to the mist and cloud to handle.

The most well known example of *shanshui* in handscroll format is Huang Gongwang's *Dwelling in the Fuchun Mountains*, the finer points of which will be discussed in detail in the chapter on handscrolls.

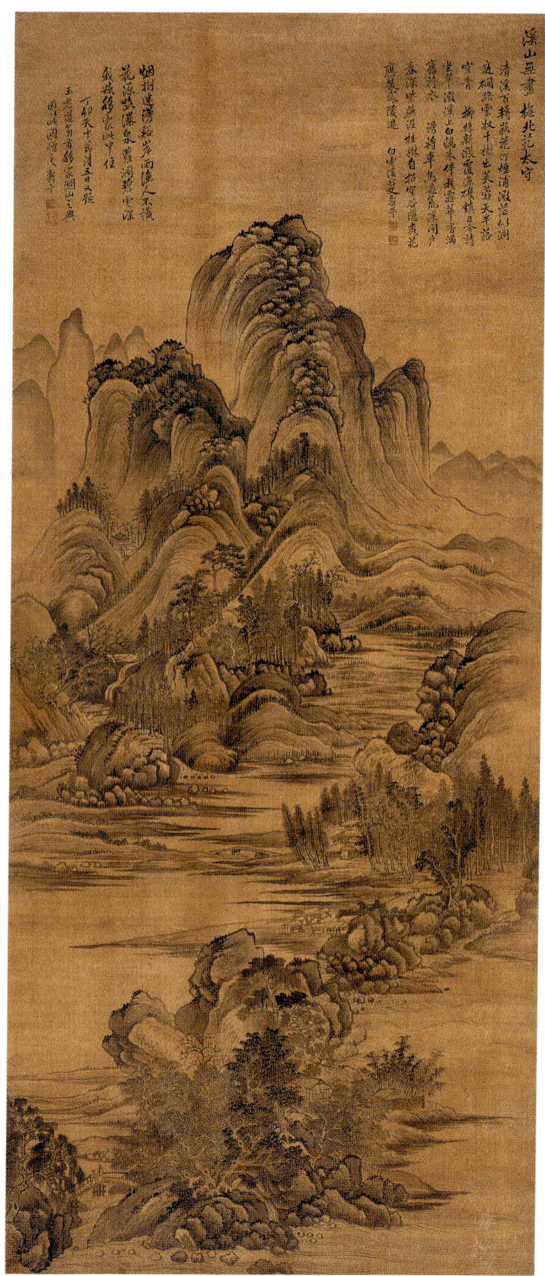

Fig. 93 *Streams and Mountains in the Style of Dong Yuan*

Yun Shouping (Qing dynasty, 1633–1690)
Color on silk
Height 184.3 cm × Width 79.2 cm
National Art Musem of China

Together with Wu Li, Wang Shimin, Wang Jian, Wang Hui and Wang Yuanqi, Yun Shouping was one of the "Six Great Masters of the Early Qing Dynasty." They believed in the theory of "learning from the ancients" and advocated the copying of the brushwork of the ancients as a creative basis.

The Realm of *Shanshui*

Apart from the fact that *shanshui* are not landscapes of a view presented realistically and that they use a three-distance perspective that offends our visual experience and makes it difficult for us to connect the image in the picture with real scenery, there is a further important reason why modern man finds them so difficult to grasp. This is that modern man is now too distant from the reality of true scenery. Surrounded as we are by forests of construction, we rarely see trees in our everyday life. Country parks are now carefully manicured scenic spots boasting modern equipment such as barbecues. Not only are they thronged with visitors like so many squid, they are filled with the modern clamor of bizarre telephone ringtones and high-decibel sound that blots out any of the music produced by nature itself. The sound of the wind, of birdsong, of running water and of falling blossom was an element of the ancient *shanshui* philosophers' understanding of the meaning of nature. How can the modern city-dweller possibly share it?

Traditional *shanshui* shows us a realm of harmonious co-existence between man and nature. It is a spiritual world in which "heaven and man are one." It may be that many people believe that this concept is peculiar to Chinese traditional culture, but a year ago I read the American polar explorer Byrd's diary of his time alone in the Antarctic. It convinced me that this concept of a *shanshui* realm was not limited to the *shanshui* artists of ancient China. Anybody who has truly experienced the embrace of nature will understand this realm of the spirit. Below is an extract from Byrd's diary:

> Took my daily walk at 4 pm today in 89 of frost … I paused to listen to the silence … The day was dying, the night being born—but with great peace. Here were imponderable processes and forces of the cosmos, harmonious and soundless. Harmony, that was it! That was what came out of the silence—a gentle rhythm, the strain of a perfect chord, the music of the sphere, perhaps.
>
> It was enough to catch that rhythm, momentarily to be myself a part of it. In that instant I could feel no doubt of man's oneness with the universe. The conviction came that that rhythm was too orderly, too harmonious, too perfect to be a product of blind chance—that, therefore there must be purpose in the whole and that man was part of that whole and not an accidental off-shoot. It was a feeling that transcended reason; that went to the heart of man's despair and found it groundless. The universe was a cosmos, not a chaos; man was as rightfully a part of that cosmos as were the day and night.[1]

Is not this a precise description of the realm of "heaven and man are one" expressed in the traditional *shanshui* art of China? Naturally, Byrd was not thinking of the *shanshui* of the Five Dynasties and Northern Song when he wrote, nor was it traditional Confucian or Daoist philosophy. Nevertheless I can imagine that had Byrd been faced with a *shanshui* from the Five Dynasties or Northern Song he would have focused very quickly and felt that sense of "heaven and man are one" that the painting expressed. Byrd's desire to remain by himself at the South Pole was born of a wish to distance himself from the world, to be close to nature and to experience absolute solitude. The result was that he achieved a realization of that realm of the unity of heaven with man. I have a number of friends who on retirement actually trod the high peaks of China and once amidst nature and away from the clamor of the modern world suddenly realized that what they saw spread before them was the realm of traditional *shanshui*.

1 Richard Byrd, *Alone* (New York: Kodansha International, 1995), page 84–85.

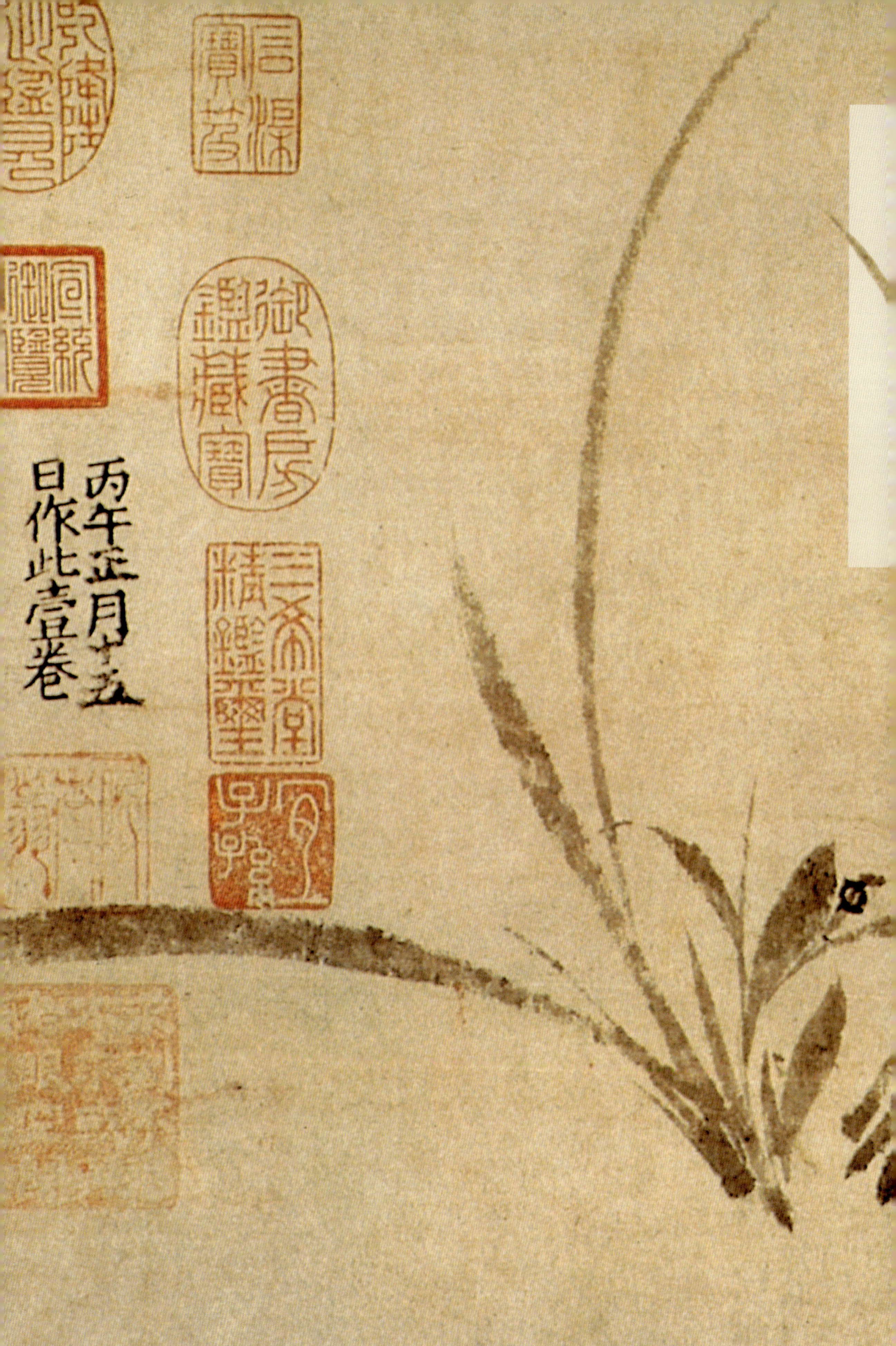
丙午正月廿五
日作此壹卷

CHAPTER FIVE
The Delicate World of Birds and Flowers

In the traditional western oil painting, a ground is first applied to cover the pure white of the canvas before the execution of the painting. By the end of the 19th century, the impressionists no longer applied a ground but painted directly on to the white canvas to achieve the tonality of original color. In fact, western artists, whether they applied a ground or not, and be it in oil, watercolor or pastel, were quite particular in their handling of background which was always completely filled in and very rarely contained blanks, the opposite of traditional Chinese painting.

The background of traditional Chinese paintings often contained large areas of blank space, rather as if the painters of ancient China were not too concerned about the handling of background. So what is the underlying reason for this?

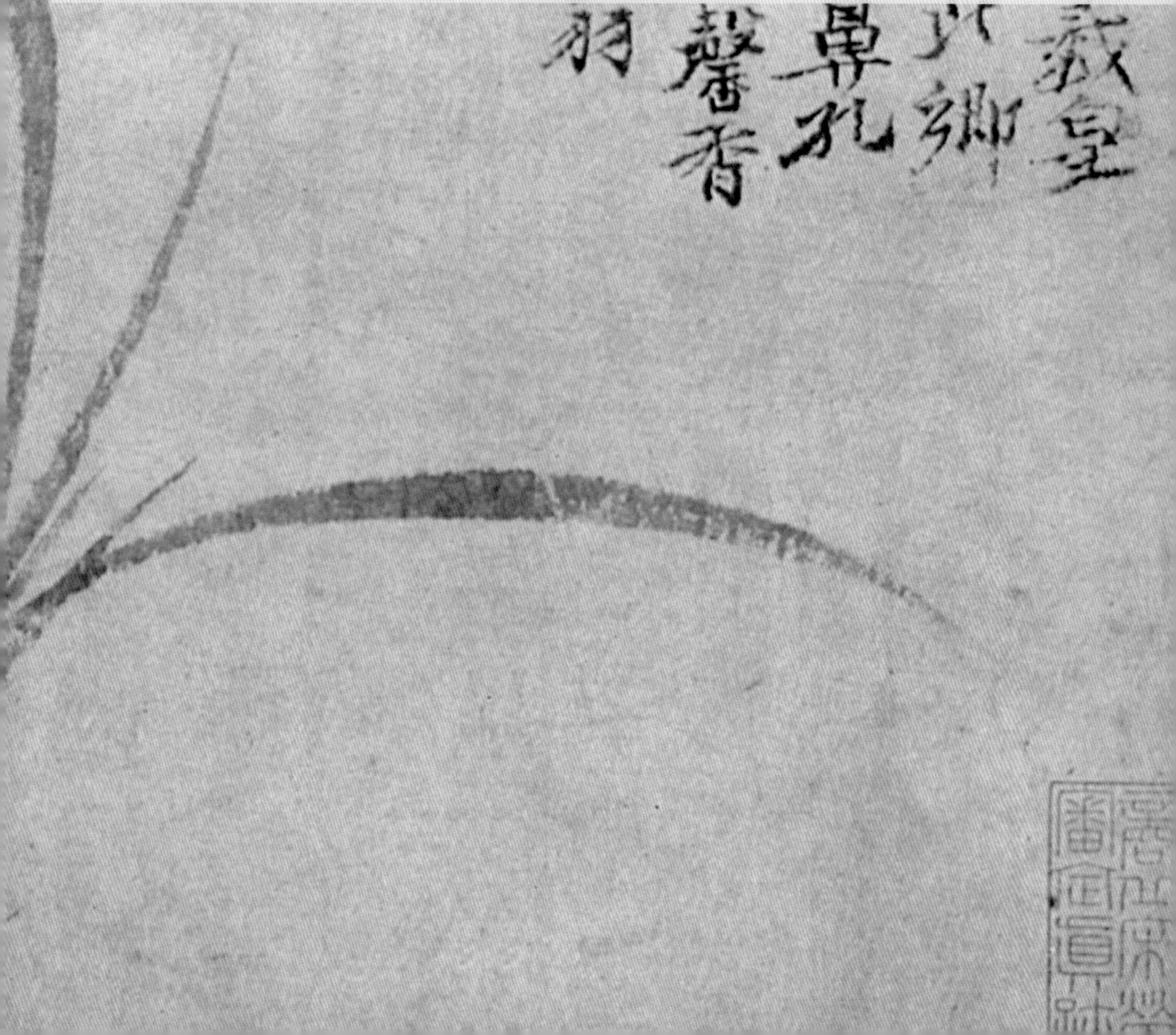

Concision of Concept

The three most frequently encountered themes of traditional Chinese painting are figure, *shanshui* and flower-and-bird. The two previous chapters explored the qualities of transmission and respect for intention in figure painting and *shanshui*. This chapter looks at the focus in flower-and-bird painting. Compared with the western still life, the composition of a traditional flower-and-bird painting is over simple. This is particularly so of those flower-and-bird paintings from the brush of literati painters where the composition consists of a few sketchy brushstrokes with no background and no detail. In fact, in traditional flower-and-bird paintings flowers never appear thrust into vases as they so frequently do in a western still life (fig. 95). Nor do they contain the detailed studies of inanimate objects (fig. 96). The underlying reason remains that aspiration towards respect for intention in Chinese art.

From the very beginning, the development of Chinese art was in the direction of "imaging the spirit through form." It is "spirit" that is the focus of Chinese art. In figure painting, *shanshui* and flower-and-bird painting, the depiction of the subject and its background is always in order to secure the expression of the

Pages 94–95
Fig. 94 *Ink Orchid* (detail)
Zheng Sixiao (Southern Song dynasty, 1241–1318)
Ink on paper
Height 25.7 cm × Width 42.4 cm
Osaka Municipal Museum of Art

Zheng Sixiao was a minister under the Southern Song dynasty who retired to a hermetic life in Suzhou on the overthrow of the dynasty by the Mongol Yuan dynasty. In order to identify himself with the Southern Song, he changed his title to "Of the South" (*Suo Nan*). The painting was executed in the tenth year of the Yuan Emperor Dade (1306). The focus is not upon the detail of flower and leaves but upon the absence of roots. Zheng had once said: "Our land has been stolen away, did you not know?" The painting expresses Zheng's sorrow at the rootlessness of the era in which he found himself.

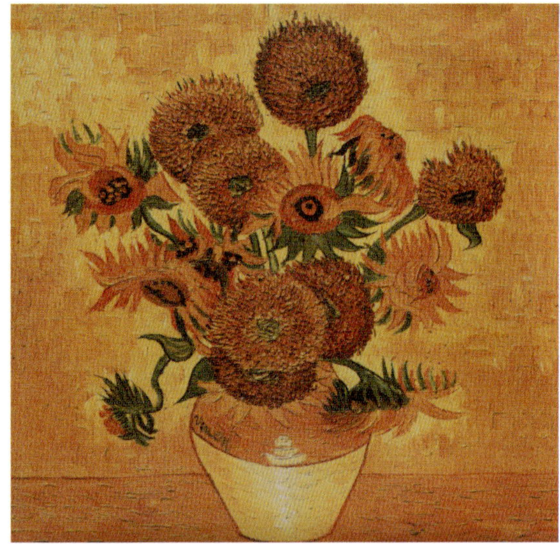

Fig. 95 *Still Life: Vase with Fifteen Sunflowers*
Vincent Van Gogh
Oil on canvas
Height 76.4 cm × Width 59.2 cm
Van Gogh Museum, Amsterdam

Flowers in western paintings are almost always displayed in a vase.

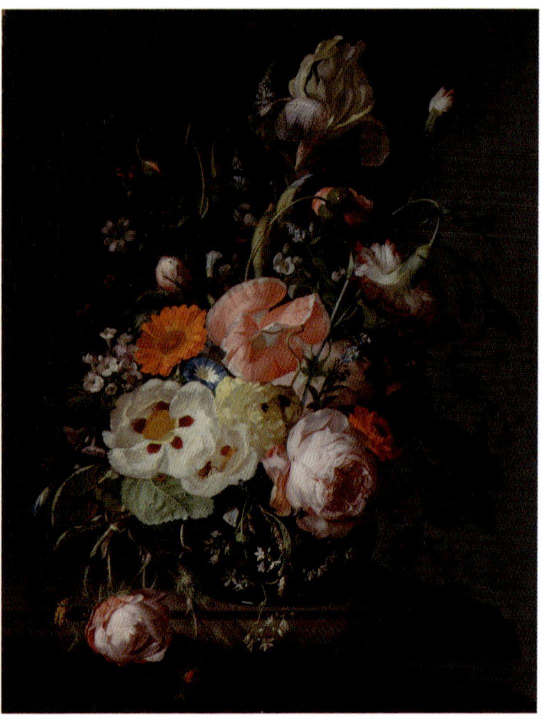

Fig. 96 *Still Life with Flowers on a Marble Tabletop*
Rachel Ruysch (Netherlands, 1664–1750)
Oil on canvas
Height 48.5 cm × Width 39.5 cm
Rijksmuseum

Flowers are often the subject of the 17th century Baroque still life and are mostly shown in vases.

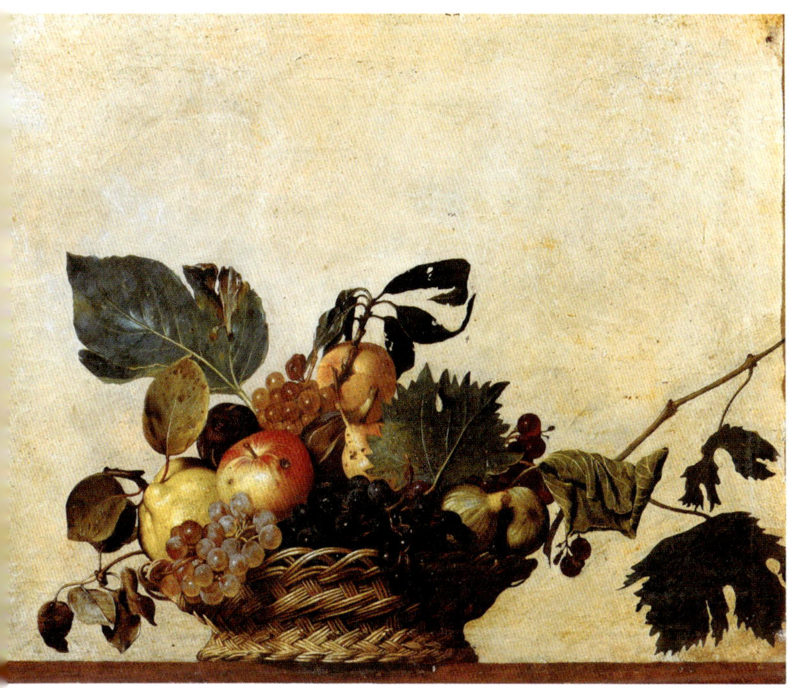

Fig. 97 *Still Life with a Basket of Fruit*

Michelangelo Merisi da Caravaggio
Oil on canvas
Height 46 cm × Width 64.5 cm
Pinacoteca Ambrosiana, Milan

The painters of the Baroque era set great store by naturalism and depicted their subjects with great accuracy and detail. If we look at this work we can see that the details, such as the wormhole on the apple, the different stages of withering in the leaves and the texture of the basket, are generally, like the overall space and treatment of light and shade, rendered so precisely as to call forth gasps of admiration.

essence of the subject. "Spirit" is an abstract concept which perhaps does not rely upon the depiction of a great deal of detail but is an evocation of the imagination inspired by the painting. The depiction of detail should only be lightly touched upon and too much detail tends to limit our imaginative space. We can explain the reasoning behind this through the example of one western and one Chinese painting.

By the 17th century the ability of western artists to observe and depict objects had reached the point of "to see is to feel." In this, Caravaggio led the field. His works are models of the Italian art of the Baroque, famed for their minute observation and depiction of nature. There is a still life of his, *Still Life with a Basket of Fruit* (fig. 97). It is a finely detailed and meticulous depiction of the form, color and luster, even of the degree of freshness of grapes, apples and pears. Look at the apple in the center, it has a wormhole; the leaves attached to the fruit are at different stages of withering; and the texture of the basket is so realistic as to be almost tangible. Underneath the basket there is a horizontal strip of table and the background consists of different tones of gray-blue rather as if it were a wall behind the table. Each object depicted in the painting is crystal clear and if we look more closely further detail emerges. But because the detail is so accurate it leaves no room at all for the exercise of conjecture or imagination, so that when we have had our fill of the detail, the deepest impression left on our minds is still just of the detail itself and of the admirable painterly skills of the artist.

Now let us look at the Southern Song literati painter Zheng Sixiao's (1241–1318) *Ink Orchid* (see fig. 94 on pages 94 and 95). In comparison with Caravaggio's still life, and in point of composition, the subject has been placed in the center of the painting. What is different is that Zheng Sixiao's orchid consists mainly of a number of orchid leaves in ink, whilst the single orchid flower that they accompany still lacks color and is rendered in ink alone. Neither leaf nor flower possess color, or light and shade, or texture, nor is there a trace of any other detail. Particularly notable is the fact that the background to the orchid is a blank so that the whole orchid seems suspended in the center of the painting. A poem appears to the right of the orchid and is signed with Zheng Sixiao's title, "Old

Man of the South" (*Suonan Weng*). There is a further poem to the left which has been added later by others and there are a large number of seals added by later collectors. It is not difficult to imagine that Zheng's original composition was extremely simple and consisted of an ink orchid and a single verse with the remaining space left blank. The purpose of this simplicity of construction is to force us to concentrate upon the orchid and the poem, since beyond them there is nothing else to see. As we concentrate upon this orchid in ink we realize that it has no roots and as our attention moves to the poem we read:

> Head bowed I asked the father of our race,
> Who are you that comes to this land?
> And before lifting my brush,
> I opened my nostrils
> To the fragrance that filled the heavens
> Of the past.
>
> *Old Man of the South*

Ink Orchid clearly lacks detail and in this respect cannot stand comparison with Caravaggio's still life. Those well versed in the history of Chinese painting will know that Zheng was a member of the College of Supreme Learning under the Southern Song. When the Southern Song dynasty was destroyed by the Mongol Yuan dynasty he retired from court and lived as a hermit in Suzhou (now in Jiangsu province). In order to demonstrate his attachment to the Southern Song he always sat facing south and never north and even changed his title to "of the South." We should know that the literati painters of ancient China like Zheng Sixiao painted in order to express their inner emotions and ideals. In the act of creation they paid no heed to the commonality of viewers and consequently saw no need to depict the detail of objects. It is to this category of literati painting that *Ink Orchid* belongs, where the weight of concentration is not upon the display of detail but upon the internal expression of the artist.

It must be said that *Ink Orchid* is no ordinary flower or plant picture. It is a strong political statement. This painting was executed in the tenth year of Emperor Dade of the Yuan dynasty (1306). The reason that the orchid in the painting has no roots is because Zheng Sixiao said: "Our land has been stolen away, did you not know?" This rootlessness represents the sad times in which he found himself. The beginning of the poem describes Zheng's longing for the previous dynasty and his grief at the destruction of the nation. The end is a metaphor in which the orchid stands for the character and aspirations of the artist, virtuous, resolved and like the orchid, complete in every detail, willing to grow in seclusion where it emits clouds of fragrance.

Leaves and flowers are not the subject of this painting, the subject is the abstract symbolic significance that lies behind them. Thus, the scanty leaves on the one hand point up the orchid blossom as the subject, reminding us of the symbolic significance of the orchid in Chinese culture. On the other hand, the lack of detail in the painting obliges us to concentrate not only on the specific shape of the stems and leaves but also on the artist's use of brush and ink. If we carefully examine the line that goes to make up the leaves, it is not difficult to discover the power of their brushwork. They appear straight and tough, but have softness with strength. The plain, empty background lends the whole painting an air of simple calm that matches the symbolic seclusion of the orchid. It is the simplicity of construction and the utterly blank background that are the principal factors contributing to the brilliance of this painting. This kind of composition has an ethereal expression that assists both emotion and perception.

The Literati Painter's Preference for Ink over Color in Flower-and-Bird Painting

The tradition of the literati painting originated in the Song dynasty and reached its zenith in the Yuan dynasty because of the large number of educated men who, like Zheng Sixiao, were unwilling to serve the foreign Yuan regime and would rather return to the countryside and live as hermits. Painting, for them, was a means of expressing their ideals and emotions. The Four Yuan Masters represented the heights of the literati *shanshui* tradition. The literati painters preferred to use ink over color and consequently mostly used ink in flower-and-bird paintings. Even if color was used there was a preference for lightness and simplicity of tone. In choice of subject there was a tendency to concentrate upon the so-called "four gentlemen" of the plant kingdom: plum blossom, orchid, chrysanthemum and bamboo. Apart from Zheng Sixiao and his *Ink Orchid*, there were other artists. Zhao Mengfu (1254–1322) and Ke Jiusi (1290–1343) renowned for bamboos in ink and Wang Mian (1287–1359) and Yang Wujiu (1097–1169) famed for their plum blossom (fig. 98). The

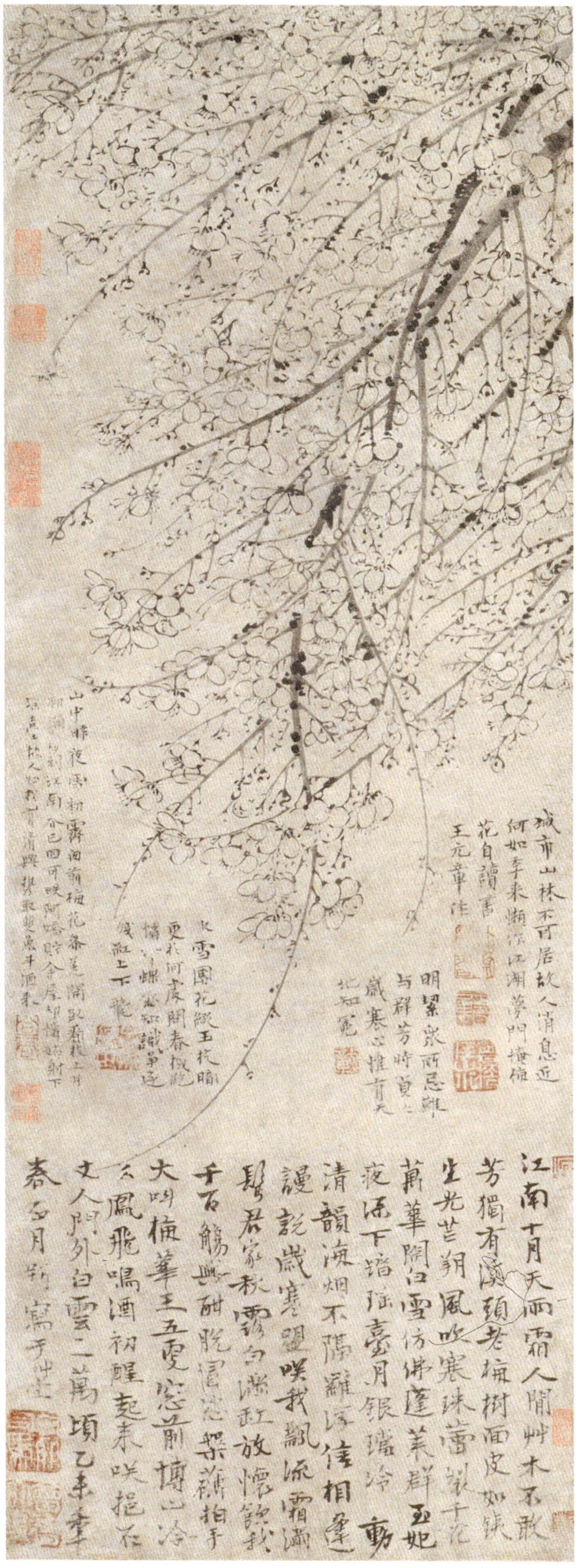

Fig. 98 *Plum Blossom*
Wang Mian (Yuan dynasty, 1287–1359)
Ink on paper
Height 67.7 cm × Width 25.9 cm
Shanghai Museum

Orchid, plum blossom, chrysanthemum and bamboo are the "four gentlemen" of the subject matter of traditional Chinese painting. The literati painters of ancient China liked to use them as subjects and adopted their characteristics as metaphors for the human character. The orchid was aloof and secluded, the plum blossom resistant to cold and unbending, the chrysanthemum private and airy and the bamboo modest and segmented.

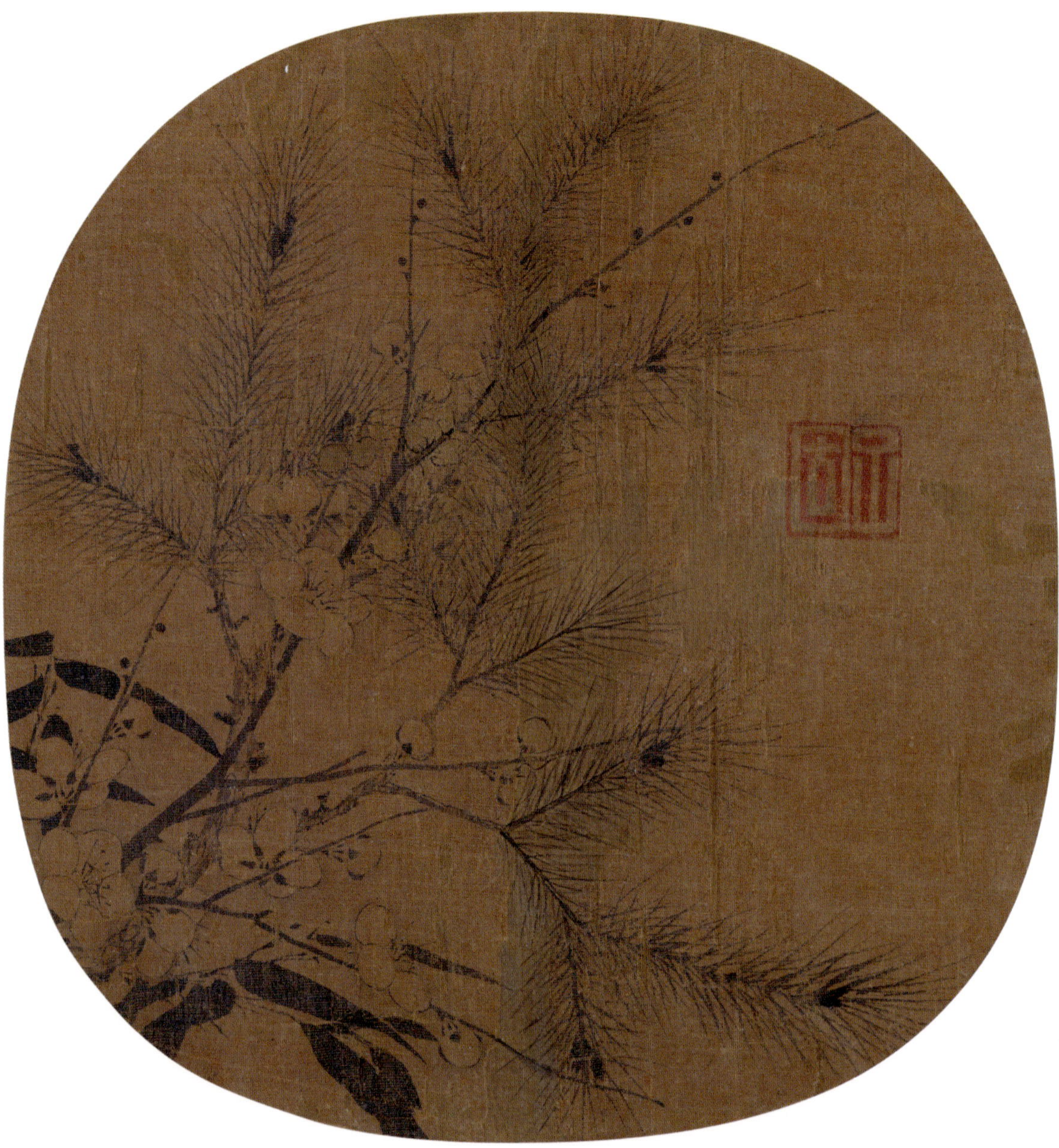

Fig. 99 *Winter's Three Friends*

Zhao Mengjian (Southern Song dynasty, 1199–before 1267)
Ink on paper
Height 24.3 cm × Width 23.3 cm
Shanghai Museum

Winter's three friends are the plum blossom, bamboo and pine, all with the ability to withstand bitter cold and revered by the ancient literati painters as exemplars of the spirit of perseverance.

literati used these four plants to represent the innate values that they esteemed. A plum blossom in full bloom resplendently in freezing conditions represents perseverance and the ability to withstand cold; the solitary but a fragrant orchid that does not catch the eye stands for the gentleman who lives in seclusion unknown to the world; and the chrysanthemum derives from a poem by Tao Yuanming (c. 365–427) that describes a secluded realm beyond material desire.

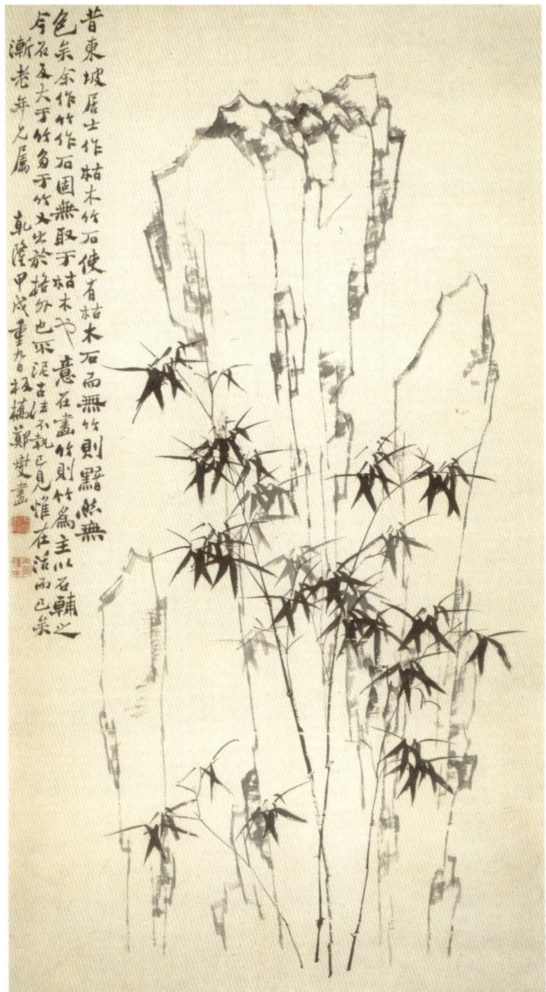

Fig. 100 *Bamboo and Rocks*
Zheng Xie (Qing Dynasty, 1693–1765)
Ink on paper
Height 217.4 cm × Width 120.6 cm
Shanghai Museum

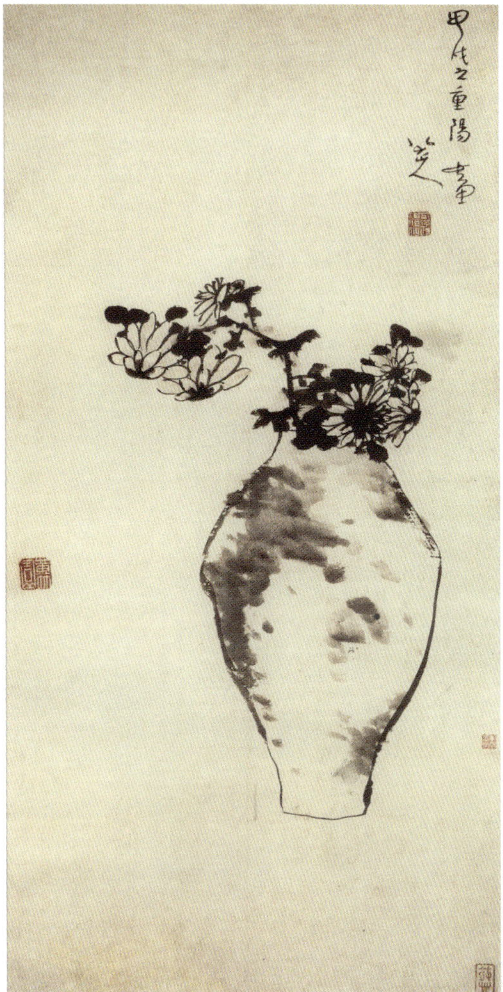

Fig. 101 *Chrysanthemums in a Vase*
Bada Shanren
Ink on paper
Height 90.5 cm × Width 46.5 cm
Private Collection

Figs. 100–101 Please refer to fig. 98 on page 99.

For the literati, to love the chrysanthemum is to recall the virtuous moral solitude of Tao Yuanming; the bamboo because of its segmentation and its perfectly straight growth suggests the integrity and modesty to which the cultivated man should aspire (figs. 99–101).

Foremost amongst the literati flower-and-bird painters of the Ming dynasty was Xu Wei (1521–1593) (figs. 102–103 on next page). There were also Chen Chun (fig. 104 on page 103) and Wen Zhengming (1470–1559) (fig. 105 on page 103). In the Qing dynasty there were the better known Bada Shanren (fig. 106 on page 104) and Shi Tao (fig. 107 on page 104), together with the later Eight Eccentrics of Yangzhou (fig. 108 on page 105). There was a kind of interlinked transmission between them. For example, the shadow of Xu Wei falls upon Bada Shanren and the Eight Eccentrics of Yangzhou and the young Chen Chun was apprenticed to Wen Zhengming, the works of both share the same quality of elegant simplicity.

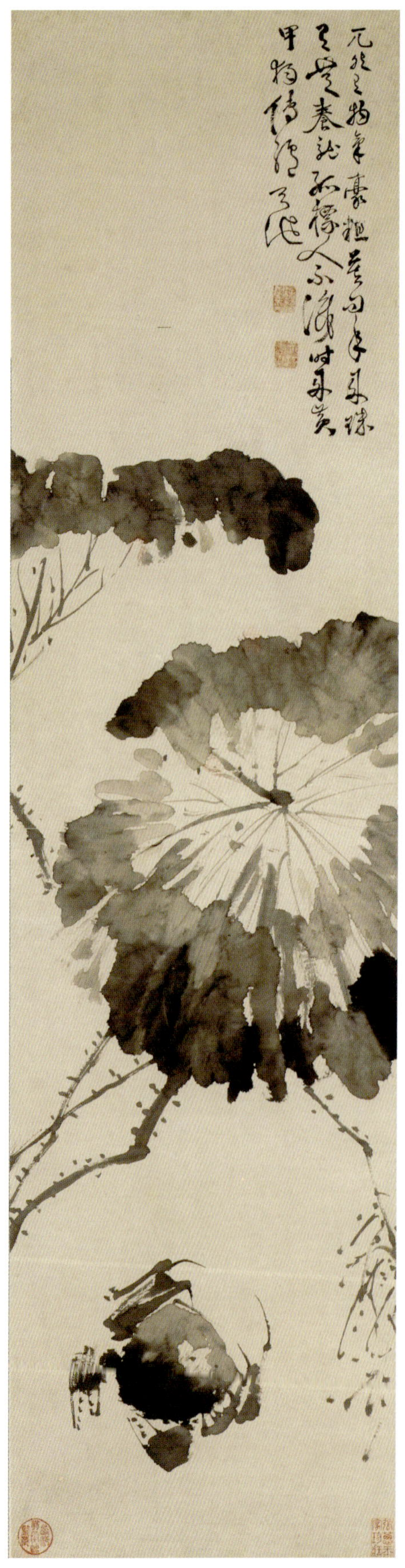

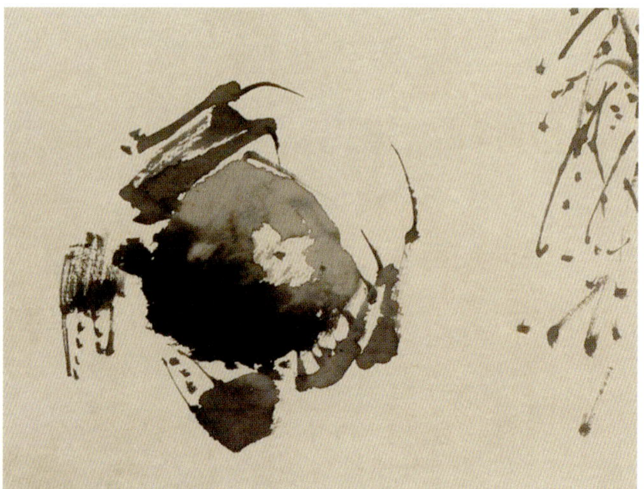

Figs. 102–103 *Yellow-Shelled Crab*
Xu Wei (Ming dynasty, 1521–1593)
Ink on paper
Height 114.6 cm × Width 29.7 cm
Palace Museum, Taibei

Xu Wei was a distinguished Ming writer, calligrapher and playwright. He served as a general during Ming resistance to Japanese pirate raids and as adviser to Hu Zongxian, governor of Zhejiang province. When Hu lost power and was imprisoned, Xu Wei, maddened by anxiety and apprehension, attempted suicide nine times and was later condemned to seven years imprisonment for killing his wife in a fit of madness. He subsequently traveled extensively in the south and sold off a library of several thousand volumes. His later years were spent in poverty. Xu Wei's paintings were in the unrestrained splash style that sought to convey the spirit of an object rather than its form. He was skilled in *shanshui,* figure painting, flower-and-bird painting and bamboo and rocks. He excelled in flowers and plants. He had a considerable influence on later painters such as Bada Shanren and the Eight Eccentrics of Yangzhou.

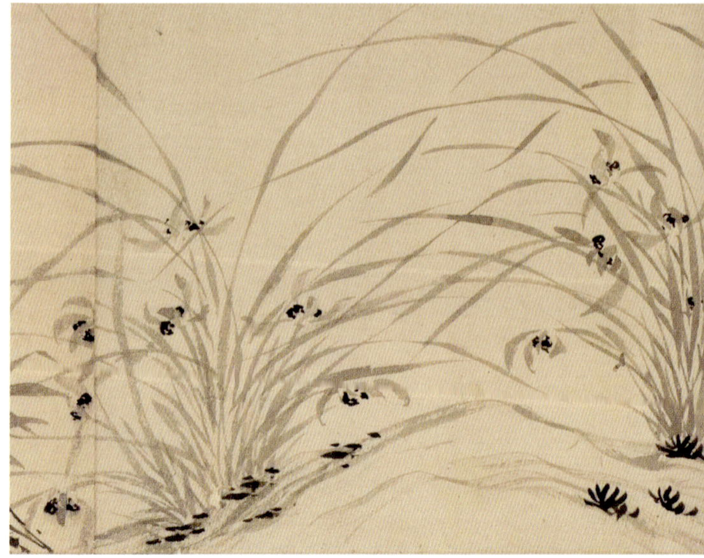

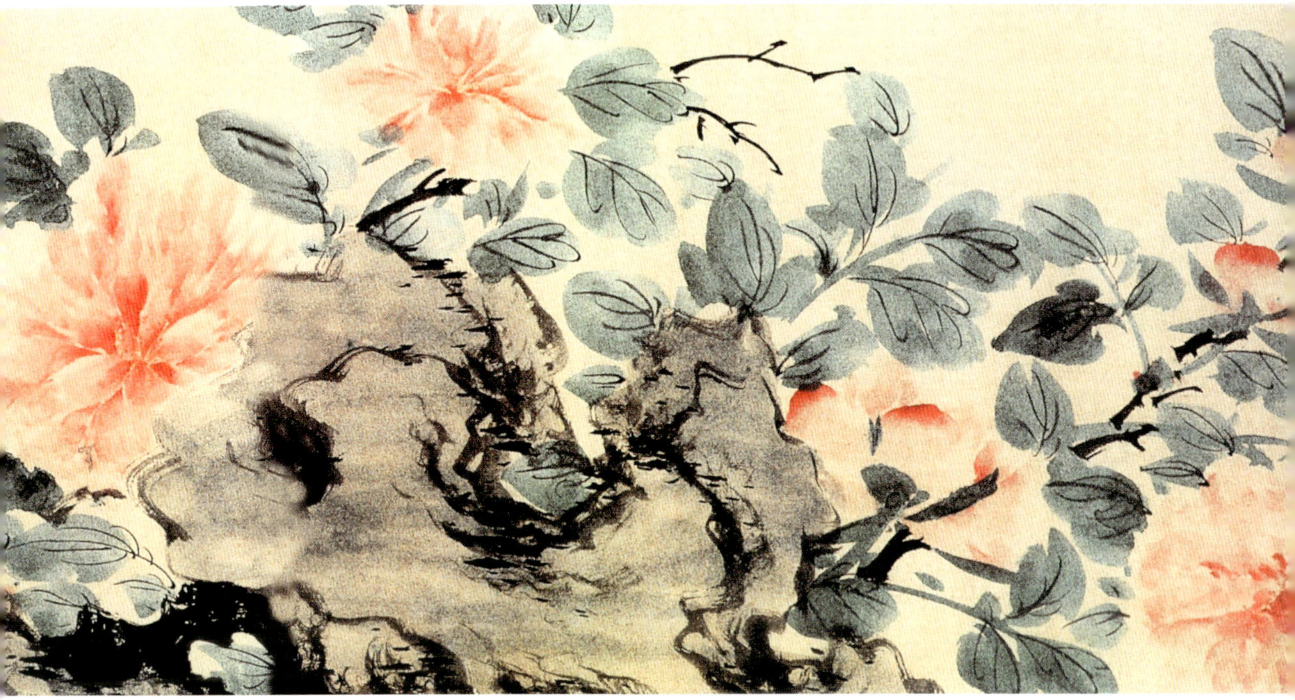

Fig. 104 *Spring at Luoyang* (detail)
Chen Chun
Ink and color on paper
Height 26.5 cm × Width 111.2 cm
Nanjing Museum

Chen Chun was a literary adept and calligrapher who excelled in painting. He was a pupil of Wen Zhengming. His freehand flowers, simplicity of style and freedom of brushwork were much praised by the cultivated classes of the Ming dynasty.

Fig. 105 *Orchid and Bamboo* (detail)
Wen Zhengming
Ink on paper
Height 26.8 cm × Width 730 cm
Palace Museum, Beijing

Wen Zhengming was a Ming artist and calligrapher who served at court but never succumbed to those in influential position. Unwilling to paint pictures for the vassal princes or eunuch officials he soon returned to his home in the countryside. His attainments in painting and calligraphy were wide and included poetry, essays calligraphy and painting where he was known as the polymath of the "Four Perfections." He co-founded the Wu School with Shen Zhou.

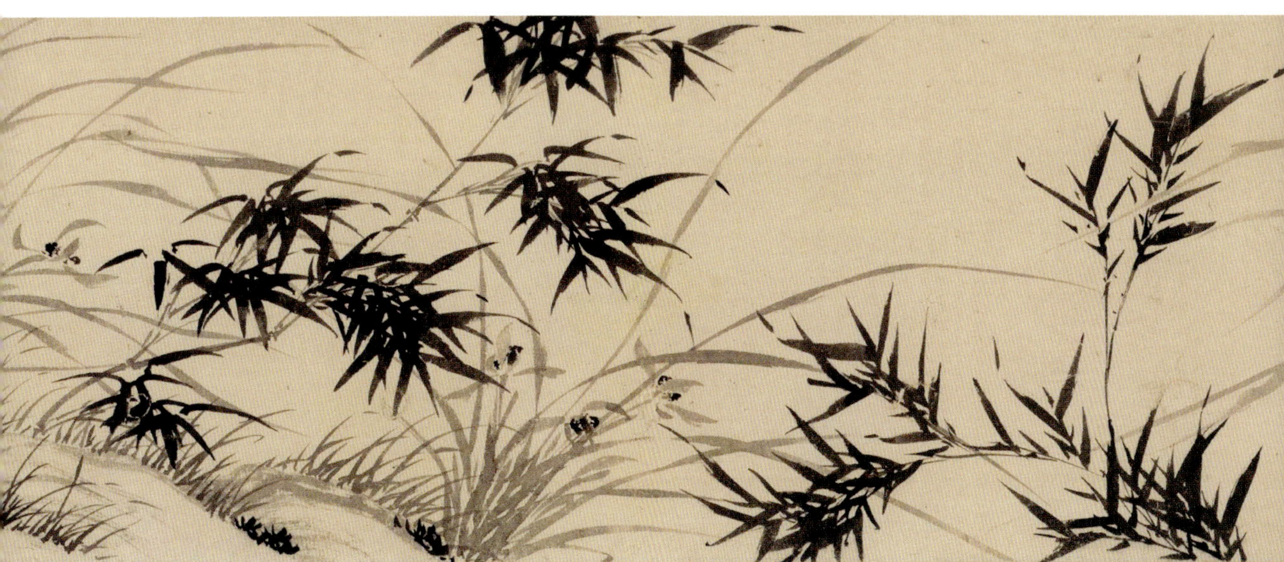

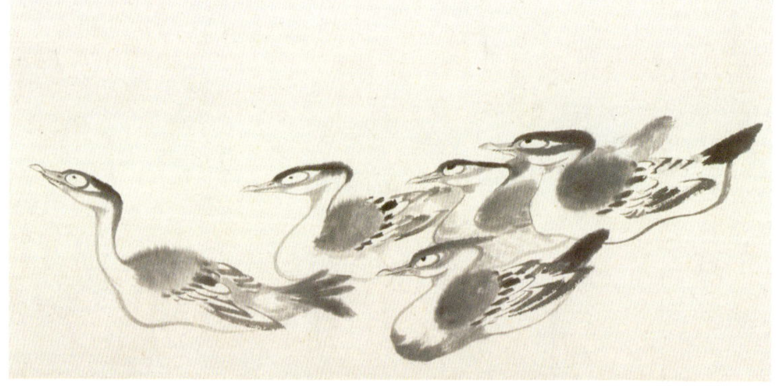

Fig. 106 *Fish with Ducks* (detail)
Bada Shanren
Ink on paper
Height 23.2 cm × Width 569.5 cm
Shanghai Museum

Bada Shanren, original name Zhu Da, a descendant of the Ming imperial family took the tonsure as a Buddhist monk on the fall of the dynasty, though he later became a Daoist. His works employed symbolism to express his feelings and his fish, ducks and birds were painted with empty eye sockets to show his embittered sense of isolation and unbending obstinacy. His brush work has an elegant vigour. His composition is simple with an air of calm and sense of remoteness. He had great influence on later generations.

Fig. 107 *Flower Album* (detail)
Shi Tao (Qing dynasty, 1641–c.1718)
Ink and color on paper
Height 25.6 cm × Width 34.5 cm (each page)
Freer Gallery of Art and Arthur M. Sackler Gallery, Washington D.C.

Shi Tao was an early Qing painter, original name Zhu Ruoji. He had a number of other names, such as Big Dizi, Old Man of Qingxiang, Bitter Melon Monk, and Blind Buddha. His Buddhist names included Yuan Ji and others. He was the son of Zhu Hengjia a descendant of the Ming imperial family and together with Hong Ren, Kun Can and Bada Shanren was a member of the group known as the Four Monks of the Early Qing. On the fall of the Ming dynasty he left home to become a Buddhist monk. He spent much of his life in religious wandering, supporting himself by selling paintings. His style was clear and upright but with fluid, uninhibited and flexible brushwork. He advocated "learning or copying from nature" (*shi zaohua*) and propounded the idea of "searching out curiously formed mountains to sketch" (*soujin qifeng da caogao*). He is one of the most important figures in the history of Chinese painting.

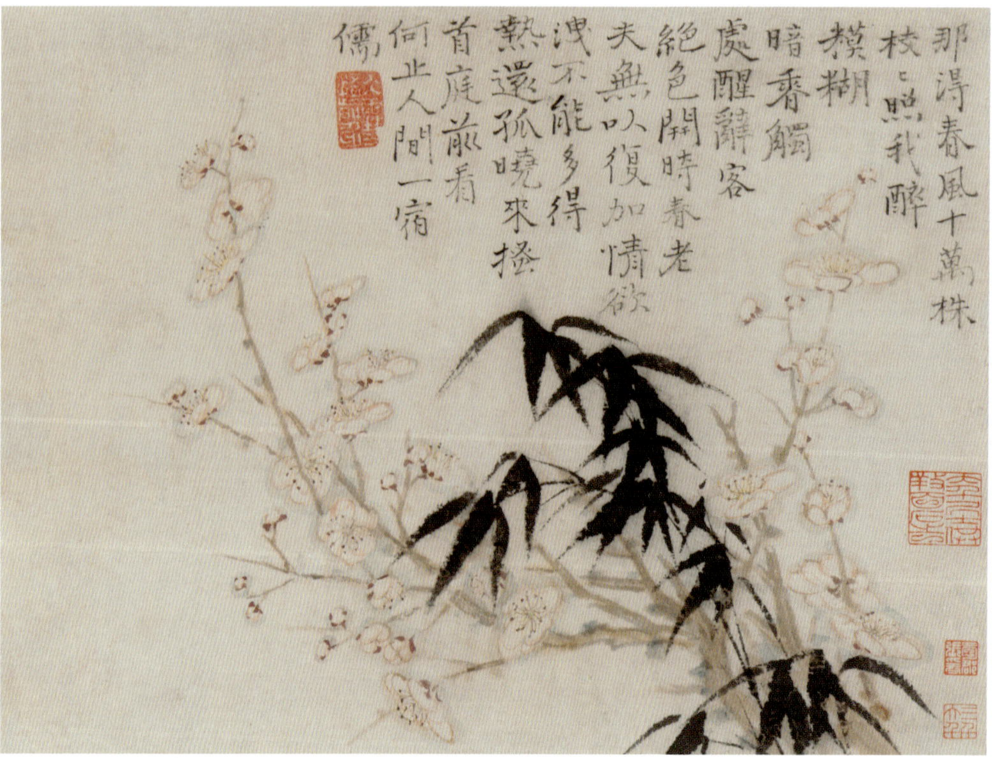

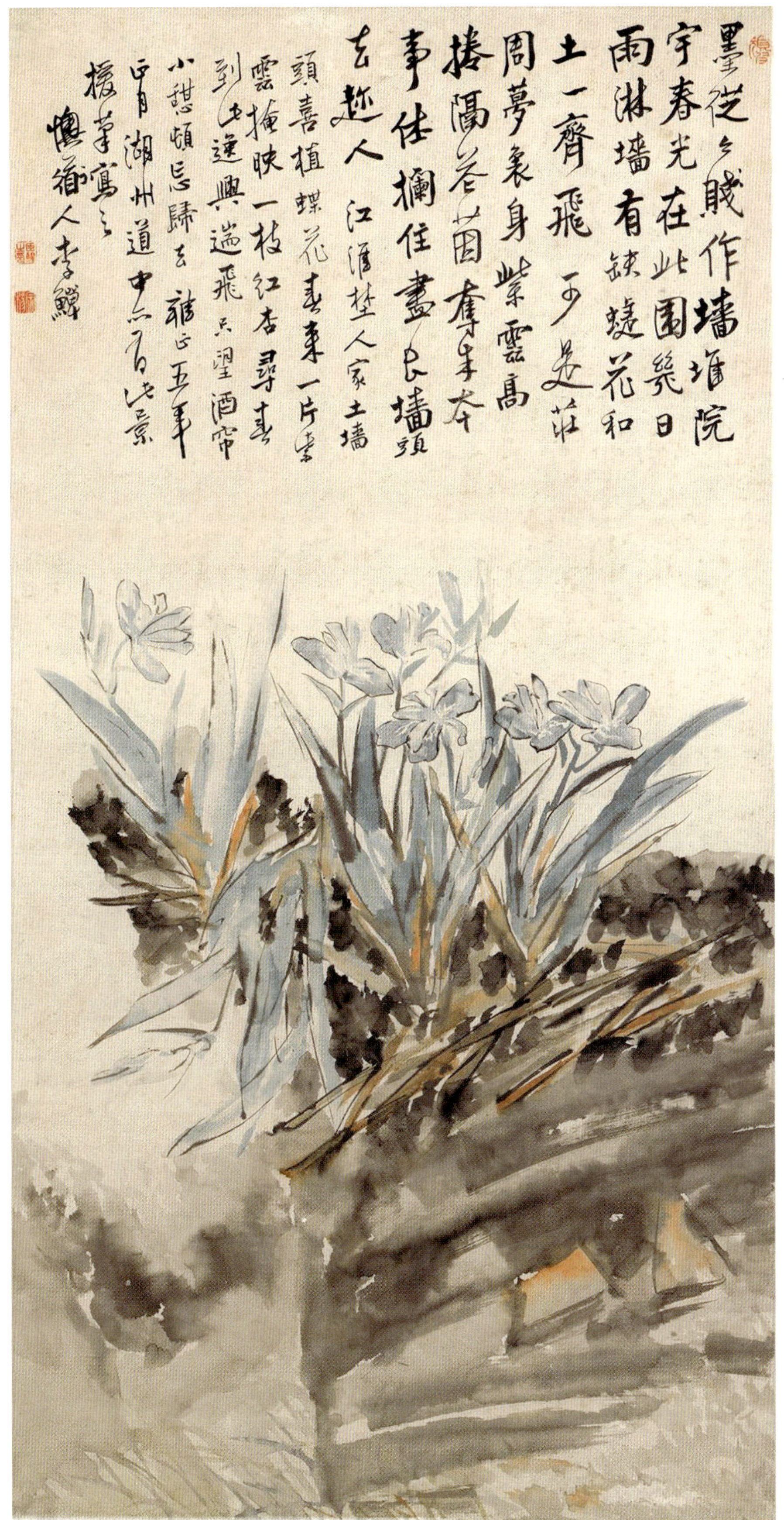

Fig. 108 *Butterflies and Flowers on a Wall*

Li Shan (Qing dynasty, 1686–1762)
Ink and color on paper
Height 115cm × Width 59.5 cm
Nanjing Museum

Li Shan, a noted Qing painter, was one of the Eight Eccentrics of Yangzhou. He was a court painter during the reign of Kangxi but retired to hermetic obscurity because of his failure to adapt to court politics. He later sold paintings in Yangzhou (now in Jiangsu province). He excelled in flower-and-bird painting, insects and fish. His early style was quite meticulously detailed but in later years he employed more freehand. His brushwork had strength and vigour and his works are full of interest. This painting breaks with the literati tradition of the use of the "four gentlemen" (plum blossom, orchid, chrysanthemum, bamboo) by making its subject wild flowers on top of a wall.

The Song Painting Academy Opens up a New Tradition in Flower-and-Bird Painting

A mature tradition of flower-and-bird painting already existed before the fashion for literati flower-and-bird painting took hold. There was, however, a considerable difference in style between the two and the mature tradition derived from the court. Its early masters can be traced back to Huang Quan (?–965) of the Five Dynasties and the Southern Tang Xu Xi (before 975).

Huang Quan entered the academy as an artist at the age of 17. He liked to paint rare and auspicious birds and his style was delicate and meticulous. His use of color was superb and because of his outstanding artistry he was granted the rank of an official of the third degree (fig. 109). Xu Xi excelled at bamboo in the wild, waterbirds, insects and fish and vegetables and fruit. He mostly used ink and tended to follow his own ideas, differing in style from the meticulous depictions of Huang Quan. Few genuine examples of Xu Xi's work survive. One regarded as genuine is his *Bamboos in Snow* (fig. 110). The styles of

Fig. 109 *Rare Birds from Life*
Huang Quan (Five Dynasties, ?–965)
Ink and color on silk
Height 41.5 cm × Width 70.8 cm
Palace Museum, Beijing

Huang Quan was a painter at the court of Shu (934–965), a state that followed the Five Dynasties and Ten Kingdoms (907–960). He was skilled at painting flowers, bamboo, fur and feathers, Buddhist and Daoist scenes, figures and *shanshui*. His style was delicately resplendent. This painting is believed to be a genuine example of his "drawing from life" work.

Fig. 110 *Bamboos in Snow*
Xu Xi (Five Dynasties, before 975)
Silk base
Height 151.1 cm × Width 99.2 cm
Shanghai Museum

Xu Xi, an outstanding painter of the Five Dynasties Southern Tang period was a member of a well-known clan in Jiangnan who refused to accept office and maintained a state of elegant self-reliance throughout his life. He was skilled in painting flowers and bamboo, birds and fish, fruit and vegetables and grass and insects. A Song treatise on painting described his bamboo thus: "The root, branch, segments and leaves are all applied with dark ink and coarse brushstrokes, and the knots between stems lightly dotted in with green, while the tips have an air of brushing the clouds." This points up his heavy use of ink but sparing use of color.

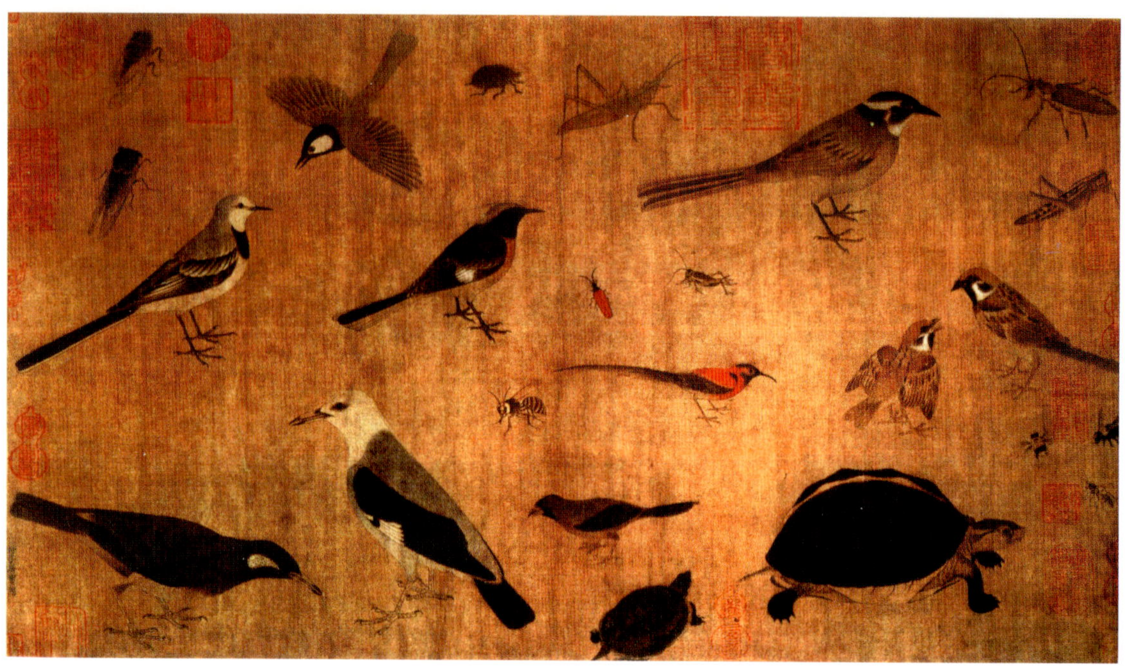

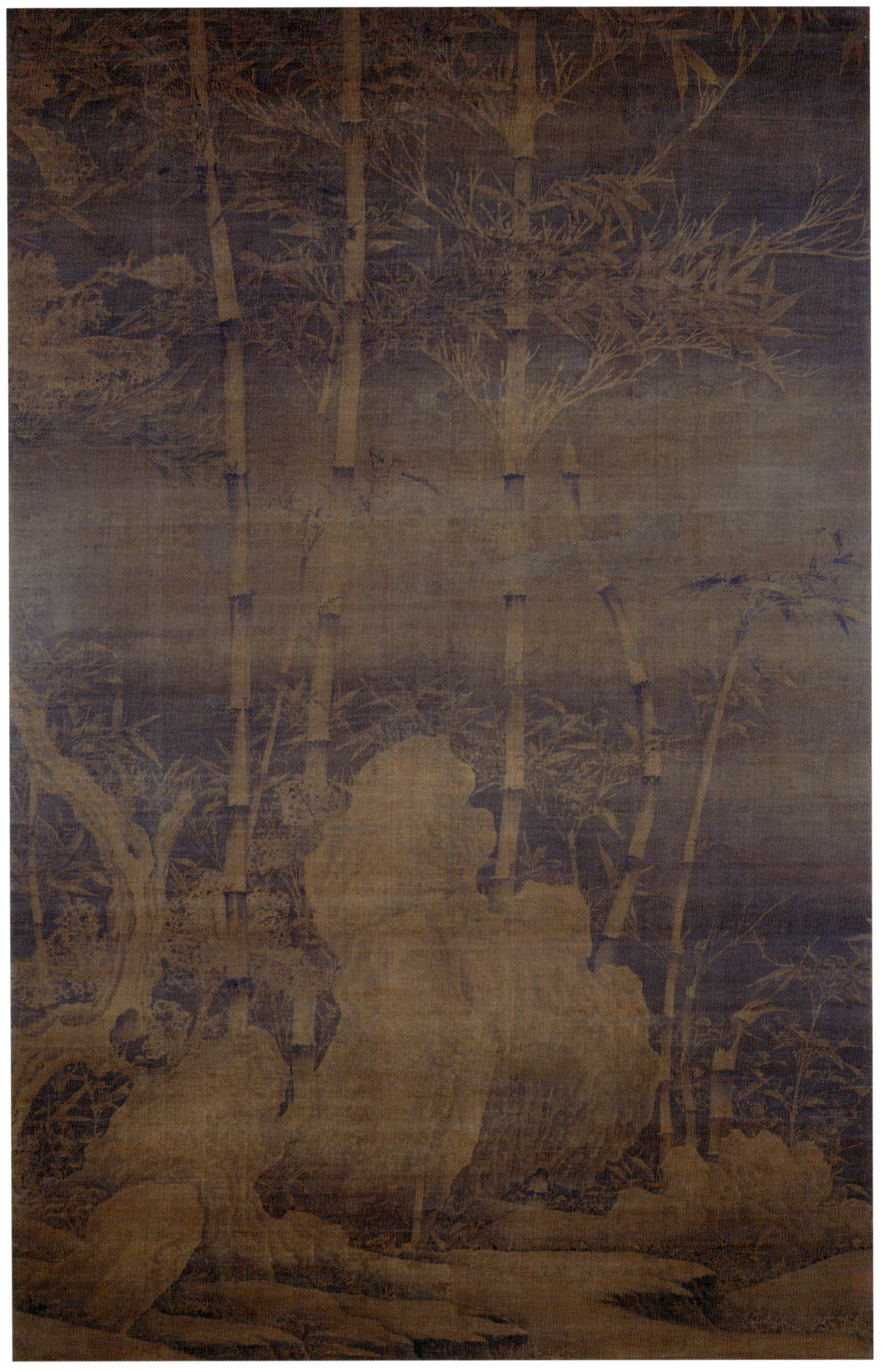

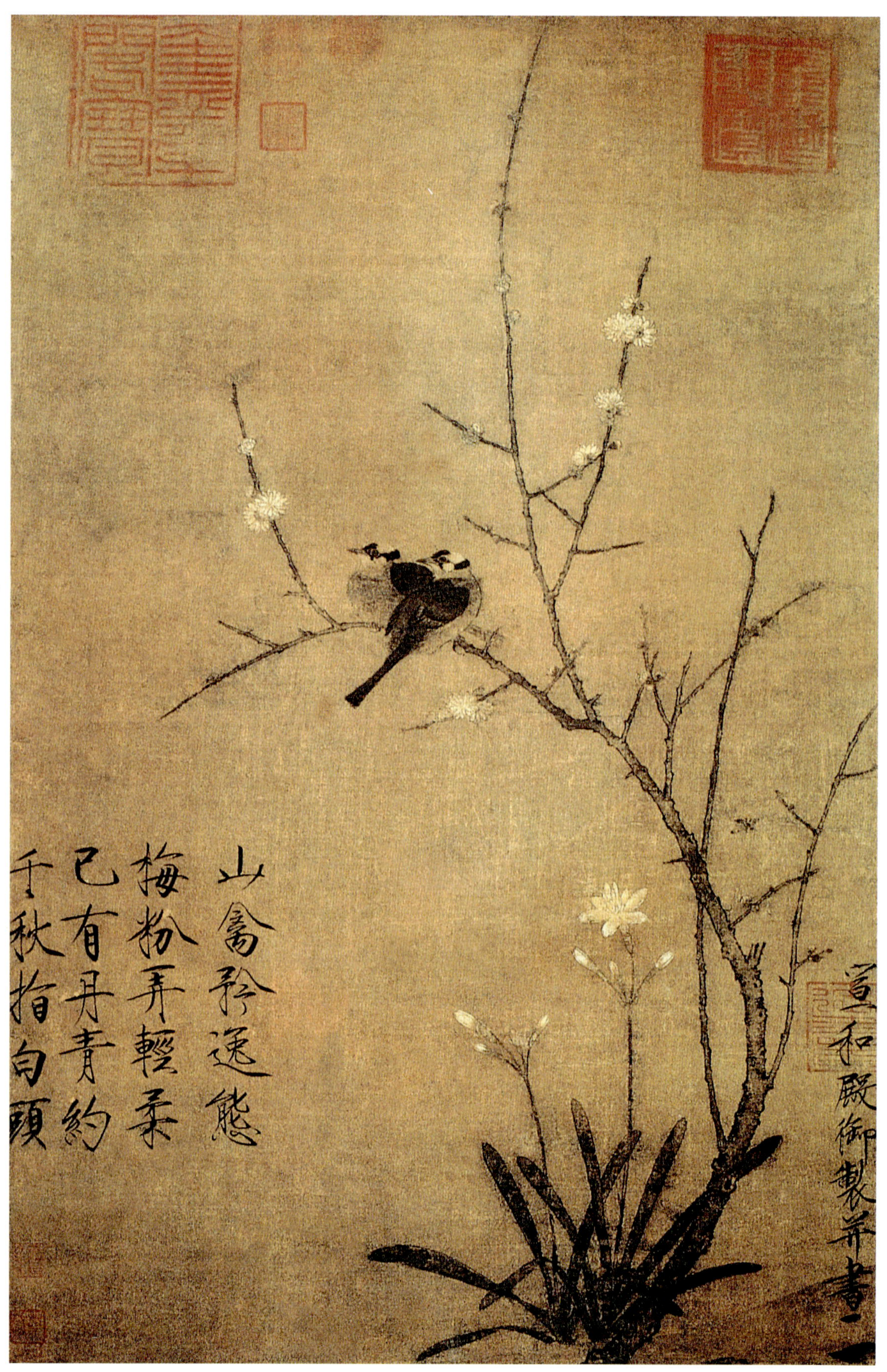
山禽矜逸態
梅粉弄輕柔
已有丹青約
千秋指白頭
宣和殿御製并書

both Huang Quan and Xu Xi were praised in historical treatises on painting and both had a definite influence on the development of flower-and-bird painting.

The Song Emperor Huizong established a Painting Academy and incorporated flower-and-bird painting into the formal categories of art. The style of the two Song Painting Academies followed the meticulous tradition of Huang Quan. However, because of Emperor Huizong's passion for literature and under his influence and encouragement, the academy's masters of the flower-and-bird genre integrated painting with literature and created a fresh tradition that combined poetic sensibility with artistic charm and in style added serenity and the flavor of poetry to delicacy.

Let us look at *Plum Blossom and Mountain Birds* reputedly by Emperor Huizong. A plum blossom grows upwards joint by joint from the ground and here and there on its slender twigs there blossom brilliant plum blossom flowers, surrounded by specks of white that represent the floating snowflakes of a cold winter. On the central branch two bulbuls nestle against each other sniffing at the plum blossom scent in the powdery snow. At the bottom left of the painting there is a poem in the hand of Emperor Huizong:

Fig. 111 *Plum Blossom and Mountain Birds*
Zhao Ji
Ink and color on silk
Height 82.8 cm × Width 52.8 cm
Palace Museum, Taibei

Zhao Ji, the Song Emperor Huizong, was the eighth Song emperor. He achieved nothing politically but his artistic achievements were outstanding. He was a genius and polymath rarely found in ancient China. His style of calligraphy was later known as "slender gold." He was passionate about poetry and literature and flower-and-bird painting. He established the Song Painting Academy and integrated poetry with painting.

"Two bulbuls perch at ease
And scented plum blossom softly fills
the air.
This painting is the promise
Of hoary age spent together."

The first two lines set the scene and the last two describe the feelings. It is written by Huizong himself, a metaphor for a ruler who loved painting and a regret at the way in which fate deals with man. The words in the poem such as "ease," "scented plum blossom," "softly" and "hoary" offset the images in the painting and poeticize the feeling and sense in it, so that the mood of the painting is given form (fig. 111).

Starting with the Northern Song dynasty there were a series of new developments in flower-and-bird painting. The Southern Song Painting Academy succeeded to the Northern Song tradition of delicacy and refinement of style and established a model for later court painters in the genre. For example, in the Qing dynasty, Jiang Tingxi's (1669–1732) *Willow with Cicadas* (fig. 112 on page 110) and Leng Mei's (late 17th century) *Two Rabbits under a Wutong Tree* (see fig. 117 on page 115) are both deep in the shadow of the flower-and-bird painters of the Northern Song dynasty. However, on closer examination, the flower-and-bird paintings of the Qing dynasty show none of the influence of the Song tradition of Huizong, they lack the sense of poetry and have come under foreign, particularly western, influence.

During the reign of Emperor Kangxi western priests were engaged as court painters, the best known and most influential being Lang Shining (Giuseppe Castiglione) (1688–1766). Let us now try and compare Leng Mei's *Two Rabbits under a Wutong Tree* with the Northern Song painter Cui Bai's (fl. 1050–1080) *Double Happiness* (fig. 18). In the former, the presentation of space and especially the modelling of the shadows on the ground shows obvious signs of

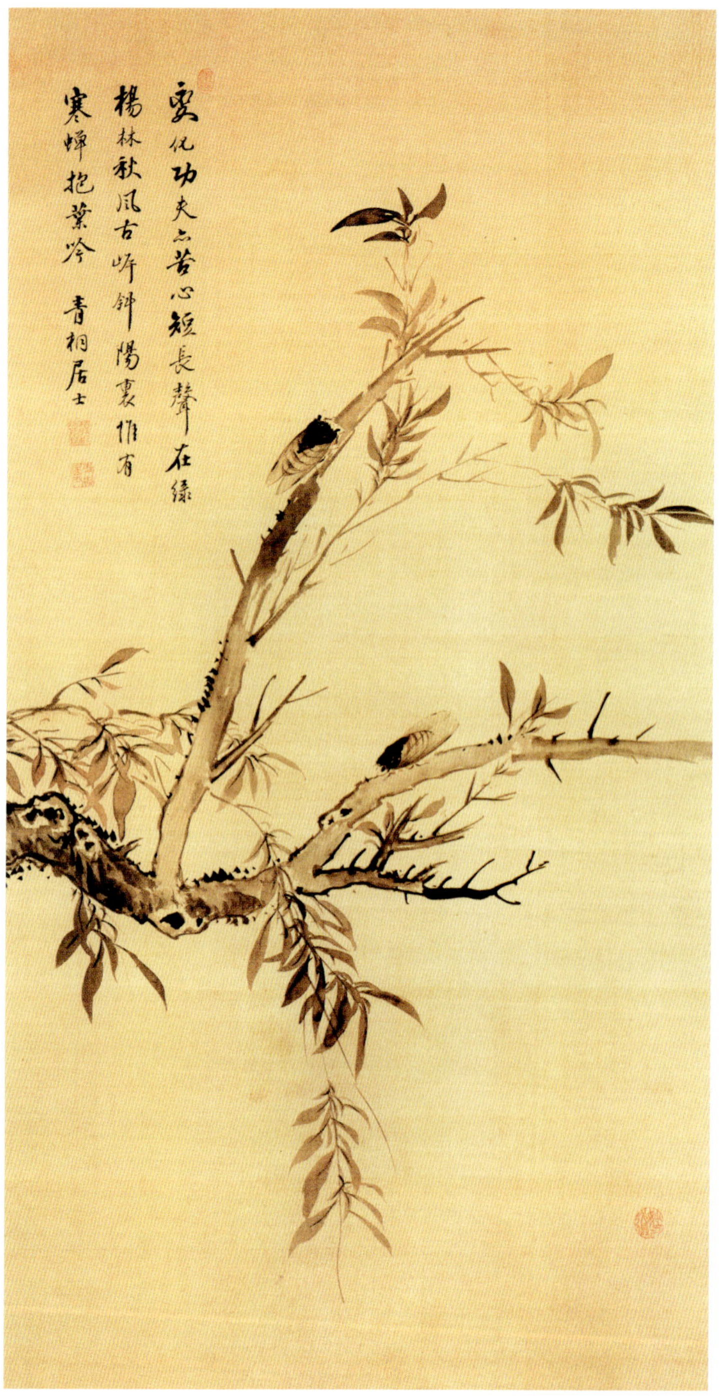

Fig.112 *Willow with Cicadas*
Jiang Tingxi (Qing dynasty, 1669–1732)
Ink on silk
Height 94 cm × Width 48.5 cm
Palace Museum, Beijing

Jiang Tingxi was a Qing philologist, book collector and painter skilled in flower-and-bird painting. In his youth his style was relatively delicate. He later liked using a "boneless method" technique, which means without outline, to paint twigs.

the influence of western techniques. In addition, Leng Mei applies rather more ink to the texture of objects than does Cui Bai. These are new concepts not to be found in the Song dynasty *Double Happiness.*

Thus, traditional flower-and-bird paintings can be divided into two major classes, the first the meticulous and richly colored academy style, and the second the literati style with its simple composition, use of ink and the four gentlemen of the plant kingdom as its typical subjects. At a glance it would seem that flower-and-bird painting never escaped from these two categories. However, a detailed analysis would suggest that the academies of different periods had different achievements. Insofar as the paintings of the literati tradition were concerned, they may have been similar in composition but artists differed in their use of brush and of ink and the interest and focus lay in the abstract values of brush and ink (*bimo*). Herein lies the reason why such importance is placed upon the appreciation of *bimo* in traditional Chinese painting. But whether in the flower-and-bird paintings of the academies or in the literati tradition, the focus was upon the "conceptual sense", and "leaving blank" was the major means of achieving it.

The Wonder of *Liubai*

In traditional Chinese painting the background is usually a large blank. We call this phenomenon *liubai*, leaving blank. The basic concept of *liubai* is not to regard "blank" space as an empty nothing. The concept of regarding nothing as something is closely related to the theories of the Daoists and of the *Book of Changes* in Chinese culture. The so called pairs, "void and solid" and "existence and non-existence" appear to be opposites, in fact they are complementary and each fills the gaps of the other to achieve harmony. This is the theory of "two elements one body." Consequently the ancient worthies and philosophers did not regard "non-existence" and "void" as negatives. In chapter 11 of the *Daodejing* Laozi discusses the use of non-existence and says: "In molding clay into a vessel, what is not there becomes of use to the vessel. In chiseling doors and windows to make a room, what is not there becomes of use to the room. Thus, what there is, is a matter of profit and what there is not, is a matter of use." What he is pointing out is the value of emptiness. A vessel can hold matter precisely because it contains an empty space within it; a room becomes a space in which people can live only when windows and a door have been cut. We may ask, what degree of wisdom is required before the value of "solid" and "existence" within "emptiness" and "non-existence" becomes apparent? Influenced by traditional philosophy the artists of ancient China were, from the very start, well aware of the concept that "void" embraced "solid" and that "blank" was not an emptiness.

Liubai is one of characteristics of traditional Chinese painting and has an extraordinary effect. The previous example of Zheng Sixiao's *Ink Orchid* involved the values of the aspirations of the literati towards an aesthetic concept of elegant purity and abstract *bimo*, and even in a work based upon realism, *liubai* could have an effect that drew gasps of admiration. The best and simplest example is Qi Baishi's (1864–1957) painting of shrimps (see fig. 3 on page 4).

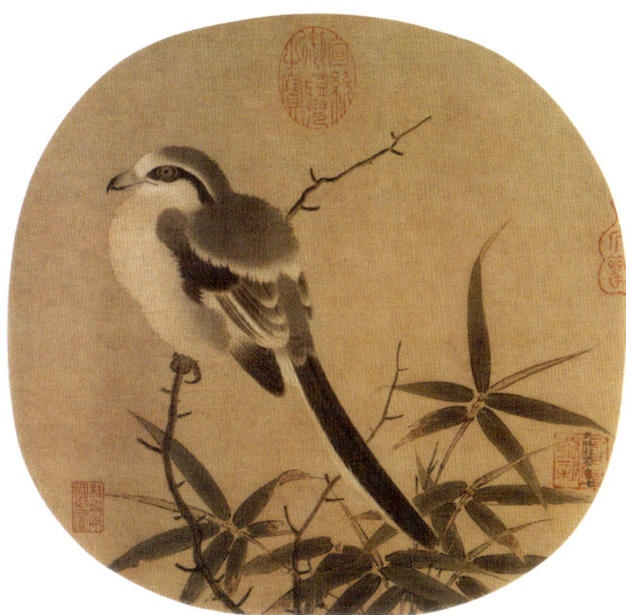

Fig. 113 *Bamboo with Turtle-Dove*
Li Anzhong (Southern Song dynasty)
Ink and color on silk
25.4 cm × 26.9 cm
Palace Museum, Taibei

Large expanses of *liubai* are often found in the background of traditional paintings, their role being rather like that of a modern telephoto lens, to draw scenes in the distance towards you so that they become the focal point of the camera shot, leaving the background to the viewer's imagination.

Qi Baishi excelled in painting shrimps and in his paintings, the background is an expanse of blank nothing. His shrimps are fresh, lively and brim with translucence. Qi Baishi's consummate brush and ink (*bimo*) technique convinces the viewer that beneath his brush the shrimps are happily swimming in a pool of clear, limpid water. But what we have failed to see is that the background to Qi Baishi's shrimps is actually the paper of the picture itself. Without the shrimps it is a blank expanse; but with the shrimps the blank expanse at once becomes a stretch of lake water. This piece of *liubai* provides the picture with limitless space and had the background

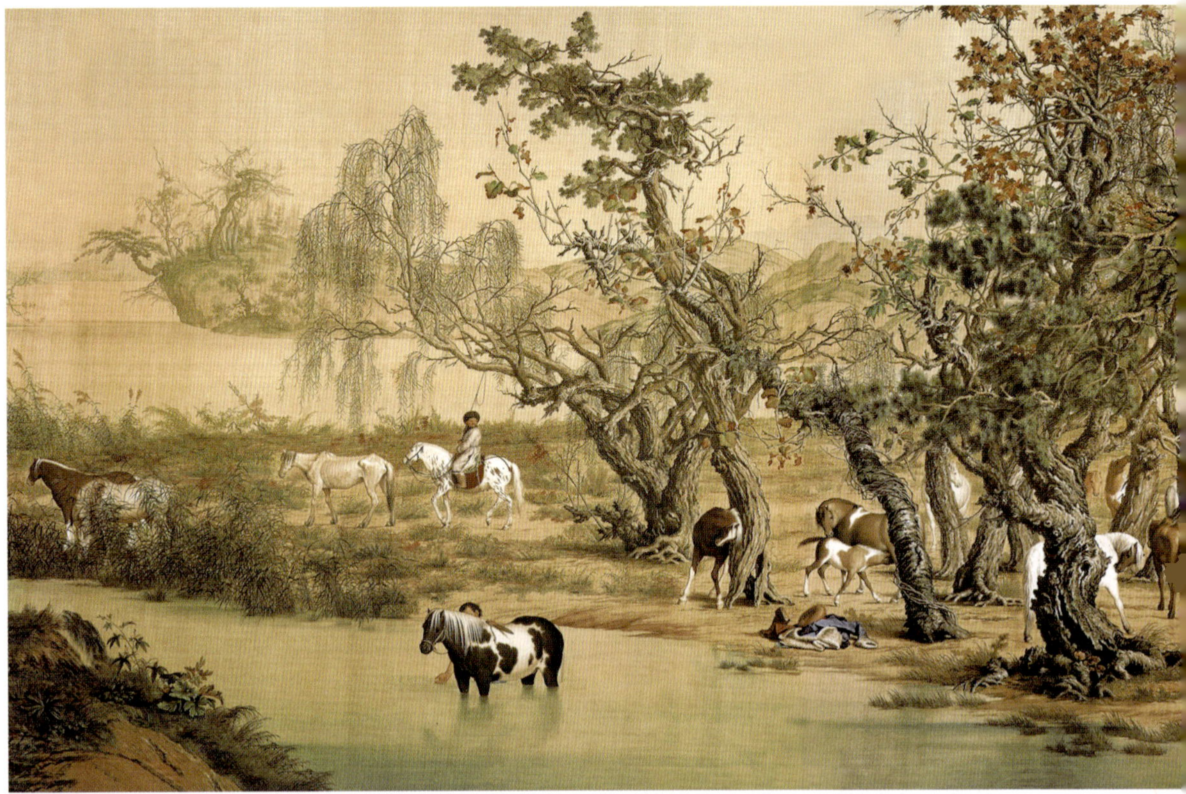

Fig. 114 *One Hundred Colts* (detail)
Lang Shining (Italy, 1688–1766)
Ink and color on silk
Height 94.5 cm × Width 776.2 cm
Palace Museum, Taibei

Lang Shining was the Chinese name of the Italian Jesuit priest Guiseppe Castiglione who came to China as a missionary in 1715 and was then appointed a court painter. He served for over 50 years during the reigns of the emperors Kangxi, Qianlong and Yongzheng. He had a considerable influence upon the painters of the Qing Painting Academy. His paintings are in an obvious western idiom; for example, in the pronounced western characteristics of the handling of the fore, middle and backgrounds and the depiction of light and shade in this painting.

been filled with ripples or waterweed, it would, as it were, have spoilt the view.

As we look at Qi Baishi's shrimps we cannot doubt the existence of water, we do not even need to ask where these shrimps are. This is the marvel of *liubai* in traditional painting. It is the same with the Song Painting Academy's flower-and-bird painting. Take Li Anzhong's *Bamboo with Turtle-Dove* (see fig. 113 on page 111), although all that can be seen are some flowers on a twig without any definite distant view, yet we feel that both the bird and the flowers are on a tree in a forest, rather as if we are using a telephoto lens to bring the distance towards us as the focus of our shot, rendering the background unimportant.

Liubai has always been a characteristic of traditional painting and became subject to the onslaughts of western influence during the Qing dynasty when a number of painters, particularly professional painters and the painters of the Qing court made changes to the composition of *liubai*. Western painting was introduced into China by missionaries from the Ming dynasty on. Although in the beginning it found no acceptance, in the Qing dynasty, Lang Shining, obtained the favor of Emperor Kangxi and was appointed a painter in the court academy. He served through three reigns, those of Kangxi, Yongzheng and Qianlong and under him much western painting became influential, one particular influence being in the handling of background.

Lang Shining's paintings often used

Fig.115 *Double Happiness*
Cui Bai (Northern Song dynasty, fl. 1050–1080)
Ink and color on silk
Height 193.7 cm × Width 103.4 cm
Palace Museum, Taibei

Cui Bai was a Northern Song painter who excelled in the depiction of bamboo and fur and feathers. His working methods adhered to the ancient requirement for equal attention to both form and spirit. Whilst drawing from life he also searched for the inner vitality of the plants, birds, and animals that were his subjects. This painting depicts a chance encounter in a wood between a wild rabbit and a pica bird (magpie). It is delicately executed and depicted with vitality and realism. It has a rich sense of rustic ease.

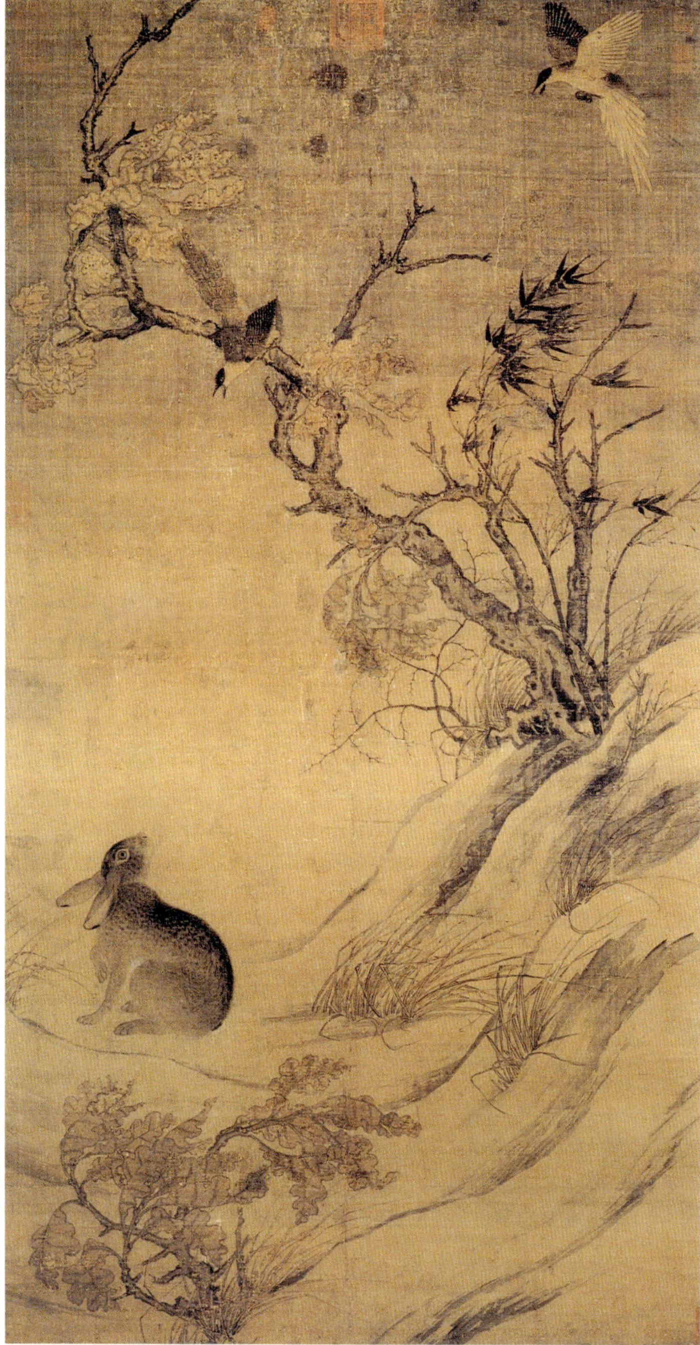

western perspective thereby increasing the detail of the background. For example, in his *One hundred Colts* (fig. 114), the fore, middle and backgrounds are very neatly arranged and the lower half of the painting is full, leaving no blank space and reducing the attraction of the compositional flavor of traditional painting.

Western influence broke down or at least reduced the element of *liubai* in traditional painting with results that were both good and bad. We can compare the Northern Song painter Cui Bai's *Double Happiness* (fig. 115) with the Qing Leng Mei's (who was active during the reign of Kangxi) *Two Rabbits under a Wutong Tree*.

Double Happiness is a representative work of the Northern Song Painting Academy under Emperor Shenzong. Cui Bai was renowned for his flower-and-bird painting and deeply influenced later painters of the genre. The picture depicts the scene as a wild rabbit on a mountain path who spies two pica birds in a tree, stops and gazes upwards at them. The composition is basically angled from bottom left to top right. The bottom left is occupied by a rabbit as it looks up into the tree branches, the right shows the path lightly sketched in simple line and ink. Above, there is a branch extending from the right to the

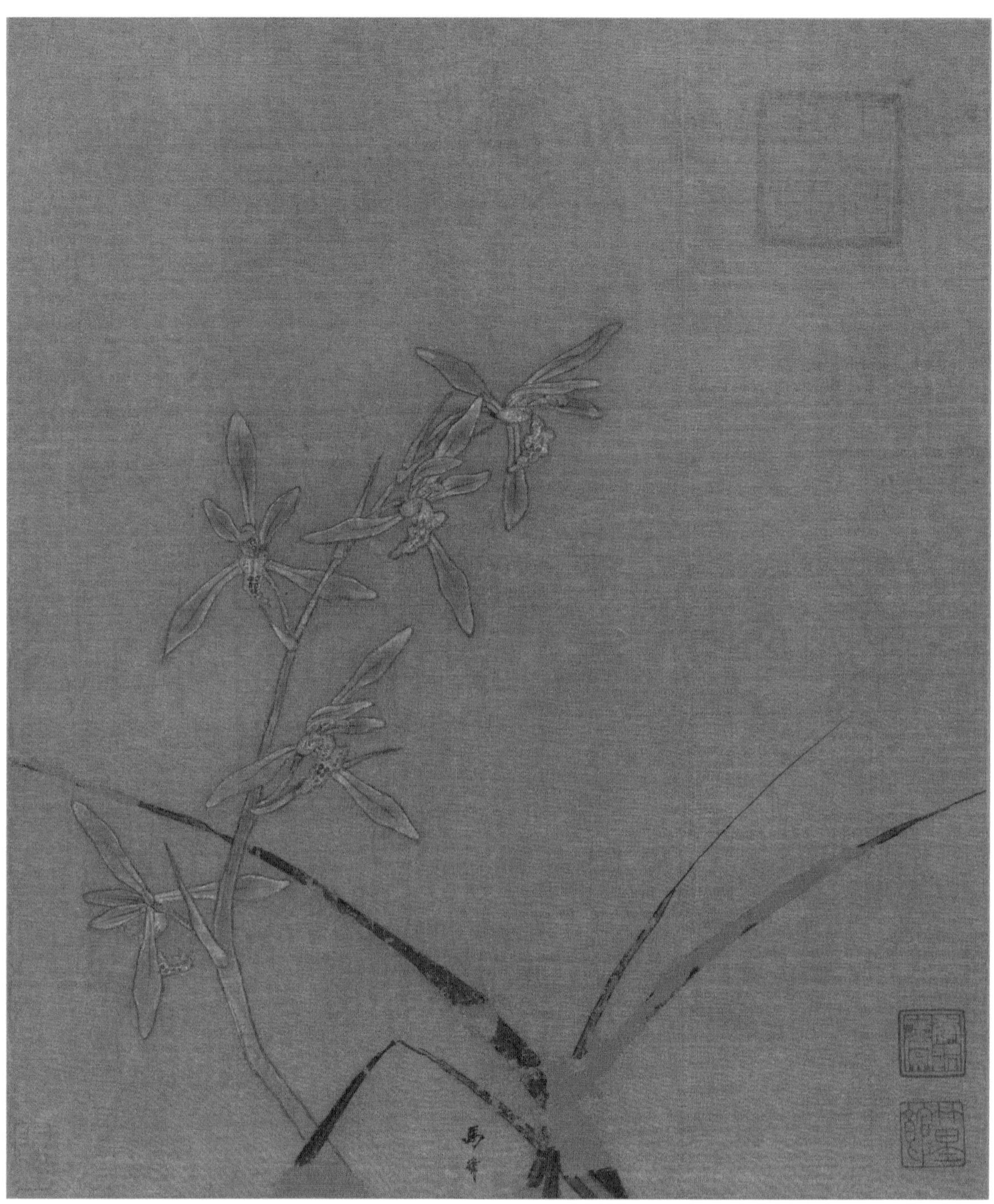

Fig. 116 *Secluded Fragrance*

Ma Lin (Southern Song dynasty, c. 1180–after 1256)
Ink and color on silk
Height 26.5 cm × Width 22.5 cm
The Metropolitan Museum of Art, New York

The basic concept of *liubai* is that areas that are "blank" should not be regarded as an empty void. In this painting the area of *liubai* is a space that brims with secluded fragrance.

upper left and on it perches a pica bird whilst another flies towards a branch from the upper right corner of the picture. The *liubai* portion of the background occupies about one third or more of the picture.

The composition of *Two Rabbits under a Wutong Tree* shows clear traces of the influence of *Double Happiness.* There is the same arrangement of angle, though left and right have been interchanged and the two rabbits appear opposite each other in the lower right with the Wutong tree extending from the middle left towards the right. Compared with *Double Happiness*, the foreground and background of *Two Rabbits under a Wutong Tree* contain much more defined detail. For example, Leng Mei used a western perspective for the rocks in the foreground and the bamboo fence in the background, the size of objects also accords with their distance from the viewer and the distant hills in the background are lightly inked in.

Although *Two Rabbits under a Wutong Tree* is not the same as a western painting with its crowded background, the correctly proportioned size of objects together with the hills in the distance express a feeling of the space in the picture with some clarity and thus considerably reduces our freedom to imagine space for ourselves. By contrast, when we look at the *liubai* background of Cui Bai's *Double Happiness,* the absence of defined indicators of space creates a sense of the ethereal existence of mountain and forest which allows this feeling for the abstract to roam freely both within the painting and without. This is the marvel of *liubai*. To an extent, *Two Rabbits under a Wutong Tree* resembles Caravaggio's *Still Life with a Basket of Fruit* where too much detail is not a good thing.

The analysis above more or less explains how the concept of *liubai* in traditional painting provides space for the imagination, and simplicity of composition aids the

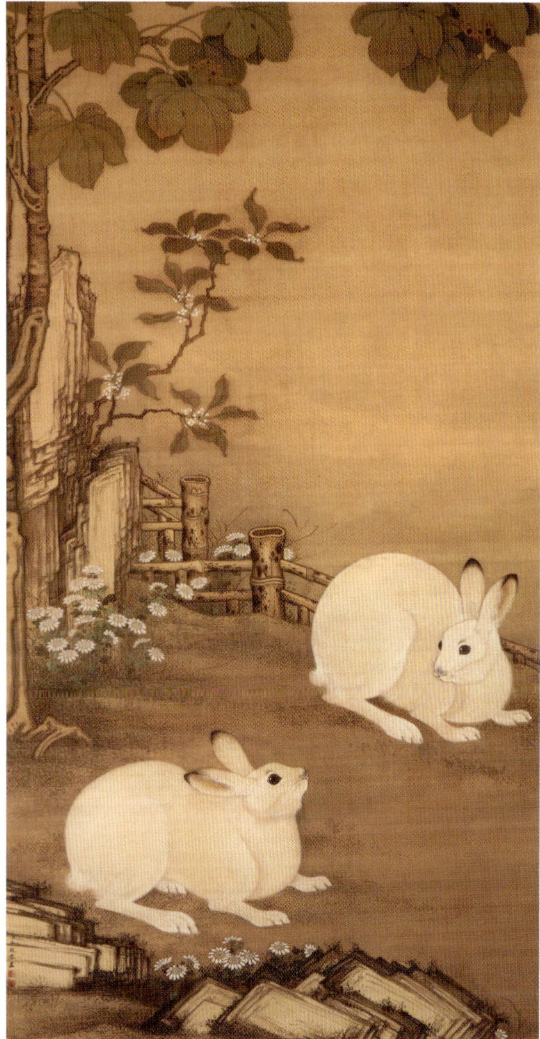

Fig. 117 *Two Rabbits under a Wutong Tree*
Leng Mei (Qing dynasty, late 17th century)
Ink and color on silk
Height 176.2 cm × Width 95 cm
Palace Museum, Beijing

Leng Mei was a Qing court painter skilled in figure and architectural painting and was particularly adept at paintings of court ladies. His style had a delicate beauty and his colors were harmonious and brushwork delicate. This painting reminds us of the Song painter Cui Bai's *Double Happiness*.

expression of the ethereal. Let us now look at several further examples. Ma Lin (c. 1180–after 1256) was the son of Ma Yuan (12th–early 13th century) and both father and son were court painters at the Southern Song Painting Academy. Ma Lin's painting of an orchid under the title *Secluded Fragrance* (fig. 116) differs from Zheng Sixiao's *Ink Orchid*.

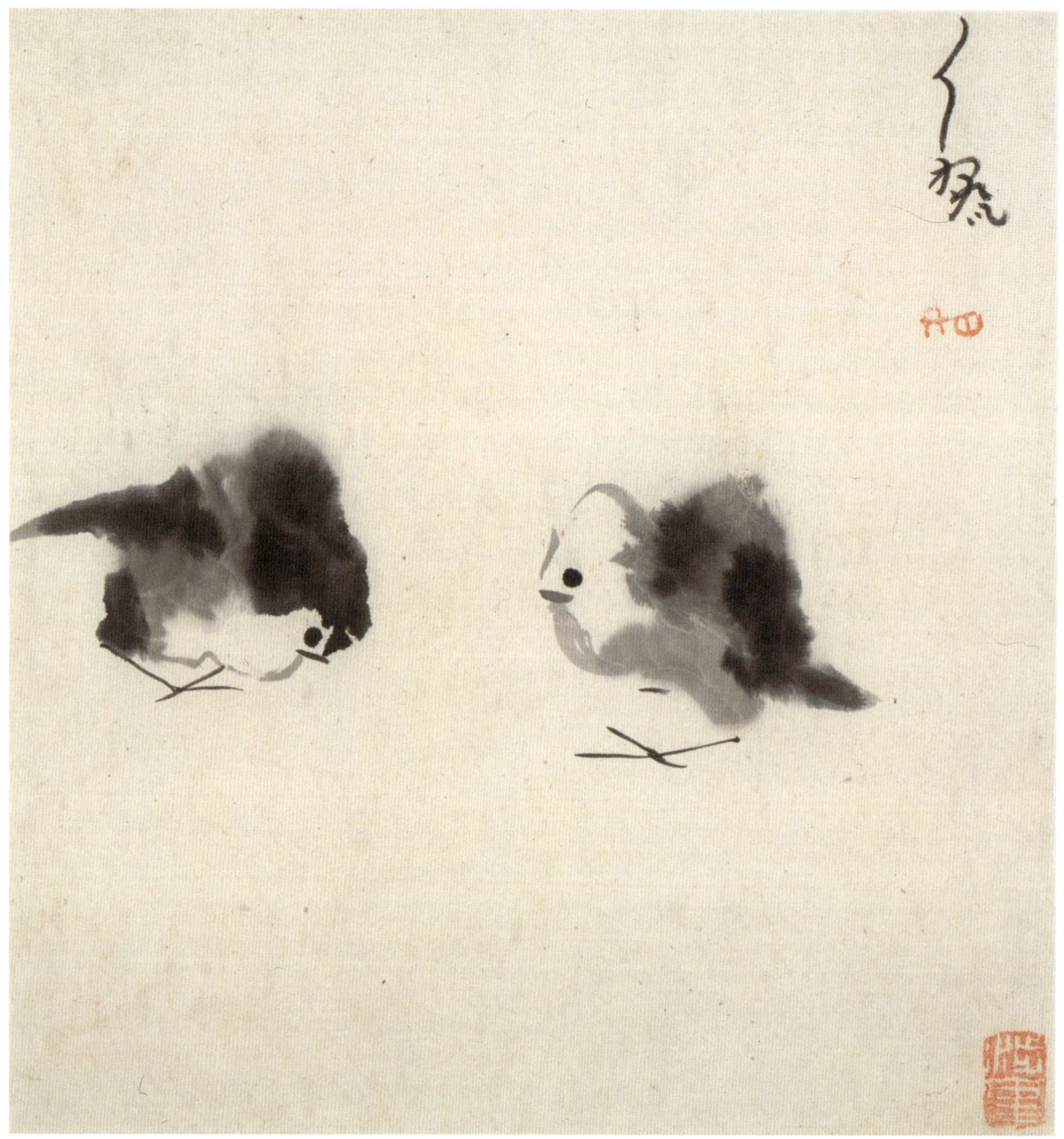

Fig. 118 *Squabs*
Bada Shanren
Ink on paper
Height 24 cm × Width 23 cm
Shanghai Museum

"Table top paintings" are improvisatory minor works executed by literati painters on the top of a table. They have rather the flavor of "ink play" (*ximo*) and are loosely composed with a considerable extent of *liubai* that focuses our attention on the delights of their brush and ink.

It is imbued with color and the brushwork is meticulous. It is more detailed in its treatment of the form of the flower and of the changing direction of the stem. This is because Ma Lin as a professional painter in the court academy, though he concentrated on capturing the spirit of objects, did not neglect their form either. Despite the differing style of these two paintings they have in common a simple composition with a large area of *liubai.*

Ma Lin's *Secluded Fragrance* represents just half a plain orchid that extends from the bottom left to the top right of the painting. The area of *liubai* occupies more than half the painting and simplicity is at its extreme. Apart from form, it was, more importantly, the essence of the orchid that Ma Lin wished to capture in this painting, an abstract expression of seclusion and of fragrance. The large expanse of *liubai* creates an atmosphere of serenity and seclusion that is neither expansive nor busy. It is not difficult to imagine that if Ma Lin had painted in a rich and well defined background, even of deep valleys, how much that atmosphere of secluded fragrance would have been diminished and weakened. The title is not *Orchid* but *Secluded Fragrance* thus adding point to the painting. As we enjoy the beauty of the orchid in it, we can, because of the lead given by the title, imagine the secluded fragrance, while the large expanse of *liubai* can stand for a space filled with faint scent. With a background congested with detail, there would be nowhere in the painting in which our dreams could linger.

If we look at the Yuan painter Qian Xuan's (c.1239–c.1300) *Pear Blossom* again (see fig. 10 in Chapter Seven) with its single pear tree and its empty background, it seems like a shot through the lens of a camera. The pear tree blossoms in rich profusion, making it seem as if we are standing in the midst of an orchard of pear trees. The elegantly detailed brushwork expresses the scent of the pear blossom so that it is possible to say that this painting depicts not just a single pear tree but a whole orchard scented with the fragrance of pear blossom.

The format of Qian Xuan's *Pear Blossom* is a handscroll, different from the hanging scroll *Bamboo with Rocks* by Zheng Xie (1693–1765) mentioned previously. The layout of the former places the viewer in the horizontal, so that the elegance of the painting unfolds to left and right; in the latter the thickets of bamboo ascend in order from the bottom of the painting towards the top, concentrating our vision on the dense spread of the stems of bamboo so that we can appreciate the way that the ink and color interweave and interact with the line of the painting.

Flower-and-bird paintings are often found in the form of album leaves which, because of their generally small size belong to the improvisatory class of minor works, much beloved by literati painters as "table top paintings." These improvisatory works are usually simple in composition, where a single bamboo or blossom amounts to the complete painting. In the Qing painter Bada Shanren's *Squabs*, apart from two very small chicks, the remaining two thirds of the painting is *liubai* (fig. 118). *Liubai* lends prominence to the squabs and concentrates our attention. As we enjoy the charm of the simple construction and of the brushwork, what we see is the inner realm of the artist. This is because the areas of *liubai* are an integral part of the composition.

Traditional Chinese painting values sensibility and serenity and good paintings resonate with their external sense even after the viewer has finished looking at them. Ethereal construction is one of the keys to this sense. The 20th century master of traditional painting Huang Binhong wrote in the preface of his 1954 *Shanshui Album*: "In painting, the ancients were diligent in the places where there was neither brush nor ink, it is difficult to follow in their footsteps, to perceive the empty space and yet hold back the ink. The achievement of this mystery is difficult to describe in words." What he is describing is exactly that deep mystery of the function of *liubai* in traditional painting. If we can understand its ethereal qualities, it will expand our ability to feel pleasure in the appreciation of a painting and there will be no end to its wonder.

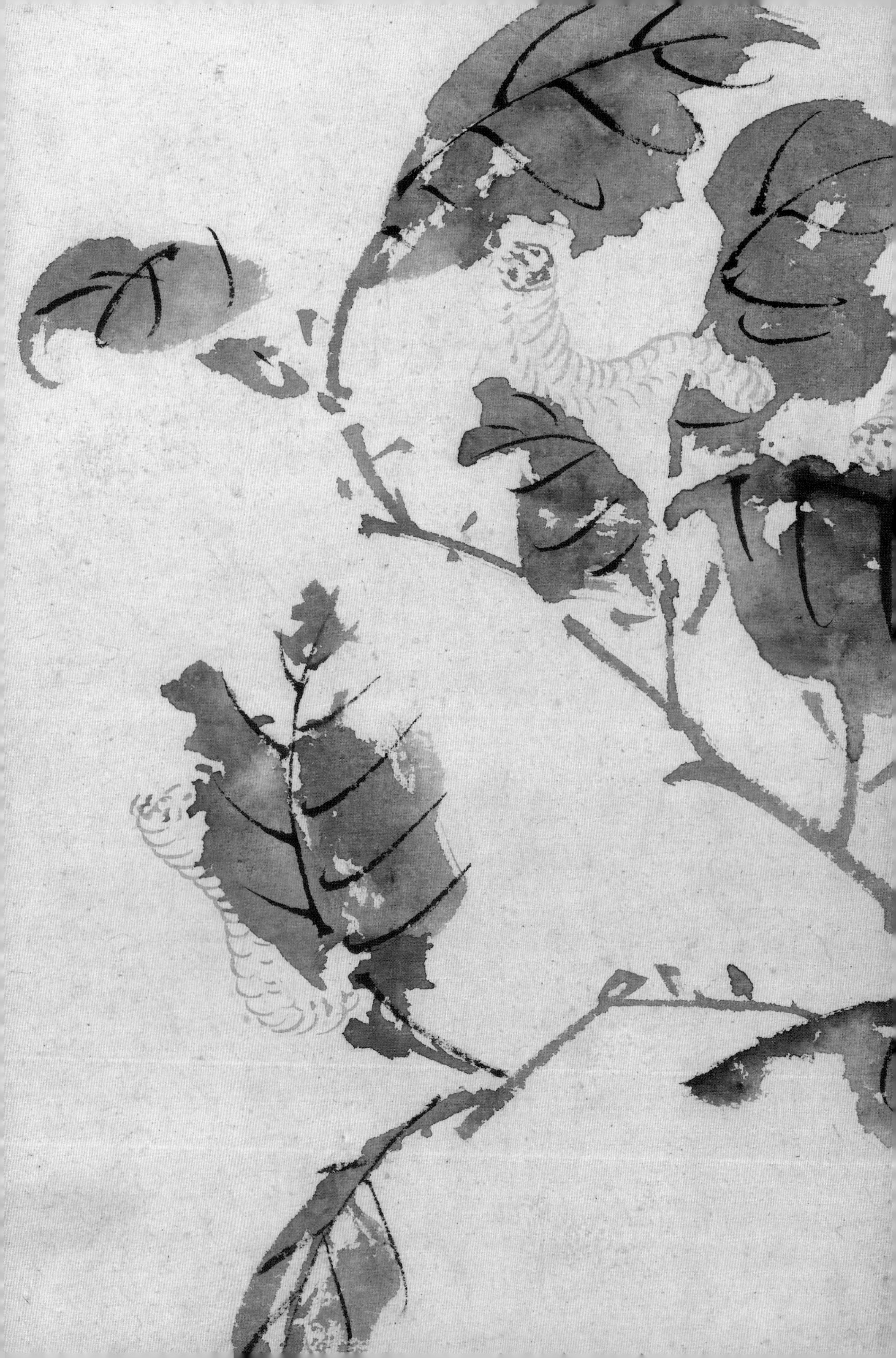

CHAPTER SIX
The Abstract Qualities of *Bimo*

The word *bimo* (brush and ink) is often on the lips of those who appreciate traditional Chinese painting. But for those who know nothing of Chinese painting, this runs the risk of giving *bimo* divine status, because, in the end, *bimo* is only one phrase amongst many. What is it that makes *bimo* so special when compared with, say, composition, color, and modelling? This chapter will examine the significance of *bimo* in traditional Chinese painting.

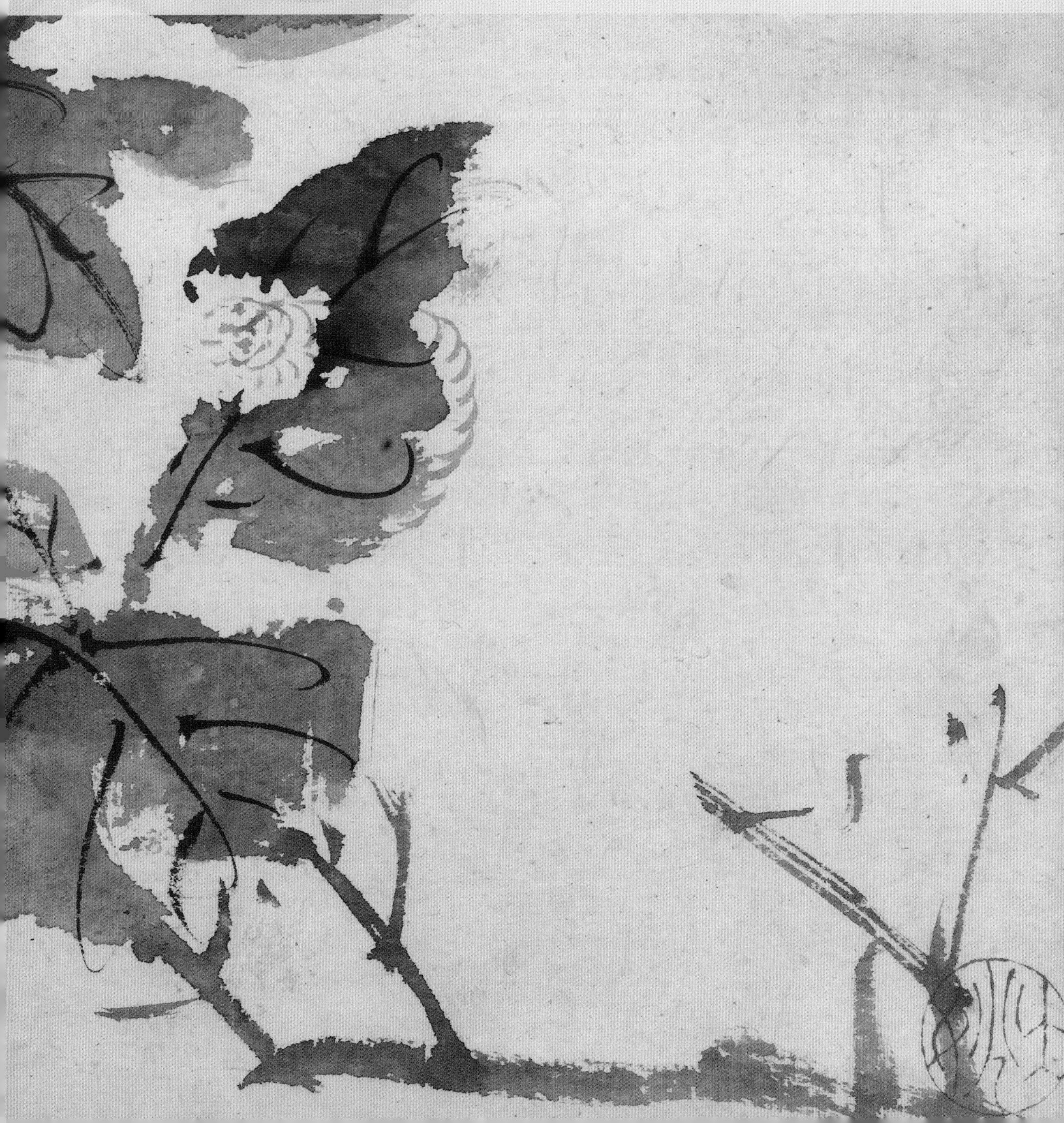

Bimo Is Not to Be Ignored

Bimo seems to be a term peculiar to traditional Chinese painting. There is nothing like it in western painting where the closest approximation is "brushwork" (*bichu*). In the works of the 20th century western modern abstract impressionist painter Willem de Kooning (1904–1997) for example, the brushwork is wild, coarse, even brutal in its pursuit of the flavor of primitive savagery. Vincent Van Gogh is another who excelled in a distinctive brushwork (fig. 120). However, *bimo* in traditional Chinese painting refers to more than just the results that appear in the painting itself. Behind the results there stands a whole range of specific content and value systems.

There are countless treatises on the study of *bimo* by the painters of ancient China, to the extent that they provide considerable evidence of a common view of the role of *bimo* in the development of traditional Chinese painting. This is particularly so of the Ming dynasty, where following the appearance of the theory of the "North and South Sects" promoted by the Ming painter and calligrapher Dong Qichang (1555–1636), the value systems expressed by *bimo* achieved a more clearly defined norm (fig. 121). Dong's

Pages 118–119

Fig. 119 *Album: Flowers* (detail)
Chen Chun
Ink on paper
Height 28 cm × Width 37.9 cm
Shanghai Museum

This work of Chen Chun's from life employs no artistic language, for example that of color or light and shade, other than *bimo*. Nevertheless, the wriggling of the silkworms on the mulberry leaves, the shape of the upper and lower surfaces, even the curls in the leaf are vividly and accurately displayed through the rise and fall and twists and turns of the brush and the presence or absence and strength or weakness of the ink. It reflects the fact that the skill of the artist's *bimo* has reached a point where the hand responds instinctively to the mind and where there is no constraint upon the exercise of either brush or ink.

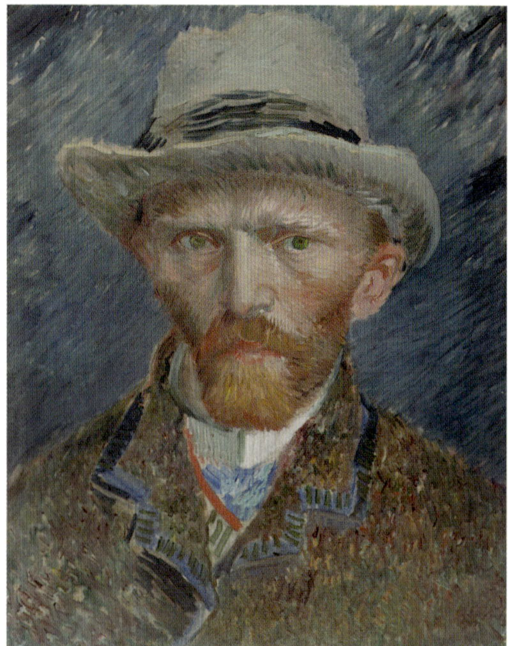

Fig. 120 *Self-Portrait*
Vincent Van Gogh
Oil on pasteboard
Height 42 cm × Width 34 cm
Rijksmuseum

There is *bichu* (brushwork) in western painting as well, as in the works of Van Gogh where the brushwork is characteristically rough and distinct. But the *bimo* of traditional Chinese painting is not just confined to what appears on the surface of the painting. Beyond ideas of how brush and ink are used there stands a whole range of specific content and value systems.

Fig. 121 *Album: Eight Views at the Height of Autumn* (detail)
Dong Qichang (Ming dynasty, 1555–1636)
Color on paper
Height 53.8 cm × Width 31.7 cm
Shanghai Museum

Dong Qichang was a well-known Ming calligrapher and painter. Courtesy name Xuan Zai, assumed names Si Bai, Si Weng, alias Xiang Guang. By the seventh year of Wanli (1589) he had achieved high office at court. In the sixth year of Tianqi (1626) he resigned and retired to his home in the countryside. He wrote extensively about painting and advocated the copying of ancient paintings. His influence on the development of later literati painting was considerable. He excelled in *shanshui* and was a pupil, at a distance, of Dong Yuan, Ju Ran, and Huang Gongwang. His style and sense of brushwork were gentle and relaxed and had a fresh grace.

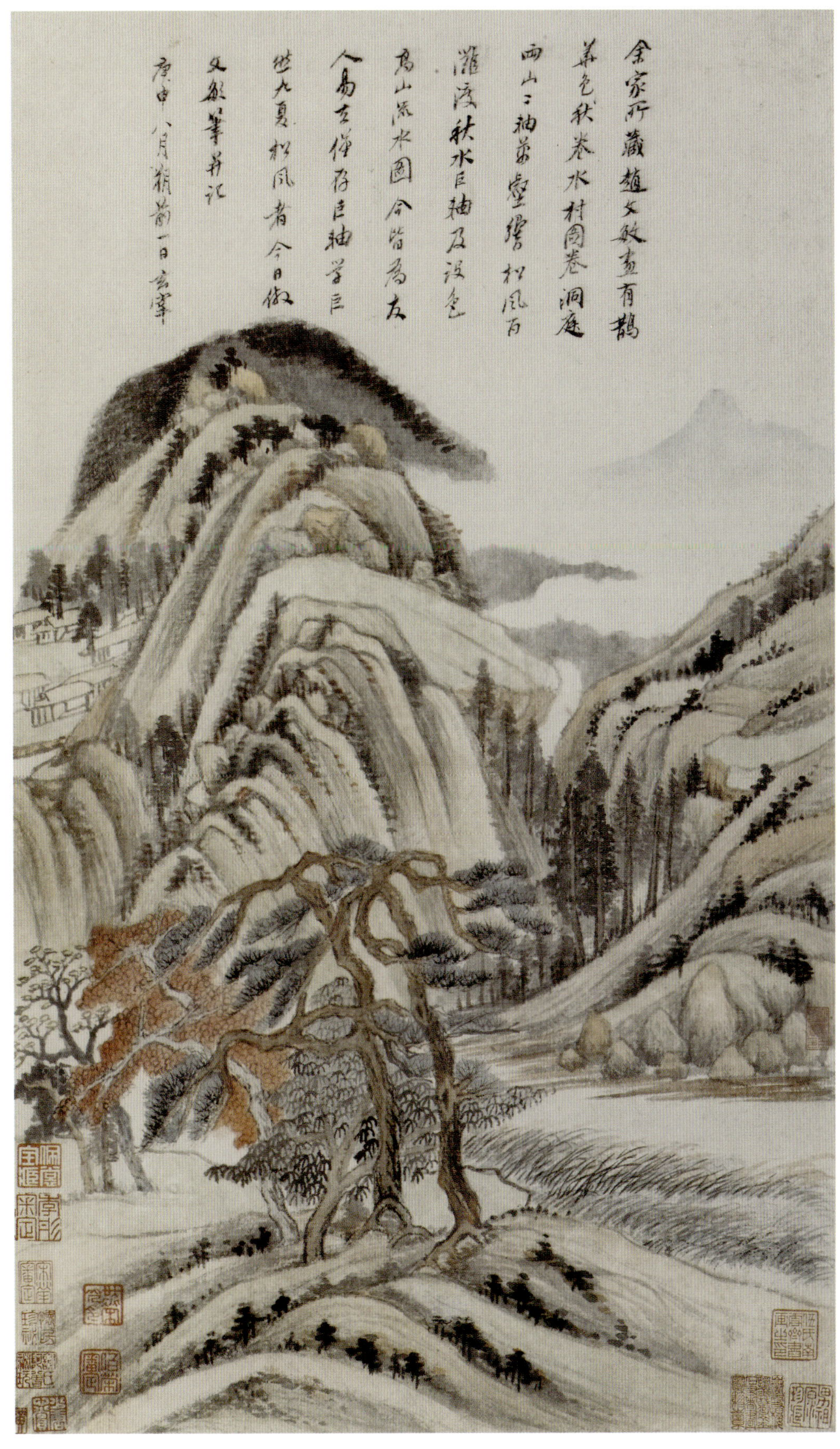

official position was that of Minister of the Board of Rites. He excelled in calligraphy and painting and had a decisive influence on the development of the later tradition of literati painting. He borrowed the Zen concept of Northern and Southern Schools or sects and divided the historical painters of *shanshui* into two traditions; the Northern, going back to the Northern Song with Li Cheng and Guo Xi at its head, and then traced back to the Southern Song Painting Academy, with the *shanshu* painters Ma Yuan and Xia Gui, and then on to the Ming court painters, like Dai Jin (1388–1462). At the head of the Southern School stand Dong Yuan and Ju Ran of the Five Dynasties and Northern Song dynasty followed by Mi Fu and the Four Yuan Masters. This is rather a rough division. There is none of the necessary transmission from teacher to pupil but it does cleverly and antithetically juxtapose court painters with literati painters. Since the motivation of literati painters lay in their own pleasure and the expression of their inner emotions, the focus was not upon the depiction of form but upon abstract values in the use of brush and ink. Dong Qichang said: "If considering the curiosity of scenery, then *shanshui* do not represent real hills and water; if considering the delicacy of *bimo*, then real hills and water do not resemble *shanshui*." This formulation elevates *bimo* to the highest of the values held by the literati painters and is an essential element in the appreciation of traditional painting.

There may be readers who consider that the reason for the importance with which *bimo* is regarded in traditional Chinese painting is that ink is more used in Chinese art and color more used in western art. This is an assumption, *bimo* applies just as much to the use of color in traditional Chinese painting as to ink.

Failure to understand the importance of *bimo* to Chinese painting compared with western painting is to ignore the distinctly different characteristics of the media used in each, particularly the difference between the brush and fine paper used in Chinese painting and the paintbrush and canvas of western art. There is an accepted view of how the literati painters used their brushes and how they applied their ink before it could be considered "good *bimo*." This view gradually became part of the content of *bimo* itself, brushwork is merely a link in the chain that goes to make up *bimo* and not even the most important link.

There are two levels to the *bimo* of traditional Chinese painting. First is technical skill in the use of brush and ink, followed by the intrinsic expressionism and set of values that *bimo* is capable of displaying. All this amounts to the commonly held view of the manifestations of *bimo* accumulated over the centuries and referred to above.

To take technical skill first, in whatever era, at home or abroad, an artist must have a proper command of the media that he employs, such as oil, watercolor or ink. However, the skills involved in the use of the paper, brush and ink employed in Chinese painting have particular characteristics of their own and differ very considerably from the skills involved in the generality of western paintings. If we remain blind to these esoterica it becomes difficult to understand the subtleties of the technical demands involved in Chinese painting.

In terms of what constitutes *bimo*, ever since the time of Gu Kaizhi in the Jin dynasty, the artists of ancient China had been involved in never-ending discussions of how to use brush and ink. As time progressed the discussions multiplied so that the theories, values and views, even prejudices involved could have formed a history of Chinese painting on their own. Consequently, *bimo* became the indispensable focal point of any discussion or appreciation of traditional Chinese painting. Let us now take a look at the subtleties of technical skill, the first level of *bimo*.

The Structure of the Chinese Brush

An understanding of the Chinese brush is integral to any discussion of the technical skills of *bimo*. The Chinese brush is a superb instrument for calligraphy and painting. The western paintbrush is generally flat-headed with stiff, short bristles. Consequently the western artist uses a number of brushes of different sizes and with heads of different lengths. Moreover, there tends to be very little variation in the brushstrokes produced by any particular brush. Compared with the western paintbrush, the variety of brushstrokes of which the Chinese brush is capable comes as a pleasant surprise.

In the 80s, the author studied painting with Yang Shanshen (1913–2004), a master of the Lingnan School. Master Yang possessed a much-loved Japanese brush made from horsehair, which, after years of use had almost completely lost its hair. Master Yang liked using this brush to paint pine trees. Under his direction and as if by magic and to the wonder of the viewer, rough cast pine trunks, large pieces of fallen dried bark, solid branches and even sharp young pine needles appeared one by one as the worn old brush travelled across the surface of the painting. Master Yang often said that as long as you had the ability to control the brush in your hand you could produce whatever brushstroke you wanted, the brush was your emissary in the creation of the myriad phenomena of the world.

The secret of the ability of the brush used for Chinese calligraphy and painting to produce such rich results lies in its construction. The head of a Chinese brush is not flat but is a reversed cone where the bottom fits into the round brush handle and the brush gradually tapers towards the tip where it ends in a small point. The head of a Chinese brush is generally two to three centimeters long, though there are brushes with a length of seven to eight centimeters, much longer than the head of a western brush. Brushes are usually made from a very soft goat's hair known as *yanghao*. There are also brushes made from the stiffer wolf's hair (*langhao*) and the horsehair (*shanma*) as well as the mixed hair (*jianhao*) brush made from both hard and soft hair.

The conic shape and softness of the Chinese brush lend it a dynamism of its own. With the brush we can paint a dot as small as a speck of dust or as large as the shape of, say, the base of a bun. In the first case we just lightly use the tip of the brush and it's done. In the second we use the whole of the brush pressed down towards the shaft and what appears is not a dot but a large ink blot.

We can imagine that from the tip to its bottom, the same brush is, in the hands of a painter, capable of an infinity of change according to how much it is raised or lowered; and that the slightest difference in the strength and speed with which it is raised or lowered will result in subtle changes that cannot be fudged or concealed. Nowadays most people no longer use a brush and this kind of experience is gradually disappearing so that the special characteristics of the brush are generally overlooked.

The fact that a single brush can produce such a permutation of changes of brushwork demonstrates that the Chinese brush is a painting tool of extraordinary plasticity and sensitivity. A painter only has to make the slightest adjustment in the height of the brush to produce a change in the nature of the brushwork and to display a different *bimo*. Imagine that we have a brush in our hand and that, without any training we are asked to draw a straight line four inches long, what would the result from our brush look like? It is easy to imagine that we would first discover that the thickness of our line was uneven and that even if it did not wriggle like an earthworm, our line would not be straight.

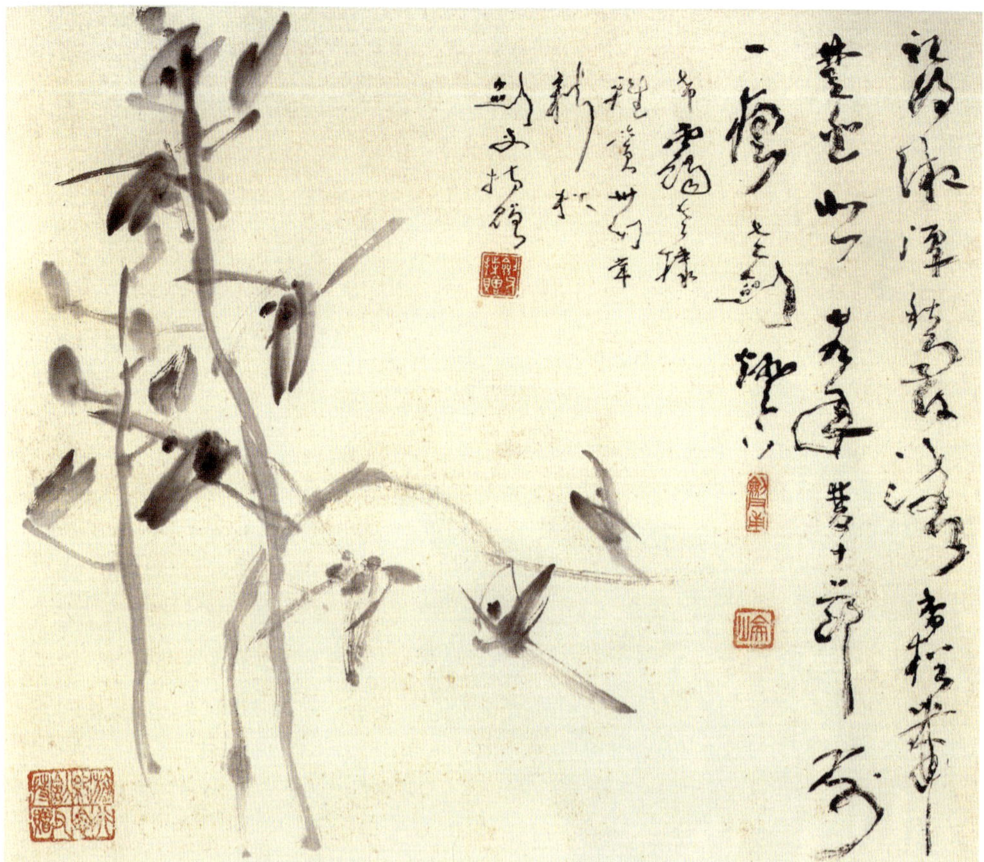

Fig. 122 *Ink Orchid*
Gao Jianfu (1879–1951)
Ink on silk
Height 38 cm × Width 44 cm
Collection of the Yicui Shantang

Gao Jianfu was a 20th century master of the Lingnan School. The focus of the appreciation of this painting is entirely upon its employment of *bimo*, on how the line in the painting displays the rise and fall, turns and pauses of the brush as well as the changes in the ink from dry to damp to thick to weak.

We would also discover that the degree of ink of the line always differed between the point at which the brush was applied to the paper and its end.

It is not difficult to explain why this should be so. Differences in the thickness of the line arise from an unevenness in the strength with which the brush is controlled. However light it may be, any involuntary lateral or vertical movement of the brush will immediately produce an unevenness and crookedness in the line. Changes in ink shade derive from the fact that at the start the tip of the brush is loaded with ink and will produce brushwork that is dark, lustrous, and damp. By the end, as the ink in the brush is used up, the brushwork will appear dry and exhausted and the line will be utterly different in degree of color and feeling from that at the beginning. That is to say, any change in the shade of color or degree of saturation in the brush will influence the degree of color and balance of dry and wet in the line that the brush produces.

Experience has once again shown that the Chinese brush is an exceptionally sensitive painting (and writing) instrument. The proper use of the brush demands a degree of accuracy in its control, the slightest shift in the vertical and lateral planes or pause in the movement of the brush will be reflected immediately in the line that it produces (fig. 122). Consequently, the artist who wishes to express the brushwork that is in his mind, requires total control of the brush, a basic requirement in the skills of using a brush.

The Technique of Driving a Brush

The calligraphers of ancient China frequently said: "Man should use the brush and not the brush the man," meaning that if the calligrapher lacked the ability to drive the brush, it would take over and he would be unable to direct it and to express what was in his mind, a real case of "strength not following the mind." The brush used in Chinese painting is related to that used in calligraphy but in comparison is far superior, since calligraphy is a monochrome art but painting is multi-colored.

The ancient literati painters preferred ink to color, so that the brush is associated with the use of ink. When different amounts of water are added to the ink it will produce an infinity of different gradations of color, from light grey to jet-black. Thus, to create a painting the traditional artist required an understanding of the use of ink as well as skill in handling the brush. The skill of *bimo* is the skill of driving the brush and of using ink. This requires lengthy practice and long training. Thus, the historical masters of *bimo* expended the energy of a lifetime before they reached the state where hand instinctively responded to mind and they could use brush and ink without constraint (fig. 119 on pages 118 and 119).

In a painting, the information that a painter can convey basically divides into two: "description of the concrete image" and "expression of the abstract image." For example, if the picture is of a flower, its form and color and luster all belong to the former; whilst the flavor it emits, such as lightness of petals and remote fragrance belong to the latter. There are, of course, ways of painting that have completely broken away from a description of the concrete, for example, the abstract paintings of the modern western formalist masters Mondrian (1872–1944) and Kandinsky (1866–1944) (fig. 123) who have attempted to escape the confines of any concrete thinking in pursuit of the expression of the pure abstract.

Any description of the concrete relies

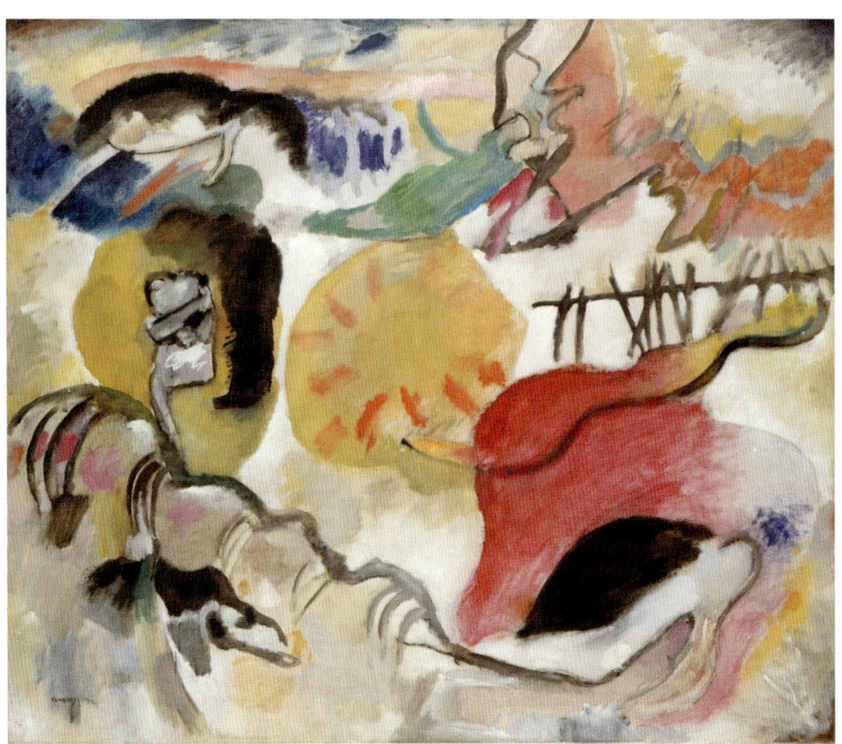

Fig. 123 *Improvisation 27 (Garden of Love II)*
Wassily Wassilyevich Kandinsky
Oil on canvas
Height 120.3 cm × Width 140. 3 cm
The Metropolitan Museum of Art, New York

The Modernist paintings of the west include a number of pure abstracts by such well known figures as Mondrian and Kandinsky.

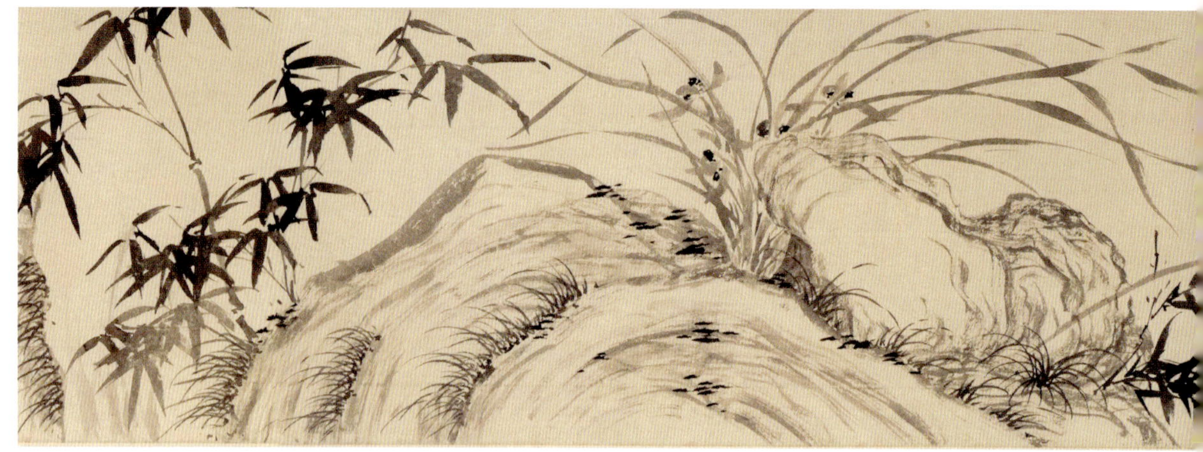

Fig. 124 *Orchid and Bamboo* (detail)

Wen Zhengming
Ink on paper
Height 26.8 cm × Width 730 cm
Palace Museum, Beijing

In traditional Chinese painting, good *bimo* expresses not only the external form of the subject, it includes the abstract state of objects as well. As, for example, the way the orchids in this painting sway in the wind, the dancing of the flowers, and even the quality of soft resilience in the way the twigs of bamboo support their leaves.

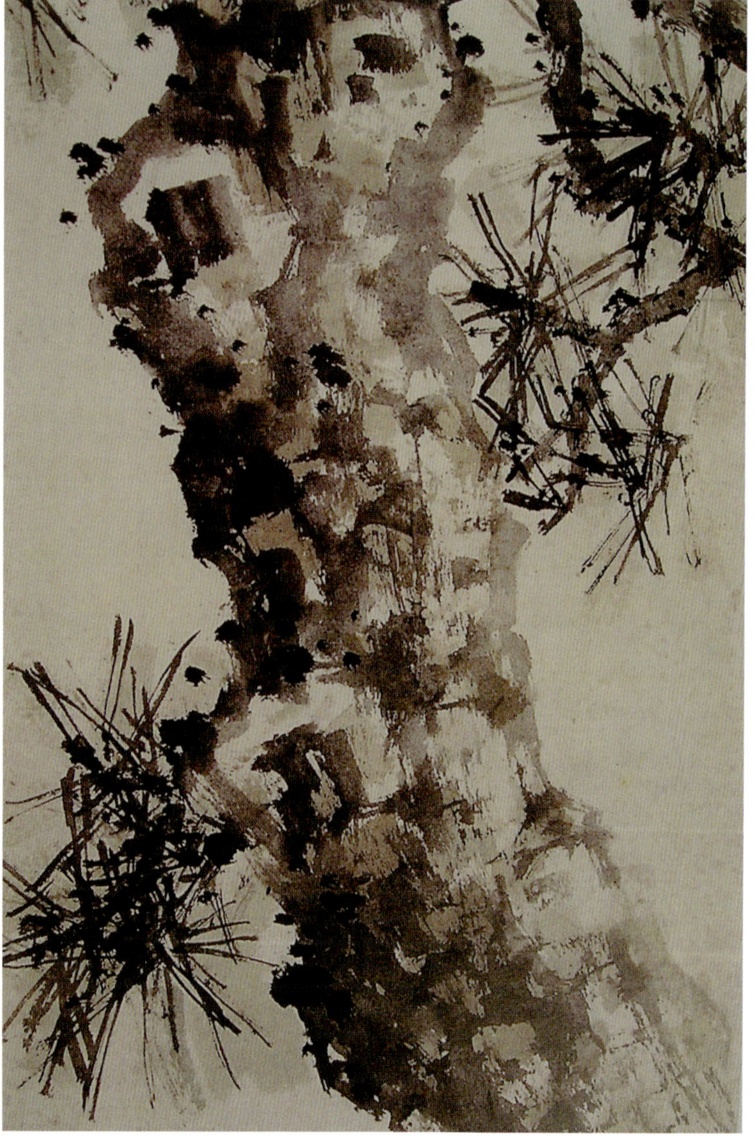

Fig. 125 *Ancient Pine* (detail)

Gao Jianfu
Color on paper
Height 131 cm × Width 57 cm
Hong Kong Chinese University

This painting relies solely on the ability of *bimo* to faithfully display both the form and quality of the trunk and needles of the pine.

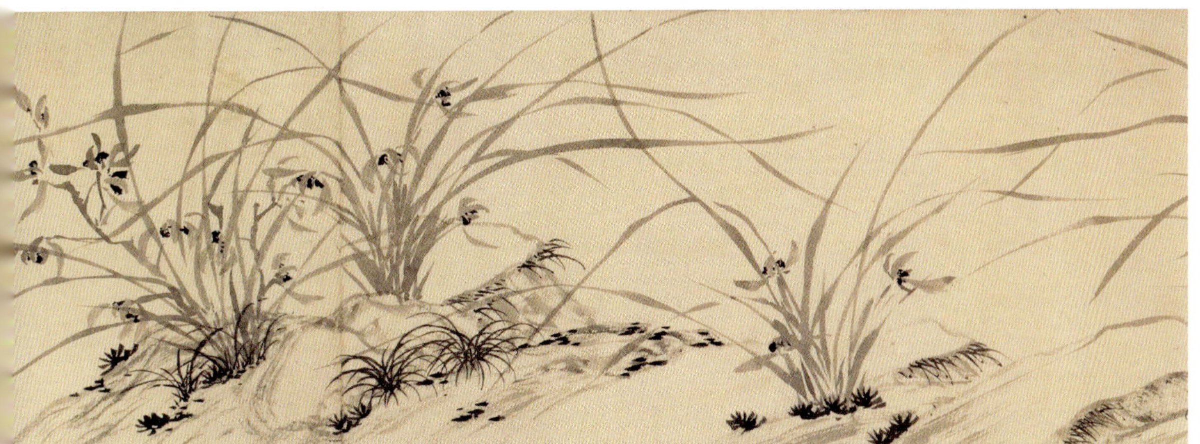

upon the scientific observation of an object by the artist in order to portray its form. On this point, both western and Chinese artists do not differ. In painting a flower, for example, the shape of the flower and the posture of growth both have to be delineated. But there is a very great difference between Chinese and western artists in the expression of abstract qualities, such as the lightness and softness of petals.

Western artists excel in the handling of light and shade and the adjustment of color to reflect the tender texture of petals; by contrast the traditional Chinese artist relies upon the twists and turns and changes in pressure of one or two brushstrokes to capture the soft pliability of the petals (fig. 124). The process by which Yang Shanshen (above) painted pines is also a very good example. Relying only on brush and ink, Master Yang could express the different textures of every part of a pine tree, rather like Gao Jianfu's *Ancient Pine* of 1930 (fig. 125). This demonstrates that the brush and ink of Chinese painting can, at the same time, fulfil the functions of expressing both the concrete and the abstract.

Let us now take another example to explain the function of *bimo* in expressing the abstract. An artist trained in the use of brush and ink can use a brush to draw two lines of similar thickness and length to represent objects of two totally different textures. One line may be a willow wand and the other a narrow strip of iron. Although both lines may appear to differ little in form, a skilled *bimo* technique can represent both the suppleness of the willow and the hardness of the iron distinctly and unequivocally, so that the viewer will instantly distinguish which is the willow and which is the iron. It is this that is the trick of *bimo*.

Beyond the ability to express the abstract texture of an object, the *bimo* of Chinese painting can also express the purely abstract such as mass, lightness, beauty, grandeur, density and boldness. This may be explained by way of traditional calligraphy. Generally speaking, different styles of calligraphy have different requirements in terms of brush technique and rhythm and consequently give rise to different artistic outcomes. For example, the technique required by seal script (*zhuanshu*) is at heart ponderous and seeks the artistic expression of a massive heaviness; the emphasis of cursive script (*caoshu*) is on the expression of inner feelings and as the brush moves the rise and fall of emotion is transmuted into the ebb and flow of *bimo*. Wild cursive script (*kuangcao*) can even have a touch of an uneven gallop about it. Thus, cursive script seeks to express a sense of free-floating agility. Calligraphers differ in personal character and this lends their use of brush and ink individual habits and characteristics, so that the same script in the hand of a different calligrapher will produce a completely different feeling, for example the elegance of Zhao Mengfu's semi-cursive script (*xingshu*) but the boldness of Huang Tingjian's (1045–1105) (figs. 126–127 on next page).

Fig. 126 *Scroll: Treatise*

Huai Su (Tang dynasty, 737–799)
Cursive script
Ink on paper
Height 38.5 cm × Width 40 cm
Liaoning Provincial Museum

Fig. 127 *Scroll: Thousand Character Classic*

Zhao Ji
Cursive script
Ink on paper
Height 31.5 cm × Width 1172.1 cm
Liaoning Provincial Museum

Figs. 126–127 Traditional calligraphy is the art of line. Different calligraphers have different temperaments and different habits and characteristics in their use of brush and ink. Different calligraphers writing the same cursive script will give a completely different feeling.

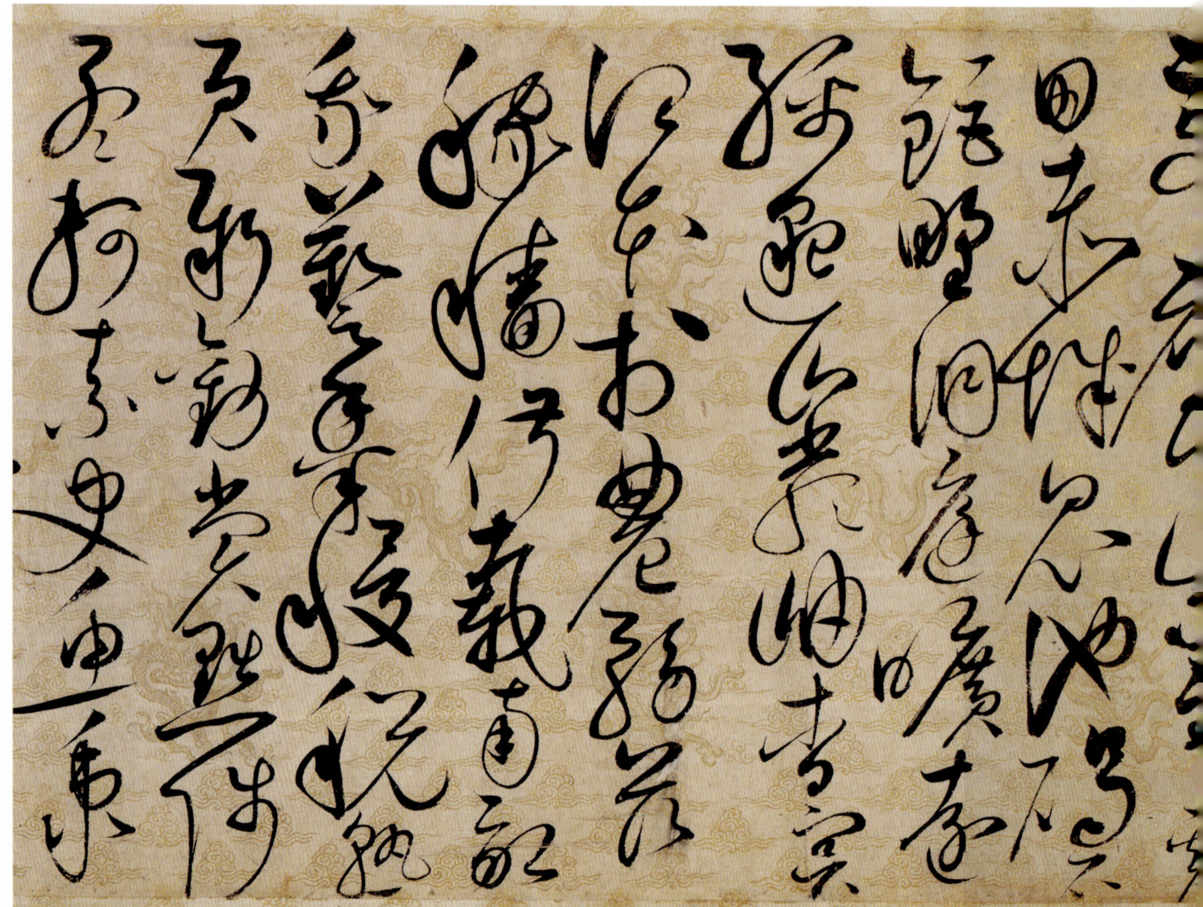

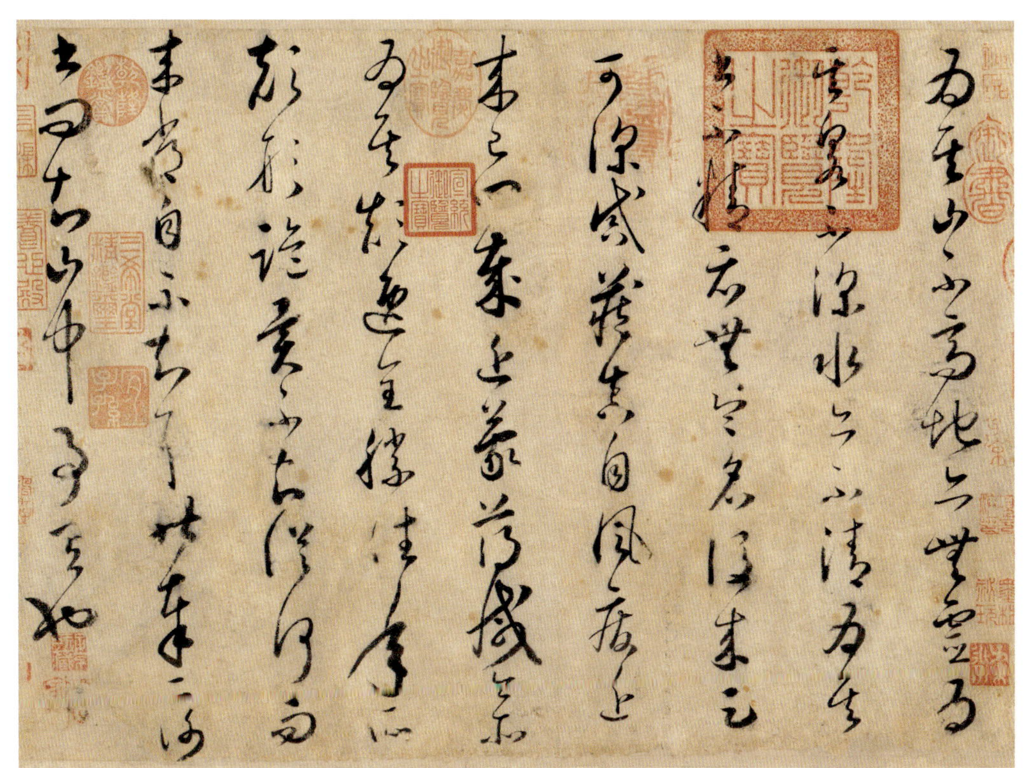

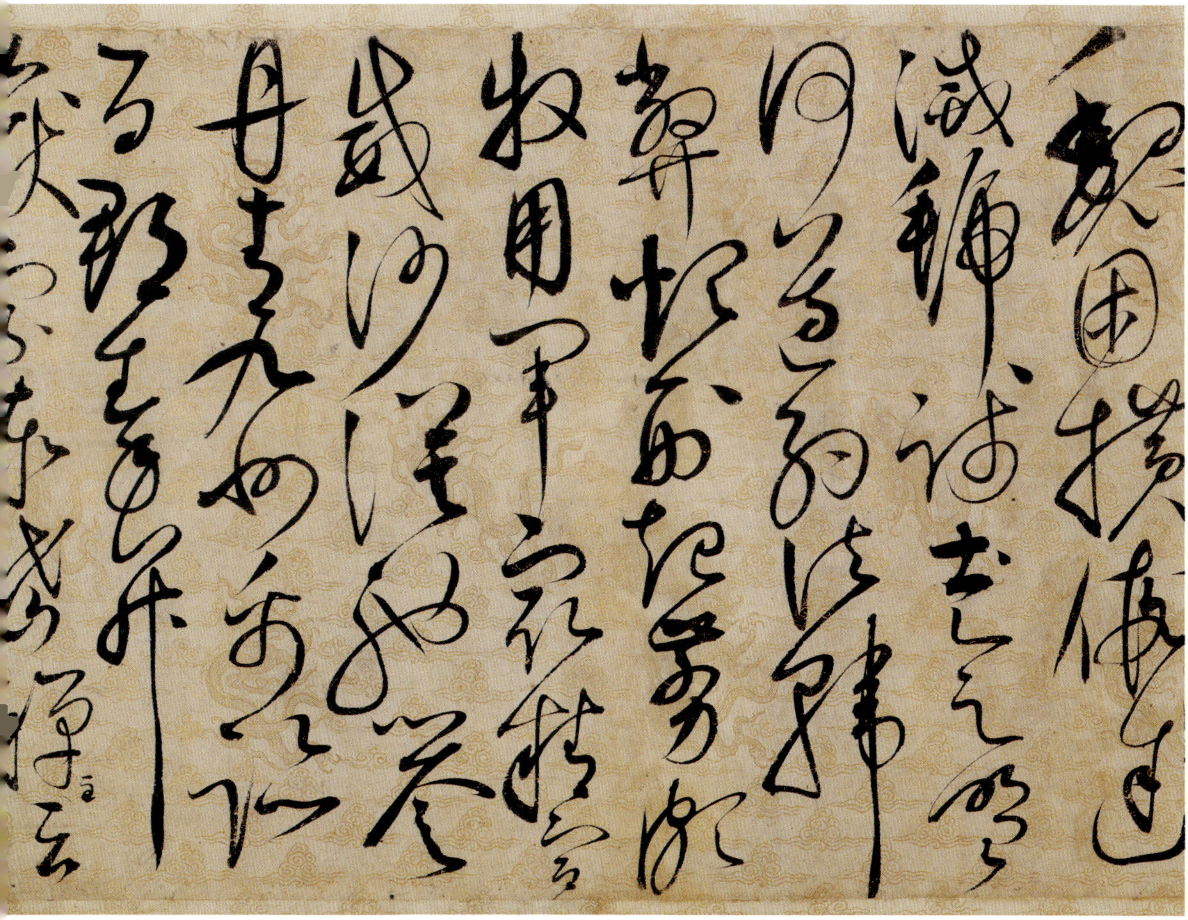

Expressing the Innermost Feelings of the Artist through Abstract *Bimo*

Although the historical discussions of Chinese painters on the topic of *bimo* could fill a volume of a history of Chinese painting, limitations of space in this book only allow a simple summary of some of the basic concepts involved in its techniques and values as a basis for discussion and appreciation, including the use of the brush and of ink.

The painters and calligraphers of ancient China discovered very early on the rich abstractions of the *bimo* idiom. Thus, the literati painter strove to achieve the flavor and expression of the abstract that *bimo* could convey. It would be fair to say that, in fact, the objects in the paintings that flowed from the brush of the literati painter were all a kind of vehicle. What the abstract *bimo* presented was not the external material world but the perfected internal world of the painter, so that it was *bimo* itself that was the painter's subject. To take Bada Shanren as an example, whether he painted fish, or flowers, or *shanshui*, the subjects may have been different but they were infused with the same *bimo* throughout and expressed his own internal world and artistic values (fig. 128).

In Europe, artists regarded painting as a form of self-expression, though this aspiration did not find its full flowering until the Romantic Movement of the 18th century. With the paintings of Goya (1746–1828) and Turner (1775–1851) western art gradually turned from the description of the concrete to the expression of the abstract, right up until the beginning of the 20th century and the emergence of the purely abstract modern art (fig. 129). In fact, in China, an aspiration towards the abstract had been one of the artistic principles of literati painters ever since the Song dynasty. The Yuan dynasty literati painter Ni Zan explained his motivation for painting as follows: "My so-called paintings are merely the careless strokes of an idle brush, they do not seek likeness and are for my own pleasure." This simple, direct statement suggests that Ni did not aspire towards the creation of likeness but towards the internal expression of an individual, and

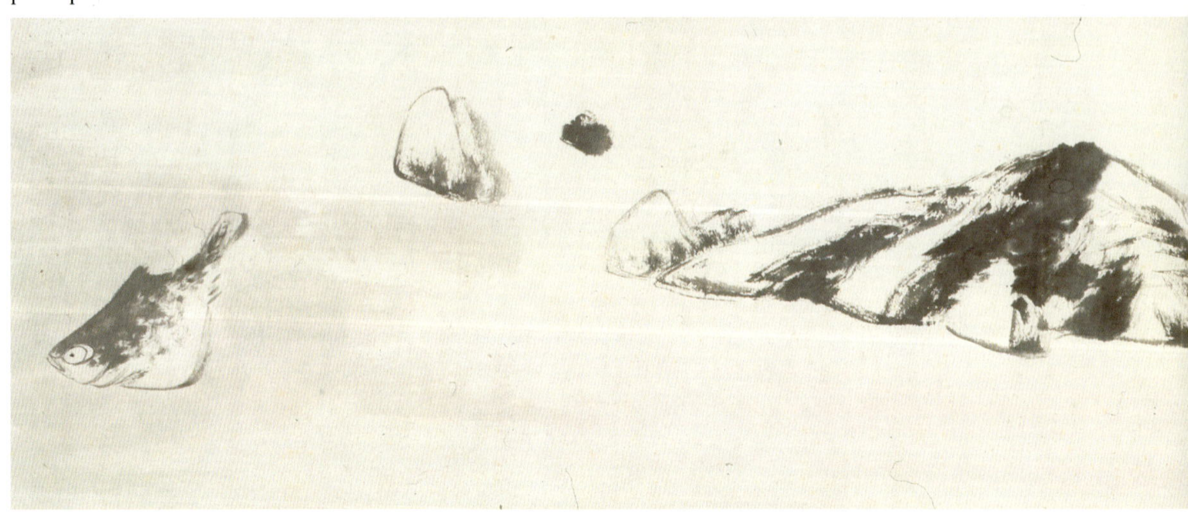

Fig. 128 *Fish with Ducks* (detail)
Bada Shanren
Ink on paper
Height 23.2 cm × Width 569.5 cm
Shanghai Museum

For Bada Shanren, the function of painting was to express his internal world and beliefs. His fish, flowers and *shanshui*, though they may have different subjects, were suffused with a *bimo* throughout that gave expression to a stubborn resolve to uphold his principles.

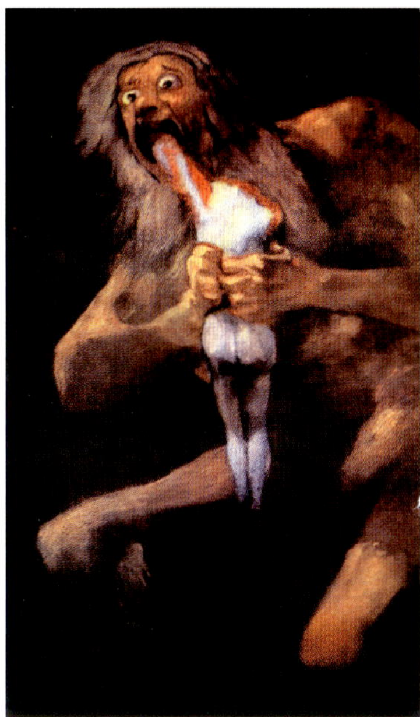

Fig. 129 *Saturn Devouring His Son*
Francisco Goya
Oil on canvas
Height 146 cm × Width 83 cm
Prado Museum, Madrid

In late life Goya lived by himself in a two story house and before his death painted a number of paintings (the so-called "black paintings") where the subject matter seemed deranged and the images weird. They reflected his despair at life and his disturbed mental state.

that the abstract values of *bimo* were both the vehicle for the internal expression of the literati painters and their true creative aspiration.

Based on their pursuit of the artistic goal of the abstract, modernist western painters of the early 20th century promoted Formalism, where the creative focus shifted from the content of the subject to the terminology of art, such as line, color and space. In "art for art's sake" the responsibility of the artist lay not in an expression of the external world but in the internal values of artistic form, the abstract value of form itself. For example, the blaze of red or the flexibility of a curve. We said earlier that *bimo* was a rich abstract idiom, we can thus regard the aspirations of the literati painters of ancient China towards a pure *bimo* as the pursuit of a kind of formalism.

After over a thousand years of discussion and practice that took place throughout the history of Chinese painting, the ancient painters and calligraphers established a broad common understanding of *bimo* as a painting form. When these painters came to choose their methods of using brush and ink, their choice was not only based on purely individual preference but also on the common understanding of the use of brush and ink and its values that had obtained in the past. If, in our enjoyment of traditional painting, we can grasp the common understanding of the theories of *bimo* reached by the ancients, we shall deepen our own perception of *bimo* as a painting form.

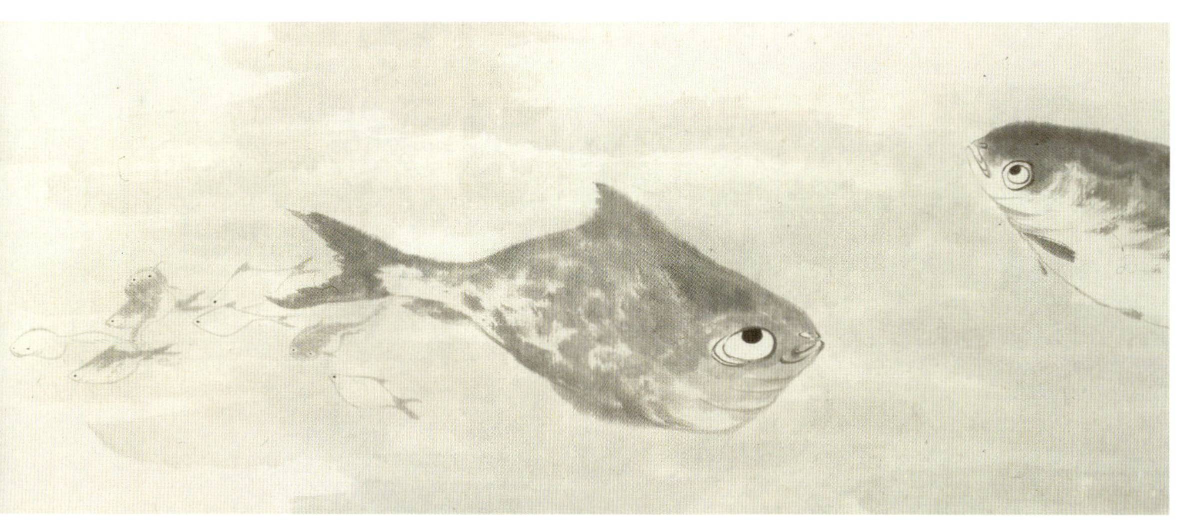

Using the Brush with Precision

There are two aspects to the use of the brush, holding it (*zhibi*) and moving it (*xingbi*). Holding refers to the way in which the hand grips the shaft of the brush when painting. There are basically two ways of doing this, the so-called upright position (*zhongfeng*) and the angled position (*cefeng*). In the upright position the artist holds the brush vertically so that the shaft is at an angle of 90° to the paper, that is to say, during the process of writing or painting the tip of the brush maintains a central position so that the dots (*dian*) and lines produced in writing or painting give a sensation of "roundness." This is because the brush is round and if the tip is kept in the dead center, its horizontal cross-section will be circular and the dot produced by the tip will naturally be round. Where line is concerned, because the tip of the brush is centralized, pressure is applied equally to both left and right and produces a line which appears perfectly round.

In the angled position the artist holds the brush at a slight angle so that the shaft of the brush is at a slight slope to the surface of the painting. Because the angle between the shaft of the brush and the surface of the paper is not 90°, that is to say, when writing or painting the brush tip is not centered at the point of contact with the paper, the cross-section will not be circular and the dot will appear as an oval. Again, where line is concerned, since the tip of the brush is offset from the center of the shaft and the pressure unequal as between left and right, heavy at the tip but light at the point where the shaft lifts, the line gives an appearance of "sharpness."

Moving the brush, refers to the speed of painting and writing. Slowness of speed means that the brush is in contact with the paper for a relatively long time and the resulting brushwork will appear heavy; on the other hand, a relatively fast movement of the brush will mean less contact with the paper and a lighter feeling to the resulting brushwork. Where the speed of movement is too fast and the brush seems to slide across the paper, the brushwork will sometimes appear to be absolutely weightless and give a "floating" feeling.

There is a further important consideration in the use of the brush in Chinese painting and calligraphy, something called "strength of brush" (*bili*). This is inherent in how the brush is applied and the application of the brush is always related to one's breathing. I once studied with the Hong Kong calligrapher Zeng Rongguang. Watching Master Zeng execute a piece of calligraphy was like watching him practice *qigong*. He

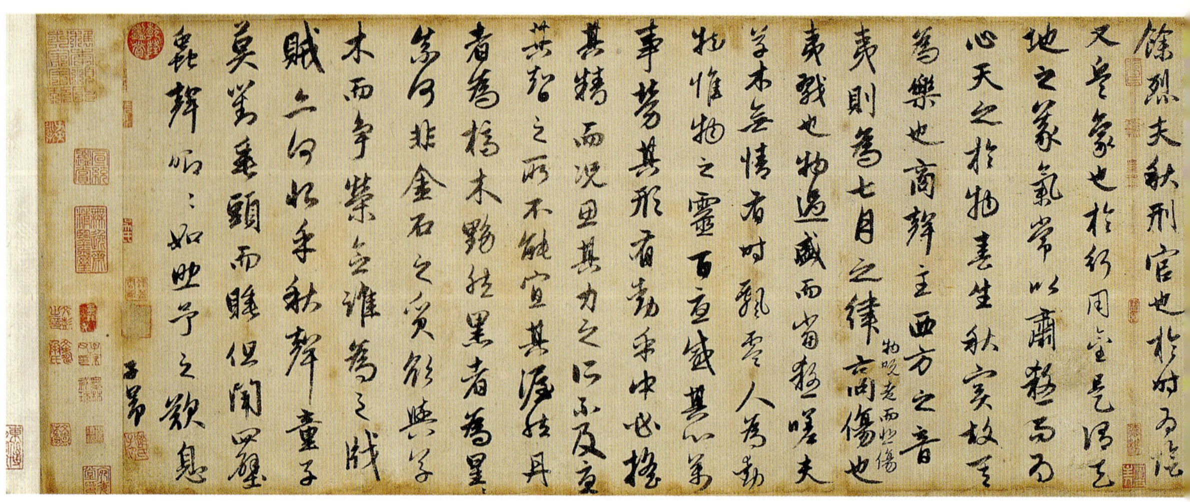

Fig. 130 *Album: The Enveloping Scent of Flowers*

Huang Tingjian (Northern Song dynasty, 1045–1105)
Semi-cursive script
In on paper
Height 30.7 cm × Width 43.2 cm
Palace Museum, Taibei

The slowness of the brush, the weight with which is applied, its direction and the way it turns, all influence the overall feeling of a piece of calligraphy, for example, its strength or boldness.

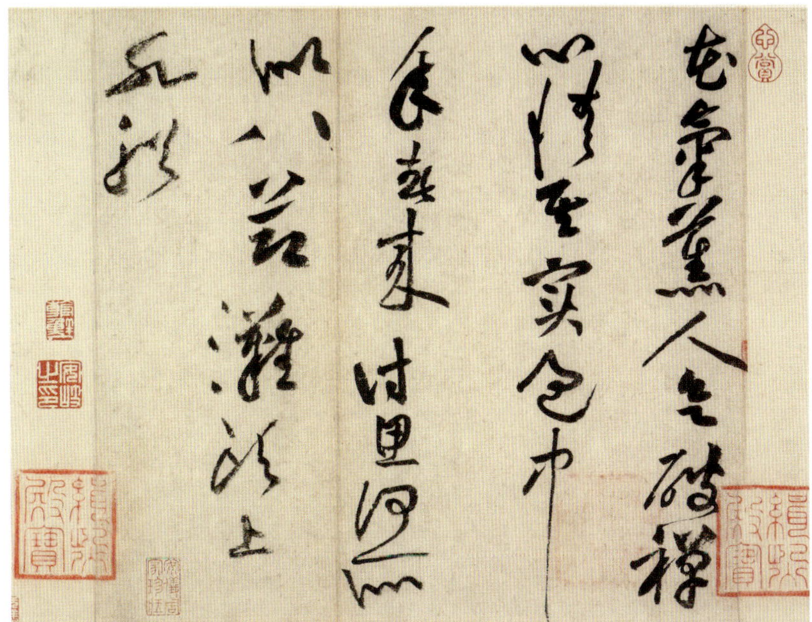

would first look at the whole piece and once he had gathered his mind, would lift his brush and write right through in a single breath. Although his brush paused between characters and between lines, he did not relax his concentration from start to finish and he only let out his breath after he had completed the final character. "Strength of brush" encapsulates the way in which the breath reaches the tip of the brush from the depths of the mind and is then transmitted to the paper. Viewing the work of masters with a powerful strength of brush, one can feel how the strength has penetrated the very paper on which it is written(figs. 130–131).

Fig. 131 *Handscroll: The Sound of Autumn by Ouyang Xiu*

Zhao Mengfu
Semi-cursive script
Ink on paper
Height 34.8 cm ×Width 182.2 cm
Liaoning Provincial Museum

The appreciation of traditional calligraphy lies in the acquisition of a sense of the rising and falling relationship that exists between brushstroke and brushstroke, between character and character and between line and line. This results in the relative density of composition of a whole piece of calligraphy which is then expressed in a single breath or *qi* that infuses it all.

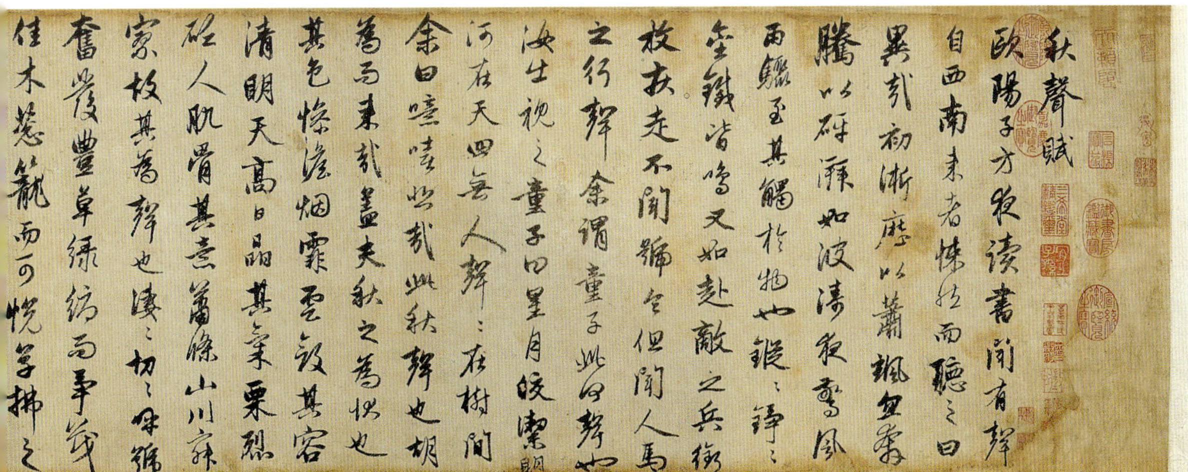

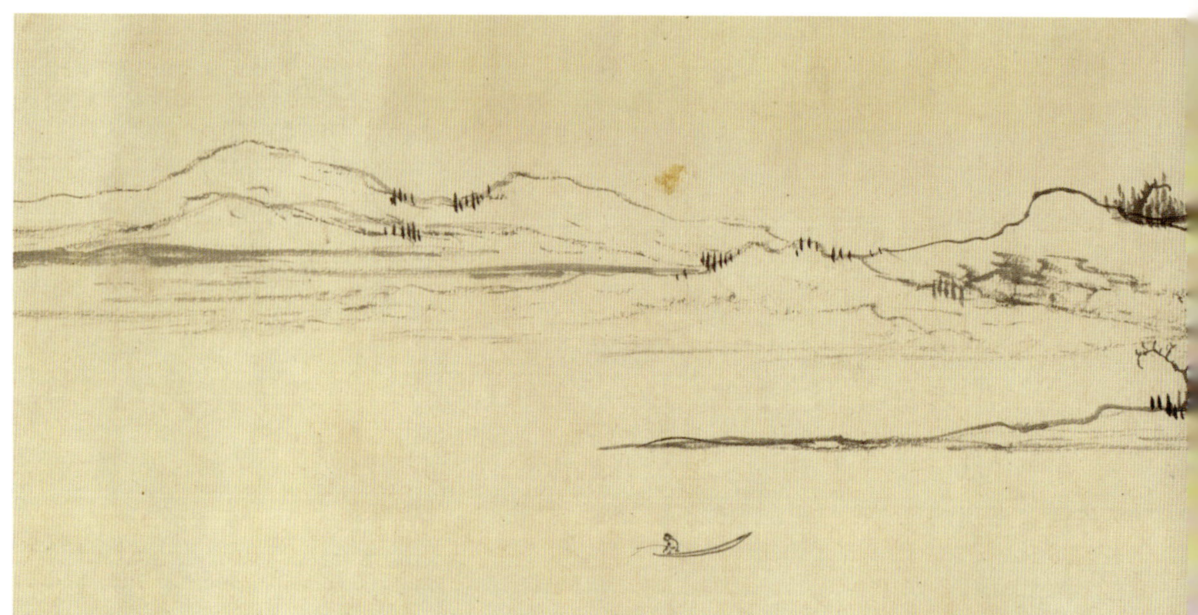

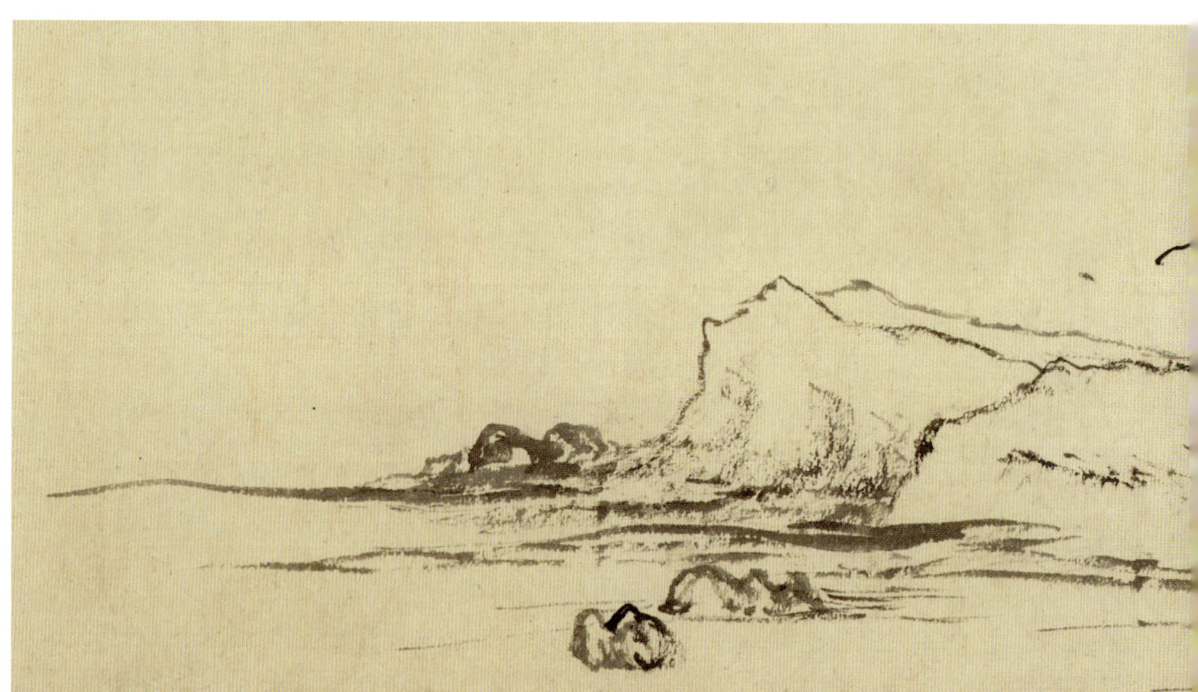

Figs. 132–133 *Two Pines in Level Perspective* (detail)
Please refer to fig. 4 on pages 6 and 7.

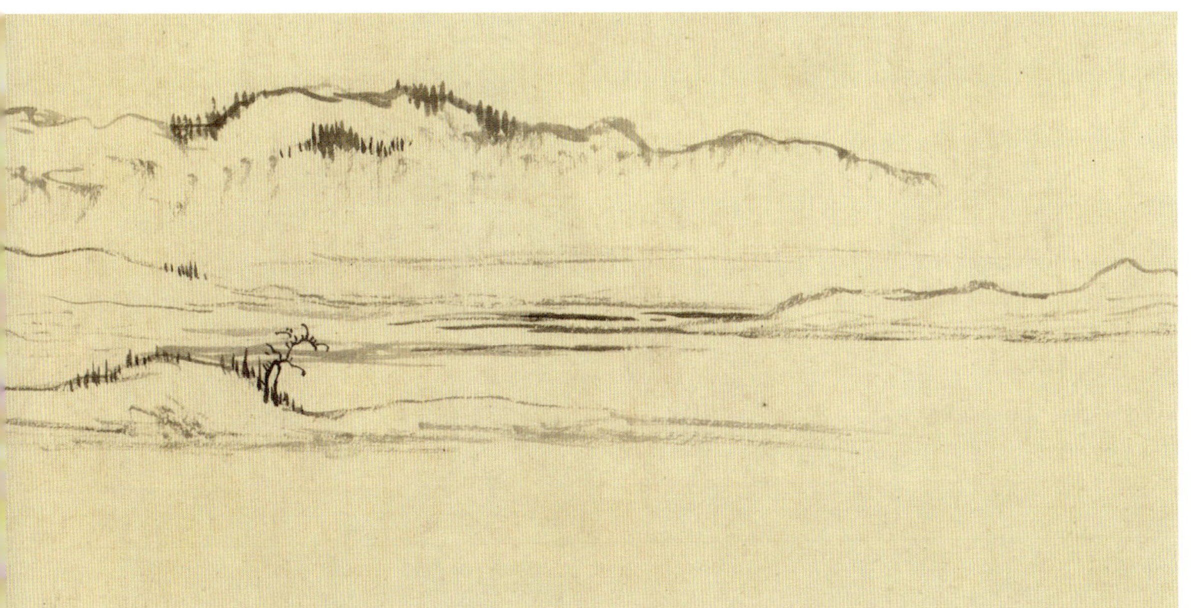

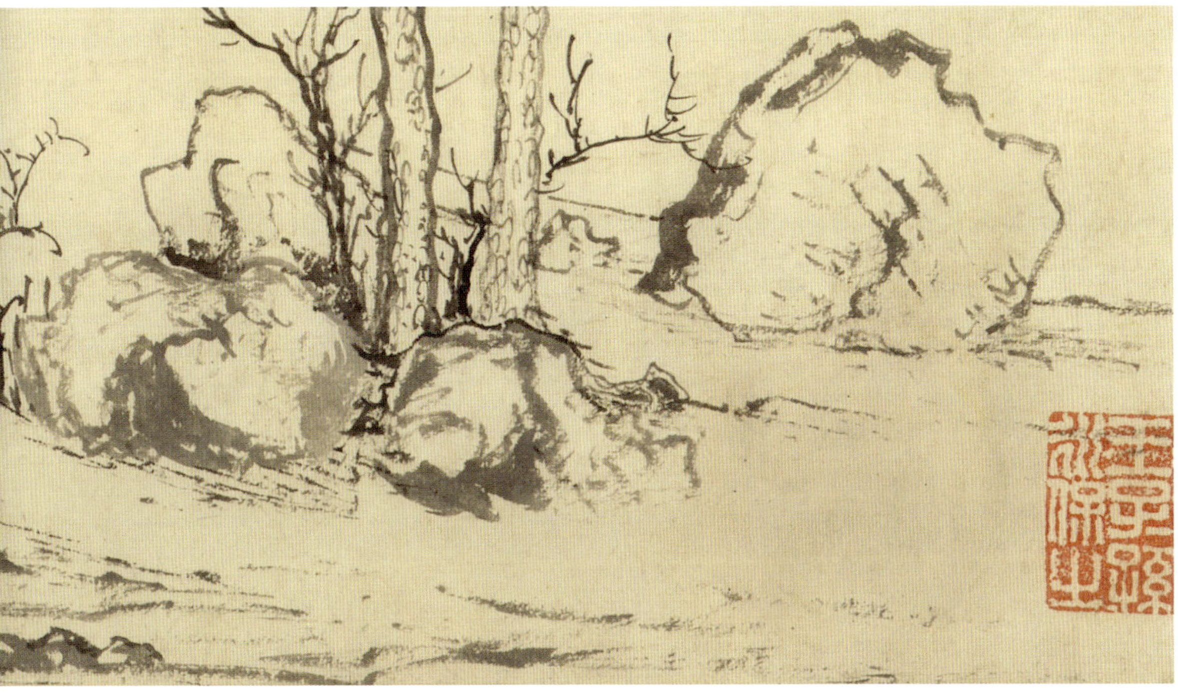

The term *qiyun* is referred to frequently in China's ancient treatises on painting and calligraphy. Both *qi* and *yun* are abstracts. The historical theorists of painting and calligraphy contain numerous interpretations of *qiyun*, both ancient and modern, and though we could grandly cite Daoist and other theories to describe it, in simple terms *qi* (vital energy) is expressed through the use of the brush. Just as in the description of the use of breath in the previous passage, *qi* is the expression of a kind of strength, a continuous rhythm where, if "the brush stops and the energy does not," it will seem as if there is ink in places in the painting where there is none, so that a rising and falling fluid strength extends throughout it. So much for *qi*. References to *yun* in ancient treatises mostly related to the use of ink. A discussion of the use of ink and then of *yun* follows below (figs. 132–133).

Using the Brush Freely

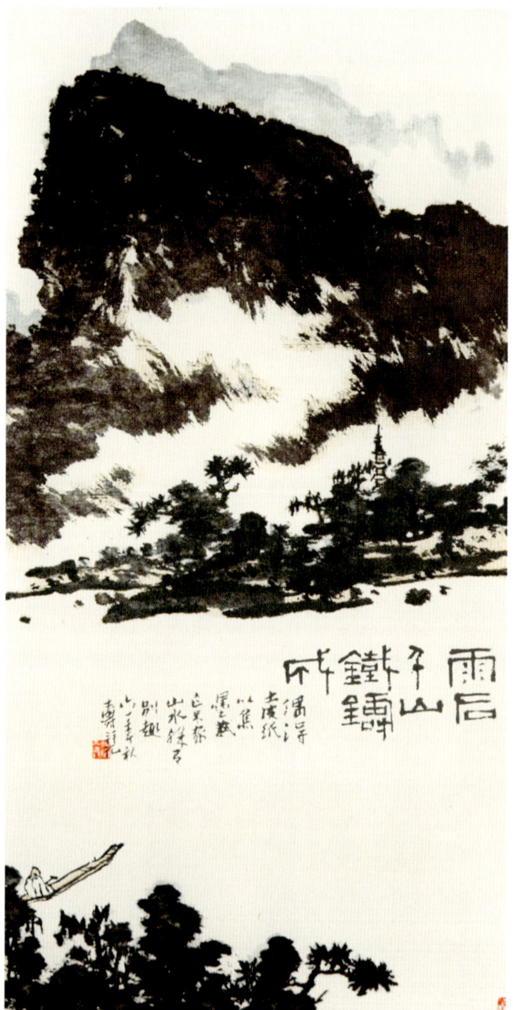

Fig. 134 *Mountains Moulded in Iron after Rain*
Pan Tianshou (1897–1971)
Color on paper
Height 89.9 cm × Width 45.9 cm
China Fine Art Gallery

Chinese artists often prefer ink over color. In fact, changes in how ink was used were no less than in the use of varieties of color. Ink used well displayed more than just a dull, dead patch of ink, it produced a sensation of breath flowing within ink that was as black as lacquer. For example, the lacquer black of the mountains in this painting has both weight and texture and the trees have direction and density.

The painters of ancient China used ink rather than color. In fact, changes in how ink was used were no less than those in the varieties of color. As early as the Qin (221–206 BC), Han, Wei (220–265), Jin and Northern and Southern Dynasties (420–589) the ancient ink makers understood how to make ink from a variety of materials. Categories of ink included the so-called stone ink, lamp-black ink and pine smoke ink. Good ink had a bright lustrous color. Historical records indicate that an ink maker of the Wei dynasty by the name of Wei Dan made ink from high-grade nicotine that resembled a "drop of lacquer" meaning that though the drop was as small as a sesame seed it shone like lacquer and brought a gleam to the eye of the beholder.

Nowadays, when we look at ancient calligraphy in a museum, the ink of some original specimens is still bright and lustrous despite the passage of years. Looking at it is like appreciating fine brandy, thick but not oily, rich but not overstated. The color of ink is determined by the amount of water with it, different amounts of water can produce infinite shades of black. Apart from changes in color, the degree of moisture of the ink can produce different flavors. For example a brush well saturated with ink will give a flavor of richness but a dry one a bitter flavor (fig. 134).

After color, luster and moistness, the crux of using ink lies in the skills of "use." In the same way that they theorized about the use of the brush, historical calligraphers and painters also had theories about ink. At this point, I am going to use what I learned from Master Yang Shanshen to give a simple outline of the main points in the use of ink. Master Yang said that the principal element in the use of ink was "dynamic free-flowing" in the sense of lack of obstruction. He explained that if ink was used properly there would be no sense of blockage, so that even if the image was a mass of ink, the impression it gave the viewer should be one of fluidity and the ability to breathe within, only then would the image come alive. This hard won knowledge was the result of the Master's practices of several decades. Ink has to be used so that it lives, a skill not acquired overnight.

If we say that *qi* is the manifestation of a kind of strength, then *yun* is the manifestation

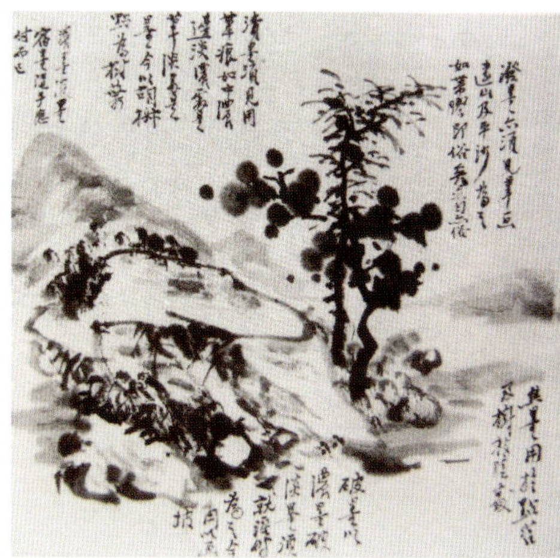

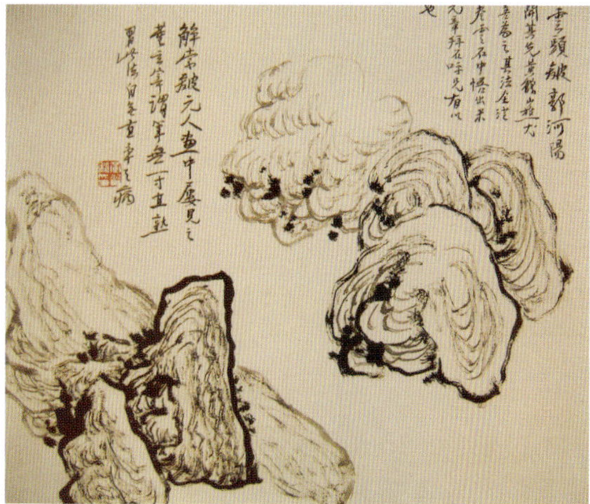

Figs. 135–136 Illustration of Huang Binhong's Use of Ink

Huang Binhong was a 20th century master of Chinese painting. His treatise "five brushes and seven inks" is an important signpost to the understanding of the creation and appreciation of *bimo* in traditional painting.

of a kind of quality, a type of flavor that is distributed between the differing shades of ink, between wet and dry and between concentration and dispersal.

Huang Binhong, one of the great 20th century masters of traditional painting was a power in the study of *bimo* and his theories were profound. He said: "*Qi* lies in strength of brush and *yun* in variety of ink." His theory of "the five brushstrokes and the seven inks" is a summary of the values of *bimo* in traditional painting.

The five brushstrokes are "even, round, heavy, preserved and changeable." The seven inks are "thick, faint, smashed, splashed, soaked, dry and overnight ink (where the ink stick has been soaked overnight and the water has evaporated leaving the color sticky and very dark)." The "even" brushstroke should be like drawing in sand with an awl, using a consistent strength of brush and keeping the tip of the brush in position; from a distance the stroke should appear even and seen close-up it should appear to twist and turn. The round brushstroke should give a sense of the circular where a hook and a horizontal will produce a circumference; where the line twists the strength should remain even and pliable. The "preserved" brush stroke should appear like the stains of leaking water preserved on a wall where dots become a line and the brush should not be lifted too quickly. The "heavy" brushstroke should give an appearance of weight and strength, but not ponderous, like a boulder rolling down a mountain. The "changeable" brushstroke is varied in interest, its inner beauty relying on being ordered and yet disordered in size, slope, length, spread and girth (figs. 135–136).

The theories of "five brushstrokes and seven inks" involve on the one hand the skills of using brush and ink and on the other the preservation of the traditional content and values of *bimo*. Considerable scholarship is involved here and there may be later opportunities for a deeper discussion. However it should be pointed out that the system of values and aesthetics and common consensus about *bimo* accumulated in the development of Chinese painting, derive from the choices made by traditional painters as they worked.

When we look at the *bimo* of the masters what we see is a reflection of each master's individual recognition of different artistic concepts. For example, the "preserved," "round" and "heavy" brushstrokes of Huang Binhong's "five brush strokes" all demand an upright position of the brush and slow speed. This is a recognition of a *bimo* that expresses simple strength, weight and self-restraint, all artistic concepts of the literati painting tradition's aesthetic values of simple sincerity.

Vitality of *Qiyun*

No discussion of *bimo* can exclude *qiyun* and no discussion of *qiyun* can exclude "vitality of *qiyun*" (*qiyun shengdong*), one of the "six methods" advocated by the Southern Dynasty fifth century artist Xie He. The six methods have had a wide influence on Chinese painting, particularly on the development of *shanshui*. Historically, painters after Xie He produced fresh interpretations of the meaning of vitality of *qiyun*. The abstract nature of the values and concepts involved was more and more confusing to those who had no understanding of the theories of traditional painting and with the addition of rumor became more mysterious in the telling. The purpose of this book is to focus upon traditional painting and it will not cover any deeper discussion of *bimo*. However, in simple terms, *qiyun* lies in the use of brush and ink and "vitality of *qiyun*" may be interpreted as "*qiyun* with vitality," the use of brush and ink with vitality.

There is a further particular uniqueness about *bimo* in traditional painting and that is it cannot be altered or corrected. The brushwork of western painters in oils can be altered, in other words, if an artist makes a mistake he can over-paint it and failing the use of X-ray technology, it is extremely difficult to detect traces of the over-painting once the painting has been completed. However, the type of paper, ink and brush used in traditional Chinese painting, leaves no room for alteration or correction. The merest touch of the brush on the fine paper used in painting produces a watermark round the black of the ink even with the weakest ink. An additional brushstroke, even with relatively dense ink, cannot obliterate the previous watermark though its ink may have been weaker. On the contrary, the watermark will become more pronounced at the points where the two brushstrokes overlap and

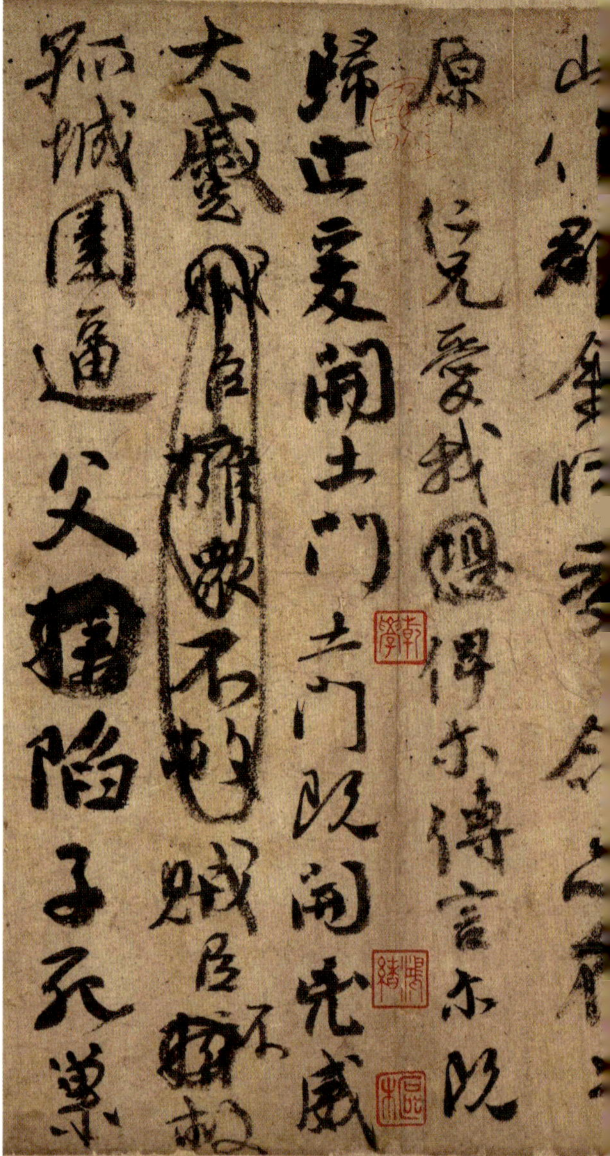

it becomes impossible to conceal traces of alteration (fig. 137)

Calligraphers skilled in *bimo* and knowledgeable connoisseurs are able to determine from the *bimo* of a single piece of calligraphy or painting the stroke by stroke sequence of the *bimo*. Consequently there are some western scholars who liken traditional Chinese calligraphy to a kind of abstract performing art, a theory based on the fact that *bimo* cannot be eradicated.

The starting point for an appreciation of *bimo* is an understanding of the skills necessary in the use of brush and ink;

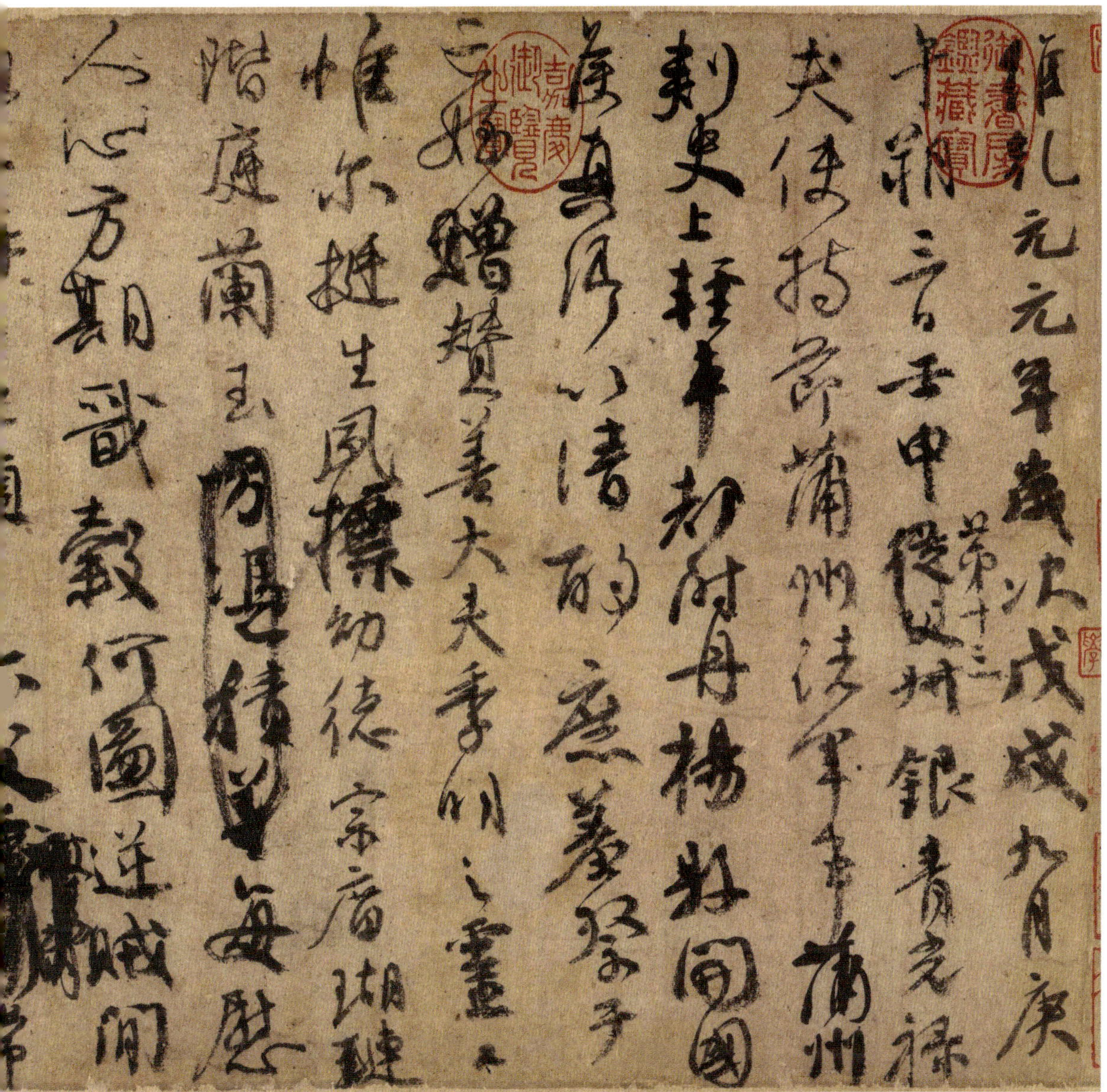

Fig. 137 *Memorial for a Nephew* (detail)
Yan Zhenqing (Tang dynasty, 708–784)
Semi-cursive script
Ink on flax paper
Height 28.3 cm × Width 75.5 cm
Palace Museum, Taibei

A characteristic of Chinese painting is that the original initial brushwork is non-erasable and cannot be corrected. Once the brush touches the paper it leaves traces that cannot be covered, unlike oil painting where previous brushwork can be corrected or over-painted.

understanding the *bimo* content in the development of Chinese traditional painting is a step forward in the discussion and appreciation of *bimo*. There are objective standards for the so-called "proper handling of brush and ink," these are the content and skills of *bimo*. *Bimo* is an artistic language that expresses an internal life. Whether it is the strength expressed by the brush or the flavor expressed by the ink, the aim is the achievement of a kind of living rhythm, a realm of communication, the "vitality of *qiyun*" of ancient painting theory that is so frequently mentioned.

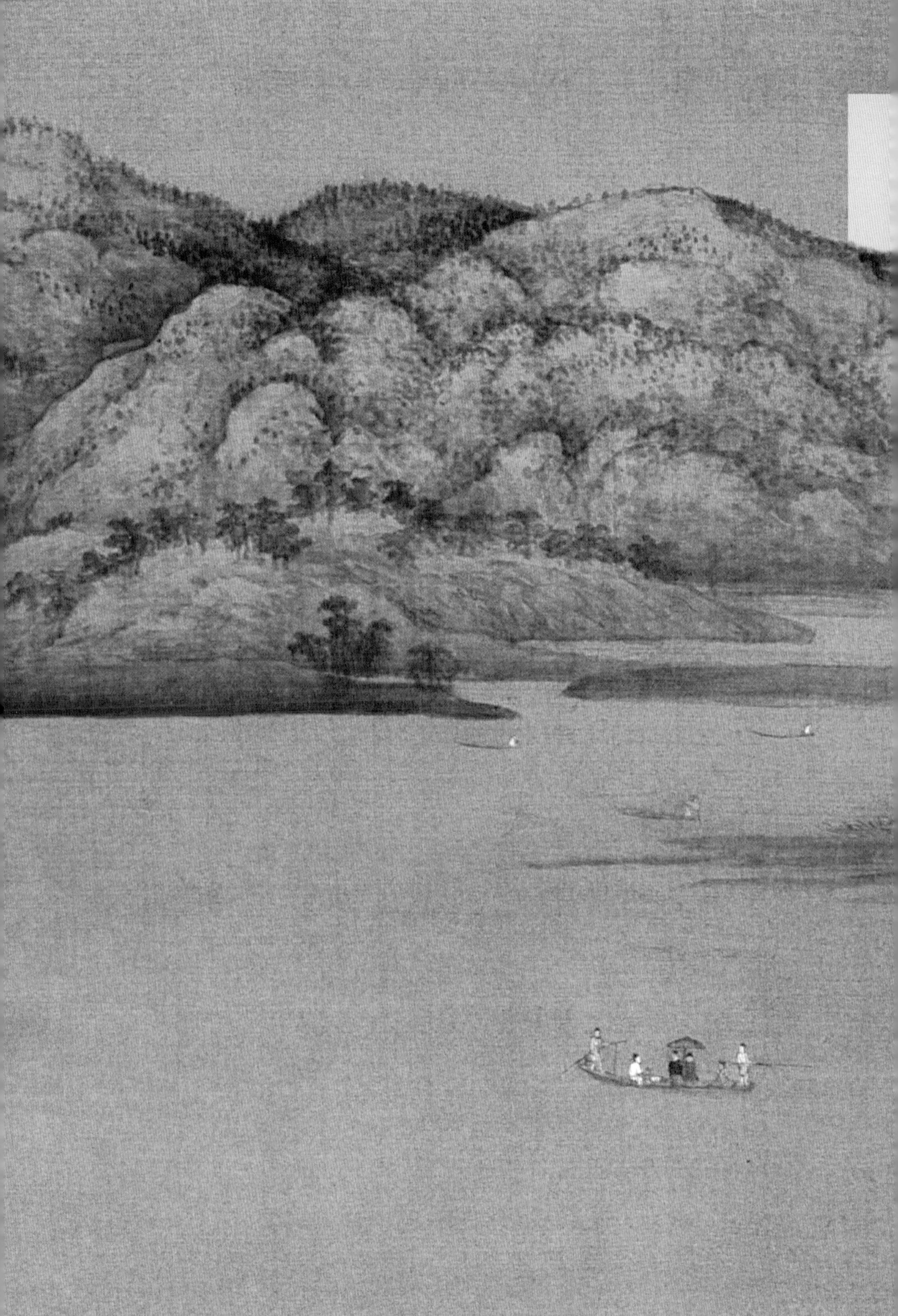

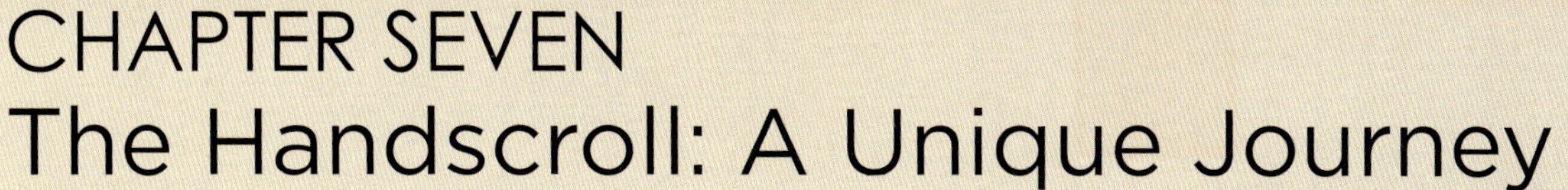

CHAPTER SEVEN
The Handscroll: A Unique Journey

The handscroll is a pictorial form peculiar to Chinese painting which is absent from the art forms of the western painting tradition. The way in which handscrolls are displayed is unusual. The creative concept of handscroll is closely linked to the emphasis upon *xieyi* and the freedom from the tyranny of the view found in the traditional painting tradition. In ancient times the appreciation and enjoyment of handscrolls was a very private and particular form of artistic exchange: today, alas, the appreciation of handscrolls has lost the sense of that intimacy.

The Aesthetics of the Handscroll Form

In terms of an art form, the creation, display and appreciation of handscrolls is unique and is only to be found within the tradition of Chinese painting. There is an important link between the emergence of the handscroll and the artistic aspirations and ideals of the painters of ancient China. Rolled up, the handscroll looks no different from a rolled up hanging scroll. Once unrolled however, the hanging scroll displays a painting as a vertical oblong, whereas a handscroll unrolls from right to left displaying the painting as a horizontal oblong (fig. 138 on pages 140 and 141, figs. 139–140).

Generally, handscrolls are between about 30 and 40 cm in height though some are not much higher than 10 or so cm. Rolled up, they fit neatly into the hand with a feeling of intimacy. There are no rules governing their length which can depend upon the mood and interest of the artist at the moment. Short handscrolls vary in length from one meter to several; whereas long handscrolls can vary from several meters to several tens of meters and are known as "long scrolls."

The famous handscroll *On the River during the Qingming Festival*, reputedly by the Northern Song dynasty painter Zhang Zeduan (late 11th–12th century) measures 24.8 cm in height with a length of 528 cm and falls into the category of long scrolls (see figs. 141–142 on pages 144 and 145). The 20th century painter Zhang Daqian's handscroll *Ten Thousand Li of the Yangtze* is 53.2 cm high and 1979.5 cm long, that is to say very nearly 20 meters in length, a really long scroll.

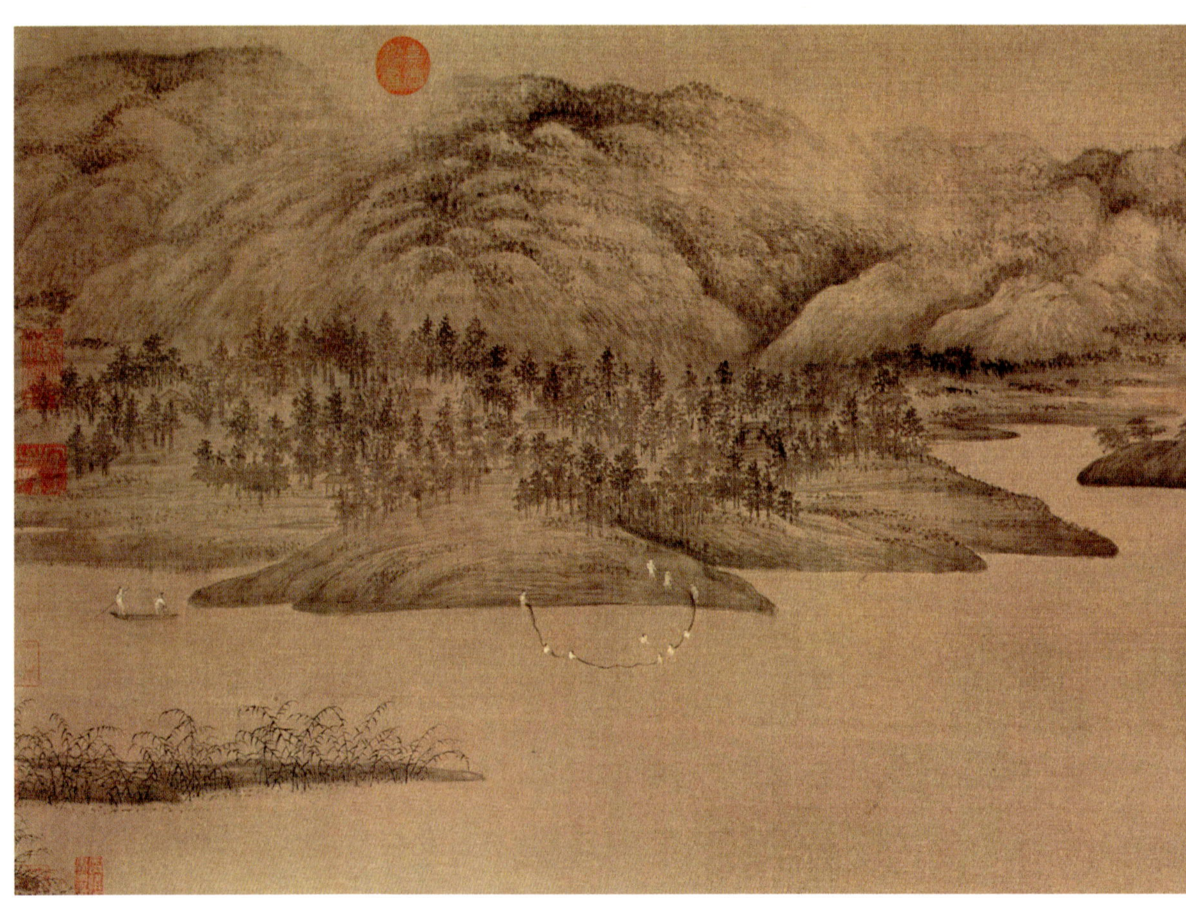

Figs. 138–140 *Xiaoxiang River*

Dong Yuan (Five Dynasties, ?–962)
Color on silk
Height 50 cm ×Width 141.4 cm
Palace Museum, Beijing

Dong Yuan was a painter of the Southern Tang period and *Xiaoxiang River* is the work most representative of his style. The subject material of this painting is drawn from the gently rolling hills of the Jiangnan area of east central China. On the river, a boat approaches whilst a group of welcomers at the riverside rush forward in greeting. A density of trees covers the shoreline, half-concealing a few peasant huts. Several people are fishing with nets in the water. The painting is woven together with dots and lines that throws into prominence the horizontal stretch of the hills and the rise and fall of the range. An accretion of heavy and light ink dotting in the haze of the hills produces a thin misty cloud from which the damp, moist climate of Jiangnan flows like oil.

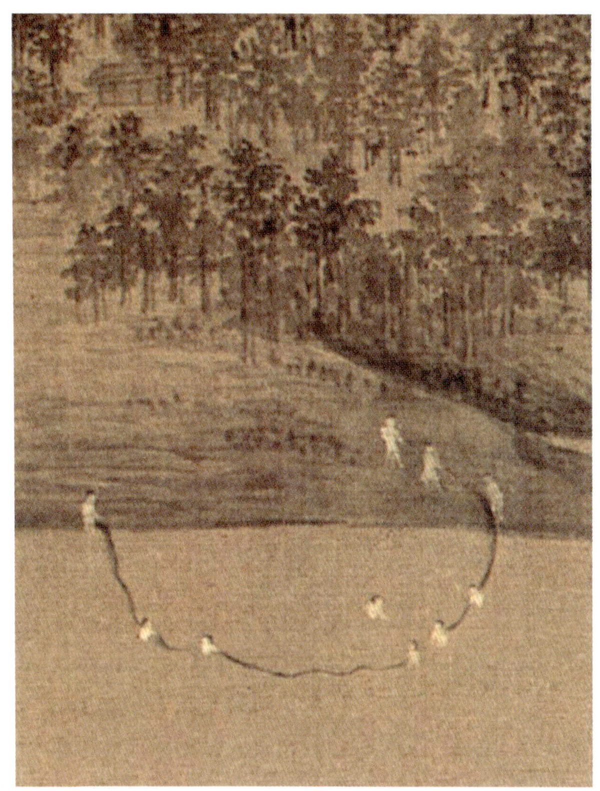

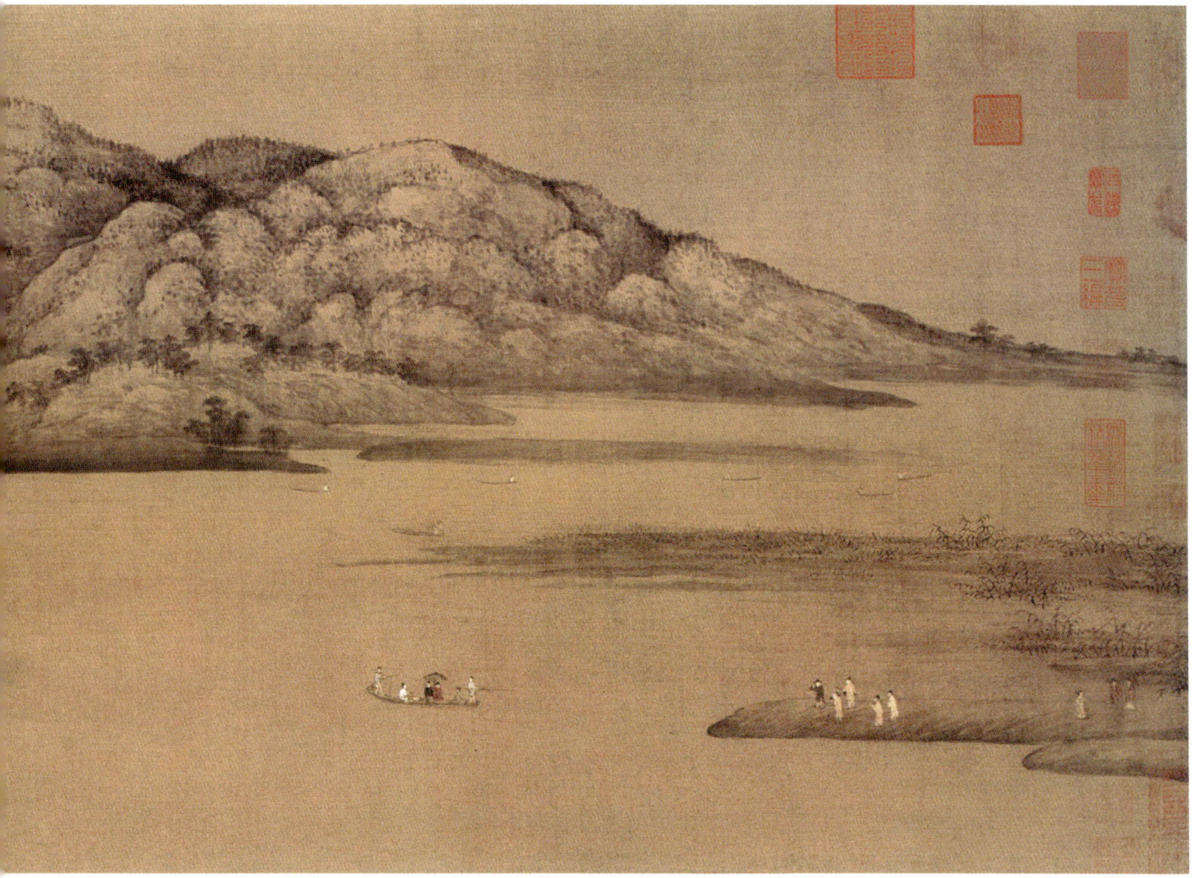

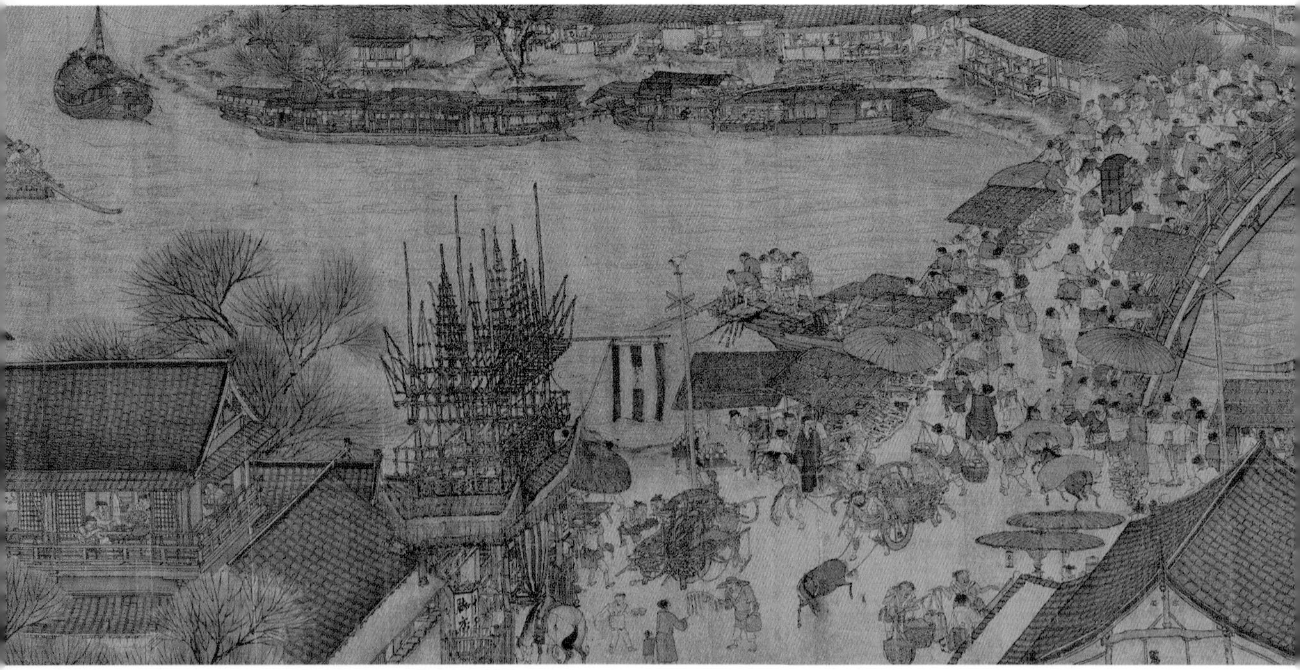

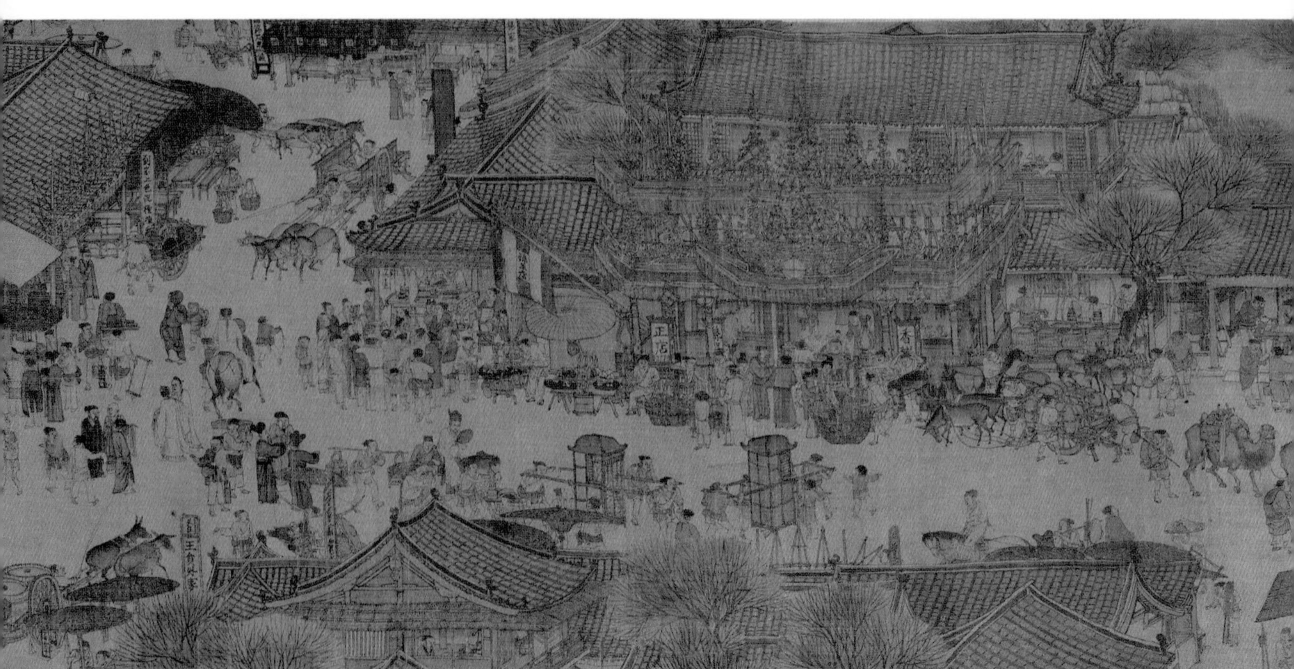

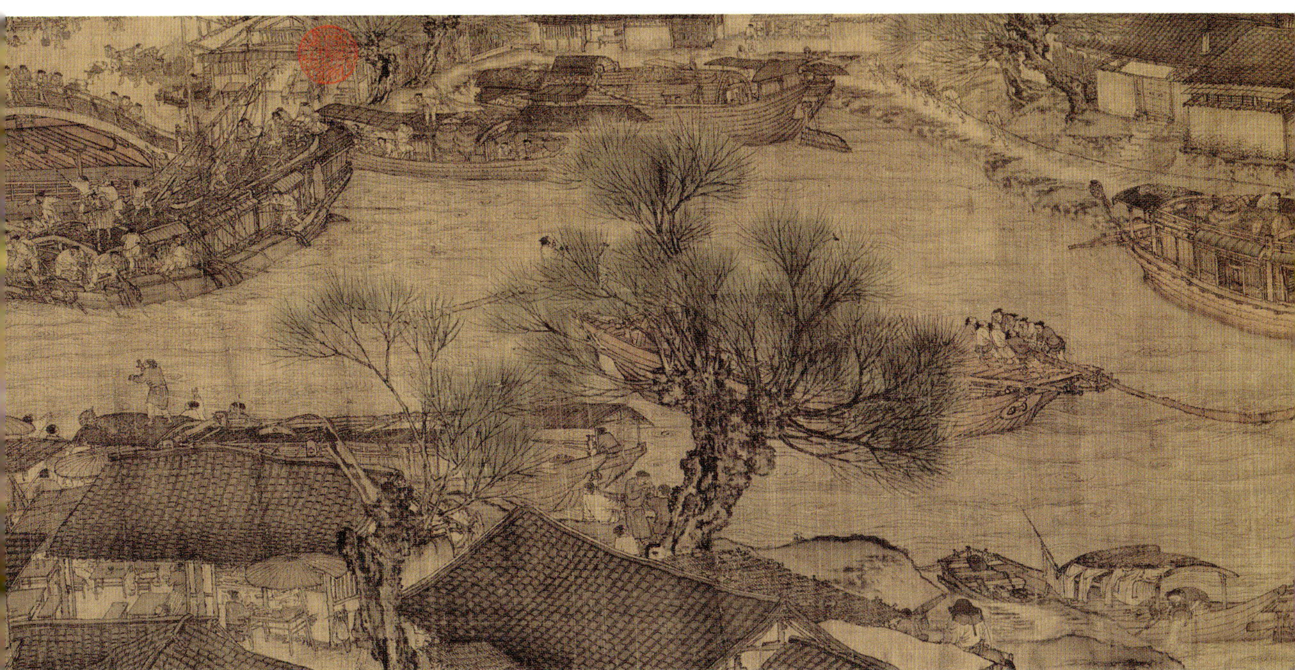

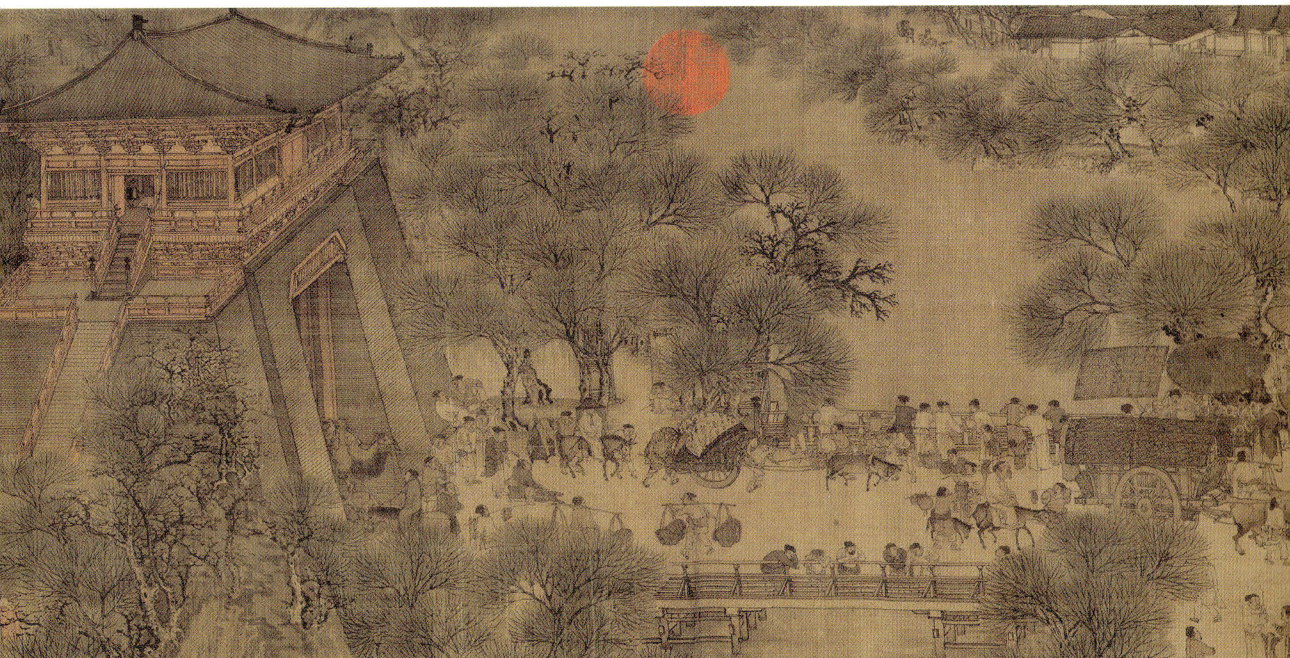

Figs. 141–142 *On the River during the Qingming Festival* (detail)
Zhang Zeduan (Northern Song dynasty, late 11th–12th century)
Color on silk
Height 24.8 cm ×Width 528 cm
Palace Museum, Beijing

This scroll, handed down over centuries, illustrates the scene on both banks of the river at the Northern Song capital of Bianhe. Panel upon panel of scenery, from village, to town and city unrolls in the form of a long scroll, faithfully depicting in detail the life and scenery of the river banks. The scroll depicts up to 814 people, more than 60 head of cattle, 28 boats, more than 30 dwellings, 20 carts, 8 sedan chairs and 170 trees. The rich yet orderly lay-out of the activity and scenery of the scroll reflects the urban and rural development of the Song dynasty.

The Secret of Reading Handscrolls

When we look at a handscroll in a museum, it is displayed in the same way as a hanging scroll in that the whole painting is on show for all to see. The hanging scroll hangs on a wall vertically and handscrolls are usually laid horizontally in a glass case so that viewers can examine them in detail. In the case of long handscrolls and in order to give the viewer an unobstructed view, museums will sometimes provide a special viewing case that allows a complete view of the whole scroll. In fact, this total display method is the only one that works in modern museums. However, it is not the way that handscrolls were originally displayed. Moreover, to a considerable extent, it destroys the unique way in which handscrolls were originally viewed and enjoyed.

To enjoy handscrolls as handscrolls, they should be hand held. The proper way of enjoying a handscroll is not to take in the whole scroll in a single glance but to look at it section by section. The viewer should be seated with the scroll in the palm of the left hand and the scroll stave that opens the scroll in his right and then slowly open the scroll to the right to the extent of the distance between the two shoulders. At this point, we can begin to appreciate the images in the first section of the scroll. Having looked at this section of the painting, the viewer then first uses his right hand to roll up the scroll to the left, and when his right hand reaches his left, that is to say when the images in the first section he viewed have been completely rolled up, he relaxes his left hand and allows the right once more to draw out the scroll to the same distance as before and display the completely new images in the second section of the scroll. In this way, the scroll is slowly enjoyed section by section, until the whole scroll has been viewed.

There were no museums in the ancient past and painters, calligraphers and collectors could not exhibit their complete works or collections at the same time. The appreciation of painting in ancient society was the joint enjoyment of friends, and the appreciation of handscrolls was a particularly intimate form of enjoyment in private cultural gatherings because, unlike hanging scrolls, which could be hung on a wall and viewed by four or five close friends at a time, the handscroll could only be held by a single person at a time thus creating an intimacy between the viewer and the work (or its creator). We can imagine a cultivated scholar, a bowl of fragrant tea beside him and scroll in his hand, calmly and minutely enjoying the scenery and *bimo* of the painting it displays. Perhaps, through the depiction and content of the scene or possibly because of the abstract expression of the *bimo*, the heart of the viewer is moved as the images change scene by scene, a feeling of fluid tranquility and of real joy.

Thus, the appreciation of a handscroll is an extremely intimate and private experience. No modern museum can provide such an private viewing space for its visitors, much is the pity, but at the very least, the next time we view a handscroll, it should be section by section, slowly, and from right to left.

It is only by viewing a handscroll section by section that we can experience its unique creative form. The creative form of a hanging scroll derives from its vertical state which lends itself to the depiction of towering, lofty mountains and expanses of water. By contrast, the handscroll develops horizontally and its uniqueness lies in a sense of extension and change. From previous chapters we know that the painters of ancient China were not bound to the creation of "views" so that the scenery that flowed from their brush could alter as they saw fit and create a picture formed from different points of view and spread across the painting. The creative freedom provided by this transcendence of fixed point perspective is known as "three-distance perspective" when it appears in a hanging scroll. When it is used as a creative medium in a handscroll it is called "floating perspective" (*yuli toushifa*).

Floating Perspective

As with three-distance perspective, when painting a handscroll, the Chinese artists of the past were cleverly adept at linking scenery viewed from different points. However, unlike a hanging scroll, the scenery was not laid out and linked from top to bottom but horizontally, extending along the length of the painting as the artist seamlessly joined up scenery observed from different viewpoints.

Appreciating and enjoying a handscroll, the process of looking at it section by section, allows the viewer to move unconsciously from one viewpoint to another and is like undertaking a tour. The subtle trick that creates the illusion of being on tour lies in the use, peculiar to handscrolls, of floating perspective. Taking the Yuan master Huang Gongwang's painting *Dewelling in the Fuchun Mountains* as an example, let us examine how floating perspective takes us on a tour of the mountains.

Dwelling in the Fuchun Mountains is one of the great historical works of Chinese painting and is the reason for the respect that Huang Gongwang is shown as a literati painter. The *bimo* of the painting is filled with the air of the literati and the painting itself is a model of the literati painting tradition. Before looking at the painting, let us first understand the background to this handscroll and to Huang Gongwang the man. Huang Gongwang was a minor judicial official who was imprisoned for involvement in a political case and who, when he left prison, became a Daoist. He followed the "Whole Truth" sect of Daoism, abandoned an official career and devoted himself to the practice of Daoism, preaching and telling fortunes in the area of Hangzhou, Songjiang, and Yushan. He fell in love with the countryside but only started to paint *shanshui* in late middle age. His later years were spent as a hermit in the Fuchun Mountains.

Dwelling in the Fuchun Mountains, the masterpiece of Huang's late years, was three years in the painting and was completed between 1347 and 1350. The handscroll is in ink on paper and is 636.9 cm long and 33 cm in height. It was revered by collectors over the years and by the time of the Qing dynasty was in the possession of the collector Wu Hongyu. Wu more than loved this scroll to the extent that he called the study where he housed his collection, the "Fuchun Pavilion" and never displayed the scroll in front of people. As death approached Wu instructed his nephew to burn the scroll as a sacrifice. Not daring to disobey, Wu Zhendu, the nephew, reluctantly put the scroll in the fire but fortunately, seized the opportunity of Wu's lack of concentration as he died to retrieve it from the flames. However, the first section of the scroll had been destroyed. The remnant was later divided into two and remounted and circulated as two scrolls. Since 1949 the two halves have been stored separately in the Zhejiang Provincial Museum and the Palace Museum in Taibei (see figs. 143–145 on pages 148 and 149).

In his personal inscription on the scroll Huang Gongwang wrote: "In the seventh year of Zhizheng (1347) I retired to the Fuchun Mountains accompanied by the Useless Master and during days of leisure in the Southern Chamber I painted this scroll. In our excitement we pressed on with untiring diligence. When it was nearly done I added to it here and there. The reason that it has not been finished in three or four years is that the painting has remained in the hills while I travelled abroad ..." The Useless Master (*Wuyong Shi*) is a reference to a fellow adept of Huang's in the Whole Truth sect whose original surname had been Zheng and style name Wuyong. This postscript explains Huang's hermetic retirement to the Fuchun Mountains. Also how, having acquired experience there over a number of years he would wander abroad, and then on return and in the excitement of the moment put

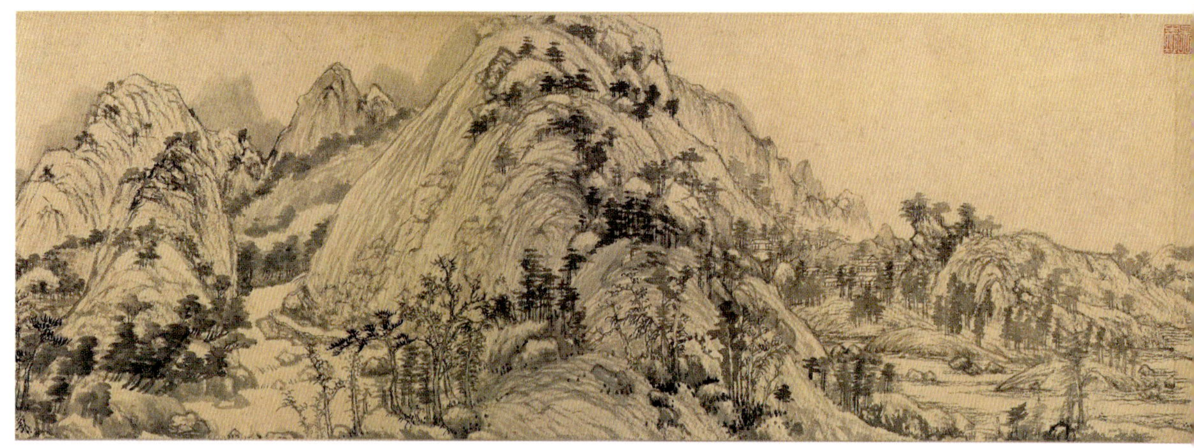

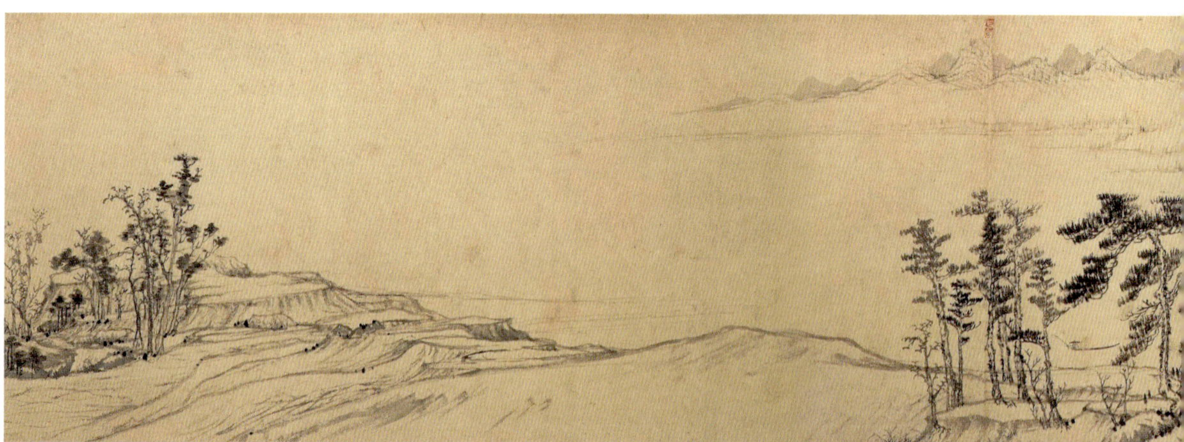

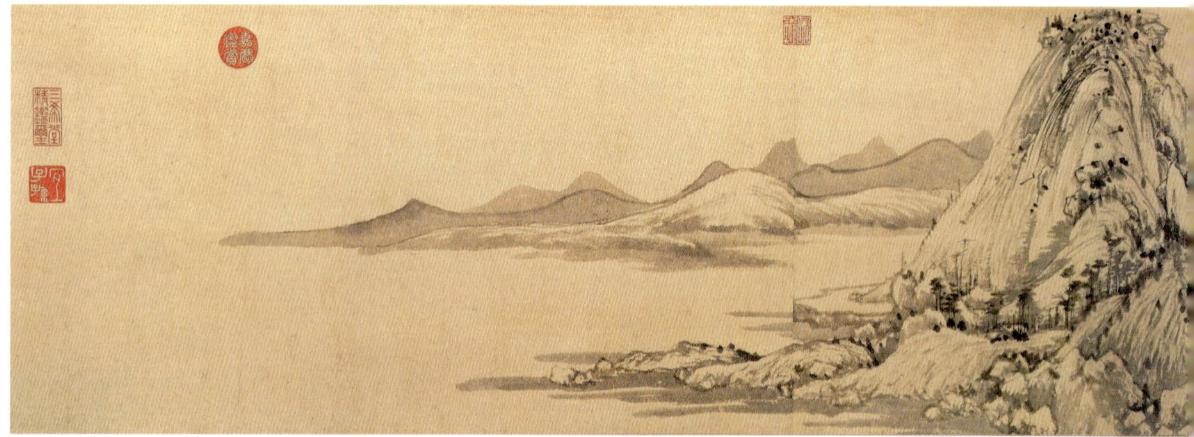

Figs. 143–145 *Dwelling in the Fuchun Mountains—The Useless Master's Scroll* (second half of the scroll)

Huang Gongwang
Ink on paper
Height 33 cm × Width 636.9 cm
Palace Museum, Taibei

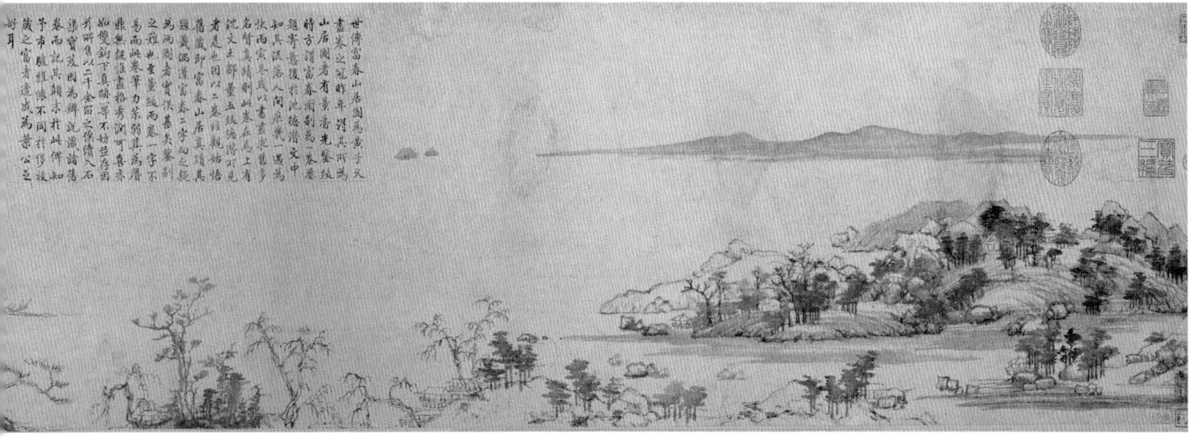

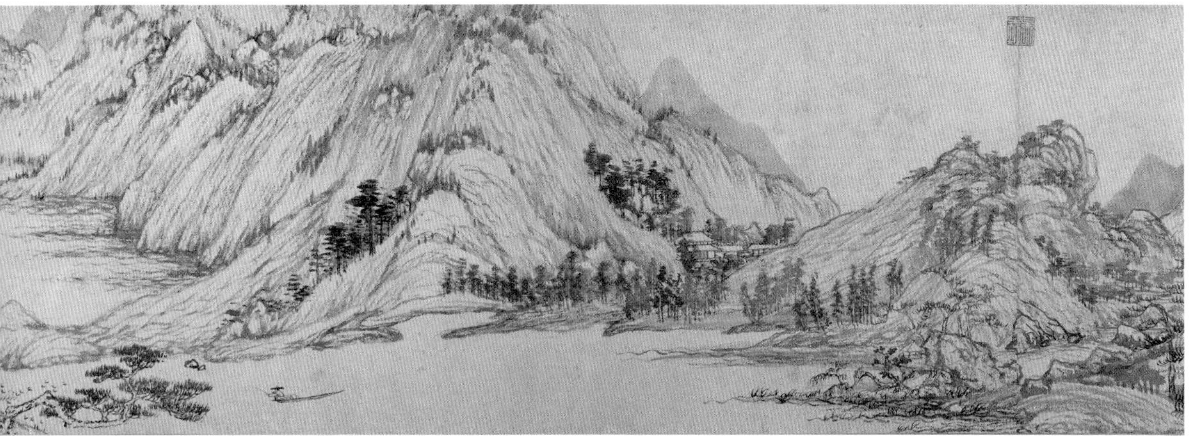

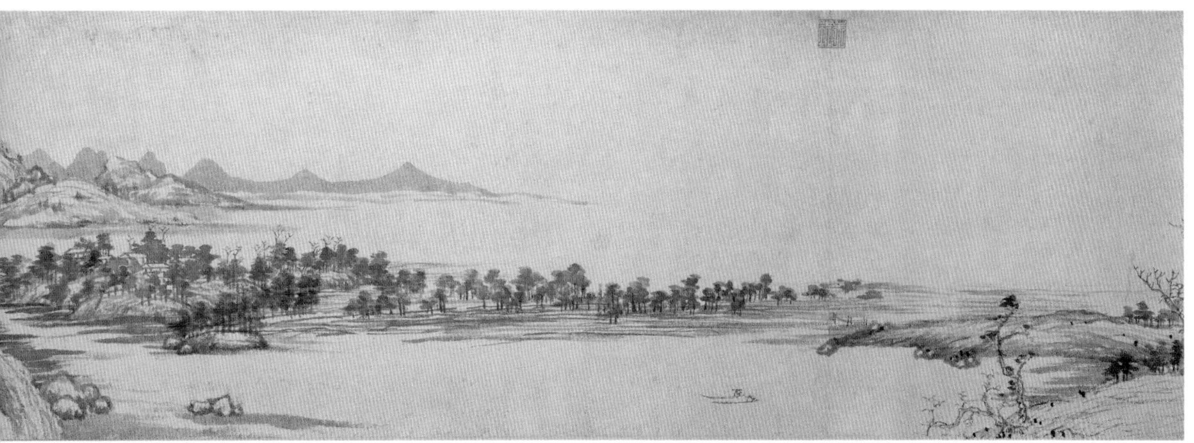

Hunag was one of the most respected literati painters in history. *Dwelling in the Fuchun Mountains* is his late masterpiece. It was revered by collectors over the centuries and by the time of the Qing dynasty was in the possession of the collector Wu Hongyu. Wu more than loved this scroll and when death approached instructed his nephew to burn it as a sacrifice. Fortunately, the nephew retrieved it from the flames. However, the first section of the scroll had been destroyed. The remnant was later divided into two and remounted and circulated as two scrolls. Since 1949 the two halves have been stored separately in the Zhejiang Provincial Museum and the Palace Museum in Taibei.

brush to paper, and how after several years of this improvisatory work, he would finally complete the scroll.

As a practitioner of Daoism and during many years of tramping the mountains and forests Huang Gongwang arrived at a perception of nature both as a creator and as a path to be followed. In 1347 Huang Gongwang was already over 80 and he now knew more than most men, in terms of the mystery that lay between *shanshui* and nature. The Fuchun Mountains are the subject of this scroll, the place where Huang Gongwang spent his late years in hermetic retirement. The Fuchun Mountains are no lofty sacred mountains and have none of the grandeur of high peaks. In fact, they are a range of low hills in part of Zhejiang Province, ordinary, bare and like hermetic life in the hills itself, without anything imposing about them, they are just dull.

At the start of the scroll and on the right of the painting there is a small hill where a few simple village houses are glimpsed through a density of low trees. The village is surrounded on three sides by a river and a light ribbon of ink runs the other side of the hill, symbolizing a range of distant hills. The view point is as if we have just stepped on to a path that leads up the hill and we are looking across the river that divides us from the village, the foreground consists of the rocks beneath our feet and luxuriantly growing trees.

When we roll up the first section of the scroll and open the second, we see an extension of the scattered rocks as they gradually become larger, the scenery of the hills also gradually becomes more distinct. By the third section we seem to be at the foot of a mountain peak as the scroll displays the whole shape of the mountain. It is not an awe-inspiring sight and lacks the imposing grandeur of a true peak, nor are there any strangely shaped rocks. The opposite in fact, smoothly shaped rocks are veined with a scattered pattern of moistly gleamimg moss dots that induce a feeling of placid lushness leading to a sense of the harmony between man and nature. Another range of hills rises and falls behind the hill, high then low, responding to the at times dense then sparse undergrowth, as if beating out the rhythm and pulse of nature, brimming with life but peaceful.

In the fourth section of the scroll we seem to have travelled from the front to the rear of the mountain and are able to survey a distant range of hills. A river flows at our feet and on it floats a boat carrying an old fisherman wearing a grass rain hat who is fishing from its stern. Further on, we seem to have descended from the heights into a plain. Tree shapes are clearer and more easily made out and the surface of the river as smooth as a mirror, reflects the level path beneath our feet.

As the scroll unrolls we can see some low-lying land close to the water by the river where a dense wood of low trees gradually ascends from the bottom to the top of the connected small hill. A few small huts are scattered about, half-concealed here and there in the wood. Close by on the water there is another small boat, does the fisherman it carries come from this small fishing hamlet? There is a mountain peak to the left of the hamlet, still smoothly patterned with gleaming moss but its shape climbs upwards, fold by fold telling us that we are at the foot of the mountain, looking up at its bare peak in the distance. There is a light streak of ink behind the peak of the mountain that extends from right to left, becoming narrower as it rises and falls until its end ceases in the center of the painting, giving the feeling of a piece of music slowing down and decreasing in volume at the last note until the sound has stopped altogether. The area of *liubai* that follows gives room to ponder the lingering sound that remains in the heart, a placid moment of peace.

External Scenery as a Vehicle for the Inner Spirit

As we look at *Dwelling in the Fuchun Mountains* we are unconsciously allowing Huang Gongwang to take us on a tour, the scenery unfolding step by step as we start from the view-point looking out from the path at the beginning of the scroll. Each section of the scroll displays scenery seen from a different view-point as the artist cleverly guides us up the hill from the bottom and then, having reached the top of the slope that faces us, through to the rear of the hill and then slowly down, across a plain and back to the foot of the hill.

This method of composition, incorporating different view-points, was known early on in the Chinese painting tradition, there was nothing novel about it. However, when artists using the unique horizontal form of the handscroll applied the different viewpoints to the painting it resulted in the visual experience known as floating perspective.

It took Huang Gongwang over three years of work to complete *Dwelling in the Fuchun Mountains.* Whenever the time was ripe he would add to the painting, cleverly linking together the different scenery from his mind in a result that was rather like the composition of a movement of a symphony.

On the face of it, the Fuchun Mountains are a group of not very large hills, like many others in the Yangtze River basin, and so ordinary as not to be worth the three years spent painting them. What this painting really portrays is the state of leisured privacy of Huang Gongwang's late years. It exhibits the fruits of his journeys in the hills over several years and his perception of the varieties of scenery. It was this scenery that was the only vehicle through which he could express his inner world. Everything in the scroll, whether distant hills or nearby scenery is plain and unadorned; there is a rhythmic harmony to the rise and fall of the hills and the spacing of trees and rocks; the use of the brush is rich but not overdone, the dotting and use of ink is smooth but not dazzling. As you look at the scroll you feel at peace and at ease, while in the extensive *liubai* of the scroll's final section, the ink is fading and tapers off to end in a tail as if resonating a decrescendo in a piece of music.

The handscroll, which presents us with a visual experience in the form of a tour, is unique to the tradition of Chinese painting and in good hands, like those of Huang Gongwang in *Dwelling in the Fuchun Mountains* it can truly resemble a beautiful piece of music. The way in which a handscroll appears section by section suits a narrative form of composition and favors the personal narrative. Gu Kaizhi's *Admonitions of the Instructress to the Court Ladies* displays, section by section, the standards of moral and personal integrity required of womanhood in ancient times (see figs. 146–148 on pages 152 and 153). The Tang dynasty Zhou Fang's handscroll *Court Ladies Adorning Their Hair with Flowers* and the Five Dynasties' Gu Hongzhong's *Chancellor Han Xizai's Evening Banquet* are both classic handscroll figure paintings of Chinese painting history.

By the Yuan dynasty there was also a fashion for handscrolls of flowers and plants amongst literati painters. A well-known example is Qian Xuan's *Pear Blossom* (see fig. 149 on pages 154 and 155). There were later collections of different kinds of flowers and plants displayed in a single handscroll known as "hundred flower scrolls" (*baihua juan*). These hundred flower scrolls mainly consisted of flowers displayed according to their season, but the hundred flower scrolls of the noted Ming literati painter Chen Chun took an improvisatory approach and broke with the time hallowed lay-out by allowing the responses to the demands of composition

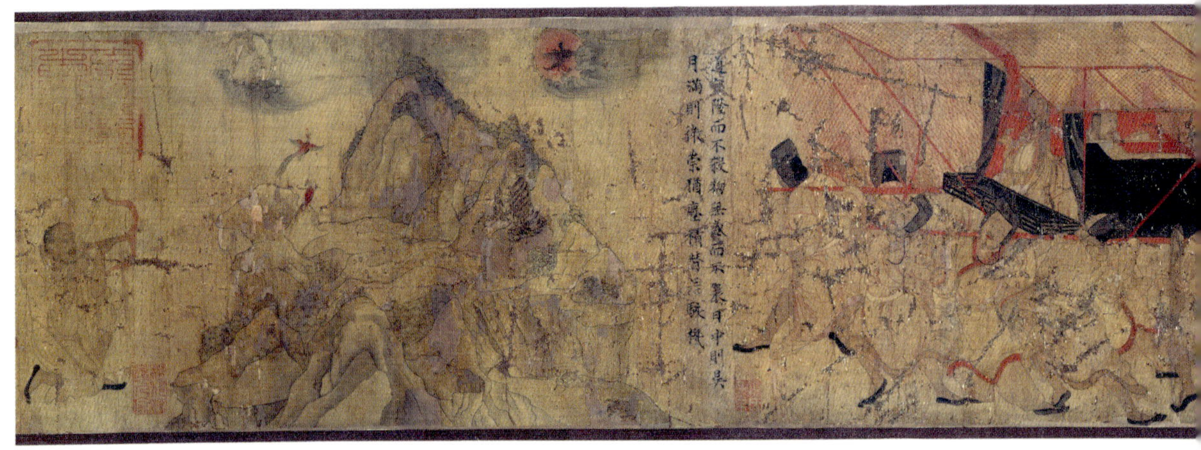
道罔隆而不殺物無盛而不衰日中則昃
月滿則微崇猶塵積替若駭機

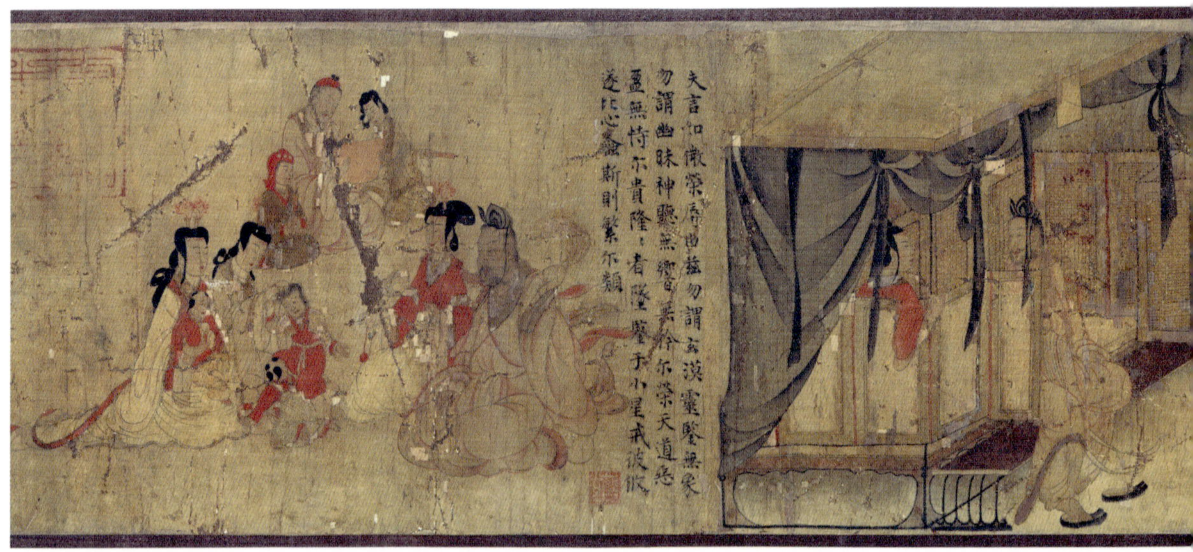
夫言如微榮辱由茲勿謂玄漠靈鑒無象
勿謂幽昧神聽無響無矜爾榮天道惡
盈無恃爾貴隆隆者墜鑒於小星戒彼攸
遂比心螽斯則繁爾類

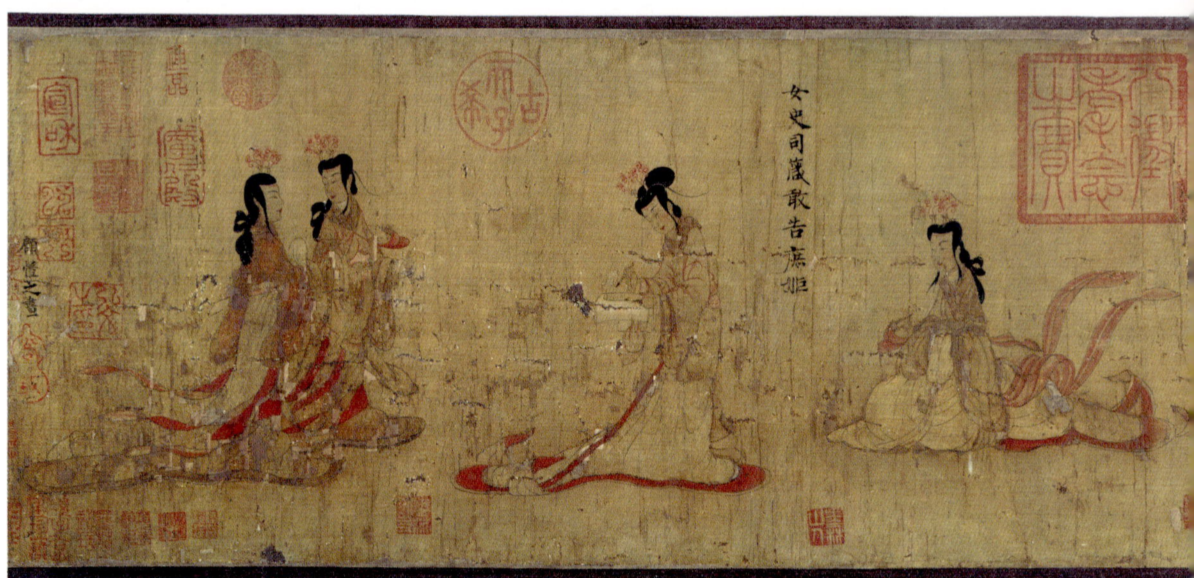
女史司箴敢告庶姬

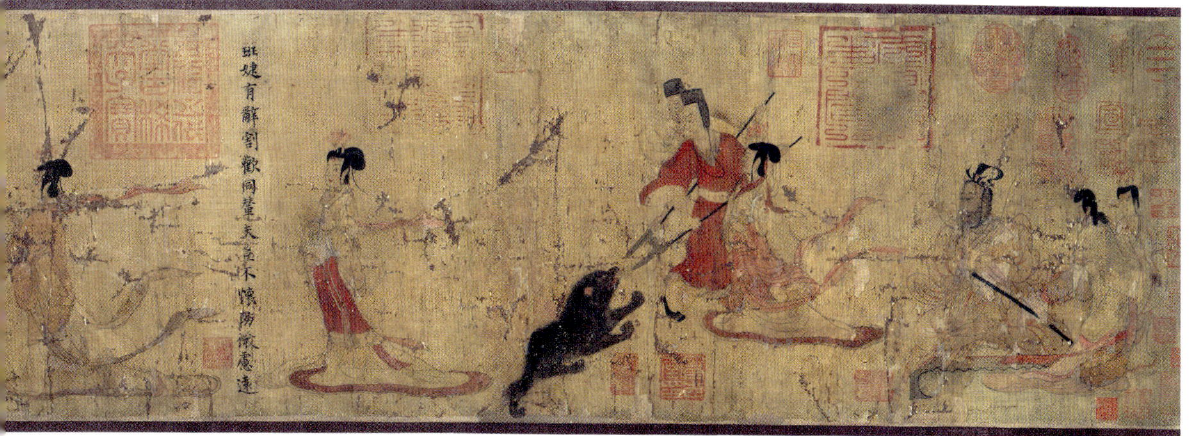

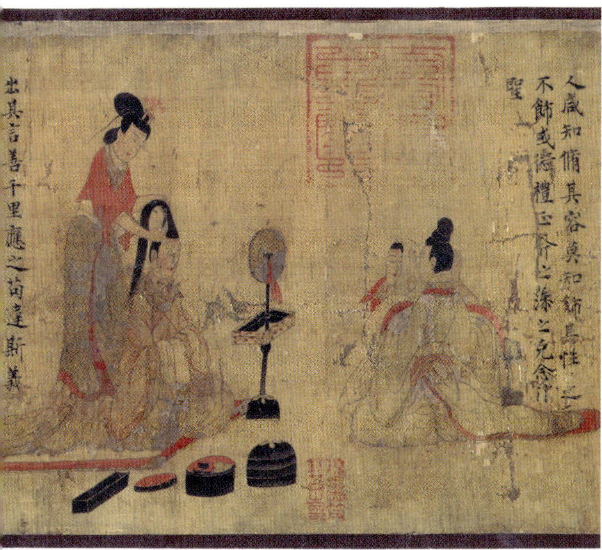

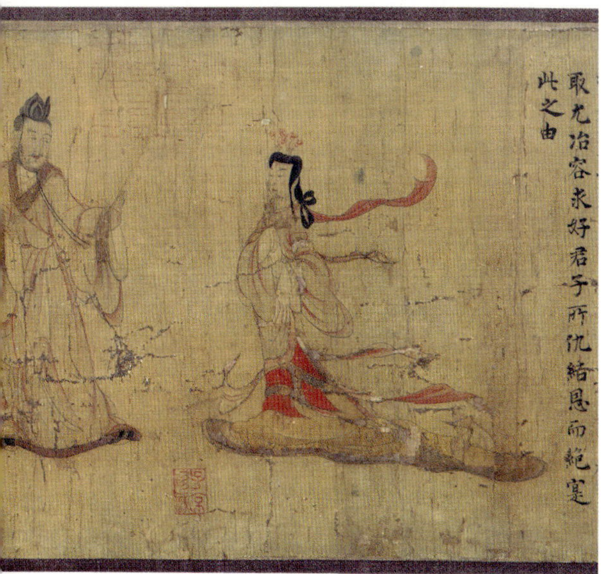

and the direction taken by the *bimo* to become a guide (see fig. 150–152 on pages 156 and 157). He also employed the idea of composition that was "part calligraphy" and "part painting" in the development of the handscroll, combining poetry, calligraphy and painting into one, while, at the same time, displaying the idea of a single source for calligraphy and painting.

The handscroll has been a brilliant chapter in the history of Chinese painting. Once we understand the subtleties of the handscroll form, it will provide much creative space for the art of painting.

Figs. 146–148 Copy of Gu Caizhi's *Admonitions of the Instructress to the Court Ladies*

Anonymous (Tang dynasty)
Color on silk
Height 24.8 cm × Length 348.2 cm
British Museum

It is believed that *Admonitions of the Instructress to the Court Ladies* is a copy of a painting of the same name by Gu Kaizhi, made between the 5th and 8th centuries. It is one of the earliest known long scrolls in the history of Chinese painting. It is based on the text of *Admonitions of the Instructress to the Court Ladies* written by the Jin poet Zhang Hua in 292, admonishing the imperial concubines to honor womanly virtue.

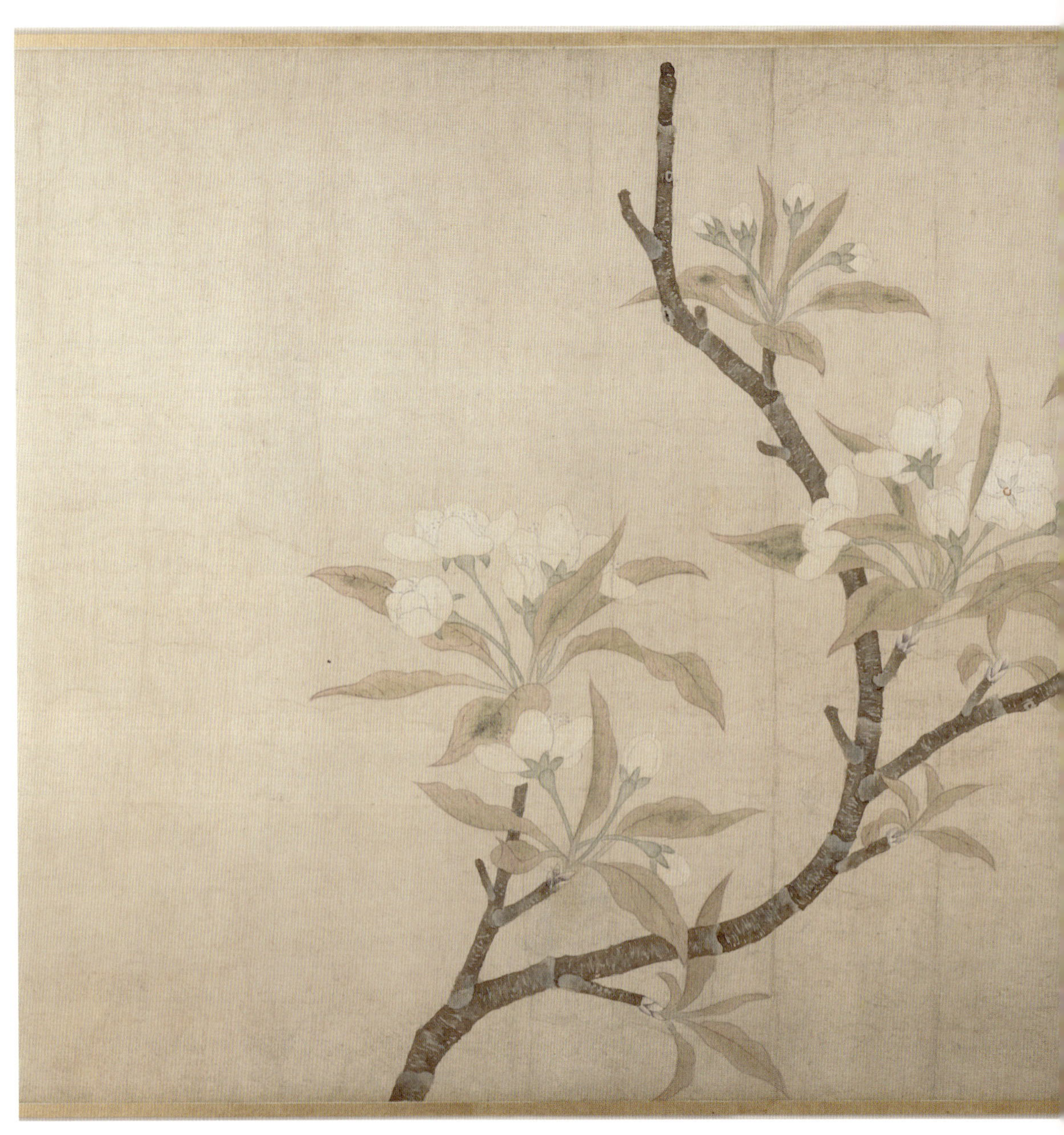

Fig. 149 *Pear Blossom*

Qian Xuan
Color on paper
Height 31.7 cm × Width 95 cm
The Metropolitan Museum of Art, New York

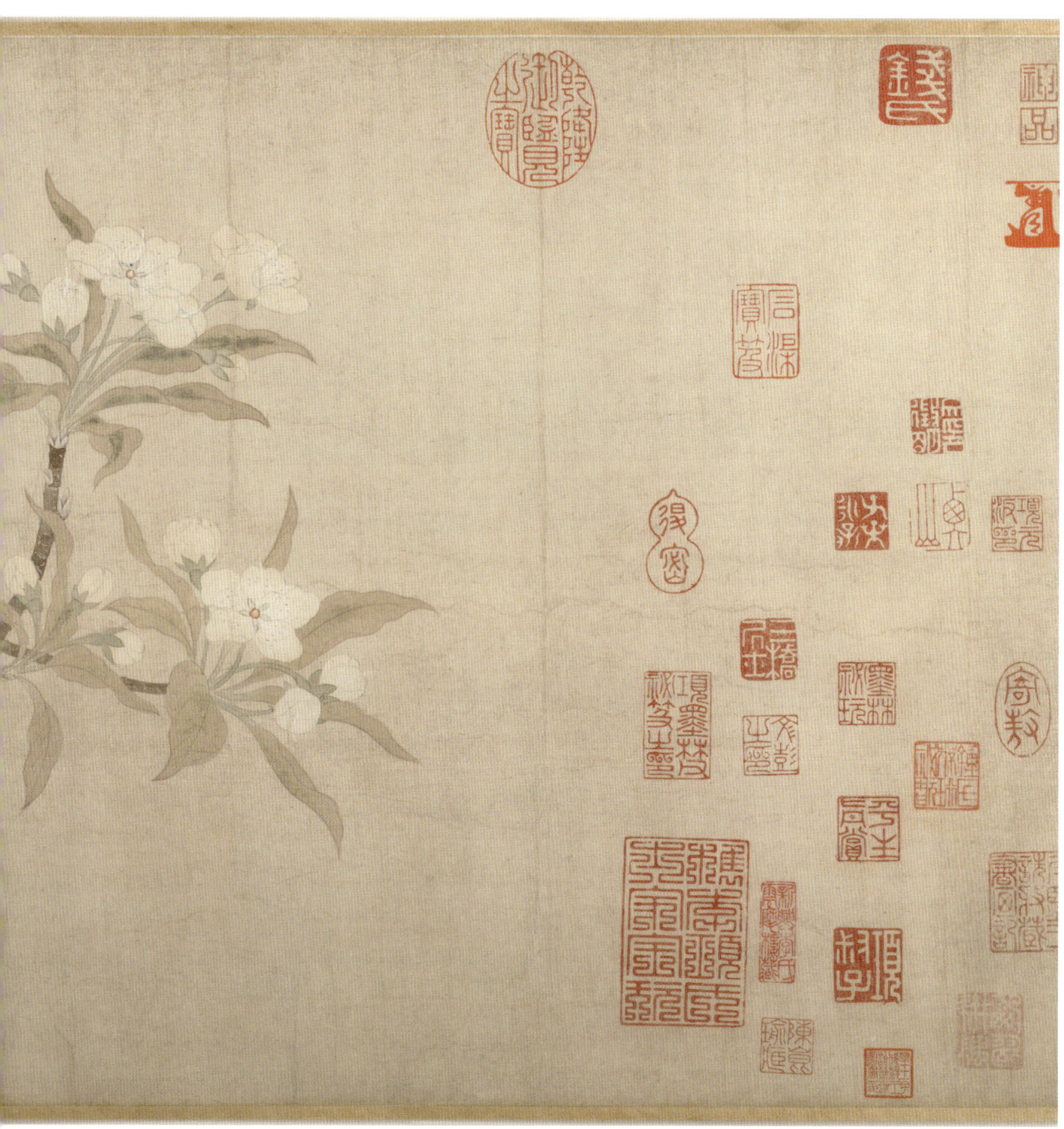

Qian Xuan was a well-known literati painter whose life spanned the Southern Song and Yuan dynasties. On the fall of the Song dynasty, he was unwilling to hold office under the Yuan dynasty and resigned himself to becoming a professional artist, making a living by selling paintings. He was expert in the theory of the tuning of musical instruments and excelled in poetry. He frequently expressed his inner feelings in poems inscribed on those of his paintings that pleased him, thereby developing the literati tradition of inscribing poems on paintings. This scroll is representative of his flower and plant work, the pear tree branch, flowers and buds are represented vividly and naturally in simple elegant color. He has inscribed a poem at the end of the scroll.

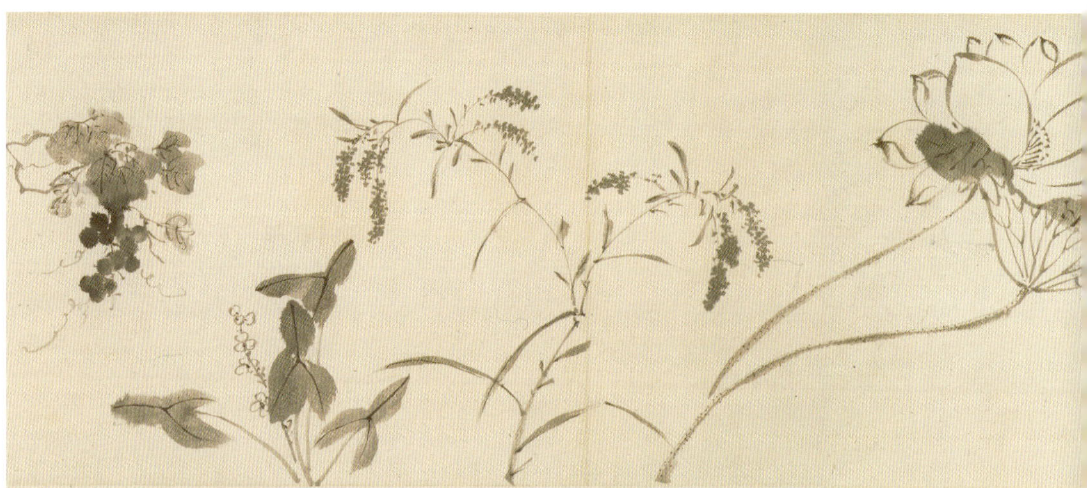

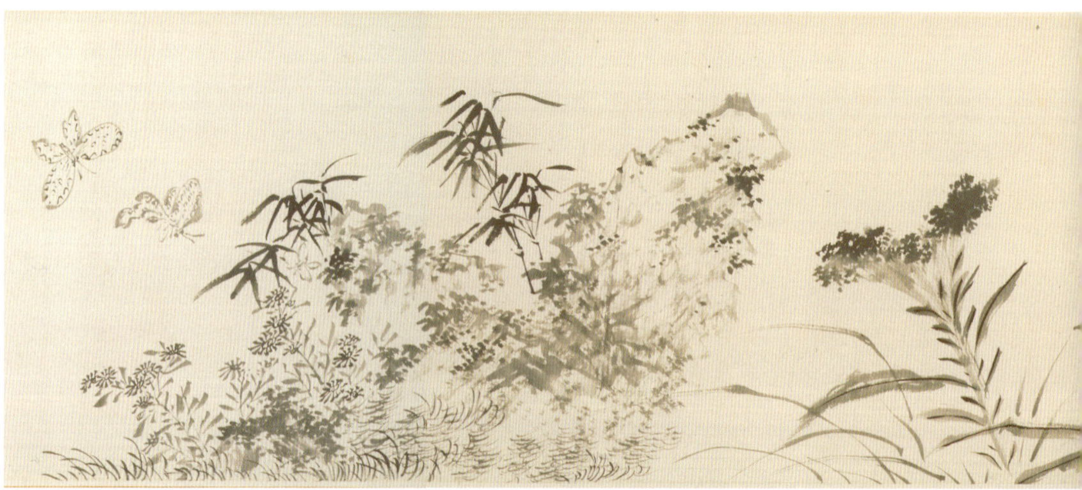

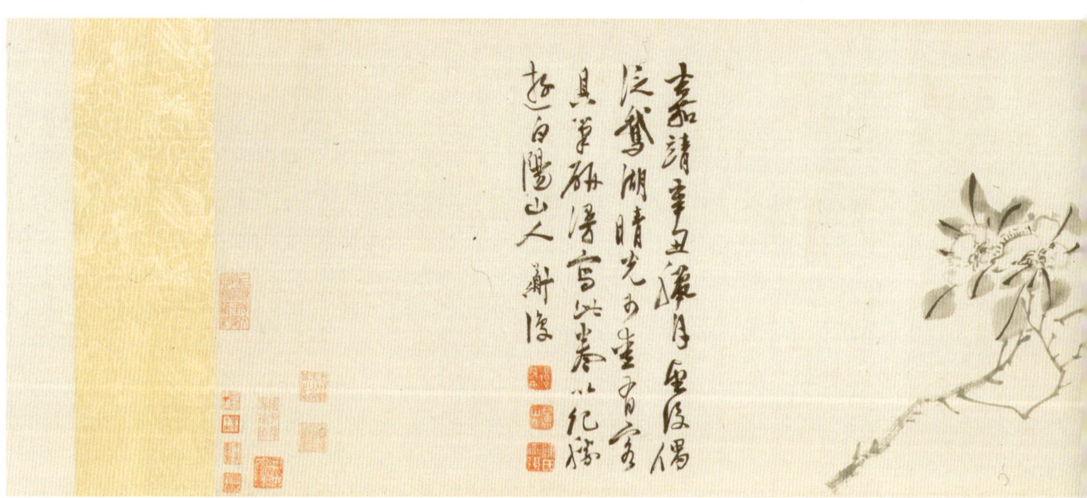

Figs. 150–152 *Flowers and Plants*

Chen Chun
Ink on paper
Height 34.3 cm × Width 527.4
Shanghai Museum

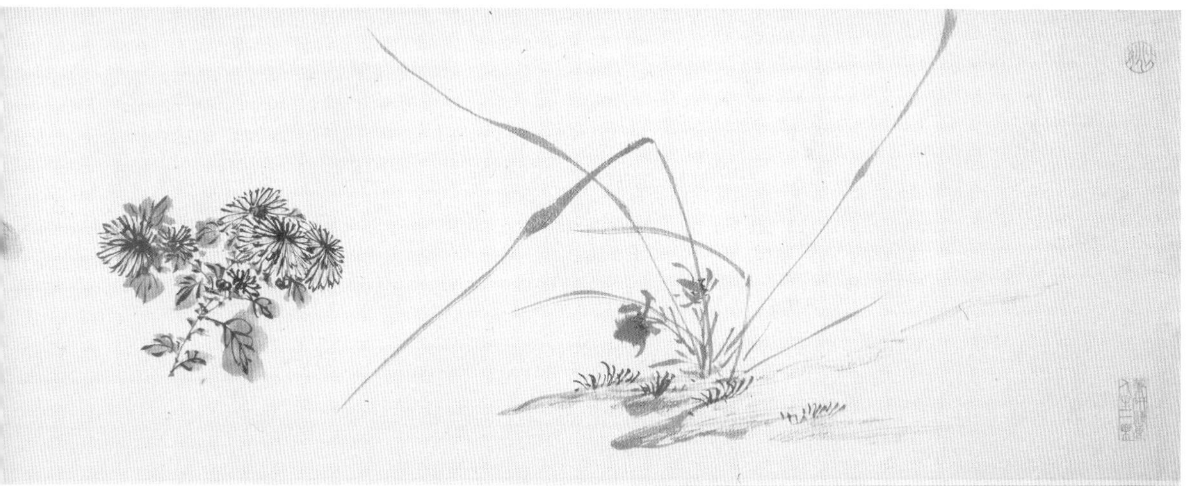

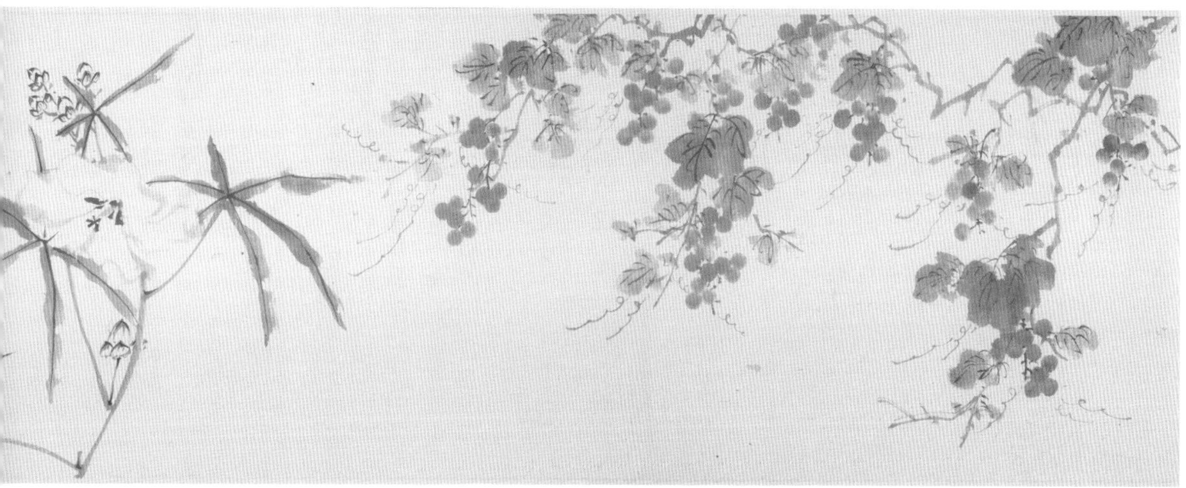

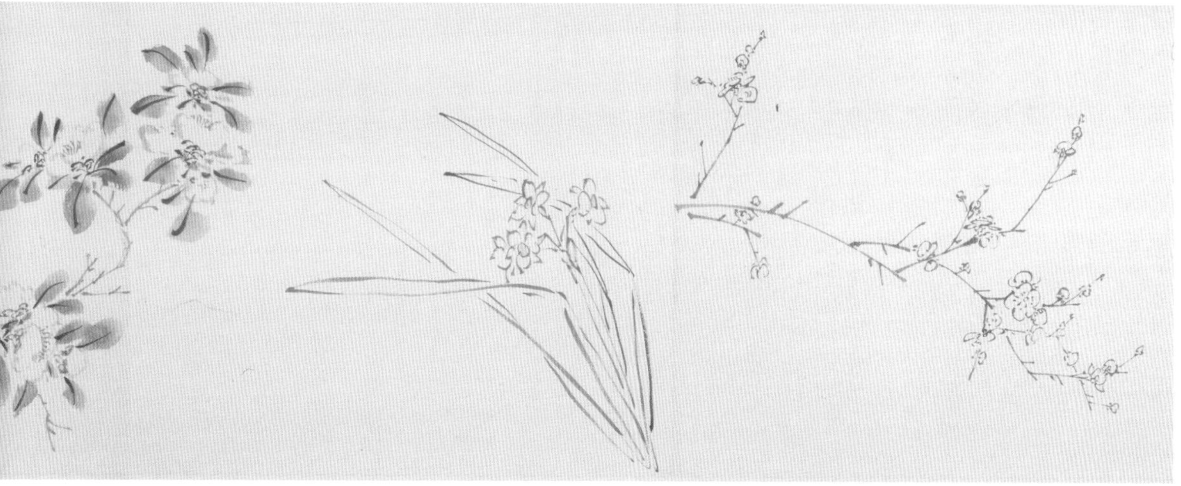

Chen Chun was a well-known Ming dynasty literati painter. In this handscroll he depicts nearly a dozen different kinds of plant in a freehand ink style including orchid, chrysanthemum, lotus, sunflower, bamboo and narcissus. Although there is no linkage between each plant, the posture of the plant, whether it droops or leans sideways in attractive disorder, is in response to those to the left and right. At the same time, the use of brush and of ink has an unrestrained naturalism and agile fluency which lends an air of vigor to the whole scroll.

Translator's Postscript

For the translator, every translation is a voyage of discovery. This one was also an education. There are many excellent books on Chinese painting by western scholars. They tend, however, to address other experts and to present Chinese painting in terms of personalities, categories, schools and influences.

Sophia Suk-mun Law, who has taught courses in Chinese painting for many years, has taken a different approach and seeks to equip her readers with fresh eyes that can look at a Chinese painting and enjoy and appreciate it to the full for what it is, an experience totally different to admiring the Mona Lisa and based on different criteria. Religious iconography stands outside the main-stream tradition of Chinese painting.

The criteria may appear esoteric but are not difficult to grasp. The biblical view of the universe as created by God for the use and enjoyment of humanity would not resonate with the early Chinese philosophers, who, particularly the Daoists, were green to a man. They possessed a sense of nature and of man as part of it that informs the thousand year tradition of Chinese *shanshui* (landscape) painting, so that *shanshui* are not so much about the scenery of a particular spot as about the perceived essence of nature itself.

There are two broad sets of factors that effect the criteria that Professor Law describes: intellectual and technical. Intellectually, they reflect a concern for essence over appearance and technically they reflect a difference of means and material that profoundly influences technique, the difference between oil paint on canvas or water and ink on paper or silk.

It is Professor Law's examination of these factors that can help the readers towards a new perception and enjoyment of Chinese painting. On the way there will be encounters with unfamiliar concepts and terms for which no precise English equivalent exists. The original Chinese version of this book was designed for a Chinese readership that may have shared the cultural background but was largely unfamiliar with the means (few write characters with a brush nowadays). I have done my best to help the readers by, as it were, erecting signposts along the way and the editors have provided a glossary of terms.

This translation would have been impossible without the enthusiastic support of the author and the steadfast editorial assistance of Zhang Yicong and Wu Yuezhou. I am deeply grateful to all of them.

Tony Blishen

APPENDICES

Catalogue of Chinese Paintings and Calligraphies

Painting and Calligraphy (English)	Painting and Calligraphy (Pinyin and Chinese)	Artist (Pinyin and Chinese)	Period	Museum	Page
A Solitary Temple amidst Clearing Peaks	Qingluan Xiaosi Tu 晴峦萧寺图	Li Cheng 李成	Five Dynasties	Museum of Art, Kansas City	86
Album: Flowers	Huahui Ce 花卉册	Chen Chun 陈淳	Ming dynasty	Shanghai Museum	118–119
Ancient Pine	Gu Song 古松	Gao Jianfu 高剑父	Modern	Hong Kong Chinese University	126
As One Would Wish Year upon Year	Nian Nian Shunsui Tu 年年顺遂图	Li Fangying 李方膺	Qing dynasty	Yangzhou Museum	39
Bamboo and Rocks	Zhushi Tu Zhou 竹石图轴	Zheng Xie 郑燮	Qing dynasty	Shanghai Museum	101
Bamboo with Turtle-Dove	Zhujiu Tu 竹鸠图	Li Anzhong 李安忠	Southern Song dynasty	Palace Museum, Taibei	111
Bamboos in Snow	Xue Zhu Tu 雪竹图	Xu Xi 徐熙	Southern Tang period	Shanghai Museum	107
Bamboos in the Wind	Xiaoxiang Fengzhu Tu 潇湘风竹图	Li Fangying 李方膺	Qing dynasty	Nanjing Museum	38
Butterflies and Flowers on a Wall	Tuqiang Die Hua Tu 土墙蝶花图	Li Shan 李鱓	Qing dynasty	Nanjing Museum	105
By the Bank of a Stream	An Bo Tu Juan 岸波图卷	Shen Zhou 沈周	Ming dynasty	Suzhou Museum	23
Chancellor Han Xizai's Evening Banquet	Han Xizai Yeyan Tu 韩熙载夜宴图	Gu Hongzhong 顾闳中	Five Dynasties	Palace Museum, Beijing	13, 62–63
Chrysanthemums in a Vase	Pingjü Tu 瓶菊图	Bada Shanren 八大山人	Qing dynasty	Private Collection	101
Copy of Gu Kaizhi's *Admonitions of the Instructress to the Court Ladies*	Nüshi Zhen Tu 女史箴图	Anonymous 佚名	Tang dynasty	British Museum	152–153
Copy of Gu Kaizhi's *The Nymph of Luo River*	Luo Shen Fu 洛神赋	Anonymous 佚名	Northern Song dynasty	Liaoning Provincial Museum	28–29, 36–37
Court Ladies Adorning Their Hair with Flowers	Zanhua Shinü Tu 簪花仕女图	Zhou Fang 周昉	Tang dynasty	Liaoning Provincial Museum	44–47, 60
Crags and Trees	Cengyan Congshu Tu 层岩丛树图	(Attributed to) Ju Ran 巨然	Five Dynasties	Palace Museum, Taibei	75
Deep River in the 5th Month	Wuyue Jiangshen Tufu 五月江深图幅	Wen Zhengming 文征明	Ming dynasty	Suzhou Museum	8
Double Happiness	Shuangxi Tu 双喜图	Cui Bai 崔白	Northern Song dynasty	Palace Museum, Taibei	113
Dwelling in the Fuchun Mountains: The Remaining Mountain	Fuchun Shanju Tu: Shengshan Tu 富春山居图 · 剩山图	Huang Gongwang 黄公望	Yuan dynasty	Zhejiang Provincial Museum	90
Dwelling in the Fuchun Mountains: The Useless Master's Scroll	Fuchun Shanju Tu: Wuyong Shi Juan 富春山居图 · 无用师卷	Huang Gongwang 黄公望	Yuan dynasty	Palace Museum, Taibei	148–149

Painting and Calligraphy (English)	Painting and Calligraphy (Pinyin and Chinese)	Artist (Pinyin and Chinese)	Period	Museum	Page
Early Spring	Zaochun Tu 早春图	Guo Xi 郭熙	Northern Song dynasty	Palace Museum, Taibei	84
Eight Views at the Height of Autumn	Qiuxing Bajing Ce 秋兴八景册	Dong Qichang 董其昌	Ming dynasty	Shanghai Museum	121
Elegant Gathering in the Wei Garden	Weiyuan Yaji Tu 魏园雅集图	Shen Zhou 沈周	Ming dynasty	Liaoning Provincial Museum	78–79
Elevated Ease	Gaoyi Tu 高逸图	Sun Wei 孙位	Tang dynasty	Shanghai Museum	2–3, 58–59
Fish with Ducks	Yü Ya Tu Juan 鱼鸭图卷	Bada Shanren 八大山人	Qing dynasty	Shanghai Museum	104, 130–131
Fisherman's Hut beneath an Autumn Sky	Yuzhuang Qiuji Tu 渔庄秋霁图	Ni Zan 倪瓒	Yuan dynasty	Shanghai Museum	43
Flower Album	Huahui Ce 花卉册	Shi Tao 石涛	Qing dynasty	Freer Gallery of Art and Arthur M. Sackler Gallery, Washington D.C.	104
Flowers and Birds	Hua Niao Tu 花鸟图	Qian Xuan 钱选	Yuan dynasty	Tianjin Municipal Museum	15
Flowers and Plants	Huahui Tu Juan 花卉图卷	Chen Chun 陈淳	Ming dynasty	Shanghai Museum	40
Flowers and Plants	Huahui Tu Juan 花卉图卷	Chen Chun 陈淳	Ming dynasty	Shanghai Museum	156–157
Hills and Streams with Boats	Xishan Fanting Tu 溪山泛艇图	Cao Zhibai 曹知白	Yuan dynasty	Shanghai Museum	35
Humming beneath the Pines	Songxia Xianyin Tu 松下闲吟图	Ma Yuan 马远	Southern Song dyansty	Shanghai Museum	65
Image of Self	Zi Hua Xiang 自画像	Jin Nong 金农	Qing dynasty	Palace Museum, Beijing	32
In the Style of a Ju Ran Shanshui	Lin Jü Ran Shanshui Tu Zhou 临巨然山水图轴	Wang Jian 王鉴	Qing dynasty	Shanghai Museum	27
In the Style of the Shanshui *of Da Chi (Huang Gongwang)*	Fang Dachi Shanshui Tuzhou 仿大痴山水图轴	Shen Zhou 沈周	Ming dynasty	Shanghai Museum	24
In the Style of the Shanshui *of Wu Zhen*	Fang Wu Zhen Shanshui Tu Zhou 仿吴镇山水图轴	Wang Yuanqi 王原祁	Qing dynasty	Shanghai Museum	27
In the Style of Zhang Xuan: Ladies Preparing Newly-Woven Silk	Dao Lian Tu 捣练图	Zhao Ji 赵佶	Northern Song dynasty	Museum of Fine Arts, Boston	52–53
Ink Orchid	Mo Lan 墨兰	Zheng Sixiao 郑思肖	Yuan dynasty	Osaka Municipal Museum of Art	94–95
Ink Orchid	Mo Lan 墨兰	Gao Jianfu 高剑父	Modern	Yicui Shantang	124
Ink Shrimps	Moxia Tu 墨虾图	Qi Baishi 齐白石	Modern	Liaoning Provincial Museum	4

Painting and Calligraphy (English)	Painting and Calligraphy (Pinyin and Chinese)	Artist (Pinyin and Chinese)	Period	Museum	Page
Listening to the Qin	Ting Qin Tu Zhou 听琴图轴	Zhao Ji 赵佶	Northern Song dynasty	Palace Museum, Beijing	16–17
Lotus	Yehe Tu 野荷图	Bada Shanren 八大山人	Qing dynasty	Shanghai Museum	11
Memorial for a Nephew	Ji Zhi Wengao 祭侄文稿	Yan Zhenqing 颜真卿	Tang dynasty	Palace Museum, Taibei	138–139
Mountain and Mist in the Style of Mi	Fang Mishi Yunshan Tu 仿米式云山图	Wen Zhengming 文征明	Ming dynasty	Palace Museum, Beijing	72–73
Mountains and Cloud	Yun Shan Tu 云山图	Wang Shimin 王时敏	Qing dynasty	Shanghai Museum	21
Mountains Moulded in Iron after Rain	Yuhou Qianshan Tie Zhucheng 雨后千山铁铸成	Pan Tianshou 潘天寿	Modern	The National Art Museum of China	136
On the River during the Qingming Festival	Qingming Shanghe Tu 清明上河图	Zhang Zeduan 张择端	Northern Song dynasty	Palace Museum, Beijing	144–145
One Hundred Colts	Baijun Tu 百骏图	Lang Shining 郎世宁	Qing Dynasty	Palace Museum, Taibei	112
Orchid and Bamboo	Lanzhu Tu Juan 兰竹图卷	Wen Zhengming 文征明	Ming dynasty	Palace Museum, Beijing	102–103, 126–127
Pear Blossom	Lihua Tu Juan 梨花图卷	Qian Xuan 钱选	Yuan dynasty	The Metropolitan Museum of Art, New York	154–155
Pines amongst Ravines	Wanhe Songfeng Tu 万壑松风图	(Attributed to) Ju Ran 巨然	Five Dynasties	Shanghai Museum	1, 83
Plum Blossom	Momei Tu Zhou 墨梅图轴	Wang Mian 王冕	Yuan dynasty	Shanghai Museum	99
Plum Blossom and Mountain Birds	Lamei Shanqin Tu 腊梅山禽图	Zhao Ji 赵佶	Northern Song dynasty	Palace Museum, Taibei	108
Portrait of Dongpo	Dongpo Xiang 东坡像	Zhao Mengfu 赵孟頫	Yuan dynasty	Palace Museum, Taibei	57
Portrait of Feng Ping	Feng Ping Zaoxiang 冯平造像	Anonymous 佚名	Northern Song dynasty	Freer Gallery of Art and Arthur M. Sackler Gallery, Washington D.C.	70
Portrait of Li Qingzhao	Li Qingzhao Xiaoxiang 李清照小像	Jiang Xun 姜埙	Qing dynasty	Wuxi Museum	67
Portrait of Wang Shimin	Wang Shimin Zaoxiang 王时敏造像	Zeng Jing 曾鲸	Ming dynasty	Tianjin Municipal Museum	68
Rare Birds from Life	Xiesheng Zhenqin Tu 写生珍禽图	Huang Quan 黄筌	Five Dynasties	Palace Museum, Beijing	106
Reading at the Window in Autumn	Qiuchuang Dushu Tu 秋窗图书图	Liu Songnian 刘松年	Southern Song dynasty	Liaoning Provincial Museum	64
Reading in the Hills in Spring	Chunshan Dushu Tu 春山读书图	Wang Meng 王蒙	Yuan dynasty	Shanghai Museum	20
Secluded Fragrance	Youxiang Tu 幽香图	Ma Lin 马麟	Southern Song dynasty	The Metropolitan Museum of Art, New York	114

Painting and Calligraphy (English)	Painting and Calligraphy (Pinyin and Chinese)	Artist (Pinyin and Chinese)	Period	Museum	Page
Seven-Character Regulated Poem	Qilü Shi Zhou 七律诗轴	Wen Zhengming 文征明	Ming dynasty	Liaoning Provincial Museum	35
Shanshui *Imitating Dong Yuan*	Fang Beiyuan Shanshui 仿北苑山水	Wang Shimin 王时敏	Qing dynasty	Shanghai Museum	26
Spring at Luoyang	Luoyang Chunse Tu Juan 洛阳春色图卷	Chen Chun 陈淳	Ming dynasty	Nanjing Museum	103
Squabs	Chuniao Tu 雏鸟图	Bada Shanren 八大山人	Qing dynasty	Shanghai Museum	116
Streams and Mountains in the Style of Dong Yuan	Fang Dong Yuan Xishan Wujin Tu 仿董源溪山无尽图	Yun Shouping 恽寿平	Qing dynasty	The National Art Museum of China	92
The Emperor Carried in Procession	Bunian Tu 步辇图	Yan Liben 阎立本	Tang dynasty	Palace Museum, Beijing	48–49
The Enveloping Scent of Flowers	Huaqi Xunren Tie 花气熏人帖	Huang Ting Jian 黄庭坚	Northern Song dynasty	Palace Museum, Taibei	133
The Impoverished Official	Suanhan Wei Xiang 酸寒尉像	Ren Bonian 任伯年	Qing dynasty	Zhejiang Provincial Museum	69
The Scholar He Tianzhang Listening to Music	He Tianzhang Xingyue Tu 何天章行乐图卷	Chen Hongshou 陈洪绶	Ming dynasty	Suzhou Museum	10–11
The Sound of Autumn by Ouyang Xiu	Ouyang Xiu Qiusheng Fu 欧阳修秋声赋	Zhao Mengfu 赵孟頫	Yuan dynasty	Liaoning Provincial Museum	132–133
The Thirteen Emperors	Lidai Dihuang Tu 历代帝皇图	Yan Liben 阎立本	Tang dynasty	Museum of Fine Arts, Boston	50
Thousand Character Classic	Caoshu Qianzi Wen 草书千字文	Zhao Ji 赵佶	Northern Song dynasty	Liaoning Provincial Museum	128–129
Tramping through the Snow to Visit a Friend	Taxue Fangyou Tu Zhou 踏雪访友图轴	Sun Zhi 孙枝	Ming dynasty	Suzhou Museum	80
Travelers among Mountains and Streams	Xishan Xinglü Tu 谿山行旅图	Fan Kuan 范宽	Northern Song dynasty	Palace Museum, Taibei	19
Treatise	Lunshu Tie 论述贴	Huai Su 怀素	Tang dynasty	Liaoning Provincial Museum	129
Two Pines in Level Perspective	Shuangsong Pingyuan Tu 双松平远图	Zhao Mengfu 赵孟頫	Yuan dynasty	The Metropolitan Museum of Art, New York	6–7, 134–135
Two Rabbits under a Wutong Tree	Wutong Shuangtu Tu 梧桐双兔图	Leng Mei 冷枚	Qing dynasty	Palace Museum, Beijing	115
Willow with Cicadas	Liu Chan Tu 柳蝉图	Jiang Tingxi 蒋廷锡	Qing dynasty	Palace Museum, Beijing	110
Winter's Three Friends	Suihan Sanyou 岁寒三友	Zhao Mengjian 赵孟坚	Southern Song dynasty	Shanghai Museum	100
Xiaoxiang River	Xiaoxiang Tu 潇湘图	Dong Yuan 董源	Five Dynasties	Palace Museum, Beijing	140–143
Yellow-Shelled Crab	Huangjia Tu 黄甲图	Xu Wei 徐渭	Ming dynasty	Palace Museum, Taibei	102

Brief Glossary of Some Chinese Painting Terms

Many terms in the vocabulary of Chinese painting lack precise equivalents in English or describe concepts that have no parallel in western art. Although the terms are generally explained in the text, it may help the reader to find them more concisely expressed in one place.

Bimo 笔墨
Bi—brush, *mo*—ink. The quality of brushwork both technical and artistic. The term is widely used and conveys a sense of more than just skill, it has a spiritual dimension as well. A painting can be described as having "good *bimo*."

Cunfa 皴法
Cun—roughness of skin, *fa*—method. Texture method. A brush technique used to express the texture of rocks and mountains.

Diantai 点苔
Dian—dot, *tai*—moss. Dotting. A brush technique that employs different sized dots of ink to represent moss on rocks or vegetation or trees on distant mountains.

Gongbi 工笔
Gong—work, *bi*—brush. Fine-work. The delicate and meticulously detailed depiction of form, e.g. in flowers and plants.

Jubei shanshui 巨碑山水
Monumental landscape. A term derived from the sheer scale of the scenery of hills and rivers that appear in the *shanshui* of the Five Dynasties and Northern Song period.

Linmo 临摹
Copying as a means of study. It takes two forms. *Lin* where a painting is copied mechanically by eye and *mo* where the painting is traced through paper, brushstroke by brushstroke.

Liubai 留白
Liu—leave, *bai*—white. To leave blank. Dynamic emptiness. An integral part of the composition of a painting with an active function in relation to the rest of the painting.

Sandian toushifa 散点透视法
Multi-point perspective. In Chinese painting this comprises three distinct perspectives incorporated into a single whole known as *sanyuan toushifa* (三远透视法)—three-distance perspective whose elements are:

Gao yuan. Upper distance. The top of a mountain viewed by someone standing at its foot.

Ping yuan. Level distance. The far distance and the view below seen by someone standing on a mountain.

Shen yuan. Deep distance. The hypothetical observer is situated facing a mountain but able to see beyond it, from near to far, thus giving a sense of depth.

Shanshui 山水
This term (*shan*—hill, *shui*—water) is often translated as "landscape." This does not convey the full meaning of the term which stands more for scenery recollected by the artist and later recreated in essence than for the visual reproduction of a specific view.

Xieshen 写神
Xie—write, *shen*—spirit. The quality of abstract essence in a painting as opposed to the reality of likeness. Not to be confused with *xiezhen* below.

Xiesheng 写生
Drawing from life (*sheng*).

Xiezhen 写真 and **Xieyi** 写意
Two terms that are linked philosophically where they stand in opposition. *Xiezhen* (*xie*—write, *zhen* —true) true likeness, the concrete and realistic manifestation of the appearance of an object based upon the detailed observation of the artist.

Xieyi, by contrast, where *yi* means sense, is the abstract manifestation of an image beyond its actual appearance. In its technical sense, *xieyi* may also be termed a simple, spontaneous "freehand" but "painterly impression" conveys more of the overall meaning. A roughly equivalent concept might be to regard Turner as a master of *xieyi* and Canaletto as a master of *xiezhen*.

Yijing 意境
Yi—sense, feeling, *jing*—state. Conceptual or creative sense. Also found in traditional Chinese philosophy and literature.

Dates of the Chinese Dynasties

Xia Dynasty（夏）	2070–1600 BC
Shang Dynasty（商）	1600–1046 BC
Zhou Dynasty（周）	1046–256 BC
Western Zhou Dynasty（西周）	1046–771 BC
Eastern Zhou Dynasty（东周）	770–256 BC
Spring and Autumn Period（春秋）	770–476 BC
Warring States Period（战国）	475–221 BC
Qin Dynasty（秦）	221–206 BC
Han Dynasty（汉）	206 BC–220 AD
Western Han Dynasty（西汉）	206 BC–25 AD
Eastern Han Dynasty（东汉）	25–220
Three Kingdoms（三国）	220–280
Wei（魏）	220–265
Shu Han（蜀）	221–263
Wu（吴）	222–280
Jin Dynasty（晋）	265–420
Western Jin Dynasty（西晋）	265–316
Eastern Jin Dynasty（东晋）	317–420
Northern and Southern Dynasties（南北朝）	420–589
Southern Dynasties（南朝）	420–589
Liang Dynasty（梁）	502–557
Northern Dynasties（北朝）	439–581
Sui Dynasty（隋）	581–618
Tang Dynasty（唐）	618–907
Five Dynasties and Ten Kingdoms（五代十国）	907–960
Five Dynasties（五代）	907–960
Ten Kingdoms（十国）	902–979
Song Dynasty（宋）	960–1279
Northern Song Dynasty（北宋）	960–1127
Southern Song Dynasty（南宋）	1127–1279
Liao Dynasty（辽）	916–1125
Jin Dynasty（金）	1115–1234
Xixia Dynasty (or Tangut)（西夏）	1038–1227
Yuan Dynasty（元）	1279–1368
Ming Dynasty（明）	1368–1644
Qing Dynasty（清）	1644–1911

Index

Q

R

S

T

U

V

W

X

Y

Z